OCR
RECOGNISING ACHIEVEMENT

HODDER
EDUCATION

Official Publisher Partnership

OCR BUSINESS STUDIES for GCSE

SECOND EDITION

D1328729

PETER KENNERDELL

ALAN WILLIAMS

MIKE SCHOFIELD

DYNAMIC
LEARNING

HODDER
EDUCATION
AN HACHETTE UK COMPANY

Orders: please contact Bookpoint Ltd, 130 Milton Park, Abingdon, Oxon OX14 4SB.
Telephone: (44) 01235 827720. Fax: (44) 01235 400454.
Lines are open from 9.00–5.00, Monday to Saturday, with a 24 hour message answering service.
You can also order through our website www.hoddereducation.co.uk

If you have any comments to make about this, or any of our other titles, please send them to
educationenquiries@hodder.co.uk

British Library Cataloguing in Publication Data
A catalogue record for this title is available from the British Library

ISBN: 978 0 340 98349 2

First Edition Published 2001
This Edition Published 2009
Impression number 10 9 8
Year 2014

Copyright © 2001, 2009 Peter Kennerdell, Alan Williams, Mike Schofield

Hachette UK's policy is to use papers that are natural, renewable and
recyclable products and made from wood grown in sustainable forests.
The logging and manufacturing processes are expected to conform to the
environmental regulations of the country of origin.

Artwork by Oxford Designers and Illustrators
Cover photo © iLexx/iStockphoto.com
Typeset by Dorchester Typesetting
Printed and bound in Dubai for Hodder Education, an Hachette UK company, 338 Euston Road, London NW1 3BH

Contents

PEOPLE

PART THREE PRODUCTION, FINANCE AND EXTERNAL BUSINESS ENVIRONMENT

PRODUCTION

FINANCE

EXTERNAL BUSINESS ENVIRONMENT

Preface

This book, based on the very popular first edition, has been revised specifically for the new specifications in GCSE Business Studies for first teaching in September 2009. It has been designed and written with GCSE candidates of all abilities in mind to allow them to develop a better understanding of the way in which the business world operates.

The book is not intended to be a scheme of work, but a resource that both students and teachers can use in the process of preparing for a GCSE examination in Business Studies. The effectiveness with which this resource is used will depend on the skill and professionalism of the teacher and the commitment and determination of students. Material in the book will need to be adapted and supplemented with clear explanations designed to suit the needs of the candidates.

OCR GCSE Business Studies specification

The highly successful and popular OCR GCSE Businesses Studies Specification has been revised for first teaching from September 2009. The revised specification has been based on the previous one but amended to meet the requirements of the Qualifications and Curriculum Authority 2007 GCSE Business Studies subject criteria.

The new specification employs an analytical, evaluative and investigative approach to the study of business studies. This will require candidates to both understand the dynamic environment in which business operates, and appreciate the many and varied factors that impact upon business activity and behaviour in the twenty-first century.

The unitised design of the specification enables candidates to be assessed in particular aspects of business activity and business behaviour. The specification is divided into three units of assessment; each unit comprising discrete content:

Marketing and enterprise (25 per cent). This unit is internally assessed via a controlled assessment.

Business and people (25 per cent). This unit is externally assessed by means of an unseen question-and-answer style of examination paper.

Production, finance and the external business environment (50 per cent). This unit is externally assessed by means of a question-and-answer style examination based on pre-released case study stimulus material.

About this book

Although the material in the book has been written to support the OCR GCSE Business Studies specification, large amounts of the material will be relevant to specifications offered by other awarding bodies, as they have all been written to the same subject criteria.

The content of the book is not intended to be a definitive work, beyond which examiners cannot go in seeking ways to assess the assessment objectives where candidates are expected to:

● recall, select and communicate their knowledge and understanding of concepts, issues and terminology

● apply skills, knowledge and understanding in a variety of contexts and in planning and carrying out investigations and tasks

● analyse and evaluate evidence, make reasoned judgements and present appropriate conclusions.

The limiting factor to what an examiner may set as a question in an examination is the specification content. For this reason, teachers must plan their teaching around the specification content using the material in the book as a resource upon which to draw. It is the specification content that is being assessed and not the book content. However, we have tried, as far as possible, to use our experience and knowledge of teaching and examining GCSE Business Studies over a long period of time, to include in the book a body of knowledge and range of activities which we feel are essential in underpinning the GCSE Business Studies subject criteria.

We also believe in providing students with the necessary background information to support topics on which they will be examined. For this reason, some concepts and facts relating to businesses studies have been included even though they are not included in the OCR GCSE Business Studies specification.

It must also be remembered that GCSE question paper writers are extremely skilled and inventive when seeking new ways to test the abilities of candidates entered for a GCSE examination in Business Studies. For this reason, it is vital that teachers prepare their candidates to apply the information they have available in providing a detailed and relevant answer to the question which has been set.

How to use this book

The book is organised into three basic parts, which reflect the specification content. At the beginning of each of the three modules is an *introductory activity*, which gives an overview of the specification content for that module.

Each part contains a *unit* detailing the way in which it will be *assessed*. Each of the specification's three units is assessed by a different examination technique, which has been designed to assess different skills in different contexts. Both teachers and candidates will need to understand and master the different techniques if they are to achieve success. The nature of the unitised course allows candidates the opportunity to attempt the modules either at the end of the course, or as they progress through the course. The opportunity to retake modules where performance has been disappointing is also available.

Each part is split into several *sections* which are then subdivided into *units* upon which a programme of study can be based. Each unit has:

● the learning outcomes that the user of the book should expect to have achieved after studying the unit.

● a brief **introduction** designed to get candidates thinking about some key issues related to the broad area of business studies on which the unit is based.

- a *body of knowledge* based around the specification content relevant to that unit.

- a series of **activities** designed to reinforce learning and understanding.

- **evaluation points** designed to get the reader thinking analytically about key concepts and problems faced by business.

- In Part 1, **assessment activities**, designed to replicate controlled assessment type tasks have been included to help underpin and reinforce the knowledge, concepts and theories relevant to each unit of study.

- In Parts 2 and 3, **examination-type questions**, adapted from past examination papers, together with advice from examiners on what they are looking for in answer to the question. Where the specification content is new, and has not previously been examined, practice questions similar in style to those used in examinations have been included. These questions should help to reinforce and support learning, as well as providing an opportunity for candidates to become accustomed to the type and style of questioning that they can expect to experience on certain topics. Our interpretation of what the examiner was looking for, gives guidance on how candidates will need to respond in order to answer the question successfully. When preparing candidates for the examinations, the attention of candidates should be drawn to the use of **command words** in questions which provide a clear instruction as to what is required when answering the question.

- **Key facts** which provide a summary of the unit content

- a list of the **key terms** and definitions relevant to the unit content. For candidates to be successful, they will need to have a sound understanding of basic business terminology, which they can use when developing answers to examination questions.

Interactive dynamic learning electronic resource

It is our intention to make available, to help support the learning of GCSE Business Studies candidates, an **interactive dynamic learning electronic resource** on CD for use primarily by teachers. We recognise that the way in which GCSE candidates are engaged in learning has changed with time. While paper-based materials can serve a useful purpose, the development of electronic technology presents a whole new range of learning activities. The content of the CD will complement the materials in the book to improve further the GCSE Business Studies learning experience. Activities in the book will be included on the CD. However, it is important to point out that both this textbook and the CD resource have been designed to be stand-alone resources. They may be used independently of one another, or in conjunction, to allow teachers to 'build' lessons in the way they feel is most appropriate to their students. It is for individuals to decide on how they wish to use the materials available.

Acknowledgements

We are grateful to a number of people in helping us to prepare this book. In particular, our families, who have, once again, been very patient with us while the preparation of the material for this revised edition was being carried out. The OCR Business and Society Subject Team, especially Matthew Buttler, Jane Weir and Emma Russell, have been very supportive and helpful throughout. Finally, without the drive, foresight and determination of Colin Goodlad from Hodder Education, this publication would not have been possible.

Acknowledgements

The authors and publishers are grateful to the following for permission to reproduce illustrative material:

Apex News and Pictures Agency/Alamy p2 (l); Colin Palmer Photography/Alamy p2 (r); © Car Culture/Corbis p13, p45 (t), p386; Steve Stock/Alamy p13(b); © Hulton-Deutsch Collection/Corbis p30; PSL Images/Alamy p32, p126 (r), p368; Gregory Wrona/Alamy p33; Robert Convery/Alamy p46; Trinity Mirror/Mirrorpix/Alamy p49; David Burner/Rex Features p54; © Courtesy of lastminute.com p57 (l); Rolf Marriott/BBC Photo Library p80; Derek Hudson/Getty Images p81; Courtesy of Shell Livewire p85; © Somos Images/Corbis p102; Courtesy of Vodafone p114; Alex Segre/Alamy p117 (1c, t), p158 (t); geogphotos/Alamy p117(1c, m), p184 (l); LH Images/Alamy p117 (2c); JHB Photography/Alamy p124 (t); picturesbyrob/Alamy p124 (m); Colin Underhill/Alamy p124 (b); Charlie Bishop/Alamy p125 (1c, t); © Rainer Jensen/epa/Corbis p125 (1c, m); © Bananastock/Photolibrary Group Ltd p125 (1c, b); Greg Balfour Evans/Alamy p125 (2c, t); Jack Sullivan/Alamy p125 (2c, b); PA Archive/PA Photos p126 (l); © James Leynse/Corbis p128; courtesy of Cargill p133 1c; Markos Dolopikos/Alamy p133 (2c, t); Courtesy of Direct Accident Management Ltd p133 (2c, b); Chris Howes/Wild Places Photography/Alamy p158 (m); Tim Graham/Alamy p158 (b); Helene Rogers/Alamy p165 (l); Glyn Thomas Photography/Alamy p165 (r); Nick Hanna/Alamy p166 (t); Koichi Kamoshida/Getty Images p166 (b); North River Images/Alamy p174 (t); VStock/Alamy p174 (m); Terry Harris Just Greece Photo Library/Alamy p184 (r), p227; Johnny Green/PA Archive/PA Photos p209; workingwales/Alamy p215; Steven May/Alamy p220; ©Photodisc/Getty Images p230, p244, p344, p346; Bob Johns/expresspictures.co.uk/Alamy p232; © Diego Azubel/epa/Corbis p246; London Aerial Photo Library/Alamy p289; Leslie Garland Picture Library/Alamy p308, p365; Linda Kennedy/Alamy p309; Rex Features p326; Moodboard RF/Photolibrary Group p328 (t); Oliver Knight/Alamy p328 (m); graham jepson/Alamy p328 (b); Tristar Photos/Alamy p331, p347; Chris Ratcliffe/Rex Features p332; Tim Ireland/PA Archive/PA Photos p336; Flab/Alamy p357; Don Tonge/Alamy p358; David Pearson/Alamy p364 (1c); © Paul Brown/Rex Features p364 (2c); Paul Souders/Corbis p366.

Key: 1c = 1st column, 2c = 2nd column, t = top, m = middle, b = bottom, l = left, r = right.

The authors and publishers are grateful to the following for permission to reproduce copyright material:

Article on p208 © NI Syndication Ltd; Article on p245 (t) courtesy University of Nottingham. © Crown Copyright material is reproduced with the permission of the Controller of HMSO.

Every effort has been made to trace and acknowledge ownership of copyright. The publishers will be glad to make suitable arrangements with any copyright holders whom it has not been possible to contact.

MARKETING & ENTERPRISE

PART 1

Introductory Activity

Learning Outcomes

By studying this unit you will be able to:

● Understand the ways in which businesses research the market for their products and services

● Explain and evaluate the importance of different marketing strategies used by businesses

● Understand and explain the part played by enterprise and planning in a business context.

Bligh Sound and Vision has many larger competitors

Rory Bligh owns Bligh Sound and Vision, a small shop selling electrical goods located near the town centre in Wakefield, West Yorkshire. The business was started in the early 1960s by his uncle, and Rory has run the business since 2003. He does not think of himself as enterprising, but he has had to work hard on marketing to keep the business running successfully.

Sales in the shop mainly come from LCD televisions, DVDs, radios and a small number of washing machines. A rental service is also offered, something which other local businesses do not do. A reasonably priced repair service is also available to Rory's customers. The business has built up a loyal local customer base, especially amongst the elderly and disabled, who are given informed and friendly help and advice personally by Rory before they buy.

The electrical goods market is very competitive, with Rory's much smaller business having to compete with Currys, Comet and Argos as well as the large supermarkets. Rory feels that he can beat the larger electrical businesses on customer service, with free installation and a good back-up service if things go wrong – something which his larger competitors do not do as well as Bligh Sound and Vision. The business is part of a large buying group of 700 shops, which enables Rory to purchase goods for sale at a favourable price.

Rory puts the continuing success of the business down to first-rate service and selling quality products (Panasonic, Toshiba, Samsung, Roberts, etc.) which has produced a trustworthy local reputation, with recommendations being made to others by satisfied customers. He feels that advertising the business in the newspaper is a waste of time, though will sometimes use direct mailshots, which are more effective.

Rory, like others who run their own businesses, is taking a risk. With many competitors selling the same products, Rory has managed to keep this risk to a minimum, by keeping to a small range of products that he knows will sell well. He admits that he does not 'chase' younger customers who want every new electronic gadget. He knows that televisions will sell well and concentrates on that area of business – for his older customers, of course.

Questions

1 Who are the competitors of Bligh Sound and Vision?

2 Why might some consumers not use a shop such as Bligh Sound and Vision?

3 Who are Rory's main customers? Why might these customers use Rory's shop?

4 Considering the customers who use Bligh Sound and Vision, explain why Rory might have taken his decisions on how to advertise the business.

5 Make a list of the reasons why Bligh Sound and Vision is still a successful business despite the competition from larger businesses such as Comet and Currys.

6 Using the list in your answer to question 4, which do you think are the main two reasons why Rory's business is successful? Give reasons for your answer.

7 In marketing, a business will often use price, product, place and promotion (advertising) as headings to look at its marketing activities. Use the same headings to explain whether Rory could do any more in marketing to improve the success of Bligh Sound and Vision. Give reasons for your answer.

Requirements of the controlled assessment

Learning Outcomes

By studying this unit you will be able to:

- **Understand what you are expected to produce for the controlled assessment**
- **Understand how you will work whilst completing the controlled assessment**
- **Understand how the controlled assessment will be marked.**

What is in a controlled assessment?

The controlled assessment is new to Business Studies GCSE courses from 2009 onwards, and replaces the coursework that was part of the final GCSE grade. Its aim is to make sure that work completed for assessment at GCSE is *only* the work of the candidate. This is done by completing the work in a *controlled* place, which would normally be within your business studies classroom. You will be able to complete some research work outside the classroom, but the writing of the work will only be allowed when supervised by a teacher in your normal workplace in school or college.

For the controlled assessment you will be given information on a business situation. This information will be in written form as well as numerical data. Using this data, your own business studies knowledge (on marketing and enterprise) and research, you will complete three tasks called

A good controlled assessment will need careful planning

Investigations. Investigation one is marked out of 10, with investigations two and three being marked out of 25. The work you produce should be detailed, as it is 25 per cent of your final business studies grade!

For investigation one you will need to use the data provided by OCR, together with some background knowledge and understanding of marketing and enterprise. For investigations two and three you will need to collect data of your own in order to fully complete the work.

How you will be expected to work in the controlled assessment

The nature of the controlled assessment is the level of control your teacher will have over the completion of your work. There are different levels of control for the different stages of completing the controlled assessment. These are described below.

Research work

You will be expected to complete some research to help you to complete the controlled assessment. This may be in the form of primary research (questionnaire/ interview work), as well as secondary research (for example, internet, books, magazines). This stage of your work can be completed *outside* the classroom *without* the direct control of your teacher.

You must make sure that you have completed all your research work in the time you have been given, so that you have the necessary information to complete the writing stage that will follow. You will be allowed to complete graphs, charts, diagrams, photographs, etc. in this stage, but *not* any written work that will come from the use of this information. You can make notes to help you with the writing stage, but these must only be notes and not a first draft of your final work.

Writing up your work

At this stage of your work, your teacher will have *direct* control over your writing, and so this will be completed *only* in your classroom. You will only be allowed the notes you have made during the research stage, and the graphs, chats, etc. you have already completed. There is *no* allowance for you to

use the internet, etc. when you are writing up your work, so make sure that you have all your notes ready.

Analysis of data needs careful thought and attention

Data provided for the controlled assessment

The data provided for the controlled assessment will be in the form of background information to the business(es) that form the basis of the work, and numerical data. The following are examples of some numerical data you may expect and the ways it may help you to complete the controlled assessment.

Socio-economic groups

(See also Unit 1.3.1.) This data will provide you with an indication of the type of town or city where a business is located, or is considering locating. It will show, for example, whether a town has a high proportion of richer consumers with a large number of A and B groups. If there are a larger proportion of C2, D and E groups shown by the data then this will point out that there are rather more people with less money to spend.

Differences in socio-economic groups will clearly have a direct effect on the products that are sold in different towns and cities. With a high proportion of A and B groups in a town, a business selling expensive cars such as Aston Martin has rather more chance of being successful. If a town has a higher proportion of D and E groups then budget shops are more likely to be found.

The socio-economic groups within an area will also affect the promotional activity that a business might undertake. In advertising, for example, the newspapers read by groups A, B and C1 are different to those read by C2, D and E. This will mean that a business has to think of the product or service it is selling, its target market, and then where best to advertise in order to reach potential customers.

Income

This may be given as well as, or instead of, socio-economic groups. The income of residents in an area will have the same impact on decision making as in socio-economic groups detailed above. The higher the level of income, the more likely those businesses selling more expensive goods and services will succeed. In the same way, lower income levels for people in an area will mean that goods and services aimed at the budget market are likely to have some success.

Age groups

This data will simply split the people living in an area into different age groups. It is useful in identifying whether there are enough consumers for a particular product or service. For example, a service such as an old people's home needs an area with elderly people. A product aimed at young families will need consumers of a different age group. Look carefully at such data to identify the target market for a product and to see if there are a large number of those consumers in an area.

Competitors

When any business is considering opening in an area, it should look at the potential competition. Data on competitors will show just what a new business is up against, and whether perhaps it needs to think of a new way of selling a product or service if the competition is fierce. Obviously, if there is no competition then there is rather more chance of success *providing* there is demand for the product.

Transport links

Whilst a large town will have more consumers than a smaller town, if there are good transport links to the smaller town, more consumers may be able to travel in to buy products and services. Always consider the total number of possible customers for a business, which might not simply be the number living in the town or city itself.

Transport facilities may also affect the location of a business. If customers are more able to get to a particular location because of good roads, bus and train services then such an area may be a good location for many businesses.

Employment

This will give details of the type of work undertaken by those employed in an area. It could be in the form of employment sectors, dividing the workforce into primary (raw materials, e.g. mining), secondary (manufacturing, e.g. furniture making) and tertiary (service e.g. shops). This can be used to help make decisions on whether there is the *type* of workers in an area for a business thinking of where to locate. If a car maker was interested in locating a new car factory, one consideration would be if there are the correct skills available in the workers (e.g. secondary). However, a business may consider that it can easily train workers and so this type of data is not going to influence their decision. Look at the business you are investigating and think whether or not this type of data will have any effect on its decision making.

Unemployment figures may also be important to a business. High levels of unemployment would indicate that there is a ready supply of workers for a business. This would normally mean there will be no problem in recruiting workers, *providing* that the unemployed workers have the required skills or can be re-trained easily. Higher levels of unemployment may also mean that there will be less demand for expensive goods in an area. These factors should be taken into account when evaluating a particular location.

Comparative data

This could relate to any of the examples given here. Data will change over time, and businesses that are planning for the future may well want to see the *future estimates* of how a particular set of data could change. It may be the case that there are, for example, few families in an area, but with the building of large new estates the expectation is that the proportion of families will rise in the years ahead. This will affect any product or service that parents of children or children themselves are likely to buy. While this might cover most items, certain services, such as childcare, should see business growth in the future.

Questionnaire

This data would be information collected by one of the businesses in the controlled assessment information provided by OCR. It may be part of a questionnaire. It may be some ideas on a questionnaire that the business has been thinking about using.

It is important that you follow the instructions in the tasks that relate to the data. You may be asked to evaluate the usefulness of the data collected, or possibly make suggestions on what other data would need to be collected in addition to that already produced. In each of these examples you need to carefully consider the product or service being provided, and the target market at which it is aimed. This should give you ideas on the usefulness of the data and how it might be improved. As in all your work, you would need to give full reasons for any ideas being put forward.

How the controlled assessment will be marked

The controlled assessment will be marked using three marking criteria. In summary these are:

1. **Select, recall and communicate knowledge and understanding.** This means that you will need to select the correct business information from your knowledge of marketing and enterprise to use in your work. You will need to show that you know and understand the business studies terms and other information you include in your work. For higher marks, you will need to show a range of knowledge and understanding of the area of study required by the investigation.

2. **Application of knowledge and understanding.** Here you need to apply your knowledge and understanding to the business situation in the investigation you are completing. For example, you may have shown that you know and understand the different sales promotion that any business may use. For this marking criterion you would need to explain how the business you are investigating uses sales promotion.

3 **Analyse and evaluate evidence.** The final marking criterion requires you to look carefully at all the data you have collected and explain what it means for the business you are investigating. You will need to use your graphs, charts, tables, etc. to help you in this section. The final step is to evaluate the evidence (data) you have. What should the business do? In coming to a conclusion and making recommendations, it is important that you use the data analysis you have completed to justify the ideas you are putting forward.

Analysing the market

Learning Outcomes

By studying this unit you will be able to:

- **Understand that businesses have different views on how to market their products**
- **Explain how the market for many products is split into different parts called 'market segments'**
- **Understand how businesses analyse different parts of the population, called 'socio-economic groups', to help them market their products or services**
- **Explain how different types of market, mass, niche and test, are used by businesses.**

Introduction

Before a business starts, it is important that the owners check exactly who their customers are likely to be. There is little point in starting a business and then wondering why you are not selling anything! Analysing the market involves looking closely at different groups of consumers called **socio-economic groups** and then examining whether you are going to sell products or services to all these groups (a **mass market**) or perhaps to a small part of a single group (a **niche market**).

This analysis of the market will normally be part of the business plan (see Unit 1.4.2), and is an important part in setting up a successful business.

Activity

Activity 1: Explanation – analysing the market for a product

It is important to analyse the market for a product before a business starts

Catherine Bird wants to start her own business making pottery. She has no business experience, but has been working part time in a small pottery business for 12 months. She realises that she must look carefully at the way she sets up the business, in particular what she should make and who she should aim her products at. She has come to you for advice and has the following questions. What advice would you give to Catherine? Give reasons for any recommendations you make.

1 Should Catherine research whether or not people will buy her product before she starts making pots? Research will take time and cost money.
2 Should she make any type of pottery, or just certain styles?
3 If Catherine wanted to find out who might buy her products, what should she do?
4 Should she make many pieces of pottery aimed at everyone, or just a few pieces aimed at a select number of customers?

Product and market orientation

When a business wishes to sell a new product or service it must be sure that customers will want to buy it. Whether the business is selling to another business, or to consumers, there is little point in providing something that customers do not want.

In the past a number of businesses were **product-oriented**, which means they took little or no interest in what people wanted and made products that they hoped would sell. At a time when people had little choice of products, this system worked quite well. More recently, this has meant that products were developed that customers did not want and that resulted in losses for the business.

Most businesses are now **market-oriented**, which means they carefully find what people want before they develop a product or service. By doing this, a business would make sure that a product or service would be a success and, it hopes, make a large profit.

Market segments

Another way in which a business will analyse the possible market for its product or service is to consider the different **market segments** at which the product may be aimed. This is called **targeting** the market and involves looking at the different types of consumers that might buy the product.

Although each product will have its own market segments, common ways in which the customers for most products can be divided are shown in Figure 1 below.

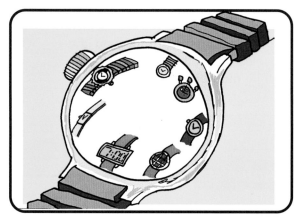

A watch is a product with many different market segments

Figure 1 Ways in which a market can be segmented

Age	Different age groups will buy different products.
Gender	Male and females will often (but not always) buy different products.
Income	People with higher levels of income will want particular products.
Region	Consumers living in different parts of the country will have different tastes and needs.
Interests	Different people have different hobbies and interests. This will mean that a range of products is needed to satisfy all tastes.

Activity

Activity 2: Explanation – Market segments of different products

Divide the following products into as many different segments as you can.
Use the information just given on market segments to help you. You could illustrate your work in a similar way to the cartoon of a watch.

1 Jeans

2 PCs

3 Magazines

Activity

Activity 3: Research – The targeting of consumers by banks

Go on the website for Halifax Bank (www.halifax.co.uk). Look up the different types of savings account. Explain who you think the different accounts are being targeted at. Give reasons for your answer.

Socio-economic groups

An important way in which businesses analyse a market is to divide consumers into different groups. The groups are based on the occupation of the head of the household. The occupation a person has obviously affects the amount of money they earn, and will affect the way in which a business will target its products. Aston Martin will target their cars at one group and Fiat will target their cars at a very different group.

Consumers in groups A, B and C are more likely to have a higher **disposable income.** This is money left after all the essential bills such as mortgage, rent, gas, electricity, etc. are paid. Businessess will look at the disposable income of different groups when they are targeting their products or services.

When a business wants to advertise a product aimed at a particular socio-economic group, it will need to be sure that the advertisement is being seen by that group. This will affect the choice of newspaper or magazine a business chooses to use for its adverts.

Mass, niche and test markets

When a business is looking at the market at which to aim a product, it needs to consider how many customers it hopes to attract. A product or service aimed at lots of people is a **mass market product**. This will include things such as popular chocolates, family cars and household electrical goods such as TVs.

Figure 2 Socio-economic groups

Socio-economic group	% of total workforce	Examples of occupations
Group A - Higher professional	3	Doctors, judges, company directors of large businesses
Group B - Intermediate professional	20	Teachers, department managers, solicitors
Group C1 - Skilled non-manual	28	Supervisory workers, secretaries
Group C2 - Skilled manual	21	Electricians, plumbers
Group D - Part skilled	18	Assembly line workers, cleaners
Group E - Unskilled	10	Unemployed, casual workers, state pensioners

Figure 3 Examples of occupations in socio-economic groups

Group A	Group B	Group C1	Group C2	Group D	Group E

Activity

Activity 4: Research – Socio-economic groups comparison

Figure 2 gives details of the *national* figures for workers in each socio-economic group. Conduct a survey of the rest of your business studies group to find the socio-economic group figures that would best represent your local area. Remember if there are two people working in a household, use the higher category if there is a difference.

a Draw two graphs, one showing the national figures for socio-economic groups and one showing the results for your group.

b What differences are there from your group results to the national figures?

c How might the differences you have identified in (b) affect the type of products and services that businesses may provide in your local area?

Activity

Activity 5: Zone activity – Occupations and socio-economic groups

Using Figure 3, insert the occupations below in the correct socio-economic group.

Occupations:
- Teacher
- Doctor
- Plumber
- Refuse collector
- Unemployed person
- Pensioner
- Waitress
- Chairman of a plc
- Experienced hair stylist.

Evaluation point

1 Most businesses will have a target market of consumers for their products. In some, but not all cases, socio-economic groups are used to examine the views of consumers when a market is being analysed

2 When looking at which socio-economic group to use when analysing a market, think carefully about who is likely to buy the product. It may be a whole range of consumers, or perhaps just one or two groups. This will then affect how and where the product is sold.

Activity

Activity 6: Explanation – Targeting different socio-economic groups

When targeting their products and services at certain socio-economic groups, businesses need to choose where they advertise very carefully. Explain where the following products should be advertised to reach their target socio-economic group.

1 An expensive car aimed at group A.

2 Furniture aimed at groups C2, D and E.

3 A laptop computer targeted at groups B and C1.

4 Clothes targeted at Groups A, B and C1.

5 A book targeted at groups C1, C2, D and E.

Niche market products are aimed at much smaller groups of people, with products made being very specialised. This type of market would include hand-built cars, made-to-measure clothes and hand-crafted pottery. As very few products are made for a niche market, they are usually more expensive than those for a mass market.

When a business is unsure about how a new product will sell, it may use a **test market**. This means that the product will be sold or tested in a particular area or with a certain group of people to test whether consumers like it. If the product sells well, the business may decide to sell it throughout the country. If consumers don't like the product, the business may decide to stop production or change the product and test it again later. By carrying out a **test market** a business hopes to make sure that the sale of a product or service will be a success, though it must be careful to make sure the **test market** is the same mix of socio-economic groups as the eventual market the business hopes to target.

Different products have different target markets

Activity

Activity 7: Missing words – mass, niche and test markets

Use the words given below to complete the paragraph on mass, niche and test markets. There are more words than spaces!

- small
- large
- televisions
- selling
- £10
- buying
- £2,000
- cheaper
- market
- expensive
- Ferrari cars

Mass niche and test markets

When a business sells a............number of products to different groups of consumers, it is said to be selling to a mass market. .... are an example of a mass market product. A niche market is where a business sells only a.........number of products which may be............, because only a small number are available for consumers to buy. A dress costing............would be said to be targeting a niche market.

Larger businesses may test market a product. This will mean...............it only in a small area which represents the general target............... they will eventually sell to if the test is successful.

Assessment Activity

Alison Gray has always loved food and has worked in a restaurant in Dinchester for ten years. She now wants to open a restaurant of her own so that she can fulfil a lifetime ambition and, she hopes, to make money out of something that has always been a hobby. Her idea is for an up-market restaurant for customers who like a quiet atmosphere and quality food.

She now has to decide where to locate the business, and is trying to decide between Dinchester, where she has worked, or nearby Newtonham.

The following data has been collected by Alison to help her make the decision. She now needs your advice.

Figure 4 Socio-economic group data

Social Class	Job type	Newtonham	Dinchester
A	Doctors, judges, company directors of large businesses	5%	9%
B	Teachers, department managers, solicitors	15%	27%
C1	Supervisors, clerical workers, sales assistants	32%	33%
C2	Skilled manual workers, plumbers, electricians	25%	20%
D	Semi-skilled workers – assembly line workers, cleaners	15%	8%
E	Unemployed, casual workers, state pensioners	8%	3%

Figure 5 Age group data

	Newtonham	Dinchester
Total Population	135,000	140,000
Age 0 to 11	15,000	9,000
Age 12 to 19	20,000	8,000
Age 20 to 29	35,000	30,000
Age 30 to 59	40,000	45,000
Age 60+	25,000	48,000

Question

Using the information in Figures 4 and 5, advise Alison on which location, Dinchester or Newtonham, would be most suitable for her bookshop. Give reasons for your advice, using the data as necessary.

Advice on how to answer the question

The question is centred on an up-market restaurant selling quality food. The question, then, to ask yourself is what *type* of person will most likely want to use such a restaurant. Is it older people, younger people, richer people, poorer people, families or couples on their own?

Once you have you have decided on the features of this target market, you then must use your knowledge of socio-economic groups to decide which group fits this target market for Alison. Then look at each town, along with the age group data. The one with the highest number of the target market will be the one to recommend.

Remember to use the data in your answer. You should be using figures from Figures 4 and 5 to support any ideas you put forward.

Key facts

- Most businesses are market-orientated rather than product-oriented.
- Most products are targeted at a number of different market segments.
- Socio-economic groups are an important method by which businesses analyse a market.
- The amount of disposable income a consumer has is important to a business when targeting its products.
- Mass and niche markets are opposites. 'Mass' means large; 'niche' means small.
- Test markets are used by businesses to try out products before full production takes place.

Key Terms

Make sure you can explain each of the following key terms:

Socio-economic groups A method of dividing up the population based on the occupation of the head of the household.

Mass market Making a product or providing a service aimed at a large number of customers.

Niche market A small market for a specialised product.

Product-oriented Where a business makes a product and hopes to sell it without first analysing the market.

Market-oriented Where a business analyses the market and consumers' needs for a product before starting production.

Market segments How the market for a product or service is divided – for example, by age or gender.

Targeting When a business aims a product or service at a particular group of consumers it is said to be targeting that group.

Disposable income The amount of money a consumer has to spend after paying essential bills.

Test market Where a business tests its product in order to see whether consumers will buy it.

Market research and data collection

Activity

Activity 1: Explanation – Using market research

Market research is an important ingredient for business success

Mark Hanson has worked in an Italian restaurant for two years. He has always dreamt of starting his own restaurant business but is worried whether such a thought is really a good idea. He knows that to start a business he must do some research first in order to check that people will want to use it, and they will like what he wants to serve. His problem is that he has no clear idea as to where he should start in his research. He has thought about asking his friends and relatives to see what they think.

1 Explain why Mark may choose to ask friends and relatives.

2 Advise Mark why asking friends and relatives might not be a good idea.

3 Suggest three questions that could help Mark in his research. Give the reasons why you think these questions are appropriate.

4 Mark has been advised to look at whether other Italian restaurants are successful in the local area. Explain what Mark may learn from this exercise.

What is market research?

Market research is how businesses collect information on whether their products or services will be bought. It is important that a business carries out this research before it begins production, so that time, money and effort are not wasted on products that people do not want to buy.

What type of information should a business collect and why?

A business may need to collect information on the following:

● **Whether customers will buy the product or service.** This is a basic question, as if there is no interest at all then the business should not continue with developing the product or service

- **How often customers will buy the product.** Even if a lot of customers will buy the product it is important to find out if they will buy the product every week, every month, and so on. For example, a restaurant may find that enough customers will buy a meal, but only once every year. This might mean that the restaurant business is not really worthwhile.

- **The price that customers are willing to pay.** This is an important part of market research, as consumers may be very willing to buy a product that has a low price. However, the price must be high enough for the business to cover its costs and make a profit.

- **The type of customers interested in the product.** This information will help the business to target its product at the correct market segment. This may include details such as age and occupation (see 'Analysing the market' in Unit 1.3.1).

- **Where the product should be sold.** It is important that a business knows where a product will sell. This could be in a certain part of the country or in a type of shop. For example, will teenagers buy expensive trainers in a supermarket or is it better to sell them in specialist sports shops?

Methods of market research

There are two types of market research a business will use. These are **primary research** and **secondary research**. Primary research is also known as 'field research' and secondary research is sometimes called 'desk research'.

Primary research

Primary research means collecting information first hand. This means that the business designs and collects the information itself, or perhaps pays a research organisation to collect the information for it.

The benefits of using primary research are:

- The business asks the questions it wants in any research. This means it can find out exactly the information required.

- The information collected is up to date. Any research information must be as up to date as possible, as the opinions of consumers do change.

- The research can be designed in such a way that the information collected can be analysed easily.

Methods of collecting primary research information

Businesses will use one or more of the following methods when they use primary research:

- surveys

- consumer panels

- testing and observing.

Surveys

Surveys are the most common way of collecting primary information. They are usually in the form of **questionnaires**, which may be sent to consumers in the post, or put in with guarantee forms for products. **Interviews** are conducted in which consumers are asked questions and the person asking the questions (the interviewer) fills in the answers. Group interviews are sometimes used where a group of consumers are asked the same questions at the same time. Interviews can also take place over the telephone to collect information.

Advantages of using surveys

- The questions can be designed to provide exactly what the business requires, with detailed information being collected that can be analysed later.

- When an interview technique is used, the person asking the question (the interviewer) can explain any questions that the person being asked (the interviewee) does not understand.

- The correct amount of information can be collected when interviews are used. If a business requires the opinions of 1,000 consumers, then it can make sure that 1,000 interviews take place.

Disadvantages of using surveys

- The questions being asked in a survey must be clear, otherwise customers will not understand, and later analysis will be incorrect. For example, if a question asks consumers if they have seen an advertisement for a product, if they say 'yes' this does not mean they are about to buy it.

- The interviewer must not ask questions in such a way that the interviewee is made to answer in a particular way, otherwise the information collected will not be accurate.

- Collecting information by using surveys takes time and is expensive. Many smaller businesses will not be able to afford this type of research.

- When postal surveys are used, many consumers may ignore the form and throw it away. To persuade consumers to return the completed questionnaire form, a prize is often offered as an incentive. Even with this system, a business cannot be certain how many survey forms will be returned.

- Using the telephone to collect information may upset consumers, who dislike being disturbed at home – especially if they are just starting a meal when the telephone rings!

Activity

Activity 2: Explanation – Designing a questionnaire

1 Design a questionnaire on a new soft drink called Wizzfizz, an exciting combination of exotic fruits with a new energy formula. You should aim to have between eight and ten questions.

2 Briefly explain why you included each of your questions.

Consumer panels

Consumer panels are groups of consumers who are regularly questioned on test products and services. Because they are already used to the idea of market research they can give clear and detailed information that a business can use. Questionnaires would be filled in correctly and the members of the panel would need little help. The people in the panel would be carefully selected for the product they are reporting on and are usually paid for the work they complete. Once again these are often expensive to set up and keep going, which means that only larger businesses, for example, washing powder manufacturers, would use this type of primary research.

Testing and observing

This type of primary research involves consumers' reaction to products being recorded in some way. It may involve consumers being watched as they look at a new display in a shop, or consumers being invited to see if they can tell the difference between two similar products. This is sometimes done with the consumer being blindfolded and the scene used later in advertisements for television. Food products in a supermarket may be tested by consumers being invited to taste a small sample. Observers will then record the reaction to the product for later analysis.

Many products and services are not suitable for this type of primary research. Careful thought needs to be given before using testing and observing.

Primary research – whom to ask

When a business decides that it will conduct some primary research, it must carefully decide *who* it requires information from. This involves deciding what the **target market** for the product is likely to be. For example, if a business was thinking of introducing a new sports car, it would be of little use questioning children under 15 years old. However, if another business wanted to produce a new flavour of crisps, those under 15 would certainly be asked.

The use of guarantee forms for information is especially useful here as a business is collecting information from the very people who have bought their products.

Sampling

Sampling is an important part of primary research. If a business required information before developing a new product it would be impossible to question every possible customer. What is needed is a system for selecting a *number* of those consumers likely to buy the product who *represent all* the possible consumers. For example, if a school was thinking of changing its uniform and wanted the reaction of students, there would be no real point in asking *all* the students at the school. A few people from each year group could be questioned, which would represent accurately the views of the other students.

Methods of sampling

1 **Random.** This means that each person has an equal chance of being selected for questioning.

- **Advantages.** The selection of those to be questioned can be chosen easily, for example every 10th person that passed a certain point. The cost of collecting this type of data will be lower as there is often little planning. This will save businesses money which could then be used elsewhere.

- **Disadvantages.** Random sampling is not very accurate, with the data collected often not exactly what the business wants. For example, a business may want half those questioned to be under 20. Random sampling cannot guarantee that level of accuracy and because of this, any analysis of the data could be misleading.

2 **Quota.** This method of data collection involves carefully selecting the consumers who are to be questioned. The way consumers are selected is based on the target market for the product or service being researched.

- **Advantages.** This method of data collection is much more accurate. For example, if a business wanted 10% of those questioned in age group 40–60, 30% in age group 20–39, and the remainder in age group 12–19, then a quota sampling method would make sure that precisely those percentages of consumers were asked. This will make any later analysis of the data more accurate and useful for the business when planning for the future.

- **Disadvantages.** Because of the planning required and the fact that only particular people can be questioned, quota sampling is more expensive. This may mean that for smaller businesses in particular it is not a realistic choice for research.

Activity

Activity 3: Zone activity – Primary research

Complete the following chart by matching the correct starting phrase with one of the phrases below.

Figure 2: Primary research

Primary research is also known as
Primary research is often
Consumer panels are groups of consumers
Smaller businesses often don't use primary research
Sampling is
Random sampling is where
Quota sampling is where

- who are questioned by producers and test products on a regular basis
- each person has an equal chance of being interviewed
- because it can be expensive
- field research
- researching from a chosen number of consumers
- the most up to date information available
- a carefully selected number of consumers are selected

Evaluation point

When choosing an appropriate method of research to use, there are many factors to be considered. One important decision is whether a business wants precise, up-to-date information about particular consumers. If this is the case, then it is more likely that specially designed **primary research** will be used as there may not be any suitable **secondary research** available. If more general data is required, cheaper secondary research may well be suitable.

Activity 4: Explanation – Choosing a method of primary research

How would you collect primary information on the following products?

1 A new chocolate bar

2 A DVD recorder

3 Washing powder.

In your answer you should include details on the following:

- the method of primary research you would use and why it is suitable for the product
- whom you would ask
- why you would ask those consumers
- the sampling method you would use in any survey and why it is appropriate for the product.

Give reasons for your answers.

A business may further target the primary research at particular consumers – for example, by asking football fans at a match their opinions on admission prices and the cost of the new home strip. For this type of information to be any use to the business, there would be little point in asking consumers who had no interest in football.

Secondary research

Secondary research, sometimes called **desk research**, is research that another organisation has already completed. Secondary research information can be found in a number of places, such as books, newspapers, magazines and government publications through the Office for National Statistics.

Census data

For the census, every person living in Britain is questioned on how they live, what their income is, etc. The information is extremely useful for businesses, and is collected every ten years. The last census was in April 2001. The next one will be in 2011. Data collected by the Census can be seen at www.statistics.gov.uk

Internet

There is a huge amount of information available on the internet. Many companies now put information about themselves and their products on the internet, all of which can be used by others as secondary research.

Internal data

Many businesses have their own secondary data. This is in the form of past sales figures, profits from departments as well as comments from customers. This is usually kept on computers and can be used by a business when it is making decisions for the future.

Data published by other businesses

Public limited companies (plcs) must publish details of their financial performance. This can be used by other businesses as secondary research in order that they may see how they compare. These company reports can also provide a more general view of the business. The details of private limited companies can also be obtained from Companies House and used in the same way. Internet research also provides valuable information about businessess and can include data on prices, products and location.

Activity 5: Explanation – Choosing a method of secondary research

What type of secondary research could be useful in the following situations? Give reasons for your answer and try to be as precise as possible with your choices.

A business wanting to know:

1 How many banks are in the local area.

2 How many competitor businesses sell a particular range of products.

3 The number of people over 65 years of age living in a particular area.

4 The prices charged by competitor businesses.

The advantages and disadvantages of secondary research

Secondary research	
Advantages	**Disadvantages**
• As the research has already been completed by another organisation, secondary research is usually much cheaper to collect than primary research. • A wide range of data is readily available, especially with the growth of the internet.	• The research information might not be *exactly* what a business wants. Remember that someone else has completed the research. • The data may not be up to date. There are possible problems for a business which makes decisions based on outdated market research. • The data might not be in a form that the business can analyse easily. Only by designing its *own* research (primary) can a business be sure that it is in the form it requires.

Activity 6: Zone activity – Comparison of primary and secondary research

Complete the following chart, which shows a comparison of primary and secondary research. Use the statements below to help you.

Figure 4: Primary and secondary research comparison

	Primary research	Secondary research
Advantage 1		
Advantage 2		
Disadvantage 1		
Disadvantage 2		

- is often cheaper to complete
- is designed by the business so is just what the business wants
- may be out of date
- research collected may not be exactly in the form the business requires
- internet is a valuable easily accessible source of information
- precise amount of data can be collected through interviews
- may be expensive
- may take time to organise.

Activity 7: Explanation – Using primary and secondary research

Using the details from how you have completed Figure 4 on primary and secondary research, which advantage and disadvantage is most important to:

1 A new business.

2 A well-established business.

Give reasons for your choice.

SWOT analysis

SWOT stands for:
Strengths
Weaknesses
Opportunities
Threats.

A business will carry out a **SWOT analysis** when it is looking at how it is performing compared to other businesses. It can also be used by a business *before* it starts, in order to judge whether or not it has a chance of succeeding.

Strengths will examine what the business is good at doing. It may have a very good product, or it may have an office in every town in Britain so it can offer good service. A business may have extremely well-trained staff who are well motivated. When looking at its own strengths, a business must be honest and not imagine strengths that are not there.

Weaknesses will look at the opposite of strengths, and examine what the business should improve. This might be difficult for business managers who may not wish to admit having weaknesses. Only when weaknesses have been identified can action be taken to improve performance.

Opportunities looks outside the business and identifies the possible opportunities there are that the business might take advantage of. This may be on a large scale with a business hoping to succeed internationally, and on a small scale such as the building of a new housing estate, giving a window cleaner the opportunity to increase customer numbers.

Threats examines the problems that a business faces. This may be influenced by the government increasing taxes, which reduces the amount of disposable income consumers have.

Other threats may come from the competition a business faces. For example, in the computer games console market, Sony, Nintendo and Microsoft are constantly trying to bring out a better product to stay ahead of each other. A business must not fall behind its competitors for long or it may find it difficult to make up lost ground. In other situations a competitor might cut its prices and so take some of your market share. A successful business will always identify the possible threats from other businesses and plan a solution.

An example of SWOT analysis

Dyson cleaners

Strengths

- **Design.** The Dyson cleaner places great strength on its unique design, with advanced technology.

- **Bagless cleaning.** The Dyson cleaner does not need a bag to be replaced regularly like conventional cleaners. This will save money for the owner.

- **Power.** Because of the bagless operation, the Dyson does not lose power (when a bag becomes full of dust in a conventional cleaner, some power is lost) and is able to pick up more dust etc. from carpets.

- **Respected name.** Dyson has now established a well respected name in household products. This can help the introduction of further products in the future.

- **Helps asthma and allergy sufferers.** Because of its technology, Dyson cleaners claim to be the most suited for use by people who suffer from asthma and other allergies.

Weaknesses

- **Price.** Having the latest technology and advanced design does come at a price. Dyson cleaners are more expensive than some of their competitors.

- **Weight.** Some Dyson cleaners are heavier than products made by competitors. This may make those cleaners less attractive to some consumers.

Opportunities

- **Other cleaner development.** Dyson cleaners have expanded their cleaner models over the years (for example the ball cleaner) and this could continue in order to provide products for different consumers in different living conditions.

- **Different products.** The use of advanced technology at Dyson is now being applied to products other than cleaners. Examples are washing machines and hand dryers.

- **Exports.** Dyson cleaners are now sold in a number of countries. There is further opportunity for expansion in this aspect of the business.

Threats

- **Competitors.** Competitors such as Hoover and Panasonic were at first slow to react to the introduction of Dyson cleaners. Such large global businesses must however still be regarded as a threat and may develop technologies to rival Dyson.

● **Falling consumer income.** Dyson cleaners are more expensive than many competitor models. If incomes fall, then consumers may choose to save money and buy a cheaper cleaner from another maker.

Assessment Activity

Bradley and Natasha live in Dinchester. They have a small garden centre business but now feel that there is an opportunity to expand the business by providing gardening services aimed especially at older people who are having trouble keeping their gardens tidy. They need help to complete their research, but have made a start by drawing up the following questions:

● How old are you?
● Are you interested in gardening?
● Would you be interested in a weekly gardening service?
● Do you like to see your garden tidy?
● How much are you prepared to pay for a weekly gardening service?

Questions

1 Evaluate the suitability of the above questions.

2 What other questions would you think appropriate in these circumstances? Give reasons for your answer.

3 Analyse different sampling methods available to Bradley and Natasha in completing their research. Which method would you advise them to use?

Give reasons for your answer.

Advice on how to answer the questions

You must put yourself in the role of Bradley and Natasha, and look at what they are trying to do. Data is required from 'people who are having trouble keeping their garden tidy'. The information states that they are *especially* targeting older people. It does not say that they are *only* targeting older people. This will give some indication about the questions they should be asking and *whom* they should be asking.

You are asked in question 1 to 'evaluate'. This means that you must make a judgement concerning whether you would use each of the questions or not. In all cases, give reasons for any decisions you make.

The final question asks you to 'analyse'. This means explaining the advantages of different sampling methods and how they might be useful to Bradley and Natasha.

Key facts

- Market research is important to the success of a market-oriented business.
- There are many reasons why market research should be undertaken. The most important is whether consumers will buy a product at the price the business requires.
- The two main types of research are primary (or field) and secondary (or desk).
- Primary research is often more use to a business, as it can be designed for its exact needs and be up to date.
- Surveys, in the form of questionnaires and interviews, are the most common form of market research.
- Market research, especially primary, can be expensive.
- The Census is an important source of secondary data. The internet is of growing importance, but remember that not all groups of people use the internet in the same way.
- Market research should always be aimed at the target market for the product.
- Sampling means questioning a small sample of your market.
- Methods of sampling are random and quota. Quota is the more commonly used.
- SWOT analysis means looking at strengths, weaknesses, opportunities and threats.
- Not all businesses use all types of market research. Smaller businesses may use very little, if any!

Key Terms

Make sure you can explain each of the following Key Terms

Market research The collection of data on customer habits to help decision-making in marketing.

Primary research Data collected first-hand, often in the form of surveys. Sometimes referred to as field research.

Secondary research The collection of data using research or information provided by others, such as magazines, journals and the internet. Often called desk research.

Surveys Primary research data collected in the form of questionnaires and interviews.

Questionnaires A question sheet filled in by the consumer.

Interview A question sheet filled in by the person conducting the interview.

Consumer panels Groups of consumers who are paid to comment on products and services. They are often kept by a business to act as a permanent method of testing their products.

Target market The group of customers to whom a business aims to sell its products. The target market may be other businesses as well as consumers.

Sampling The method of choosing a group of customers to represent the views of the target market for a product or service.

Random sampling Choosing a sample for market research where each customer has an equal chance of being asked. A true random sample is often difficult to achieve, and is not used as much as quota sampling.

Quota sampling A method of choosing a sample that represents the target market. If females buy 80 per cent of a product, then there should be four females questioned to every male in a quota sample.

Census data Data collected by the Government every ten years, questioning the entire population on their income, occupations etc.

SWOT analysis The process of a business looking at its performance against others, examining strengths, weaknesses, opportunities and threats.

The marketing mix

Learning Outcomes

By studying this unit you will be able to:

- **Understand how the marketing mix is principally made up of the 4 Ps – Price, Product, Place and Promotion**
- **Explain why the marketing mix is important for business success**
- **Understand the role of packaging in marketing**
- **Explain and evaluate the benefits of customer service as part of the marketing mix**
- **Discuss the way in which franchising can be used in a marketing context**
- **Analyse and discuss the effects of ethics in marketing.**

Introduction

The marketing of a product or service is an important part in the success of any business. This starts with the product itself, which must be something that consumers want. The price must be right; otherwise customers simply will not buy. The product must be sold in a place where customers can get to, or, if it is not, perhaps available on the internet. Customers must be told about the product through advertising, and possibly offered special deals, or promotions to persuade them to buy.

However, even this is not enough for many businesses who want to make sure that their customers get the best available service, not only when they buy a product but also long after. A number of businesses also look to behave in a fair and morally correct way. By doing this they feel they will be able to sell more products and help others at the same time.

All this adds up to the **marketing mix**, a combination of different factors that a business will use to increase its sales through marketing.

The 4 Ps of the marketing mix

A good way of starting to study the marketing mix is the 4 Ps. These will form the basis of the marketing for most businesses. The 4 Ps are:

- Price
- Product
- Place
- Promotion.

Obviously a business must have a **product** that customers want to buy and it must be sold in a **place** that the target customers will use. In addition to this, the **price** of the product must be acceptable to the customer. If customers are to be attracted to the product, for example by advertising, the business must undertake some **promotion**.

This way of looking at marketing is known as the **marketing mix**, and is principally made up of the **4 Ps** of product, place, price and promotion. It is called a 'mix' because all of the four Ps must be 'mixed' in the correct way to make sure the product or service is marketed successfully.

Activity

Activity 1: Explanation – Using the marketing mix

There are many decisions to be made when marketing a business

Memories Ltd is a business specialising in selling souvenirs at holiday resorts in Britain. Its marketing manager, Nick Brown, is reviewing how the business should be marketed. He is interested in looking at the following and would like your advice on what you think the business should do.

● Where they should advertise the shops, or should they simply not advertise at all?

● The range of products they should sell

● What offers they could use to tempt people on holiday to buy their products

● How they should decide on the price to charge for different products

● Should they try for a sea-front location for the shops or is any location in a town suitable?

● Would they be able to sell their products in other ways, such as on the internet?

Write a short report to Nick on how you think the business should be marketed, making sure you cover all the points above. Always give reasons for any recommendations you make. Complete the work on a computer if possible to help with presentation.

Success in marketing requires the correct mix

The importance of a business having the correct mix cannot be over-emphasised. How the mix is made up will also change for businesses in different situations. For example, if a business is unknown it may have to put more into promotion (which includes advertising and special offers) than a business that has already built up a good reputation. A business that is in competition with many other businesses may have to be more careful about price than a business that has little or no competition.

The market mix is closely linked to **market research** (see Unit 1.3.2). From good market research, a business will have a clear idea of whether the product is something a customer wants to buy. Research will also have identified the price that customers are willing to pay, the places where they buy similar products and the types of promotion that interest them.

Problems with an incorrect marketing mix

If the mix is wrong in any way, then the results can be disastrous.

In the 1980s Sir Clive Sinclair invented his C5 battery car. Sir Clive was well known, and attracted a lot of publicity for the new invention, a single-seater battery car. This meant that the early promotion of the product was good. The price, at £399, was thought to be reasonable, and it was available in many places. What was *wrong* was the product itself. Without detailed market research, the car was produced in the belief that consumers would want to own this new invention. Unfortunately for Sir Clive, consumers did *not* want to go along at a slow speed (15 miles per hour) at a height that meant that exhaust fumes from lorries and buses blew straight in their faces. The C5 was a famous flop, but shows very well that even a successful businessperson (Sir Clive had made his fortune making pocket

calculators) can make costly mistakes if the market mix is not correct. However, there is now much more interest in battery powered cars.

The C5 was never a successful product – but could it return?

Activity

Activity 2: Research – Examples of marketing failure and success

1 Ask your parents if they can remember any products that were a failure, or perhaps did not last very long at all.

 What was the reason for the failure? Was the price wrong? Was it because no one wanted the product?

 Can you think of any such failures yourself?

 Write up your report on a computer if possible. Title it 'Business Failures'.

2 Now title a new piece of work 'Business Successes'. Think of a range of different products that always seem to have been with us (some food products will make a good start). What has made these products last so long? Explain how the marketing mix helps show us why these products have been with us for such a long time.

Evaluation point

When evaluating the most important part of the marketing mix, there are many considerations. An important one is simply producing a product at that time that consumers actually want to buy. The Sinclair C5 (see above) was not wanted by consumers at that time, however well it may have been advertised. A product such as Kit Kat, first sold in 1937, is something which has always been popular with consumers.

Other parts to a successful marketing mix

The 4 Ps are the main parts to the **market mix** for most businesses. There are, however, other considerations that businesses may have in the marketing of their products or services.

Packaging

Packaging is sometimes called the fifth 'P'. For many products, such as electrical goods, packaging is there simply to protect goods while being transported and plays no real part in the final sale of a product. When you see television sets for sale, they are not kept in their packaging. It would be strange to go shopping for a new CD player and simply see a pile of boxes from different companies. But for other products, such as children's toys, the packaging is vital and is often aimed at bringing the child's attention to the product. In these types of product, a great deal of care goes into the design of the packaging in order to make the product successful.

Customer service

Customer service is becoming increasingly important in the marketing of products and services. In a business, customer service can take many forms such as:

- Giving customers help and advice on different product or services with friendly well-trained staff

- Having help available through the internet or phone

- Offering free delivery on large items with a guaranteed delivery date

- Taking items back without any argument if at all faulty.

As many businesses are seeing the value of keeping their customers happy, huge sums of money are being invested in systems that will keep customers returning to buy more products. Customer services in shops will deal with items that are being returned, often taking goods back which by law they have no need to do. The belief is that customers will feel that the shop has treated them very well in a difficult situation and will return to spend more money in the future.

Ventura operate telephone customer services for businesses such as O2 and National Rail Enquiries

Some businesses have opened large call centres in order to answer customer questions and make 'courtesy' calls to make sure that customers are receiving good service. Call centres can be located in any area of the world to service the whole country. Good customer services may be *the* reason why people return to certain businesses, in the knowledge that if something *does* go wrong, then they will be treated well.

Some businesss have developed a good reputation based on well-developed customer service. The John Lewis Partnership have a policy where all the items in their shops are guaranteed not to have a higher price than other businesses. This 'Never knowingly undersold' policy has helped the business gain their reputation for good customer service.

The John Lewis Partnership: never knowingly undersold

Activity

Activity 3: Research – Investigating customer service

Search the websites of three well-known businesses that you are familiar with. Look to see what information they have under customer service. Summarise your findings in a short report or on a poster. Which business offered the most thorough customer service advice? Did any business *not* have any reference to customer service on its website?

Franchising

Franchising (see Unit 2.3.6) is a system where an established business (the **franchisor**) lets someone else (the **franchisee**) use their business name and method of operation for a fee. The franchisor will provide equipment, premises, support and training as necessary. The payment of this fee also enables the franchisor to further expand the business and pay for advertising, which in turn attracts more franchisees who are willing to pay to use the now more famous business name and successful methods.

The system started in the USA. In this country, McDonalds is possibly the most famous business which uses franchising, though there are many other businesses, large and small that use this method of developing a business.

Franchising and the marketing mix

Looking back at the marketing mix, we know that it is made up (mainly) of the 4 Ps of price, product, place and promotion. These 4 Ps are already in place for a franchisee to use to make the business a success. The relationship between franchising and the marketing mix can be seen in Figure 1.

Ethical behaviour

When a business behaves in an ethical way (see Unit 3.5.2) it behaves fairly and morally correct. This is now closely connected with marketing because businesses may advertise that they are an 'ethical' business as a way of attracting more customers who want to have a connection with an organisation that is fair and acting in a morally correct way. The Co-op Bank is one business that has always stressed its **ethical behaviour** in business in order to attract new customers.

Figure 1 Franchising and the marketing mix

Price	This is set by the franchisor, so that *all* the franchisees are selling at the same price. This will attract customers who know beforehand the price they will pay for the product.
Product	Again, this is controlled by the franchisor. All the products sold by the franchisees will be the same. Customers will become aware of the range of products being provided, and use the business because they know that certain products will be sold. For example at McDonalds, *all* of the products will be the same, down to the ingredients, the cooking time and the cooking equipment used. This will mean that a customer will know *exactly* what to expect. There is no uncertainty, which means that more customers will use the business.
Place	When a franchisor lets the franchisee use the business name and systems of operation, it is for a particular area. In this way, the franchisee knows that there will not be an identical business in that area. This lack of direct competition is another attraction of franchises.
Promotion	Because the franchisor has a larger business, they can afford much more extensive and expensive advertising and promotions. Think of a burger bar operating on their own and what promotions and advertising they can afford. Compare that to a much larger international organisation such as McDonalds and what it can do. The franchisees will clearly benefit from this system of operation, with yet more customers being attracted to the business by successful advertising.

The Co-op Bank has always stressed its ethical approach to business

Ethical behaviour and the marketing mix

Behaving in an ethical way will affect the way a business approaches its marketing mix. The relationship between ethical business behaviour and the marketing mix can be seen in Figure 2 on the next page.

Figure 2 Ethical business behaviour and the marketing mix

Price	The price charged for a product or service will be fair and not try to take advantage of the customer or supplier. An ethical business will always make sure that the people who supply it with products to sell will be paid fairly. This may mean a slightly higher price for the product, but customers have shown they will pay extra for a product if it is from an ethical business. So, if a business is seen to be ethical in its behaviour, it may be able to charge a higher price for its products than its non-ethical competitors.
Product	Ethical products are those that are produced in a fair and morally correct way. An ethical business will not buy products from countries where, for example, children are used in factories with very low wages to produce clothes. This may mean that an ethical business will not always buy the same products as other businesses.
Place	When choosing a distribution system (see Unit 1.3.6) an ethical business may choose to sell direct to consumers rather than to other shops who do not behave in an ethical way. It is important for an ethical business that they are seen to only deal with other businesses who behave in a similar way.
Promotion	An ethical business will advertise its products fairly and not try and take advantage of situations to make large profits. It will advertise the fact that it is behaving ethically. Traidcraft is one example of a business which advertises that fact that it is trying to fight poverty in the developing world through ethical business activity.

Assessment Activity

Kelly Reid owns a chain of four shops that sell small, quality ornaments that have been imported from Africa. She has tried to maintain an ethical approach to her business and has made sure that people who make the ornaments receive a fair wage and that they are kept in continuous employment.

She now wants to further market the business and is thinking about selling franchises as she hopes that the money she receives from selling them will help pay for the expansion of the business. Kelly knows that she must also change her general approach to marketing if the business grows. She is unsure what to do and would like advice on the following:

1 How should she advertise the expanded business? Where should she advertise?

2 Would there be any problem of selling franchises and keeping the ethical approach to business that Kelly feels is so important?

3 Will the expansion of the business create too many customer-service problems?

Advise Kelly on the points raised above, giving reasons for any advice you give.

Advice on how to answer the questions

In the first question you are asked to explain how you would advertise the expanded business. First of all think of the product, a small, quality ornament made in Africa. Where do you consider such a product could be advertised? Use your common sense here. Have you seen this sort of product advertised on television? If the answer is no, then don't recommend it now! Who might buy the product? When you have decided who will buy such an ornament then try and think of where such a person would see an advertisement.

You also need to write about how she should advertise. How much should she stress the ethical style of her business, or should she concentrate on, say, the quality of the product?

The second question is more difficult. Selling a franchise means that there are more people involved in the business. Will this mean that the ethical style of the business will be in danger? Could Kelly do anything to make sure that all those new people involved with her business share the same ethical values?

Customer service can be dealt with more directly if there is only one person involved in a business. Kelly has four shops and wants to expand. Will she have more customer-service problems? How do you think Kelly could deal with this, or is it *such* a problem that she should not expand the business?

Key facts

- The 4 Ps should be remembered as the basis for the marketing mix, though packaging and customer service can also be included
- All parts of the mix are important, though in certain circumstances, one part may be more important than another
- A successful business will link the results of its market research to how it uses the marketing mix
- Customer service is being seen by businesses as an increasingly important part of marketing
- Call centres are a growing part of how a business looks after its customers throughout the year
- Franchising is a popular way of extending the availability of a product or a service
- A number of businesses now stress their ethical approach in marketing their products or services

Key Terms

Make sure you can explain each of the following Key Terms

Marketing mix The parts that make up the marketing for a product or service. Often limited to the four Ps but can also include other features

The 4 Ps of the marketing mix Price, product, place and promotion

Customer service The ways in which a business looks after the interests of its customers. This can include special departments in shops or the setting up of separate call centres

Franchising A means by which an established business (the franchisor) allows another (the franchisee) to use its name, product range and expertise for the payment of a fee

Franchisor The owner of an established business who sells the franchise

Franchisee A person who buys the franchise from an established business

Ethical behaviour A term used to describe a business when it behaves in a fair and morally correct way

Price

Introduction

A business must take great care when deciding what price to charge for a product or service. The business may have many competitors selling similar products, which will influence the price that can be charged. A business may be new to consumers, who would need persuading to buy the products being offered, possibly by a price reduction.

The different situations businesses find themselves in will have an important impact on how the price of a product or service is set. For this reason, the method of deciding the price will change over time.

A business needs to look carefully at the prices it will charge

The importance of price in marketing

Most consumers take notice of the price of a product when they buy it. Only a few very rich people can afford to buy products and services without bothering about the price. Because consumers are so concerned about price, businesses must make sure that the price they charge is at a level that consumers are prepared to pay. If a business sets a price too high, it will soon see its mistake when consumers simply refuse to buy. A business cannot set a price that is too low because it will not make the profits needed both for investment and to reward those who have invested money in the business in the first place.

Activity 1: Explanation – Making decisions on price

1 Lilly Ashcroft has a market stall at a busy town market, where there are a number of other stallholders selling the same or very similar products. She has not had her stall as long as some of the other market traders and so she cannot rely on old customers coming back each week to buy from her. Lilly knows that she must get the price of her products right if she is to have a successful business. She would appreciate your views on the following, and your reasons for any advice given:

- How important is it to consider the prices charged by other stallholders?
- Will selling products for 99p a kilo rather than £1 a kilo really make a difference?
- What can Lilly do with price to try and attract customers who have always gone to other stalls? She knows the cost she pays for products and does not want to make a loss.

2 Explain how Lilly's approach to setting prices may be different from, and similar to, a much larger business such as Tesco.

Setting the correct price for a product is a complicated process

Factors that affect the price of products and services

There are many factors that affect the price a business could charge. A business may look at the price charged by competitors; it will have to consider its own costs and the level of profit it hopes to make. A new business may have to take into account the fact that consumers are not familiar with their name and may be reluctant to buy products unless the price is really low. Businesses try to solve these problems by using different pricing strategies in different situations.

Methods of pricing used by businesses

Businesses in different situations will use different pricing methods. The most commonly used methods are:

- **competitor pricing**
- **'cost plus' pricing**
- **penetration pricing**
- **skimming**
- **differential pricing**
- **promotional pricing**
- **psychological pricing.**

Competitor pricing

This method simply looks at the price being charged by competitors to give a business an indication of the price it should charge. If someone was hoping to set up a new window cleaning service, it would be sensible to see what prices any competitors were charging before the business opened. The new business may well charge slightly less than others, but the price will be based on the competition.

'Cost plus' pricing

It is vitally important for a business to look carefully at its costs before deciding on a price to charge its customers. If the costs of a business were greater than the price it charged, it would eventually close. Businesses will look at their cost to make the product and add the profit they wish to make (the 'plus' part). Calculating profit in this way makes sure a business makes a profit, *providing* that it can sell the amount it needs to.

Penetration pricing

When a business is unknown to the public it may have a problem persuading consumers to buy its products. Consumers are often reluctant to try new names, preferring to stay with the trusted brand names that they have always bought. To 'penetrate' or break into this new market, a business may reduce its price in order to tempt consumers away from the established companies. Once it has established a name, and becomes accepted by the public, the 'new' business can put its prices up to the level of the competition. **Penetration pricing** should therefore only last for a short period of time, if it has been successful. As the price is lower than the business may want it would be impossible for the lower price to remain for long. It will not usually be used by a business that is well known but simply wants to bring out a new product.

Skimming

When a business introduces a new product that is clearly superior to its competitors', especially if it is a technical product, the new product can often be sold at a higher price. This is because many consumers are prepared to pay more to have the latest products. The setting of price in this way is called **skimming**. The computer games console market is typical of this pricing method. When a new computer games console comes out, keen players are prepared to pay a very high price to be the first to use the product. After a while the product becomes 'ordinary' and consumers are no longer willing to pay the higher price.

This results in fewer customers wanting to buy the product, so companies reduce prices to encourage more consumers to buy. Like **penetration pricing**, **skimming** would normally be used for a short period of time only.

Differential pricing

This method of pricing is used when different businesses charge different prices for the same product when selling to different customers. This is common in the transport business where customers can often be charged a wide variety of prices for what seems to be the same product.

For example, on a train, there may be the following customers all paying different fares for the same journey, sitting in the same carriage:

● single ticket holders

● return ticket holders

● senior citizens

● children

● tickets holders who bought their ticket on the day of travel

● ticket holders who booked in advance.

A business will do this to attract different consumers. Whether a train is full or empty, it costs much the same to run, so it is important to attract as many different groups of consumers as possible. A train may not be as busy after the morning rush hour, so prices are lowered for the same journey to attract those people who do not mind travelling at that time. A similar style of pricing is often used on buses.

Promotional pricing

Promotional pricing is a reduction in price used either to attract customers to an existing product or to sell off old products (as in a sale). Sales of a product may be falling a little and in need of a boost, or stock may need to be sold to make room for the next range of products. In both cases, promotional pricing can help the business. As with skimming and penetration pricing, it is only used for a short period of time, though sales in certain stores often seem to go on for most of the year!

Psychological pricing

This method of pricing is very common. As £9.99 *seems* to be *much* cheaper than £10, firms will price their goods in this way to attract consumers. Whether the price is £1.99 or £9,999.99, the intention is that consumers should feel they are getting a bargain and so help to increase sales.

Psychological pricing is designed to attract attention by seeming to be cheaper

Activity

Activity 2: Zone activity – Pricing strategies used by businesses

Complete the following summary chart by using the phrases below.

Figure 1: Pricing strategies used by businesses

Differential pricing	
Skimming	
Cost plus pricing	
Penetration pricing	
Competitor pricing	
Promotional pricing	
Psychological pricing	

1 A method of pricing used when there are a lot of other businesses selling the same or similar products.

2 Prices are reduced for a short period of time, often to sell off old stock.

3 Where a business charges different groups of consumers different prices for the same product.

4 A method of pricing where the business looks at the price it paid for a product and then adds on profit to arrive at the price to be charged.

5 Where a business lowers the price of products or services to gain customers from other businesses.

6 A method of pricing where the business has a higher price than competitors because it has a better product, for which consumers are willing to pay a higher price.

7 Where prices are £9.99 rather than £10 to make the product seem much less expensive and so attract extra sales.

Evaluation point

When you are evaluating different pricing strategies to make a recommendation, never lose sight of the product that is being sold. The product may have competitors, which will affect price. The product may only be aimed at a few select wealthy customers, which will again affect the pricing strategy. The product may be new and unknown. This will again have implications for the choice of pricing strategy.

Activity

Activity 3: Explanation – Using pricing strategies

What pricing strategy would you recommend for the following situations?
Give reasons for your recommendations, which may include a range of different strategies.

1 An existing chocolate bar from a well-known maker.

2 The next Playstation from Sony.

3 A new brand of hair shampoo; the maker is unknown in the UK.

4 A restaurant introducing a new range of meals.

5 A mobile-phone service provider wanting to tempt customers from rival businesses.

6 A coach operator introducing a new long-distance service from Birmingham to London.

Activity

Activity 4: Missing words – How pricing strategies may change over time

Insert the correct word into the spaces in the paragraph below.

- profit
- promotional
- penetration
- better
- high
- lower
- skimming
- competitors

How the approach to pricing may change over time

When a business first introduces a new product it may use...............pricing if it wants to gain market share from..........If the product or service is thought to be much............. than the competition, a business might use............in order to make as much........as they can.

After time when the product becomes older, a business might have to............the price in order to keep sales..........as consumers see the product as being dated. To finally get rid of old stock when the product or model is no longer made then........pricing may be used.

Assessment Activity

Nigel Bird owns Bird Train Services, which makes and repairs model trains and control equipment for enthusiasts. He sells four different types of model engines, which he has been making for some years, and offers a repair service on these as well as on other engines a customer might bring in.

Nigel is now developing a new type of remote control for model trains and is thinking of how he should market such a product, in particular the price he should charge. He knows the new equipment will perform much better than his competitors', though he realises that other businesses may then bring out products in the future that will perform even better than his own design.

Questions

1 Analyse the pricing strategies that a business such as Nigel's might use.

2 Recommend a suitable pricing strategy for Nigel's new remote-control equipment. Give reasons for your recommendations.

3 How might the pricing strategy for the new remote-control system change over time? Give reasons for your answer.

4 How might the pricing strategy for the new remote control differ from the other products and services that Nigel sells? Give reasons for your answer.

Advice on how to answer the questions

When you are asked to analyse, make sure that you cover the advantages and disadvantages of all the pricing strategies, and remember to refer to Nigel's business.

When you have analysed all the different strategies, you need to select a suitable strategy for Nigel to use. Now you might not know too much about model train equipment, but you do know that this particular equipment is new and better than the competition, and that should be a clue to a suitable pricing strategy.

It is common to be asked about changes over time in marketing. Here you are asked about how a pricing strategy could change for the remote-control equipment. You are told that other businesses may well bring out better products in the future. What then should Nigel do with price? Can he use the same strategy as before or should it change?

Nigel sells model engines and repair services, and has done this for some time. How will the pricing strategy for these differ from the remote-control equipment, which is new, better than the competition, but which will also become outdated in the future?

Key facts

- The setting of a suitable price is vital in the marketing of a product.
- There are many factors that affect the price of a product or service.
- There are many pricing methods that businesses might use.
- Different circumstances mean that a business might use several pricing strategies.

Key Terms

Make sure you can explain each of the following Key Terms

Competitor pricing Setting a price based on prices charged by competitor businesses for a similar product.

'Cost plus' pricing A pricing method that adds a percentage for profit to the total costs of making a product. This gives the selling price.

Penetration pricing Setting a price lower than the competitor businesses. Often used by new businesses to break into a market. This should only be seen as a short-term strategy.

Skimming Where a new product is more advanced than competitors, a price is set high as some consumers are willing to pay higher prices to own the newest technology. Sometimes called 'creaming'.

Differential pricing Charging different prices to certain customers for the same product or service. Often used in the transport industry.

Promotional pricing Reducing prices to give products a boost or to sell off old stock. Most commonly seen as sales in shops.

Psychological pricing Setting a price such as £9.99 instead of £10 to make the product seem much cheaper.

Product

Learning Outcomes

After studying this unit you will be able to:

- Understand the different factors that determine the choice of product or service a business may provide
- Understand, analyse and evaluate the importance of research, development and branding in the marketing of a product
- Explain how the product mix contributes to marketing a product or service
- Understand and analyse the product life-cycle and its use in marketing
- Explain and evaluate methods of extending the life of a product.

Introduction

Product is another vital part of the marketing mix. Businesses that make products to sell must make sure that they are making products that consumers actually want to buy. Businesses that sell products (rather than making them) have to think carefully about the number of different products they sell. A large business such as Tesco will sell thousands of different products; a corner shop will sell far fewer. Whatever the number, the same question is asked: will consumers buy the product or service? If they will then fine, if not then stop selling!

The style of a product may not last forever. Some products are changed once a year or more. Others will last much longer with little change to their style or design. This, the life of a product, is another consideration for a business. Just how long can a business continue to try and sell a product or service before it has to be replaced?

The importance of product in marketing

Businesses will always try to supply products that consumers will want to buy, at a price at which the business can make the profit it requires. This will often come as a result of analysing market research, where consumer needs are identified. A business can then make the product with more certainty that it will be a success.

Even with this 'preparation', there are still some considerations that a business will have to make when marketing the product.

Considerations for marketing a product

Price

As covered in Unit 1.3.4, a business will need to decide whether the product is to be targeted at the lower 'budget' part of price, or the higher 'up-market' section.

Design

Certain products, such as clothing and furniture, will be marketed on their design. A

Activity

Activity 1: Explanation – Product and marketing

It is important for businesses to think carefully about the products they sell

Simon Jones owns a small business that sells new and second-hand computers. He is becoming concerned that the products he sells do not have a long life before they become 'dated' and lack the features of the latest models. Simon is keen to avoid having old stock which he cannot sell, but also wants to sell other products and services that will help increase the profit he makes. Another consideration for Simon is whether he should sell computers with a well-known brand name. At present he sells computers he has built himself, which can be sold for a lower price.

Write a report to Simon on how he should develop the products in his business, giving reasons for any recommendations you make. You should consider the following in your work:

● How the life of the products he has may be extended

● Other products and services that Simon may offer

● Whether or not Simon should sell new computers with a well-known brand name.

new design such as the Dyson cleaner gave the product a real advantage over competitors.

Image

How a consumer feels about owning a product may be used in marketing. It is more common in relation to exclusive products such as expensive sports cars, where consumers like to be seen to own certain goods.

Research and development

Many businesses spend large sums of money on research and developing their products. Part of the research is investigating the needs of consumers, though **research and development** (R&D) can also include testing whether an idea will work or not. In developing his bagless cleaner, James Dyson

Both image and design are used to market sports cars

built many different versions of his vacum cleaner before those we know today were ready to be sold. In the medical industry, new drugs are developed and tested over many years before they are allowed to be used on the general public. For a business to stay ahead of the competition, or even just to keep up with it, there may be large financial investment in research and development.

Activity

Activity 2: Explanation – Considerations for marketing a product

When marketing the products a) – d) listed below, which of the following considerations is most important?

1 Price

2 Design

3 Image

Products:

a Perfume

b A digital camera

c A waste-paper bin

d A laptop computer

Give reasons for the choices you make. For some products you may want to recommend more than one consideration.

The product mix

Many businesses have more than one product or service they either make or sell. This is known as the **product mix**. If a business were to make only one product, that would be fine if consumers continued to buy the product. If, however, consumers stopped buying that one product, the business would certainly fail. By having a mixture of products, if one should prove unpopular, the firm could rely on others to provide sales revenue. A business that has a wide product mix recognises that not all consumers are the same and they will have different needs. A car maker will sell different model cars that have different colours, different engine sizes, different numbers of doors and so on. The old idea of Henry Ford that a customer for his cars 'can have any colour . . . as long as it's black' would certainly *not* work in the twenty-first century!

Despite this move by businesses to have a larger product mix, some businesses, such as Aldi, the cut-price supermarket, reduce the number of different items they sell. This is done in order to save money and be able to sell the products they do have at a lower price than their larger competitors. Small, local businesses simply cannot afford to sell a wide product mix, having little room to stock many items.

Aldi restricts the number of products it sells in order to cut costs

Branding

Branding is the use of a well-known name or symbol that consumers connect with a product or service. This name or symbol is called the **trade mark**. Many consumers will only buy products where they know the name, making it difficult for unknown new businesses to be successful. In sports clothing, many teenagers will only buy products with a certain name or symbol, which is then used by manufacturers to market further products.

A business with a brand name that is trusted by consumers will sometimes use that name to market products which are not part of their normal product mix. Boots is a business with a clear brand name, and has used that name to market holiday insurance, a product not usually thought of as something sold by Boots the Chemist.

The product life-cycle

All products have a time span over which consumers will want them. This is called the **product life-cycle**. No one would buy *exactly* the same product forever. Consumers' tastes change and products have to change to meet that changed demand. Sometimes products come back into fashion after a time when they wouldn't sell, clothes being a good example where different styles come and go. Other products have a longer life-cycle; many food products have changed little over the years.

The life-cycle of a product can be shown in graph form.

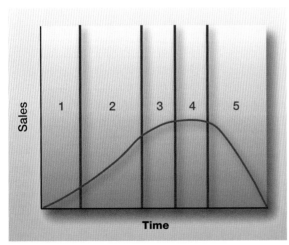

Stage 1 Introduction
Stage 2 Growth
Stage 3 Maturity
Stage 4 Saturation
Stage 5 Decline

As you can see, the graph is split into five sections, which are used to identify stages at which different marketing techniques need to be applied to the product in order to make it successful.

Introduction is where the product is launched or first put on sale. Before this a business may well have conducted some market research and invested money in developing the product. When the product is launched a business may advertise it in a number of ways, in order to make sure that it gets off to a successful start. Remember, at this stage the product is unknown and consumers need to be told about it. Sales should rise steadily.

Growth is the second stage, where the sales show their most rapid growth. Advertising and other promotion support (see Unit 1.3.7) change slightly as the product will be generally known to consumers. The product is still 'new' and will be in great demand.

Maturity is the next stage, where sales are towards their highest, but most importantly the *rate* of growth is slowing down. It may be necessary to support a product with further advertising and offers at this time to maintain sales against the competition.

Saturation. At this point the sales of the product are not growing at all, though clearly sales are still high. A business may be thinking about developing a replacement when saturation is reached, unless the life cycle itself can be extended. At saturation, a product may need some new offers to keep sales high.

Decline is the final stage in the life-cycle. Here sales are falling and though the product may be given some support in the form of further promotional offers, consumers see the product as old and switch to those of competitors or a newer replacement. It is at this stage that a successful business will have already developed a new product to replace the one that is in decline.

Activity

Activity 4: Explanation – Different stages of the product life-cycle

At what stage of the product life-cycle are the following:

a DVD players

b Digital radios

c Kellog's Corn Flakes

d Satellite navigation systems for cars

e Video recorders

Give reasons for your answers.

Activity

Activity 5: Explanation – How a product life-cycle can vary

Draw a product life-cycle to show the life of the following products. Note that some may have a very short life-cycle, some a very long one. This should be shown clearly by how you label the axis on your graphs. You must think how long they last before they are replaced and no longer sold. Give reasons for drawing your graphs in this way, and label the graphs fully.

Products:

a A Sony Playstation

b A chart single

c A car (a particular model e.g. Ford Focus)

d A mobile phone handset

Activity

Activity 6: Missing words – Description of the product life cycle

Use the words given below to complete the paragraph about the product life cycle.

● decline
● five
● time
● extend
● introduction
● replacement
● high
● maturity
● growth saturation
● life
● slowing

The product life cycle is divided into..........parts and shows the ....of a product measured against..............The first stage is called.............and is where the product is new. Advertising is often.......at this stage to make sure that consumers are aware of the product. The next stage is......................where the product is becoming well known. When the product reaches.............sales are at their highest, though sales growth is............... When the product reaches...................the sales are not increasing at all, and a business might be trying to ....the life of the product. The final stage is.................where the sales are falling and a business might be thinking of introducing a ....product.

Different products have different life cycles

Extending the product life-cycle

As can be seen from the graph of the **product life-cycle**, the highest level of sales is at the end of growth and into the maturity section. Businesses try to keep the sales of a product at this high level for as long as they can, as it will increase sales and profit.

A number of methods are used to try to *extend* the life-cycle and keep the sales as high as possible for as long as possible. These include the following:

- **Advertising** the product more widely is often used to maintain sales.

- **Price reduction.** By reducing the price, the product will be more attractive to consumers, and so help maintain sales.

- **Added value** may be given to the product to prevent sales falling. Car manufacturers often use this method, where an older model is given 'free' extra items such as air conditioning, better audio equipment, etc, to make it more attractive to consumers. A new model would not need such extras to sell it.

- **Other markets** may be developed. For example, if a business was at maturity level in Britain with a product, it might export to countries where the product was only at the introduction stage, with plenty of future sales opportunities. In other cases, a business might simply try to sell its product to a different target market than the one first used.

- **Relaunching** a product as 'new' and 'improved', with possibly a new image but little real change, may persuade consumers to continue buying the product.

Cadbury's Dairy Milk has had a very long life cycle

Evaluatio ?

It is very difficult for a business to judge the right time to replace a product. For some businesses, such as car manufacturing, the cost of designing and making a new model is very high, so will only be done every five or six years. In this case, there is a strong argument for trying to extend the life of an existing model. Where there are rapid changes in technology, such as computers and phones, new models must be brought out in order to keep up with competitors, so the life-cycle of any model is much shorter. In these businesses there is much less effort put into extending the life of the older version.

Activity

Activity 7: Research activity – How a product is developed

Research the history of Cadbury's Dairy Milk. Include in your work:

1 When it was first introduced.

2 The stage of the product life-cycle you think Cadbury's Dairy Milk is now in.

3 Changes that have been made over the years to the product (if any) and the way it is wrapped.

4 How products other than chocolate bars have now been developed by Cadbury using the Cadbury's Dairy Milk brand as a help to marketing.

Activity

Activity 8: Presentation – How to extend a product life-cycle

Choose one of the following products, or a product of your own choice. How can the product life-cycle for the product be extended? Remember that the time a product's life can be extended does vary, before it is replaced by the next model or different product. Give a short presentation to the rest of the group.

a A famous washing powder

b A bike

c An mp3 player.

Assessment Activity

JMW fashion is a large business making fashion clothing for the teenage market. It now wants to expand into the trainer market, but is concerned about the number of different styles they will have to supply. This expansion of their product mix will cost a lot to develop and the business is a little concerned about whether to go ahead.

The other concern in the business is about the life-cycle of the product. Just how long does the design of a trainer last before it has to be replaced? Is there any way of extending the life of a trainer design?

JMW would like your advice on these problems. They have a strong brand name in fashion and want to make further use of this.

Questions

1 Design a short questionnaire for your business studies group to fill in which will:

   a Identify the number of different trainer designs that JMW should consider making as part of their product mix

   b Provide ideas on how the life-cycle of a trainer design may be extended.

2   Use the questionnaire to produce a report for JMW on your findings. In your report you should analyse the different options for JMW on how they might extend the product life-cycle of a trainer design and make a recommendation as to the most appropriate action. Give reasons for your recommendation.

3   Evaluate the possible effects on JMW's strong brand name if the business decided to start selling trainers.

Advice on how to answer the questions

The advice is to have a short questionnaire that others can fill in. Keep questions to a minimum, but make sure you collect the correct information to go onto the next question.

The report on the number of trainer designs should be straightforward. Rather more difficult is the next stage, where you need to analyse. This means that you need to look at the advantages and disadvantages of the different methods of extending the life-cycle that you have covered in your work. From this you need to recommend one method for JMW to use. Make sure you give reasons why you made the choice!

The last question is on possible effects. This means that you might not be certain of what will happen, but you will need to come to some decision that is realistic for this situation. Remember the business is well known with a strong brand name. Will the introduction of trainers into their product mix make the brand better known, or is there a danger of the trainers not being successful and spoiling the brand name?

Key facts

- Many businesses invest large sums of money on research and development in order to keep their products ahead of the competition.
- Having a varied product mix is helpful to a business when the sales of one or more products start to fall.
- Branding is becoming increasingly important in the marketing of a product.
- The different stages of the product life cycle require different marketing techniques.
- The length of the product life-cycle is not the same for every product.
- Extending the product life-cycle is important if a business is faced with large investment needed to develop a new product.
- Product is but one part of the marketing mix. A business cannot simply concentrate on developing a product and ignore the other parts of the mix.

Key Terms

Make sure you can explain each of the following Key Terms

Research and development (R&D) is used to help introduce both new and existing products. The research may be testing products in a laboratory or conducting market research by interviewing consumers.

Product mix is the mixture of products or services a business markets. For example, Sony has a product mix which includes TVs, DVDs, camcorders, computer game consoles and hi-fi units.

Branding is the use of a name to market a product, e.g. Twix.

Trade mark is the use of a symbol or name to identify and market a product. It may be registered and be marked with 'TM' to make sure that other businesses cannot copy the trademark. Cadbury's is the registered trademark of Cadbury Limited.

Product life-cycle is the life of a product, usually shown as a graph divided up into five stages: introduction, growth, maturity, saturation and decline.

Added value is the extra items that are added to a product to help sales. Often used to extend the life-cycle of a product.

Relaunching occurs when an existing product is given a 'new' image to help boost sales and further extend the life-cycle of the product.

Place and e-commerce

By studying this unit you will be able to:

- Understand, explain and evaluate the importance of where a business sells its products or services
- Evaluate the different methods of distribution which a business might use
- Explain and evaluate the importance of the internet (e-commerce) in marketing
- Analyse and evaluate the advantages and disadvantages to businesses of e-commerce
- Analyse and evaluate the advantages and disadvantages to the consumer of using e-commerce
- Understand and explain the role of place in an overall marketing strategy.

Introduction

Choosing the place where a product or service is to be sold is an important decision for any business to take. What is also important is how the product or service reaches the customer. Should a business sell directly to the customer, or does it sell to a shop for that shop to then sell on to the customer?

In recent years the growth of the internet has meant that more businesses use **e-commerce** as a means of selling products rather than using a traditional shop. Customers are now buying goods and services in different ways, using price comparison sites to see where they should buy the products and services they need. Businesses have to react to these new developments.

The importance of place in marketing

It is often said that a successful business should have the right product in the right place at the right time. Though parts of price and promotion could be added to this phrase, it remains the case that a business has to have the product in the correct place for successful sales.

The **place** part of the 4 Ps is really in two parts:

1 *Where* the product is to be sold

2 The **method of distribution** to be used. In other words, how to get the product to the customer

Where to sell the product

This is linked to the location of a business, where a business may choose to sell its product or service in a town, an industrial estate, a village 'corner' shop, or in an out-of-town shopping mall. These decisions are important to a business that owns the shop itself. But what if you are a producer of a product without anywhere to sell it. What

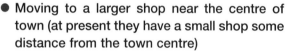

Activity

Activity 1: Explanation – Deciding how to sell a product

Brothers Mike and Peter own 'Valuables', a business which makes replica antiques. The products range from small items of furniture to larger clocks. The price they charge for the different products starts from £125 for a small cabinet to £975 for a large clock. They now want to expand their business and have recently bought a bigger factory unit, where the products are made.

Mike and Peter are now considering how they should sell their replica antiques. They are considering the following:

● Moving to a larger shop near the centre of town (at present they have a small shop some distance from the town centre)

How and where a business sells its products needs careful consideration

● Selling their products to an up-market furniture store

● Starting to sell their products direct from the factory

● Developing a website and selling through the internet.

Write a report to Mike and Peter, recommending how they should sell their replica antiques. Carefully consider the type of products they are selling, and what type of consumer is likely to buy the replica antiques. Give reasons for any recommendations you make, which may be a combination of the considerations above. If possible, use a computer to complete your work.

type of shop would be best for you? If you were making expensive furniture, would you try to sell it in a supermarket such as Tesco? Would that type of *place* suit the product? Consumers often have a fixed idea of what goods should be bought in certain places, and a business trying to sell 'different 'goods that a customer is not used to may find that this doesn't always work.

Businesses will often extend the places in which they sell their products in order to maintain growth. McDonald's first developed its restaurants in town and city centres. It then moved 'out of town' to retail parks and leisure areas. Motorway service areas have recently been targeted for further expansion. Marks and Spencer have also expanded into motorway service areas to extend the type of place where they can sell their goods (especially food) to consumers.

The methods of distribution

Distribution is all about getting the product to the consumer. It is of little use advertising

McDonald's has developed the place in which it operates

something that customers want to buy and then failing to make sure the product is in the correct place.

There are different **methods of distribution**, which are appropriate for different types of businesses.

Distribution method 1

Producer

Consumer

In this example the producer is distributing a product directly to the consumer. As the business will have to deal with each person who buys from it, this method is only possible with a small business. Imagine Heinz selling directly to everyone who wanted to buy their baked beans! The type of business where this method will be found is, for example, a small craft centre, which will sell its products direct to its customers. Small bakeries will often do the same.

A business selling its products to another business will often use this method of distribution. This is because the number of customers will once again be small and can be managed easily. As soon as the number of different customers becomes too large, a business must consider another method of distribution.

Distribution method 2

Producer

Retailer

Consumer

In this method of distribution, the producer sells to a retailer, who then sells to the consumer. This method is common in electrical goods, with producers such as Sony and Panasonic selling to shops such as Currys and Comet and consumers then buying from these shops. Once again, it would be difficult for Sony to sell its products directly to each person who wanted a television. It is easier for Sony to sell a number of products to a retailer who then sells the products to the consumer.

Distribution method 3

Producer

Wholesaler/Regional distribution centre

Retailer

Consumer

In this method of distribution, the producer sells to a **wholesaler** or sends goods to a **regional distribution centre** (RDC).

A wholesaler is a large storage centre able to take in deliveries direct from producers.

The role of a wholesaler is to 'break the bulk' of goods sent by the producer. This means buying in large quantities from a manufacturer and then selling smaller amounts to a retailer. This is especially important in the distribution of food, where small shops are often not able to store large quantities and so need to buy their stock in amounts they can cope with. Take the example of soup. Large producers such as Heinz will be unable to deal directly with *every* shop that sells its products. It will distribute the cans of soup in large quantities to the wholesaler, who will have a large warehouse to store the goods. Small retailers will then go to the wholesaler to buy, say, a tray of 24 tins of soup for sale in their shops.

Although the main role of the wholesaler is to break the bulk of goods between the producer and retailer, it does provide these other services:

- Credit can be given to the retailer, which enables the retailer to have the goods before paying for them. This 'trade credit' means that a retailer can sell the goods, which provides the money to pay the wholesaler.

- The wholesaler may be able to deliver products to the retailer. This may be very helpful when the products are bulky and heavy, or if the products are frozen and require special transport.

- A retailer may need help with a product, which the larger wholesaler will be able to provide where necessary.

- It should be remembered that the wholesaler provides a useful service to the producer, who would otherwise be unable to supply goods direct to the many consumers it might have.

The role of the regional distribution centre is slightly different. The RDC is owned by the

The Next regional distribution centre in South Yorkshire

retailer and is used to store the products it will later sell in its shops. Marks & Spencer and Next are just two examples of large businesses who use this system, where producers send goods to the RDC, which then sends the products to the shops as they are needed.

Evaluation point

When recommending a method of distribution remember that if there are a lot of buyers for a product, a business is unlikely to be able to supply directly to those customers. A retailer or a **wholesaler** is much more likely to be used.

Activity

Activity 2: Missing Words – Methods of distribution used by businesses

Use the words given below to complete the paragraph about the methods of distribution a business might use.

- regional
- product
- small
- consumer
- retailer
- wholesaler
- bulk
- direct.

Methods of distribution used by a business

Distribution is all about getting the.........to the.................. Some businesses sell...........to the consumer. These businesses are usually..........Other businesses may sell to a ....such as Comet who then sell to the consumer. Larger businesses may sell to a ....whose job it is to break.........and sell smaller amounts to a retailer. Businesses such as Tesco and Marks and Spencer have their own..................distribution centres where much of their stock is stored.

Activity

Activity 3: Explanation – Examples of distribution methods

Which method of distribution would you use for the following businesses? Give reasons for your choice.

a A business making quality jeans

b A small business making hand-made pottery in a craft centre

c A farmer selling milk

d A business selling holidays.

Activity

Activity 4: Research and explanation – The origin of products

For any 20 different products you have at home (for example, books, electrical, food, clothing, etc.) find out how they were bought. Was it:

● from a shop

● direct from the maker

● from a catalogue

● from the internet?

Display your results in a graph form with suitable illustrations. Explain why products are bought from different places.

The internet and e-commerce

E-commerce is the name given to marketing that brings buyer and seller together electronically through the internet

This grew in importance through the latter part of the 1990s, and is now being used by more and more businesses, both large and small. Older methods of marketing are now being changed in order to introduce the new technology offered by the internet. As more and more of the population use the internet, it is likely that e-commerce will become a more important part of the marketing strategy of a business. It does have its problems, with some of the early attempts at e-commerce failing.

Lastminute.com is a successful business which uses e-commerce

The pressure to change to e-commerce

There are a number of reasons why a business might feel that it *must* use e-commerce as part of its marketing activities.

Competition

When a business's competitors are offering an e-commerce service, it must seriously consider e-commerce itself if it doesn't want to lose customers. In this way, many businesses feel forced to change to e-commerce, even if they would prefer not to.

Productivity

With e-commerce, businesses are more productive, that is they can produce more with fewer workers. This saves wage costs in the business.

Increased profit

Because of the increase in productivity, profits are likely to increase. This is also helped by the opportunity in selling products to a larger market.

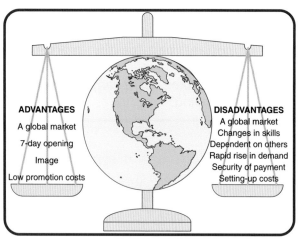

There are many advantages and disadvantages to a business when it uses e-commerce

Advantages for a *business* when using e-commerce

A global market

The potential market for a business using e-commerce is truly global. Even a small firm has the opportunity to sell to a world-wide market, even if it is only a sole trader operating from home. This brings a variety of linked advantages to a business.

Economies of scale

Selling to a **global market** increases sales, which in turn will lead to increased production and the opportunity to take advantage of economies of scale by selling goods in greater numbers.

New markets

Although a business might have reached saturation in its product life-cycle (see Unit 1.3.5) in the home market, it can sell to different markets throughout the world where the product is new. This will help to extend the product life-cycle.

New products

When a business sells to different markets, it has the opportunity of developing different products, which will help provide a variety of sales income.

Seven-day opening

E-commerce is open 24 hours a day, 7 days a week, 365 days a year. This gives massive potential for sales. As many more customers shop from home at any time of the day or night, e-commerce is the ideal way of making sure a business takes advantage of changing ways in which consumers buy products.

Image

Even the smallest business can present a professional and well-established image through e-commerce. This means that customers will see a business that they are prepared to use, even though they may not have heard of it.

Low promotion costs

When the global market that e-commerce can reach is taken into account, the promotion costs for a business are very low. This means that other methods of promoting may be dropped in favour of using e-commerce.

Disadvantages for a *business* when using e-commerce

A global market

Although the global market can bring benefits to a business, it can also bring problems. Businesses are now in competition with firms throughout the world. Just as it is a benefit for British companies to sell to Australia through e-commerce, it is also easier for Australians (and the rest of the world!) to sell to Britain. The increased competition may force prices down with the possibility that profits may be reduced.

Changes in skills

The skills needed to run an e-commerce business are different from those required for other businesses. Change may be difficult for some workers and managers.

Training

Workers will need training on customer services by computer, or in distribution skills if in a warehouse, etc. Training staff to use e-commerce will add costs to a business.

Recruitment

If there is to be an expansion of the business, new workers may have to be found. In the short term, this will add more costs to the business when there is no guarantee that the new venture into e-commerce will work.

Website building and maintenance

E-commerce demands that the website is maintained correctly. This may be beyond the skills of the workforce, resulting in specialist firms being employed, which adds further costs to the business.

Dependent on others

A business using e-commerce is dependent on others for its success. The difficulty is that the e-commerce business has no day-to-day control of the businesses that it relies upon. For example, a business using e-commerce will depend on its Internet Service Provider (ISP) for the display of the business. If there is a product to be delivered, many e-commerce businesses will rely on other firms to deliver on time. Any delay may mean lost orders in the future. Compare this to the 'normal' operation of a shop selling direct to a customer.

Rapid rise in demand

If a business is *too* successful in starting its e-commerce operations, it may be faced with so many orders that it has problems keeping to delivery promises it made. It is difficult to predict accurately the exact response e-commerce activity will bring. The reverse might also happen to a business not achieving the expected sales increase, which will then mean possible staff redundancies and poor publicity for the business.

Security of payment

Many potential e-commerce customers are worried about the security risk of using e-commerce. These worries are centred upon giving credit card details to buy goods on the internet. To give customers confidence in buying goods online, secure web pages are used, often shown using a padlock-type symbol. This method of **encryption** is aimed at making sure the personal details of the buyer cannot be copied. To process credit card payments a business may need to pay another specialist business if it does not have its own arrangements with its bank. All these additional features of e-commerce add costs to a business.

Setting-up costs

Although the promotion costs are small when compared to the potential number of

Activity

Activity 6: Zone activity – Advantages and disadvantages of e-commerce to a business

Put the following advantages and disadvantages of a business using e-commerce into the correct column in Table 1 below.

Table 1: Advantages and disadvantages of e-commerce to a business

Advantages	Disadvantages

1 A business can sell throughout the world and so has more potential customers.

2 The employees of a business may have to be retrained. This may be costly for a business.

3 A business may be able to improve its image with skilful use of websites.

4 All businesses can sell throughout the world so there is more competition.

5 A business can promote products much easier to a mass market with e-commerce. This will help increase sales.

6 There may be a need to recruit new workers with the introduction of e-commerce, which can add to business costs.

7 Other businesses may be needed to deliver goods bought through e-commerce. This may cause difficulties if they become unreliable.

8 A business is able to sell to new markets in different parts of the country or even overseas. This will help increase profits.

9 Credit or debit card details are required for payment in many e-commerce businesses. The possible security problems may put off potential customers.

10 There are costs with the building and maintenance of the website.

11 A business can be open at all hours throughout the year.

customers, designing and setting up a website can be expensive. At best it is an *additional* cost that a business did not have, though this may be helped by reducing spending on other marketing.

Advantages to *consumers* of using e-commerce

For any product or service, customers can be other businesses as well as general consumers. The following advantages (and disadvantages) should be seen from the point of view of a business buying on e-commerce and a private consumer.

Price comparison

When buying on e-commerce, prices can be compared easily, enabling the buyer to get the best possible deal and save money. There are now a number of price comparison sites, which are a business in themselves.

Seven-day availability

Just as it is an advantage for a business to open on e-commerce seven days a week, the customer can also buy at whatever time they wish.

Wide range of products

Because the internet can provide world-wide access to goods, the customer has a much wider choice of products. The correct product, at the correct price, can be chosen more easily.

There are many advantages for customers using e-commerce

Disadvantages to *consumers* of using e-commerce

Lack of personal contact

With e-commerce there is often no person to talk to directly. This may put some potential customers off using e-commerce as a means of buying goods. On the other hand, it may encourage others who prefer *not* to deal with people!

Problems returning goods

If goods purchased on the internet from a business in the UK are faulty, then consumers have the same rights as if the goods were bought from any other business. The goods must be of 'satisfactory' quality and match the description given. Despite this protection, some customers may feel that it is easier buying from, say, a shop and being able to sort problems out much more easily.

Only image of goods seen

When you buy something from a shop, you can see and touch the product, inspecting the quality. With e-commerce, only the image is available, which may not be suitable for some customers. If the customer knows the product well, such as a CD, there is less of a problem buying it with just an image given on screen.

Security

Security must be seen as a problem for the customer, as well as the business using e-commerce to sell goods and services. Credit card protection using **encryption** may be available, but this may still not be enough for some consumers.

Methods of payment

Customers wishing to pay by cash will not be able to use e-commerce. Much of the payment is geared towards credit cards, which are not used by all consumers.

Technology

To buy on e-commerce, a customer needs access to the internet. Though the number of people having internet access is increasing all the time, large groups, particularly the elderly, do not have the necessary access. A business wanting to sell using e-commerce must think carefully whether the target markets for the product are likely to be able to buy on the internet.

There are many possible problems for a customer when using e-commerce

Evaluation

When evaluating the advantages and disadvantages of e-commerce, remember to check whether it is from the point of view of the *consumer* or the *business.*

The suitability of e-commerce will be affected by the target market, and the product or service itself. Some products and services are much more suited to e-commerce than others.

The impact of e-commerce on business activity

The introduction of e-commerce is having a wide-ranging effect on business activity. It is also a fast-changing situation: you need to make sure that you have up-to-date

Activity

Activity 7: Research activity – Consumer reaction to e-commerce

1 Complete a survey of your business studies group on how they use e-commerce by buying goods on the internet. You need to make up your own questionnaire to find out:

   a What they bought through e-commerce

   b Why they used the internet rather than traditional shops

   c If they do NOT use e-commerce, what are the reasons?

2 Make a graph of your results.

3 Explain why certain goods may be bought on the internet, with other products still being bought in traditional shops.

4 Explain how your own views on e-commerce are similar to the group and how they differ from the group.

information on new developments. What *must* be remembered is that some products and services are much more suitable than others to being sold by e-commerce. Industries that have adapted well to e-commerce include some retail, travel and finance.

Already there have been changes in business activity in the following due to e-commerce:

- location
- new skill development
- levels of employment
- distribution
- customer services
- new business ideas.

Location

The locations of some parts of business activity have become more footloose than before thanks to e-commerce and now businesses are able to locate almost anywhere. A business will only need a telephone connection to take orders, this being referred to as the 'front end' of the business. A warehouse, storing goods to be sent to the customer when ordered, need not be in the same place as the office taking the order. For the warehouse, a location near the motorway network may be more suitable. In this way, locating different functions of the business needs different considerations.

New skill development

A business launching e-commerce will need the workforce to have different skills. This may be connected to the maintenance of the website, replying by email to customers or packing goods in a warehouse for delivery. All these jobs may not have been required before e-commerce. Extra training may well be required for all levels of staff. Workers may be recruited with the skills a business does not have itself. Some staff may feel threatened by the introduction of the new technology connected to e-commerce, especially if they are rather older and do not have ICT skills. Such staff need special care as they may well be vital to other parts of the business.

Levels of employment

The introduction of e-commerce may well increase and decrease the levels of employment. An existing business switching some of its operations to e-commerce may well find that it needs fewer staff due to the technology being used. Banks and building societies now offer many accounts that are available only over the internet. This enables them to reduce the number of staff needed in traditional branches.

A business may find it has to make some staff redundant who do not have the skills to transfer to e-commerce. However, a new business starting with e-commerce will recruit new workers.

Distribution

This is changing with the introduction of e-commerce.

Before e-commerce

After e-commerce

In this typical example the retailer does not have a role to play, since the goods or services are sent direct to the consumer from the producer. This may be through a warehouse, for goods such as books and CDs. It is often direct to the consumer when booking a holiday or opening an internet bank account. The continuing importance of the older distribution system for such goods and services is in some doubt if e-commerce continues to grow, though this may take some time.

Customer service

Because of e-commerce, how a business looks after its customers is changing rapidly. Unlike traditional methods, there is no person-to-person contact if there is a problem. Staff in an e-commerce business need to deal with customers by email or possibly the phone. This may need additional training and new thinking on how to cope with difficult situations at a distance without ever meeting the customer. Speed of service is vital in this situation; a customer will not return if there is a long wait for goods to arrive, or if there are other unsolved problems.

New business ideas

Since the growth of the internet, completely new businesses have been set up which previously would not have been possible. Facebook, the social site, started in 2004, and YouTube, the video and music sharing site started in 2005, are just two examples. Both these businesses use advertising to generate their profits. YouTube was bought by Google in 2006 for 1.6 billion dollars, which gives an indication of the rapid growth possible for a successful internet-based business.

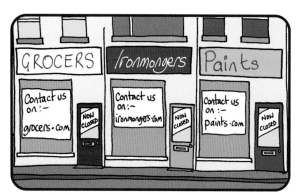

What will be the future of shops with the growth of e-commerce?

Activity

Activity 8: Explanation activity – How the internet has changed business activity

1 Explain why some businesses using e-commerce can be footloose and locate almost anywhere.

2 Many businesses using e-commerce may want to be located near the motorway network. Why is this?

3 Explain how banking has changed due to the use of the internet.

Activity

Activity 9: Explanation activity – Suitability of products for e-commerce

Explain whether or not the following products would be suitable for e-commerce businesses. Give reasons for your answers.

1 Books   4 Fresh vegetables

2 Carpets   5 Laptop computers

3 Expensive furniture   6 Suitcases.

Activity

Activity 10: Presentation – The future of e-commerce

Think of a new product or service you think would sell well, or provide a profitable service, *on the internet*. Make a short presentation to the rest of the business studies group to cover:

● A description of the product or service

● Who your target market is

● Why you believe the product or service will sell on the internet

● The location and general organisation of the business.

Assessment Activity

Jessica and Rachel own a business which makes quality aromatherapy products. They currently sell their products through specialist shops in the south of England, but Jessica in particular is concerned that they are not making the most of their products, which she thinks should be sold to a wider market.

Questions

1 Analyse the possible methods of distribution that Jessica and Rachel could use for their business.

2 Recommend which method or methods of distribution they might use in order to sell their products to a wider market. Give reasons for your recommendations.

Advice on how to answer the questions

In the first question you are asked to analyse. This will mean explaining the advantages *and* disadvantages of all the methods of distribution that Jessica and Rachel could use. You must look at a full range of distribution methods.

In question 2 you need to look at the different methods you have analysed and then recommend one or more of those distribution methods that are suitable for their business. Full reasons must be given for any recommendations you make.

Try and think 'outside the box' in this type of work. Go back to the products Jessica and Rachel are making and be inventive in exactly how they may sell this type of specialist product, which is growing in popularity.

Key facts

- Place includes both where a product is sold and the method of distribution used to get the product to the customer.
- Different products require different methods of distribution.
- More recent methods of distribution, such as direct sales and e-commerce, are becoming much more important for certain products.
- Smaller businesses usually have a more simple method of distribution; larger businesses tend to have a more complex system.
- Though the main role of the wholesaler is to break bulk, they do offer other services.
- Remember that some businesses are not as suited to e-commerce as others.
- There are advantages for both businesses and customers when using e-commerce.
- E-commerce is changing the way in which many businesses operate. This is linked to work on location, training and recruitment.
- E-commerce is used alongside other methods of marketing products and services.
- Because e-commerce is changing so rapidly, you must keep up to date with new developments.

Key Terms

Make sure you can explain each of the following Key Terms

E-commerce The bringing together of buyers and sellers electronically. Generally used as selling using the internet.

Place The part of the market mix that deals with distributing the product to the customer.

Methods of distribution The methods used to get the product to the consumer, for example: producer to retailer to consumer.

Wholesaler Part of the distribution that deals with breaking bulk between producer and retailer. A wholesaler buys large quantities from a producer and sells smaller quantities to retailers.

Regional distribution centre (RDC) Similar to a wholesaler but owned by the retailer. Used as a storage base to supply shops in a region.

Direct sales A method of selling by larger businesses direct to the customer by catalogues, TV, etc. Though smaller businesses have often sold goods in this way, the term is usually used to include more recent distribution methods.

Global market A world-wide market provided by the internet.

Encryption A method of making buying on the internet more secure by scrambling the details given by the buyer so they cannot be read by unauthorised people.

Promotion

By studying this unit you will be able to:

● **Understand and explain the aims of promotion in marketing**

● **Understand, analyse and evaluate the different methods of promotion used by businesses**

● **Discuss the importance of public relations and sponsorship in marketing a business**

● **Explain and evaluate the various advertising media used in marketing**

● **Evaluate the role of promotion in the marketing mix.**

Introduction

When a business has a good product, or is offering a good price for a service, or perhaps is moving to a new place, it needs to inform its customers. This part of promotion, advertising, is therefore very much connected with the other 'Ps' in the marketing mix. Promotion in marketing also includes all the various offers such as 'buy one get one free' that we have become used to seeing.

Much money is spent on promotion each year by businesses. Care must be taken to make sure that the money is used to good effect.

The importance of promotion in marketing

Promotion is concerned with how a business is to market its product. A business must inform customers that it has a product to sell, and make customers feel that they need to buy the product. To do this, businesses will use a variety of methods, which need to be chosen carefully to have the greatest effect on customers. Without promotion, a business may have an excellent product which is a failure because consumers were not persuaded to buy it.

Promotion in the market mix

Promotion is linked closely to the other Ps in the market mix.

Product

Clearly, a product needs to be brought to the attention of the consumer, which is normally achieved through advertising. A product coming towards the end of its life-cycle (see Unit 1.3.5) will also need further promotion if the life-cycle is to be extended. Another product with a short life-cycle may need a lot of promotion to boost sales in order to repay the development costs of the product (and make some profit!) before the end of the life-cycle.

Activity

Activity 1: Explanation – The use of promotion in marketing

No matter what the business, promotion at some stage is very important

Sarahclean Ltd offer a complete house-cleaning service in Barncaster, mainly aimed at couples who both work and have no real interest in housework. A house would normally be cleaned once a week, with Sarahclean Ltd employing local staff who appreciate being able to earn some extra money from part-time work. Services such as washing, ironing as well as dry cleaning are also available from the business.

After four years, Sarahclean Ltd now feels it should be expanding. It has the following ideas:

1 To expand into the nearby town of Donborough

2 To gain more customers in Barncaster, especially with older people who cannot do their own cleaning.

Sarahclean Ltd now needs advice on the following:

a What offers are likely to attract new customers, especially the elderly, in Barncaster who have not tried the service that Sarahclean Ltd provides?

b How and where they should advertise their services in Donborough in order to expand their business in the new location.

Write a report to Sarahclean Ltd, advising it on the above. Give reasons for your advice, using a computer if possible to complete your work. Keep in mind the type of service involved, the likely size of the business, and the target market.

Price

The price of a product should be set carefully in order to make it attractive to potential customers (see Unit 1.3.4). At certain times, the price may need to be changed to keep sales at the required level.

Place

A business may need to inform customers that it has a new shop or office opening that will improve customer service. This will need suitable advertising. A business may feel that its strength is the excellent distribution system it has, delivering products the next day. This would need to be brought to the attention of customers in order to attract further sales.

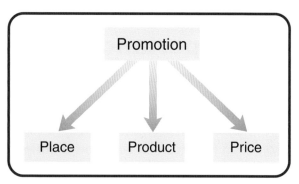

Promotion is closely linked to the other Ps in the marketing mix

The aims of promotion

Promotion has the following aims:

● to inform customers about a product or service (especially when new or changed)

- to keep a business ahead of its competitors
- to create or change the image of a business
- to maintain or increase sales.

These aims will be used as necessary by a business, though they all try to keep sales at a level which is satisfactory for the business. As a business develops, the *emphasis* of promotion will change. When a business starts, effort is put into promoting the business itself as well the products it may be selling. As the name of the business becomes established, there is less need to promote the name, and promotion is concentrated more on the product or service.

It must be remembered that even the best-known companies and their products still need promotion. Nestlé continue to promote products such as Kit Kats even though they are market leaders. This is simply aimed at *maintaining* the product as a leading chocolate product.

Methods of promotion

There are many different methods of promotion a business might use. They include the following:

1 **Sales promotion**

2 **Public relations**

3 **Sponsorship**

4 **Advertising.**

Sales promotion

Sales promotion itself can be divided into many different parts.

- **Price reductions** are often seen in shops in January in order to sell off all the old stock a shop no longer wants to keep. This will boost sales at a time when the products (such as Christmas cards) would not normally sell. Price reductions may also be used to sell off the stock of an old model, in order to make space for the newer model. In this example, consumers who know an old model is to be replaced will not want to own it, unless of course there is a large price reduction!

- **Loss leaders** are another form of price reduction, often used by supermarkets. Here a business will lower the price of one or two items to such a point that there is little or no profit. The idea is that a consumer will be attracted to the supermarket by the price reductions, but while they are there they will also buy a number of other items (at normal prices) so the supermarket makes the profit it needs.

- **Added value** is a sales promotion often used by the food industry. It involves giving 30 per cent extra free and so on. As the cost of the product to the producer has not changed much by the offer, it is a good way of drawing the attention of the consumer. A consumer may well be attracted to the product for the first time because of the added value, and then continue to buy it. Supermarkets will often offer goods at two for the price of one in the hope of consumers returning to the supermarket (saving money) and buying the product again.

- **Gifts** may be given with a product in order to increase sales. As CDs and DVDs have become cheaper to produce, they have become free gifts in many newspapers.

- **Point of sale** is a method of sales promotion used at the place where the customer will buy the product. It can often be seen in large supermarkets where there may be a large display of a certain product (often at a key point such as the entrance) which attracts attention. This may also be linked to other offers, but often the display itself can increase sales. Within supermarkets, demonstrations or free tasting also attract consumers who may be persuaded to buy a product for the first time.

- **Competitions** can be used to boost sales, where customers are entered for a monthly prize draw, offering a variety of prizes. With higher-priced products – for example, cars – the value of the prize is often very high, such as a continental holiday, or even the money you paid for the car being returned.

- **Free samples** are often used in cosmetics and other businesses to let the consumer try the product. Consumers may be reluctant to buy the full size of a product they do not know, as they may not like it and so have wasted their money. By providing a small sample, which may be simply posted through a letter box, or included in a magazine, consumers can try the sample and then buy the full size, knowing that they like it. Obviously this can only be used for certain products. A business such as Mercedes is unlikely to give away a free sample of one of its cars!

Not all products will use free samples

- **Merchandising** is becoming increasingly important in promoting certain products, especially films. When a new 'blockbuster' film is about to be released, a number of items are put on sale which are in some way connected to the film. These items can range from T-shirts to cuddly toys to key rings to posters. As with other methods of promotion, the intention is to bring the product to the attention of the consumer in order to increase sales. In the case of some merchandising, it may well make as much profit as the film!

- **After-sales service** can also be used as a sales promotion. In this case a business may offer a guarantee for a product, or extend an existing guarantee. Many businesses promise that if a customer sees a lower price in another shop they will refund the difference. This is meant to give the customer confidence when they buy a product, and so increases sales. The importance of this customer service in promoting a business was covered in Unit 1.3.3.

Public relations

The main difference between **public relations** (PR) and other methods of promotion is that PR is often free. Giving price reductions and free gifts can cost a big business many thousands of pounds, which has to be made up by increased sales. **Public relations** simply tries to bring the company and its products to the attention of the public at no cost. This is done by releasing stories to newspapers and other media about the company in the hope that the story will be printed. Where a famous personality is involved, the chance of such a story making the papers is increased. At a slight cost, a business may offer one of its products for a prize on a TV or radio show. In this way the business brings its product to the attention of the customer for little cost compared to paying for an advertisement.

Sponsorship

Sponsorship is becoming increasingly important in bringing the name of a business to different customers. It is clearly seen in sports such as football, with teams from the Premier League to local pub teams having a sponsor. Though the sponsor may have a personal interest in the team (such as the pub team) there is a clear business aim in promoting the name of the business to as wide an audience as possible. With more sport, especially football, being shown on television, there is an increasing opportunity for a business to make its products known to a world-wide audience.

Activity

Activity 2: Explanation – The use of different methods of promotion

For each of the following situations, explain what sales promotion method(s) you would use. Give reasons for your choice(s).

a A well-known trainer maker is ready to launch a new style of trainer aimed at people who go jogging. However, it has a lot of old stock left.

b Smell It Cosmetics Ltd wants to promote its deodorant range, which has not sold as many as expected.

c A soft drinks maker wants to increase the amount of lemonade it sells.

d Williams Cars feels that its new model is not selling as well as expected and it needs ideas on sales promotion.

e A famous chocolate manufacturer feels it is time to remind customers what a good product it makes, as sales have fallen slightly.

Activity

Activity 3: Matching terms – Methods of sales promotion

Match the explanations with the correct business term.

Business terms:

- Point of sale
- Added value
- Merchandising
- Loss leader.

Explanations:

1 An example is where an offer of 30 per cent extra free is made or 'buy one get one free'.

2 This is a promotion where the product or service is being sold. It can include special displays of the product, or even free tasting.

3 This promotion is where products are sold which relate to something else – for example, a toy figure from a children's film.

4 Supermarkets often use this method of reducing the price of one or two products by a large amount, in order to persuade consumers to come into the store.

Activity

Activity 4: Research – The use of sponsorship by businesses

Sponsorship is very important in promotion, especially for sport.

1 Collect information on the following:

- Ten businesses that sponsor football in some way. This may be the team itself, a league, or even a television programme.
- Ten businesses that sponsor any sport *other* than football.
- The amount that each sponsor has paid.
- What connection, if any, the sponsor has with the sport (for example, it may make football kits).

2 When you have your results, display them on a suitable chart such as the one below.

Sponsor	Who is being sponsored	Amount paid	Connection with sport being sponsored

Activity

Activity 5: True or false – Statements on promotion

Are the following statements on promotion true or false? Put a tick in the correct column.

Statement	True	False
Point of sale promotions are often used by large supermarkets		
Free samples are a type of promotion that any business could use		
Added value is making a product more expensive by adding to its price		
A loss leader is when a business makes a loss because it is in the lead		
Price reductions as a type of promotion are often used in shops in January		
When a builder's merchant sells some bricks it is called merchandising		
Gifts such as CDs are sometimes used by newspapers to increase sales		
After-sales service is when a business provides good service to customers after they have bought a product or service		

Advertising

Advertising is one of the most important parts of promotion. We all see and hear advertisements for a huge range of products. On television they often seem to be more entertaining than the programmes!

The type of advertising to be used needs to be carefully chosen as do the **advertising media** – that is, where the product is to be advertised. You would not normally expect to see the latest chart CDs and an industrial waste-disposal machine being advertised in the same way in the same place.

For some products an **advertising campaign** is launched, which involves a series of advertisements in different forms over a period of time. In this way a producer can build up consumer knowledge of a product which will increase sales or get a new product off to a successful start.

Advertising media

A business must choose carefully where it is to advertise its products and services.

In making that choice, businesses will consider the following:

● The cost of advertising. A small business may not have much money to spend.

● The target market for the product. A business selling teenage fashions will advertise where teenagers will see those adverts.

● Whether the advertisement is part of a campaign, or a single advert.

Types of advertising media used by a business

A business has a wide choice of different media to use. Figure 1 summarises the advantages and disadvantages of each.

Figure 1 Types of advertising media used by a business

Advertising medium	Advantages	Disadvantages
Television	1 Reaches a large audience throughout the country 2 Use of colour and moving images is very useful when the product itself moves eg a car 3 Can be targeted at particular consumers, e.g. advertising gardening products during that type of programme	1 The cost. Advertisements at peak times, for example during popular soaps or films, can cost many thousands of pounds for a 30-second showing
Radio	1 Much cheaper than television 2 Good targeting of customers through different radio stations. Classic FM has a very different audience to local commercial stations 3 A radio can be taken anywhere, unlike a television	1 The product cannot be seen, which is important if you are marketing a visual item 2 Not such a wide audience as television
Cinema	1 The audience will often watch cinema adverts more closely as they have paid for the experience	1 Although the number of people visiting cinemas is increasing, the audience remains small compared to television

Advertising medium	Advantages	Disadvantages
Cinema (Continued)	2 Adverts can be targeted at the audience watching 3 Advertisements not allowed on television may be shown	
Newspapers	1 Good targeting of customer by using different newspapers 2 Colour can add to the visual effect of the advert 3 Choice of local, regional and national papers 4 Different types of advertisement, display and classified	1 Not all socio-economic groups read newspapers 2 Cost. A full-page advertisement in a national paper such as *The Sun* can cost many thousands of pounds
Magazines	1 Possibly the best medium for targeting particular customer groups. All consumer interest are catered for, along with trade magazines aimed at the business buyer. This makes the advertisement very cost-effective 2 High-quality colour gloss images can make products look attractive	1 A magazine may only come out once a month. A business may need more regular adverts 2 Some magazines have few readers and are not suitable for products aimed at a mass market
Billboards and posters	1 Highly visual. Large images, often at the side of roads 2 Can be targeted at particular areas of the country	1 No real control of the people seeing the advertisement 2 Limited message can be given, as it has to be read as people pass by
Internet	1 One of the fastest growing advertising media 2 Can target particular groups according to the site a customer is using 3 Can use moving images as well as written information 4 Can be saved by the consumer 5 Allows possible direct link to the producer	1 Not used by all potential groups of customers 2 Customers may see the adverts as 'in the way' of what they really need from an internet site 3 Can be expensive to set up
Transport (e.g. buses)	1 Can be targeted at a certain area 2 Cheaper than magazines and popular newspapers	1 Space available for the advert is limited 2 Only a simple message can be given

Activity

Activity 6: Explanation – The use of different media in marketing

Which advertising media would you recommend in the following situations? Give reasons for any choices you make, bearing in mind that more than one media may be appropriate.

a A new CD from a top band

b A famous perfume brand launching a new fragrance

c A fishing rod from a new manufacturer

d A special offer from a well-known washing-machine maker

e A new high specification satellite-navigation system.

Activity

Activity 7: Explanation – Choosing an appropriate method of advertising

Julie owns the Cutting Room unisex hairdressers, which has a customer base of mainly elderly clients. After her successful move to new premises, the business is expanding, with her daughter Lindsey introducing beauty therapy in the same premises to add to the styling work done by Julie and her assistants.

Lindsey now needs advice on how to advertise the new beauty therapy service. She is considering the following:

a Local cinema

b Local radio

c Relying on word of mouth from the existing customers from the Cutting Room

d Local newspapers

e Setting up a website to advertise the styling and beauty therapy together.

Advise Lindsey on where she should advertise her beauty therapy business. Give reasons for your advice, explaining why any choices have been rejected.

Activity

Activity 8: Poster – Types of advertising

Using magazines, newspapers, the internet or any other source of information, collect at least ten advertisements, which are advertising different types of products. Make a poster of your results, labelling underneath each advertisement where it came from.

Evaluation points

1 When evaluating different methods of promotion and advertising, it is vital to consider the product and the market at which the product is targeted. Certain products are suited to particular promotion methods – for example, many liquid products add a 30 per cent extra free offer.

2 When looking at the target market, think about what type of media the target market will see before recommending where to place an advertisement.

3 The size of the business can also affect promotion and advertising. How much advertising and promotion does your local shop do compared to, say, Tesco? For many smaller businesses, advertising may be restricted to small adverts in a local newspaper, or they may decide not to advertise at all simply because of the cost.

The control of advertising

Advertising and sales promotions are controlled through the **Advertising Standards Authority (ASA)**.

The following is taken from the ASA website (September 08), and gives an indication of their work:

> *We can stop misleading, harmful or offensive advertising. We can ensure sales promotions are run fairly. We can help reduce unwanted commercial mail – either sent through the post, by e-mail or by text message – and we can resolve problems with mail order purchases.*
> **(Source: www.asa.org.uk)**

In this way, businesses must make sure that their advertising and promotions are not misleading, harmful or offensive. If they feel this is not the case, consumers can complain to the ASA and the advertisements will have to be stopped if the ASA decides the consumer is right.

Why control of advertising is necessary

Consumers need protection against false and dishonest claims that may be made by businesses. Certain groups of consumers, especially children, are easily influenced by advertisements (children's adverts have even more rules). They should not be persuaded to buy something they do not want because of false claims made in an advertisement.

The government sees certain products as being harmful – for example, tobacco. For this reason tobacco advertising is banned.

Direct marketing

This is another fast-growing method of promotion. It involves customers being sent details of a product directly to them, usually through the post. As the consumer may ignore much of the material sent to them, direct marketing is often called 'junk mail'.

Direct marketing relies on vast databases of information collected on a consumer. This may be from different sources, but is usually gathered from the different forms consumers fill in at different times. There is often a box at the bottom of a form which asks the person whether they mind the information being used by others. This information is then used to target certain consumers with products that would seem to suit them.

Activity

Activity 9: Research – The use of direct marketing

Ask your family and relations if they receive any junk mail. The chances are they will! Ask what information is being sent by this method of promotion. Find out what *type* of business is involved in direct marketing and sending the mail, and the sort of product or service that is being sold.

1 Put the businesses in the following categories:

a Those selling a service

b Those selling a product

2 For each of the above categories, make your own groups of businesses; for example, products for the home, finance and insurance, and so on. Display your results in a graph.

3 What type of product or service uses direct marketing? What do you think is the reason for this?

4 What products or services do *not* seem to use direct marketing? Explain why some businesses might not choose this method of promotion.

Assessment Activity

Ahmed owns AP holidays, which specialises in coach holidays in Britain. He has a fleet of 30 coaches and has contacts with a number of hotels, most of which are on the coast. His customers vary in age, though they are generally older couples without children. Many of the holidays are for organised groups, such as clubs, who will fill a coach. Groups such as this are offered a special price by Ahmed.

Ahmed is a little concerned that bookings are down on last year. He knows that his customers may not have as much money to spend and that some could be tempted by holidays abroad. He now needs some ideas on promotion in order to attract the customers he needs to fill his coaches.

Questions

1 What methods of promotion could Ahmed use to attract more customers? Give reasons for the methods you suggest.

2 Recommend an advertising campaign for Ahmed, including the type of advertising media he should use. Give reasons for your recommendations.

3 Evaluate the importance of advertising and promotion in Ahmed's marketing mix.

Advice on how to answer the questions

For question 1 you need to look at all of the different methods of promotion available to a business. Then think of the *type* of business in the question. It is a holiday business, taking customers, mainly older people, to the coast by coach. What method of promotion will work in this situation? Remember to give reasons for any suggestions you make.

In question 2 you have to recommend an advertising campaign. This is a series of advertisements, which should use different advertising media. You will need to choose appropriate advertising media *for Ahmed's business,* with a good answer that has a plan which will link the different advertising media. Make sure that recommendations fit the business. Ahmed has 30 coaches which does *not* make it the sort of business that can afford prime-time television advertising. Choose carefully and give reasons for your recommendations.

For question 3 you need to evaluate just how important advertising and promotion is in Ahmed's marketing mix (the other Ps plus customer service, etc.). There are references in the information to price, the product and the places the coaches go to. How important is advertising and promotion in relation to these other parts of the marketing mix? Can Ahmed do without advertising? Can he ignore sales promotion as a means of attracting customers? Always give reasons for your answer when you are asked to evaluate.

Key facts

- Promotion is a vital part of the market mix.
- Methods of promotion are varied and must be chosen carefully to fit a given business in a given situation.
- There is a range of places and methods for a business to advertise its products and services.
- Businesses must be inventive in trying to think of different ways to promote their products.
- Advertising can be expensive and must lead to increased sales that pay for the advertising that has been used.
- The internet is a fast-growing method of advertising, but is not suitable for *all* products.
- The ASA is important in keeping a check on the advertisements businesses use.
- The size of the market and money available are important considerations when choosing a method of promotion.
- Many smaller businesses may choose not to advertise at all because of the expense involved.

Key Terms

Make sure you can explain each of the following Key Terms

Sales promotions are the methods by which a business tries, over a short period of time, to boost sales; for example, by reducing prices.

Loss leaders are goods offered for sale with little or no profit for the business. They are intended to attract consumers who will buy other goods along with the loss leaders. Often used by supermarkets.

Added value is a sales promotion when an extra amount is given 'free'. An example would be seen as '30 per cent extra free'.

Point of sale promotions are used where the product is sold; for example, displays.

Merchandising is the promotion of products by selling goods in some way connected with another product or event; for example, the sale of figures of characters who appear in a major film.

After-sales service is the help given to customers after they have bought a product; for example, a guarantee to repair the product in the first year.

Public relations (PR) are the methods by which a business brings the product to the attention of consumers by articles in newspapers or other events. This is aimed at improving the image of the business.

Sponsorship is a way of advertising a business by providing money for an event or a particular team. Has grown in importance in football and other major sports.

Advertising media are the methods by which a business can advertise a product. Includes newspapers, TV and radio.

Advertising campaign A series of advertisements, often using different advertising media.

Advertising Standards Authority (ASA). Checks that adverts are not harmful, misleading or offensive.

Direct marketing involves contacting the consumer through offers sent directly, usually through the post. Sometimes referred to as 'junk mail'.

Enterprise

Introduction

Enterprise in business is nothing new. For as long as business activity has taken place, people have shown how enterprising they can be by providing a product or a service that they see others are willing to pay for. In some cases this has led to small businesses growing into world-wide operations making large profits for the owners. Larry Page and Sergey Brin started their business by meeting in a garage. That small start developed into Google, now one of the most highly valued businesses in the world.

In more recent times, television programmes like *Dragons Den* have highlighted the role of **entrepreneurs**. Here people with ideas and the energy to see their businesses prosper try to persuade already wealthy entrepreneurs to put money into the business to help it grow. Not all will succeed; such is the nature of enterprise. There are risks, but, there again, there are rewards for those who are successful.

Enterprise will not always succeed in the Den

What is enterprise?

Enterprise is something that is part of the character of a particular person, and not all people have a true enterprising personality. So what are the features in a person that will make them enterprising?

Risk-taking

Many people do not like to take risks. An enterprising person starting a business will certainly have to take a risk, possibly using their own money, which may multiply in the future or be lost forever!

Activity

Activity 1: Research activity – Researching famous entrepreneurs

Use the internet to research the backgrounds of four famous entrepreneurs. You could look up Duncan Bannatyne, Alan Sugar, Peter Jones, Richard Branson, Anita Roddick, James Dyson, Theo Paphitis, James Caen, Deborah Meaden, Walt Disney, or any other local entrepreneur your teacher may know of.

What made them successful? Do they have anything in common which made them succeed where others have failed? Write a short report on your findings, using a computer if you can.

Determination

Enterprise will include the determination to see things through. James Dyson was turned down by other recognised vacuum-cleaner makers when he showed them his idea. He did not give up, and carried on to form his own business and make millions of pounds in the process. Owners of many small businesses find that when they first start they need to put a lot of time into the business; this level of determination is not for everyone.

Persuasive

An enterprising person will need to be persuasive. Few business people will do everything themselves; they need help from others such as a bank for a loan. These other people will need to be persuaded that the business will be a success if they are going to be willing to take any part in it.

Ability to work with others

Enterprise includes an ability not only to persuade others to possibly join in a business activity, but also to continue to work effectively with them. This ability to get the best out of others around you is vital if business success is to be achieved.

Decision maker

This is linked to risk-taking. A person starting a business activity will need to be able to make their own decisions. This may come as something of a shock to someone who has worked for others and has become used to *taking* orders rather than *giving* them. An enterprising person will have no problem in making decisions.

Judgement

An enterprising person will be able to judge a situation well. They will often be very thorough in their research, take a careful look at, for example, the competition, and then be able to weigh up all these factors before coming to a reasoned judgement about what to do.

Confidence

An enterprising person will be confident that their ideas will succeed, and be able to pass on that feeling of confidence to others who are brought in to develop a business idea. An enterprising person is always very positive. 'Can't do' is *not* a phrase they would use.

Some entrepreneurs, such as James Dyson have made millions of pounds from their businesses

Activity

Activity 2: Research Activity

Use the information 'What is Enterprise?' to research the level of enterprise within your business studies group. Complete the chart below for ten members of your group *as you see them*. Put a tick in each column where you think they have that enterprising feature. Compare your results with how they see themselves. How much enterprise is in your group? Write a short report on your findings.

Name	Risk taker	Determination	Persuasive	Working with others	Decision maker	Judgement	Confidence

The entrepreneur in business

An **entrepreneur** is a person who has many, if not all, of the enterprising qualities listed above. They will also be inventive, and recognise that a business or service is needed by consumers. James Dyson realised that people wanted a vacuum cleaner that kept its efficiency, so he developed his bagless cleaner. Anita Roddick realised that consumers wanted cosmetics that were not tested on animals, so started the successful Body Shop business. These are two of the more famous entrepreneurs; there will be many less famous examples in the area where you live.

The entrepreneur is the person who will give a new business the driving force it needs to be successful, using the enterprising qualities that are listed above. It may be the case, however, that as a business grows, the personal influence of the entrepreneur who started it may well decrease. In this case, other workers and managers will be taking over some of the decision making, with, it is hoped, some of the determination and inventiveness of the entrepreneur who started it all.

The rewards and drawbacks of risk-taking

When a business starts, the entrepreneur takes a risk. This is all part of the make up of someone who is enterprising. This risk brings the potential of great rewards, but does come with some possible drawbacks.

Potential rewards for risk-taking

- **Financial.** The greater the risk, the greater the reward. This is often said when referring to the amount of money that might be made when taking a risk. Certainly some entrepreneurs have made their personal fortunes from taking a risk and starting their own businesses. Alan Sugar made his fortune by selling electrical goods through a business called Amstrad. Richard Branson made his first millions by selling records and CDs. The attraction of making a lot of money is an important factor in encouraging people to take a risk and start their own business. Financial reward for people may also come from buying shares in a business rather than starting a business themselves. The business itself may grow and the shares increase in value. It should also be said that the value of shares can go down as well as up, so there is a clear element of risk involved. Other financial rewards may come from other business activities such as buying property to rent to others, with a view that house prices would rise. This became very popular in the first years of the 21st century, but the risk has been highlighted with falls in property prices.

- **Independence.** Many people work for others and are quite happy to take orders and do the job they are told to do. Others may want to be independent, and take the risk of running their own business simply in order to be their own boss.

- **Self-satisfaction.** An entrepreneur may simply take the risk of starting their own business simply to have the satisfaction that their idea would work. They may not be interested in making a lot of money, but want to retain the satisfaction that they started, and own, their business. A business may develop out of a hobby. This will again bring satisfaction to an entrepreneur after taking the risk in starting such a business.

- **Changing consumer habits.** Some entrepreneurs are rewarded when consumers are persuaded to change their buying habits. Anita Roddick did not believe that cosmetics should be tested on animals and wanted to persuade consumers to buy products that were free from such testing. The success of Body Shop has changed consumer attitudes to choosing cosmetics, with other cosmetic businesses now offering similar products. The risk of starting the original business brought greater rewards for its founder. The move to ethical business practices has made a number of entrepreneurs start businesses in order to see the rewards of changed consumer attitudes.

Potential drawbacks for risk taking

- **Financial.** Just as there can be great rewards for risk-taking, there are also major potential drawbacks. While fortunes can be made, the life savings that are put into a business might also be lost. The possibility of losing money is one of the main reasons why people will *not* take a risk and start their own business.

- **Health.** If a business idea does not work out, or more time and effort needs to be put in than expected, the health of the entrepreneur may be affected. The strain of being in charge of a business that is in difficulty may lead to failing health. Even when a business is successful, the strain of keeping up that success may also affect a person's health.

- **Strained relationships.** Taking a risk and starting a business can be very time consuming. It may well take its toll on the health of the entrepreneur and it may also damage personal relationships, with the entrepreneur having to spend so much time developing the business. Holidays may be missed as the business takes time and money to become established.

Activity

Activity 3: Explanation – The benefits and drawbacks of risk-taking

Use the information on benefits and drawbacks of risk taking to examine your *own* attitude to risk-taking. If you *are* a risk-taker in business, what attracts you to taking risks? If you are *not* a risk-taker, what is it that puts you off taking a risk in an enterprise? Write up your thoughts, using a computer if possible.

Evaluation point

When evaluating the benefits and drawbacks of taking the risk of running a business, remember that there are often no clear correct answers. Use the information you are given to try and judge whether it is *likely* that the person involved (the entrepreneur) will make a success of the business or not.

Help available for enterprise

The government and a number of other organisations provide help to develop new business enterprises. The government feel that it is important that an 'enterprising culture' is developed in the UK in order that new business can flourish and individuals can be more independent. It is vital to the well-being of a country that it has individuals who have a 'can do' attitude and are prepared to start the business enterprises on which we all depend. Many small businesses fail within the first year of starting, which, at times, is a result of poor planning and training. By supporting these new businesses in an appropriate way, the chances of success will increase.

Government help for enterprise

Government help for **enterprise** is in two parts, grants and advice.

Government grants

Government grants are available for new business enterprise, but to receive such a grant there are certain conditions. These include:

- The enterprise should be a proposal, not an existing business.
- Matched funds are often needed. In other words, the government puts in a certain

sum into the enterprise and you must find some of the finance yourself. Sometimes, for example, in research businesses, the government may offer a grant of up to 60 per cent with the owner having to provide the remaining 40 per cent.

- The grants are usually for small/medium sized business enterprises (less than 250 workers)
- The grant may depend on where the business is located. Poorer areas will stand a better chance of being accepted for a grant.
- **Grants** are normally awarded for specific purposes – for example, buying machinery, rather than a general 'starting a business'.

The benefit of a grant is that it does not have to be repaid, as long as all the conditions agreed at the time are not broken.

Government advice

The government provides advice for enterprise through a number of routes. For example, the New Deal 25 plus is aimed at those who have been receiving Jobseekers Allowance for the last 18 months. The scheme provides training and includes a section called 'enterprise rehearsal', where an enterprise idea can be tried out. The government is also keen to support **social enterprise**. These are enterprises that are operated for the benefit of the community, where any profits made from the enterprise will be put back into community projects.

Other help for enterprise development

There are many sources for enterprise support other than government, though the government will often support organisations that are there to give help to the future entrepreneurs. Some examples of the organisations that offer help to enterprise development are shown in Figure 1.

Shell LiveWire is an organisation that supports young entrepreneurs

Figure 1 Organisations that offer help to enterprise development

The Prince's Trust (www.princes-trust.org.uk)	The Prince's Trust has helped many young people to complete their business plans and start their own business. They might be able to help you if you are aged 18–30 and unemployed or working fewer than 16 hours a week.
Enterprising women (www.enterprising-women.org.uk)	As the name suggests, this organisation aims to support females in enterprise, recognising the fact that women do not take part in enterprising activities as much as males. Located in Glasgow, grants are available to female Glasgow residents, and training is provided free of charge for women in the city.
Shell LiveWire www.shell-livewire.ork.uk)	The oil company Shell started this scheme to provide practical help to support young people (16–30) who want to set up their own business enterprise. The support offered includes a free essential business kit, advice from a local business adviser and young business mentor. Booklets provided include information on how to write a business plan (see Unit 1.4.2) and how to complete market research (see Unit 1.3.2). Shell has also set up within LiveWire a social network, which enables young entrepreneurs to share ideas, solve problems and celebrate success.
Business Enterprise Support (BES) (www.enterprise support.org.uk)	BES provides enterprise start-up support and training.
National Federation of Enterprise Agencies (NFEA) (www.nfea.com)	The NFEA provides enterprise support for people of all ages. It concentrates on small businesses that have just started or are about to start, aiming to give these enterprises a better chance of survival and growth. New Entrepreneur Scholarships are offered through the Training and Skills Council, targeted at disadvantaged areas or backgrounds. These scholarships involve training, support and mentoring.

Activity

Activity 4: Poster activity – Designing a poster on help for enterprise

Use the information above on help for enterprise, together with any further advice you can collect from the internet, to create a poster to show the help available for business enterprise. The websites for the organisations in the help for enterprise section will be a good start.

Why businesses succeed or fail

A successful business will often make use of any advice and training available

There are many reasons why businesses fail, which are often the opposite reason for businesses succeeding! Many new businesses fail in the first year of operation, though we have also seen some businesses grow to make millions of pounds for those who started them. So why do businesses succeed or fail? Some of the possible reasons are given below.

Planning

A business needs careful planning if it is to succeed. Those that are planned well will have a better chance of success. A well-thought-out business plan (see Unit 1.4.2) will not guarantee success, but it will be a good start.

Product

Rather obvious, but a product (or service) that consumers actually want is more likely to result in a successful business enterprise. With a product that only the entrepreneur likes, failure is the only result. A successful entrepreneur will recognise the need for a particular product and produce it at a price that consumers are prepared to pay.

Timing

A business might be a good idea, but simply started at the wrong time. For example, starting an estate agent business when no one is buying houses would not be the best business idea.

Experience

A lack of business experience can at times lead to business failure. This lack of experience can, of course, be corrected by taking advantage of the advice and support that is available for new business enterprises. It should also be remembered that even with experience, there is no *guarantee* of business success.

External factors

Sometimes a business is affected by things outside its control and eventually fails. These **external factors** might include a change in the law; for example, the smoking ban has reduced the sale of cigarettes, but has led to the closure of some pubs because customers are staying at home, as they can no longer smoke inside the pub with a drink.

Assessment Activity

Kieran Mulkeen has always wanted to make money, and has tried several times to set up a business of his own. His attempt to start a car-cleaning business failed when his three workers refused to work in cold winter weather for the wages they were being paid. His takeaway pizza business was doing quite well until a well-known competitor opened nearby and he lost most of his customers. He knew this was likely to happen but ignored the advice he received, believing that his style of pizza would still be popular with local people.

Kieran is now 21 years old and unemployed. His friends say that he is determined to succeed in business, and has the sort of personality that brings him many friends. Kieran feels that he has been unlucky so far and that sooner or later he will make his fortune.

Questions

1 Explain the enterprise qualities that Kieran has that should help him to be successful in business.

2 Identify any other enterprise qualities that Kieran should have if he is to run a successful business.

3 Research the possible help and assistance for enterprise that is available for a person such as Kieran. Write a short report to Kieran advising him of the help available.

4 Discuss whether Kieran has the skills to be a successful entrepreneur. Give reasons for your answer.

Advice on how to answer the questions

You first need to remind yourself of the qualities that an enterprising person should have. Which of these qualities does Kieran seem to have?

The next question follows on from question 1 and simply asks you to list the other enterprise skills that Kieran does *not* have.

Question 3 is a little more difficult and you will have to research the help that Kieran could receive for his next business idea. Look at two organisations at least that could offer help and advice. Then a *short* report is needed which should be addressed to Kieran.

The final question asks you to 'discuss'. This means that you will need to look at the good and bad points about Kieran's business activities and personality and then decide, giving your reasons, whether you think he is likely to be a successful entrepreneur. Does he have the right skills and qualities? Will he take advantage of the advice from organisations offering support? Has he just been unlucky so far? Remember, again, that you need to give reasons for any ideas you may have.

Key facts

- Enterprise is a vital part of achieving success in business.
- The entrepreneur has an important part in developing a business idea, being the main risk-taker.
- There are many qualities that make a successful entrepreneur.
- Starting and running a business has both risks and rewards.
- There are many organisations, including the government, that can help to develop business enterprise.
- Businesses can fail because of many different reasons.

Key Terms

Make sure you can explain each of the following Key Terms

Enterprise A word used to describe the skills and personality of a person that makes them successful in business, such as being determined to succeed and being confident.

Entrepreneur A person who takes the risk of starting and running a business. They will have enterprise skills which make them successful in business.

Grants Money available to support a new business enterprise and which does not have to be paid back.

Social enterprise The name given to a business enterprise that is run for the benefit of the community with any profits that are made being put back into community projects.

External factor This is something that affects a business but is outside the control of the business, such as a change in the law.

Business planning

Learning Outcomes

By studying this unit you will be able to:

- **Understand the importance of a business plan**
- **Explain the contents of a simple business plan**
- **Understand and explain how a business plan is linked to marketing**
- **Analyse a business plan to evaluate a new business idea.**

Introduction

Planning often plays an important part in being successful in life. Some people may be very lucky and have no problems to solve, but for most of us some planning will help us to succeed. Even a simple party needs some planning if it is to work well. There is no difference in the world of business. Most businesses will have planned what they want to do, and will have tried to look at possible problems ahead and then to solve the problems before they arise.

A business will usually write out a **business plan** when it starts to look at what the business will sell and how it is to be set up and organised. This is then linked to how the product or service is to be marketed, which is an important part in making the business a success.

Careful planning does not mean businesses will always succeed. There are many reasons why a business might fail; planning simply gives a business a greater chance of success.

Writing a good business plan is worth the effort

Activity

Activity 1: Research – Producing and using a business plan

Ask someone you know who owns a business whether they have ever produced a business plan. The business may be very small, perhaps only one person, or much larger, in which case you will need to talk to the person who would produce such a plan. Try and find out:

a When they produced the plan

b What they put into the plan

c Why the plan was important for the business to complete.

Write your results up in the form of a short report. Try and use a computer to complete the work if at all possible.

The importance of a business plan

When a business starts, or makes an important change, the owners would normally write a plan for the business. Planning is a vital part in making sure that the business is a success, as without some form of planning it is likely that a business would fail. A **business plan** might also include targets for the future so that the level of success (or otherwise) can be measured. It is important that a business can see whether or not it is succeeding; the business plan will help it to make this judgement. By completing a business plan, a new business, in particular, can check that it has taken all the necessary steps to achieve the hoped-for success and avoid possible failure.

The contents of a business plan

There are many possible items that could be in a business plan. A simple business plan would include:

The business idea

This may seem rather obvious, but the starting point for any business plan is a business idea that is practical and at least stands a chance of being successful.

The people running the business

Details of who is to be involved and their experience in business are often included in a plan. This is important in trying to persuade other people to invest in the business (such as a bank). It is much more likely that others will invest in a new idea if it is coming from someone who has a lot of experience in running a business.

Market research

To back up the business idea and to show consumers are interested in the product or service, some market research would be carried out (see Unit 1.3.2). The results of this will be included in the plan to show that consumers will use the business. If the market research shows that consumers are not interested in the business, then a new idea is needed!

Figure 1 The relationship between a business plan and the marketing mix

Place	The business location will be included in the plan and how the product is to reach the consumer – for example, through a shop or sold on the internet. Reasons for any choices made should be included.
Product	Detail on the product will be included in the plan. Saying you will sell electrical goods, for example, is a little vague. Are you going to sell the full range of goods (as Comet does) or specialise in, say, televisions?
Promotion	A decision will need to be made on how the business is to be advertised. This is especially important for a new business where the first few months of operation are often critical in deciding whether the business will be a success. There may be some sales promotions (see Unit 1.3.7) that the business will use to attract customers. These will also go into the plan.
Price	The price to be charged for the product or service being offered is another important part of the plan. The business might propose certain pricing strategies (see Unit 1.3.4) – for example, to attract new customers. This will, of course, be especially important for new businesses that have no existing customers, and will have to attract consumers from other established businesses.

Marketing

Here the business would look at the product or service and decide how it should be marketed. The relationship between a business plan and the marketing mix is shown in Figure 1.

Production

If the business idea involves the *making* of a product then details of how the product is to be made will also go into the plan. There may also be information on how the quality of the product will be checked, and where appropriate, details on guarantees, etc. that may be offered. Once again this is very important for a new business, where consumers will have not heard of the product and so be unsure of its quality. The offer of some guarantees may persuade new customers to buy.

Finance

The cost of setting up the business will need to be carefully calculated. A business will then include in its plan details of where the **finance** is to come from to pay for the items

A detailed business plan will help persuade others that a new idea will be successful

it needs. A new business may have to find a lot of money to pay for new premises, equipment, advertising, etc. This may come from, for example, the owners' own savings, or they may borrow the money. Whatever the source of the finance, details of where it is to come from will be in the plan.

Using a business plan

A business plan will be used to persuade others that the business idea has been carefully thought through and possible problems have been identified. If the money

Activity

Activity 2: True or false – The contents of a business plan

Is it true or false that the following statements should be in a business plan? Put a tick in the correct column.

Statement	True	False
The product being made		
The names of the owners of the business		
The price being charged for the product or service		
What school the owners attended		
Who inspired the owners to go into business		
What finance (money) is needed for the business		
The business programmes on television that the owners watch		
How the product or service is to be marketed		

is to be borrowed, say from a bank, the bank will look carefully at the business plan to judge whether it will take a risk and lend the business the money it requires.

A business plan can also be used simply to evaluate an idea. If someone thinks they have a business idea that will make them rich, sitting down and going through a business plan will help them realise what a good, or bad, idea it really was.

Remember, a business plan cannot look too far into the future. It is very difficult to predict accurately what will happen in business for more than a year ahead and in certain circumstances this time will be further reduced. A plan may have to be revised with changing circumstances and, of course, a new plan developed if a new product or service is introduced.

Evaluation point

When evaluating the importance of a business plan, remember that a business plan will usually be completed when a business starts or when a business makes an important change. While a business plan is important for both situations, it is especially important for a new business, which needs to use the plan to help judge whether to go ahead or not.

Activity

Activity 3: Explanation – The importance of a business plan

1 Explain why a business plan should be completed by *all* businesses.
2 Explain why a business plan is especially important to a *new* business.

Activity

Activity 4: Poster – A business plan and marketing

Create a poster to show the connection between a marketing strategy and a business plan. It may be helpful to use the 4 Ps of the marketing mix as a starting point.

Assessment Activity

Amanda Smith wants to start a business as a florist. She has always loved flowers and design work in general and thought she could combine these two interests and, she hopes, make money running a successful business. Her experience of business is very limited, but she realises that marketing will be important if she goes ahead and opens a florist's shop. Amanda has been told that it is important to complete a business plan before she goes any further with her ideas. She now needs further advice on what to do.

Questions

1 Advise Amanda on what she should include in her business plan.

2 How important is it that Amanda completes a business plan? Give reasons for your answer.

3 Explain how Amanda's business plan should be linked to the marketing of the new business.

Advice on how to answer the questions

The first question asks you to give Amanda advice. There is no need to give any *reasons* for that advice in this question. A bullet pointed list will be enough.

The second question asks *how* important a business plan is. You must make a decision on just how important you think it is and give reasons for the decision you have made.

Care should be taken with the final question. You will need to explain how a business plan and marketing are linked, but also to *apply* your ideas to *Amanda's* business plan for her *florist's* shop. Make sure that the marketing mix examples you use are *applied* to this type of business.

Key facts

- Planning is a vital part in the successful start up and development of a business.
- A business plan is normally written when a business starts or when an important change to the business takes place.
- A number of people, apart from the owners of the business, will be interested in seeing the business plan.
- A business plan is useful when someone is simply trying to see if a business idea will really work, before actually starting the business.

Key Terms

Make sure you can explain each of the following Key Terms

Business plan A simple business plan sets out details on the product or service being sold, where the finance is to come from to start the business, how the product or service is to be marketed, and the market research to show there is a need for what is being sold.

Finance A business word used instead of money. The finance needed to start a business is the money that is needed to do so.

PART 2

BUSINESS & PEOPLE

Introductory Activity

Learning Outcomes

By studying this unit you will be able to:

● **Explain how and why people are important for businesses**

● **Explain with an example, the main issues that businesses must think about regarding their workers**

● **Explain that different business structures suit different business situations.**

The importance of people in business

John Toner started Quality Windows and Conservatories eight years ago. At that time he employed just two other people who did most of the construction work. John ran the business. He found the customers, drew up the plans for the conservatories, organised the purchase of materials and the construction work, as well as keeping the books and doing the accounts.

Businesses need workers with many different skills

Today, Quality Windows and Conservatories employs 12 people in the firm. There are:

● two sales representatives, one specialising in sales to commercial properties, the other dealing with domestic customers

● four people work in the factory, manufacturing the UPVC window frames

● three fitters

● one bricklayer

● two full-time administrative assistants, who act as receptionists, bookkeepers and clerical assistants.

John's opinion about his workers is:

> 'People are my most important asset. Along with myself, the sales representatives find new customers and give quotations. Accuracy is critical for the factory workers. Mistakes cost money in wasted time and materials. The fitters not only install the windows, but they are the public image of the business as well. They must build good relations with the customers. Without this we would not get repeat business or word-of-mouth recommendations. The office workers are essential for keeping good records and for the general administrative work. Together we are a team, dependent on each other for the success of our jobs and the business.'

This view about the importance of people in business is common in all kinds of organisations. For many firms, appointing the right staff and getting them to work well is crucial to the success of the business. For this reason, firms often spend a lot of time, effort and expense to get the people-side of the business right.

Activity

Activity 1: Explanation – The importance of people

- Explain why the workers in Quality Windows and Conservatories depend on each other.
- List the skills and personal qualities that the different kinds of workers employed by John Toner are likely to need in order to do their jobs well.

How to get it right

Getting the people-side of organisations right is not easy. Figure 1 shows some of the things organisations consider in order to ensure that the people who work for them are effective.

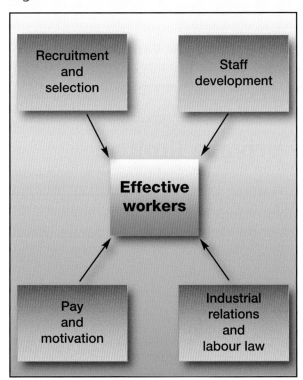

Figure 1 Effective workers

Recruitment and selection are about appointing the right kind of people to do the work. It is important to attract enough applicants so that the organisation has some choice. Information about the applications will help the organisation to decide which of the applicants will be most suitable. It can be very difficult to dismiss unwanted workers.

Motivation is about making workers work well, to produce good-quality products and services efficiently. Pay is one method of motivating workers but people do not work only for money. Organisations need to understand why people work so that they know what will motivate them to work well.

Staff development is about improving the skills that the workers have. Training is one method by which this can be achieved. Another method is appraisal. This involves reviewing the performance of the worker, identifying their strengths and weaknesses and producing an action plan to help them to improve.

Trade unions represent the interests of workers. They will try to improve the pay and conditions of the workers. They will also ensure that employers do not break the **employment laws** that are designed to protect workers and the rights of the individual. Poor **industrial relations** between managers and workers can have a very bad effect on the productivity of workers.

Activity

Activity 2: Research – Interview

Write about an employee in a local business. Write this as an article to be included in the local newspaper. You may wish to include a picture of the employee, or the premises of the organisation.

You will need to interview someone to get the information you need. The person you interview could be a relative, friend, neighbour or someone you work with during your work experience. It is important to prepare thoroughly for the interview – write down the questions that you will ask and decide how you will record the answers. You could write about:

● the organisation – its name, where it is, what it produces

● the job the person does

● the skills the person needs for the job

● the qualifications they need for the job

● what training they have had

● who they are responsible to, who they are responsible for

● how the person was recruited and selected

● how they are paid

● whether or not they are in a trade union

● what they like and dislike about the job.

The organisation may have a website that contains useful background information about what it does.

From sole proprietor to private limited company

After the first three years John Toner decided to change the form of the business. He had started the business as a sole proprietor but decided to become a private limited company.

As a sole proprietor

Being a sole proprietor had suited John at the time. He had been made redundant from his previous job in which he worked for another window and conservatory business, and he had enough money from his redundancy pay-off to buy the equipment he needed. The business was small and John was able to make all the decisions and he kept all the profit for himself.

How the business developed

As the business grew so did the risks and the business was becoming more complicated to run. John had:

- increased the amount of money he had put into the business
- increased his loan and his overdraft from the bank to buy more materials and equipment
- more customers to see, more people to manage and more windows and conservatories to install.

He knew that, as a sole proprietor, he had unlimited liability. John was worried that should the business fail, he would have to sell his private possessions to pay off his debts as well as losing what he had invested.

The other problem was the site and the factory that John had were becoming too small as the business grew. He wanted a bigger site, so he could display more examples of the conservatories he sold. He needed a bigger factory to be able to manufacture more of the windows. However, this would cost a lot of money and John did not want to use any more of his savings or borrow more money from the bank.

Not becoming a partnership

The two workers who had worked for John since he had started the business were interested in investing some money. Along with John, they had thought about changing the business into a 'partnership'. However, this would mean that they would all have unlimited liability so they decided against this.

Becoming a private limited company

By becoming a private limited company, John gained two main benefits:

- As one of the owners he would now have limited liability. This meant that there was no longer any risk to his private possessions.
- He could sell shares to the two workers who were willing to invest. They would become shareholders, as well as John, and the money could be used to buy the new site and factory.

Activity

Activity 3: Explanation – Forms of business

Imagine that you run a sole proprietor business that, like John Toner's, has been very successful. Like John, you want the business to grow further. You have two workers, who have been with you from the start, and you would like them to become shareholders in the business when you change it to a private limited company. Write down what you would say to them to persuade them to become shareholders.

Requirements of the examination: Business and people

Learning Outcomes

By studying this unit you will be able to:

● **Explain the different skills that the examination tests**

● **Explain what you have to do to answer questions that test the different skills**

● **Explain how much you will be expected to write**

● **List the main content of the specification that you will be tested on**

● **Feel confident about what you need to learn to perform well in this examination.**

What is the name of the examination?

The examination is called 'Unit A292: Business and People'.

What will the exam be like?

● The examination for Unit A292 will last for one hour.

● There will be a total of 60 marks. The marks will count for 25 per cent of your overall score in Business Studies GCSE.

● There will be two main questions. Each of these will be divided into a number of parts.

● The questions will be based on a business context. Some information will be given about the business and then a question will follow.

What will the exam test?

The examination tests three skills:

1 Knowledge. How well you can define business terms and can explain business ideas.

Example. You might be asked to define what is meant by the term 'redundancy' or to explain the advantages of sole proprietorships.

2 Application. How well you can use your knowledge to explain a business situation.

Example. You might be asked to explain how changing a business from a partnership to a private limited company affects the liability of the owners for any debts that the business has.

3 Analysis and evaluation. This is about weighing up advantages and disadvantages or pros and cons to make judgements. You may need to suggest how good or bad something is. You may need to recommend what a business should do and then give your reasons why you think this is the right thing to do.

Example. You could be asked to recommend a method of selection to use to choose between people who have applied for a particular job. You may be asked to judge if a business is using the best methods of motivating the workers it employs.

The questions on the examination paper will test different skills. Some will test only knowledge. Those that test application and analysis and evaluation will usually require some knowledge. The marks for the different skills on this paper are:

Knowledge – 27 marks
Application – 19 marks
Analysis and Evaluation – 14 marks

Note that the examination is going to test you most on your knowledge of terms and business ideas. You should learn these well!

Something extra about analysis and evaluation questions

Sometimes with evaluation questions it is difficult to come to a definite decision. In this situation you can then write that you need more information – and explain what that information is. Also, what is the right answer might depend on certain things – for example, does the owner want to keep control of the business or does he or she want it to grow. You may find the writing frame in Figure 1 helps to plan an answer for an evaluation question. The example statements in the writing frame are connected with the question below and are linked to the business situation of John Toner that has been discussed in the previous unit.

Sample question

John Toner needs to move to a bigger site with a bigger factory, for which he will need

Figure 1 Sample writing frame

Introduction
Briefly explain the problem.

Advantages/For/Good bits	Disadvantages/Against/Bad bits
Write down the advantages of something or the reasons for following a course of action.	Write down the disadvantages of something or the reasons for not doing something.
For example: *the arguments in favour of changing from a sole proprietor to a private limited company.*	For example: *the arguments against becoming a private limited company.*

Conclusion
Make your decision and explain why you have come to it. Alternatively, say what other information is needed, or what the recommendation will depend upon.
For example: *If John wants to keep control of the business, he should stay as a sole proprietor. However, if he does not have enough savings or does not want to borrow more money from the bank, he can invite his two employees to become shareholders in a private limited company. If he can get them to agree, he could be the major shareholder, which would mean he would still have a lot of control over the business.*

to raise more finance. He is considering becoming a private limited company to help with this problem. Recommend whether or not John should change from being a sole proprietor to becoming a private limited company. Give reasons for your recommendation.

How difficult will the questions be?

The questions on this examination will vary in difficulty. Some are used to test the F and G candidates, some are there to challenge the A and A* candidates. Some of the questions can be answered in different ways – a simple answer might gain a grade E or F, while a more sophisticated answer to the same question might be awarded B or A grade marks.

The people who set the examination spend hours working to make sure that the examination will be a fair test of what you, as a GCSE Business Studies student, should be able to do. They are not trying to catch you out. Please remember that the examination is supposed to be *an opportunity for you to show off how good you are at Business Studies.*

How much should I write

The number of lines that are provided for your answer is a good guide to how much you should write. If there are ten lines and you only fill two of them, you may not have developed your answer as fully as you should. Another guide is the number of marks allocated to the question. Generally, the more marks allocated the more you need to write.

Content – the knowledge

There are two main sections to Unit A292: Business and People.

The first section is called 'The structure of business activity'. There are two main parts to this:

- The need for business activity
- Business ownership, trading organisations, growth and location.

The wrong way to decide where to locate

The second section is called 'The workforce in business'. There are two main parts to this:

- Employment and retention
- Organisation and communication.

Is an interview a good way to find out about someone?

Themes for questions

The list below is designed to give you an idea of the main question themes that come up on this paper. It is not meant to be a comprehensive list. When you have finished studying this unit, you should feel confident that you could give an answer to these questions. Also, each of the units in this section of the book has examples of the types of questions that are asked on this examination.

- What are the objectives of different stakeholders and how can businesses deal with these?

- How and why has the importance of the primary, secondary and tertiary sectors of the economy changed over time?

- What are the advantages and disadvantages of different types of business structures? When are they appropriate? Why may the owners of a business want to change its structure?

- What are multi-national companies? Why have they increased in importance? Is this good or bad?

- How and why do businesses grow?

- Where should a business locate?

- What methods of recruitment and selection should businesses use for different types of workers?

- Why is training important for businesses and for workers? What methods of training are appropriate for different types of workers and to develop different skills?

- When should the different methods of motivation be used?

- What are the employment laws that businesses must comply with and what will happen if they do not?

- What interests of workers do trade unions protect and how do they protect them?

- Describe an organisation chart using the correct terms. What are the main problems with organisation charts? What are the benefits and problems of delayering?

- What methods of communication are appropriate in different business situations?

- How can ICT help businesses and what problems could it bring?

- How has the way people work been affected by the development of ICT?

Unit 2.3.1

Types of business activity

Learning Outcomes

By studying this unit you will be able to:

- **Explain and give examples of the different sectors of production activities**
- **Explain how the different sectors of production are linked together (interdependent)**
- **Explain how employment and output in the different sectors have changed in recent years in the UK**
- **Discuss the effect of these changes on employment in the UK.**

Introduction

From North Dakota to Lancashire

Where does the loaf of bread you eat come from? This is the story of the bread I used for my toast at breakfast. The wheat may have been grown in North Dakota in the United States of America. From there it is shipped to the port of Liverpool. Here Cargill's, a food processing company based in Liverpool docks, processes the wheat to make flour. The flour is then delivered by road to the Warburton's bakery in Bolton which uses it, and some other ingredients, to make the bread. The bread is then delivered to the Morrison's Supermarket in my local town.

The story of bread is typical of how complex production is. It involves three types of production – primary, secondary and tertiary. Together they form the **'chain of production'**.

Primary sector

The word 'primary' means 'first' (like a primary school). In business activity the **primary sector** is the first stage or first part of production. Businesses in the primary sector include:

- fishing
- mining and quarrying
- farming
- mineral extraction, such as oil drilling
- forestry.

All these businesses are at the first stage of production, producing *raw materials* for other businesses to use.

Secondary sector

Secondary, as the name suggests, is the second stage of production. Businesses in the **secondary sector** will use the raw materials from the primary sector and *manufacture* products from them.

The number of different secondary businesses is huge, as it includes anything that is manufactured. Some of the larger

Some businesses in the primary sector

secondary businesses include:

- car manufacturers
- furniture manufacturers
- electrical appliance manufacturers.

And lots, lots more!

Tertiary sector

The word 'tertiary' means 'third', though thinking of the tertiary sector as the third stage of production can be a little misleading. The **tertiary sector** is really concerned with providing a service for its customers and includes businesses such as:

- retailing
- banking
- insurance
- travel
- entertainment
- transport
- hotels
- customer service.

Although not really thought of as businesses, the tertiary sector also includes education, health, police, tax offices, local and national government and the armed forces.

In all of these examples, the people who work for these organisations are there to

Example of a business in the secondary sector

provide a *service* for others. At the end of their day's work they will not be able to see something they have made, unlike workers who work in the secondary sector.

Examples of businesses in the tertiary sector

How the three sectors of business activity depend on each other

No matter what sector a business is in, it will depend on businesses in the *other* sectors.

For example, diamonds are mined (primary sector); a jewellery business will use them to make a diamond ring (secondary sector). A jeweller's shop is then needed to sell the ring (tertiary sector). This is called **interdependence**. The process by which a product starts as raw materials, goes through secondary production, and is then sold in the tertiary sector is called **the chain of production**; each part is connected to the

Activity

Activity 1: Research – the chain of production

Using the internet, research the chain of production for a product. Write the story of the product you have investigated, mentioning the primary, secondary and tertiary production used. You might like to use a map of the world, or the UK, to show what happens. One website you might like to try is www.skillsspace.co.uk, which has been created by Cadbury. Use the Design Technology part of the site to find out about the making of chocolate.

Activity

Activity 2: Zone activity – Sectors of the economy

Put the business activities listed below under the correct heading – primary, secondary or tertiary – in the table.

- football club
- farm
- double-glazing manufacturer
- bank
- camera shop
- car factory
- garden centre
- diamond mine
- telephone call centre
- computer repair centre
- cinema
- washing machine manufacturer

Primary	Secondary	Tertiary

Activity

Activity 3: Research – Local business survey

a Research your local area to find different businesses in each sector of the economy. Fill in a chart like the one shown below. You should aim to find at least 20 different businesses. You could use *Yellow Pages* or a similar business directory. The local council website may also contain information about business activity in the local area.

Name of business	What the business does	Primary/Secondary/Tertiary

Local business survey

b Draw a bar graph to show the results of your survey.

other like the links in a chain. It works in both directions. The diamond mine needs the jeweller and the jeweller's shop; the jeweller's shop will have nothing to sell without the jeweller and the diamond mine.

All sectors of business activity depend on each other

Activity

Activity 4: Poster – Interdependence

Draw a poster to show how the three sectors of business activity depend on each other (interdependence) in the following products:

i   a wooden chair

ii a pair of jeans

Specialisation

When a business is in one particular sector, it will often specialise in that area, and leave other sectors of business activity to do other kinds of work. For example, the **specialisation** of a toy maker is *making* toys, leaving the *selling* of the toys to another specialist firm. By concentrating on, or specialising in, one activity the business can save money by looking at ways of reducing costs in that one area, and so producing cheaper goods.

Added value

As raw materials (primary sector) are then made into finished goods (secondary sector), the secondary business is 'adding value' to the original raw material. When the product is sold the tertiary sector is adding more value to the product by making it available to the customer. Producers pay value added tax (VAT). The amount they pay depends partly on the value that they add and partly on the rate of VAT that the government imposes.

Changes in the three sectors of business activity

Over the years, the importance of the three sectors that make up business activity in Britain has changed. What is important to understand is *what* has changed and *why* the changes have taken place.

Reasons for the changes in the primary sector

The primary sector in Britain has fallen in importance over recent years, employing far fewer people. This is because of a number of factors:

● Raw materials have been used up, resulting, for example, in the closure of many coal mines and the loss of many thousands of jobs.

● The use of machinery to replace jobs. Workers are expensive, and a business will reduce the number of workers it uses wherever it can. This has resulted, for example, in the loss of many farming jobs over the years.

● Foreign competition has meant that businesses in Britain cannot produce goods as cheaply as other countries. This has further affected industries such as coal, where the mines that remain in Britain are under threat because of cheaper fuels coming from overseas.

Reasons for the changes in the secondary sector

As with the primary sector, the secondary sector has declined in importance in recent years, with many thousands of jobs being lost. The whole process of secondary sector decline is called **de-industrialisation**, and involves the closure of much of the manufacturing sector in a country. This has happened because:

- Foreign competition has meant that many goods, which were once 'Made in Britain', are now manufactured overseas. This may be because the goods are cheaper, or because consumers in Britain feel that the quality of products from overseas is better than that of those made in Britain. This has especially affected the clothing industry, with many of the items we now wear being made in other countries. The car and motorcycle industry has also been affected in the same way, with large numbers of vehicles bought in Britain being made abroad. (See Unit 3.5.5 on Globalisation).

- The use of machinery has meant that many jobs have been lost, with workers being replaced by machines, which are less expensive. The increasing use of robotics and computer control systems has affected many businesses – for example, car assembly.

Reasons for the changes in the tertiary sector

Unlike the primary and secondary sectors, the tertiary sector has seen a large rise in importance in recent years, with many new jobs being created. This is because:

- Many tertiary sector jobs are connected to the rise in population – for example, health and education. As the population rises, more teachers and nurses will be needed. These jobs have not been affected by the introduction of machinery in the same way as primary and secondary sector jobs.

- The increase in the wealth of people in Britain means that there is more money that can be spent in shops. This, in turn, will mean more retail workers are required. Add to this, the growth of out-of-town shopping centres and the longer opening hours of shops, and there is a clear rise in the number of workers required.

- The population of Britain also now enjoys more leisure time than ever before. This means that more money is being spent on leisure activities such as sports, cinema and travel, which in turn require more workers.

- Businesses are putting more importance on customer service as a way of keeping existing customers and gaining new ones. This has led, for example, to the large increase in telephone call centres, which themselves need large numbers of workers.

- Competition from abroad is increasingly affecting the tertiary sector. Many call-centre jobs are being done by people in countries such as India – see Unit 3.5.5. on Globalisation.

Evaluation

Changes in employment in the different sectors of the UK economy will continue to happen. If the total number of jobs in primary and secondary activities continues to fall, unemployment may not occur if enough new jobs are created in the tertiary sector. However, workers may need to change the *type* of work they do and may have to work for less pay. Some workers who lose their jobs often need to retrain, which will cost them money. Older workers may find it difficult to learn new skills, or it may not be worth the expense if they only have a few years left to work. Some workers may have to take unskilled, lower-paid work.

Evaluation point

A fall in employment in a sector does not mean that the amount produced by that sector goes down. While employment in manfacturing has been reduced in recent years in the UK, the output of the sector has increased. This is because of the use of more machines that replace labour. There has been an increase in productivity – how much each worker produces. Increasing productivity reduces the costs of producing goods and services. This is very important if UK businesses are to compete in the global economy.

Activity

Activity 5: Research and calculation – Production and employment

1 At home, research where different items are made. Try to find a range of products, such as clothing, electrical, cosmetics, furniture and so on. Construct a chart similar to the one started below. Try to find at least 20 items.

Item	Country of origin

2 Draw a bar graph of your results.

3 Using the figures from your bar graph, calculate the percentage of items in your survey that are made in Britain.

4 Why do you think that only some of the items in your survey are made in Britain?

5 The following table of figures shows the number of employees in different industries for 1985 and 2000. The totals are in thousands.

Industry	1985	2000
Mining and quarrying	228	67
Textiles	278	154
Motor cars	268	211
Hotels and restaurants	940	1,412
Recreation and sport	472	605

Source: Office for National Statistics

a Draw a bar graph to show the differences in the five industries for 1985 to 2000.

b Calculate the percentage change in Mining and Hotels and restaurants from 1985 to 2000.

c Explain why the number of employees has changed in each of the five industries since 1985.

Examination questions

1 a There are three sectors in an economy: primary, secondary and tertiary. Give one example of each.

Primary _____

Secondary _____

Tertiary _____ (3 marks)

b In the county of Moorshire, over the past 15 years, employment in the secondary sector has decreased while employment in the tertiary sector has grown. The statements in the table below give reasons why these changes have taken place.

For each statement, place a tick (✓) in the column that explains the effect the statement had on employment. The first one has been completed for you.

Table: Reasons for changes in Employment in the Secondary and Tertiary sectors

Reason why changes in employment have taken place	This has caused a *fall* in employment in the *secondary* sector	This has caused a *rise* in employment in the *tertiary* sector
An increase in the population in the UK has led to an increase in demand for services such as banking.		
Imports have increased because other countries such as Taiwan and China are able to produce manufactured goods more cheaply than the UK.		
People in the UK now have more money to spend on luxury services such as eating out and going to the cinema.		
The development of new technology means that fewer people are now needed to make manufactured goods.		
People in the UK now have more time for leisure activities.		

(4 marks)

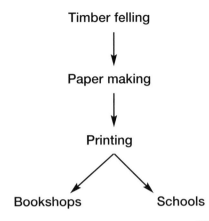

Timber felling

Paper making

Printing

Bookshops   Schools

2 Carlton Press Ltd is a publishing company that specialises in educational books. The diagram shows the typical stages of the production of one of its books.

Using examples from the diagram, explain how primary, secondary and tertiary sector businesses rely on each other.

(6 marks)

3 The table below shows the levels of employment by sector, in 1968 and 2008 in the economy of the town of Bowton.

Working population – by sector
Economy of Bowton

	1968	2008
Primary sector	1,000	500
Secondary sector	9,000	4,000
Tertiary sector	10,000	16,000

a Explain why the changes in employment in the secondary sector may have occurred. (4 marks)

b Explain why the changes in employment in the tertiary sector may have occurred.   (4 marks)

c Are the changes in employment that have taken place a problem for the people of Bowton? Give reasons for your answer.   (8 marks)

Advice on how to answer the questions

1 a You need to give one example of a business activity for each sector.

b Read the reasons in the left-hand column of the table carefully. Decide whether they explain the fall in employment in the secondary sector or the rise in the tertiary sector.

2 The command word is 'explain'. Here you are also instructed to use the diagram in your answer. Explaining without using the diagram will lose marks. There are six marks available for this question. Take each stage in turn from the diagram, and explain clearly how the different stages rely on each other. You should explain the two-way link in each case – for example, how the secondary sector depends on the primary and the primary depends on the secondary.

3 a and b State the reasons and then explain them fully.

c This is a difficult question, which needs a carefully worked out answer. Consider the overall effect on employment in Bowton. Has it increased or decreased? How will this affect workers? Then discuss how different types of workers might have been affected. For example, skilled workers in manufacturing will have lost jobs. Will it be easy for them to get new jobs? What will they have to do to get jobs – either in manufacturing or in the tertiary sector? Will the age of the worker who loses his job matter?

Key facts

- There are three sectors of the economy – primary, secondary and tertiary.
- The sectors are interdependent – one sector cannot produce without work done in another sector.
- Employment in the primary and secondary sectors in the UK is declining, while employment in the tertiary sector is increasing.

Key Terms

Make sure you can explain each of the following Key Terms

Chain of production The process of a product starting as raw materials, manufactured in secondary production and then serviced in some way in tertiary production.

Primary sector The first stage of production involving the extraction of the raw materials and natural resources.

Secondary sector The second stage of production, where the raw materials are manufactured into finished products.

Tertiary sector The third stage of production, where a service is provided for consumers

Interdependence The way in which business in different sectors of business activity depend on each other. The primary sector depends on the secondary sector to make products from the raw materials it produces. In turn, the primary and secondary sectors depend on the tertiary sector to provide the necessary services for the businesses.

Specialisation Where a business concentrates on one particular activity.

Added value When a business increases the value of a product – for example, making a car from pieces of metal or making a meal from various ingredients.

De-industrialisation The reduction of importance of the secondary sector of business activity in a country.

Business objectives and the role of stakeholders

Learning Outcomes

By studying this unit you will be able to:

- **Explain the nature of business objectives**
- **Identify and explain the differing objectives of private and public sector businesses**
- **Recognise and explain why some business objectives may be in conflict**
- **Recognise different types of stakeholders and explain why they may have an interest in particular business activity**
- **Discuss why some stakeholders in the same business may have conflicting interests.**

Introduction

Why have you chosen to study GCSE Business Studies? You must have had a particular reason or objective which you hope to achieve. Whatever we do, we usually do it with a particular reason or objective in mind. Businesses are no different.

Each business will want to achieve different objectives and will go about trying to achieve these objectives in different ways. In some cases, just like individuals, the business will achieve its objectives and in other cases it may not. Sometimes the business will need to change its objectives as it responds to changing circumstances, if it realises that the objectives it has set for itself are either too easily achieved, or if the objectives are unachievable.

This unit examines not only **business objectives** but also the individuals and groups who will have an interest in the success or failure of business activity.

Business objectives

All businesses have one or more objectives. The objectives themselves will vary according to the size and situation of the business. Normally, a large multi-national public limited company (plc), such as Vodafone Group plc, will have different business objectives from those of a local corner shop.

It has become common in recent years for a business to summarise its objectives in a **mission statement**, which is a short declaration of what the business is aiming to achieve.

Below is an extract from the Vodafone Group plc Mission of Value Statement.

WHERE DO WE WANT TO BE?

Our vision
To be the communications leader in an increasingly connected world

Our mission
Help customers to make the most of now

WHAT DO WE NEED TO GET THERE?
Our global strategic goals
- Build the best global Vodafone team
- Delight our customers
- Provide superior shareholder returns
- Be a responsible business
- Expand market boundaries

WHAT DRIVES US?
Our values
We have four core values, described internally as 'Passions'. One of our values is passion for the world around us. This is about helping people lead fuller lives through the services we provide and the impact we have on the world around us.
- Passion for results
- Passion for our customers
- Passion for people
- Passion for the world around us

Figure 1 Vodafone Group plc Mission of Value Statement

The business objectives most often set by business are shown below:

- profit
- growth
- survival
- providing a service.

There may also be other objectives that businesses attempt to achieve and these will:

- vary from business to business
- change as the business develops
- change in response to competition and changes in the market.

Clear objectives are needed to succeed in business

Profit

Most businesses will have profit as one of their objectives. For many businesses it will be the *main* objective. Some businesses may want to 'maximise profits', which means they will try to make as much profit as possible. This may, however, mean that consumers feel they are not being treated well if a business is seen to make too much profit. Sales may fall as a result.

Other businesses may aim to make just enough profit to pay for their future plans. This is called **satisficing**.

There are some businesses that will not want to pursue the objective of profit. These will include such organisations as:

- charities, which will want to maximise funds for the cause they support
- social enterprises, which may help people to return to work following an illness or accident.

Growth

Growth is important to business, as it is seen as a way to raise profits. This is especially important to larger businesses such as public limited companies, which need the growth to pay increased **dividends** to their shareholders.

Growth itself can take different forms, including:

- **Sales growth**. A business may simply want to see sales grow, which may not necessarily mean an increase in profit, as prices may have to be lowered in order to attract more customers. Sales growth is often achieved by a business opening more outlets – for example, opening shops in different towns.

- **Increased market share**. A business may wish to see its **market share** grow. This means that the business has a greater percentage share of a market. For example, if 1,000 tables were sold in a country, and a business sold 100 of those tables, it would have 10 per cent share of the market. If the total number of tables sold rose from 1,000 to 2,000, the business would have to sell more than 200 tables (10 per cent of 2,000) if it were to increase its market share. Car manufacturers often make comparisons on how much market share each manufacturer has.

- **Elimination of competition**. This is another method of increasing market share, where a business takes over its competitors, or the competitors themselves close. In these ways a business can achieve 'instant' growth. Supermarket chains often buy up other competing supermarket chains.

Survival

A rather more basic business objective is survival. This objective is particularly important to a new business for the first few months. Just to keep going after first opening a business may be something of an achievement! Other more established businesses may see survival as an important objective when they are faced with problems such as falling sales, reduced market share, and so on. In most cases survival should normally be seen as a temporary, but also vital, objective.

Providing a service

Providing a service may be closely linked to making a profit – the better the service, the more customers will be attracted and so profits will grow. For some businesses, however, providing a service may be the *main* objective, even if it means making *less profit*. This may be important in businesses which see customer satisfaction as being a high priority. With good service, the business gets a good reputation, possibly winning awards, which may well be enough to satisfy the owners of the business. Such a business may not even think of growth, being content to continue in its present form, providing a service to customers. This is often found in smaller businesses, which serve the local community.

Business objectives in the private and public sectors

The private sector

The **private sector** includes all the businesses that are owned by private individuals. All sole proprietors, partnerships, private and public limited companies are in the private sector, as they are owned by individuals rather than the government. The private sector is by far the largest part of business activity in the United Kingdom, growing in importance over the last 25 years mainly because of

Activity

Activity 1: Explanation – Business Objectives

1 a Identify the business objectives in the Vodafone Group plc Mission of Value Statement in Figure 1.

  b Explain why these objectives are important to the business.

2 a Complete the table below by selecting one of the following business objectives for each of the following business situations:

  i   profit

  ii growth

  iii survival

  iv providing a service

  b Give a reason for your choice of objective.

Business situation	Possible objective	Reason for objective
An 18-year-old school leaver just setting up a new business repairing computers		
A public limited company in the fashion business		
A local fruit and vegetable shop that discovers that a new superstore is to open 100 metres away		
A French low-cost airline starting flights from France to the UK		
A farmer who wants to diversify into home delivery of organic vegetables		

3 Imagine you were to go into business. Complete the table below by making a list of *your* business objectives in order of importance to you, adding a symbol or cartoon-type image to illustrate each objective. Explain why your objectives are in that particular order.

Name or type of business		
Objective	Image	Explanation for choice of objective

4 In pairs or small groups, compare and discuss your individual lists of business objectives from question 3. Investigate why there are differences in people's objectives.

transfer of business activity from the public sector to the private sector.

Objectives in the private sector are centred on profit and growth. A person starting a business requires some reward for taking the risk of starting the business. That reward will come from the profits of the business. Larger businesses will have to make a profit to maintain and possibly expand. Limited companies are under rather more pressure to make a profit to satisfy shareholders, who will be paid a dividend as their reward for investing in the company as a result of buying shares.

Private sector businesses come in all sizes

The public sector

The **public sector** includes all the businesses and other organisations that are controlled by central or local government. The public sector includes health, education, police, fire services and local council services. It also includes the **public corporations** such as the BBC and Post Office – see also Unit 2.3.6.

For most organisations in the public sector, providing a good service is seen as the most important objective. It would be difficult to imagine the fire service, for example, having profit as its main objective! Money is provided by local and national

government to operate the public sector services such as health and education, with no shareholders demanding to be paid dividends as in the private sector. In this way the public sector can concentrate on providing the service people need.

An example of an organisation in the public sector

Activity 2: Explanation – Public and private sector objectives

1 Explain the differences between the private and public sectors.

2 What are the differences between the objectives of businesses in the public and private sectors? Give reasons for the differences.

3 Why may it be difficult for a business to have profit, growth and improved service as objectives at the same time?

Conflicts in business objectives

Though some business objectives may work well together, such as providing a service to attract customers in order to make more profit, some of the objectives may well cause conflict in a business.

Growth versus profit

The managers of a business may see expansion as its main aim, which in turn might mean that profits are reduced for a short period of time before they rise. The

Business objectives are often in conflict with each other

owners, however, may want to see profits kept at a high level.

Growth versus service

A business may be able to offer very good service because it is small and knows its customers well. With growth, the business may lose touch with its customers and so the level of service could fall.

Survival versus profit

When a business has survival as its main objective, it is unlikely to have profit (or expansion!) as an objective. However, it may well see providing a good service as a way of surviving.

Stakeholders in business

What are stakeholders?

A stakeholder can be an individual or group(s) of people who have an interest in a business. There are many different **stakeholders** in a business, and they often go beyond the business itself.

The main stakeholders in business are:

- workers
- managers
- owners
- customers
- suppliers
- government
- local community
- competitiors
- interest and pressure groups.

There will probably be many other stakeholders who will have an interest in the business. Much will depend on the type of business and where it is located.

Workers

Workers have a clear interest in the business where they work. They rely on work for their pay, which they will use to live on. Workers will also look upon work to provide them with some security for the future, and possibly a place to meet and work with other people. A worker has every interest in keeping the business going!

Managers

The managers of a business will have a slightly different interest in it from the workers. They, too, will be employees and need the business to provide them with the money to live on, but they also have to organise the business and plan for the future, which might mean making some workers redundant if the business is not performing very well. This will put their interests in conflict with those of the workers.

Owners

The owners of a business are not always workers or managers in a business. In a limited company (see Unit 2.3.5) the shareholders are the owners of the business and their interest in the business may be only for the dividend they receive from the profits earned by the business. How the business makes that profit might be of little interest to them. One way of making more profit may be to reduce the number of managers or workers in the business. Once again, there is a conflict of interest here between groups of stakeholders.

Customers

Customers want to see low prices and receive good service from a business. Some may be pleased if a large superstore opens in the area because it will give them a choice of shops and possibly lower prices. However, customers of the local corner shop which then closes because of competition from the superstore will not be as pleased!

Suppliers

A business that supplies goods and services to another business will clearly want that business to continue and to grow. If a business fails for any reason, other businesses are often affected in some way. A business which feels that one of its business customers is about to fail may stop supplying that business in order to reduce the risk of losses.

Government

The government has an interest in all businesses succeeding as this means that more people are in work and paying taxes, which gives the government more money to spend on areas such as health and education. With more people in work, the government also has to pay less unemployment pay – once again saving money.

Local community

The local community as a whole has an interest in business development. This may not mean that *every* business is welcome in an area. A business dealing in toxic waste processing may well provide jobs for some people, but the local community as a whole may be against such a development. Successful business will also bring general prosperity to a local community, which could help to reduce crime and contribute to local projects by donations and other support.

Competitors

Businesses in competition will want to see how their rivals are running their business and will also look to see if they can develop and improve on their business ideas. Businesses will want to see their rivals doing less well than they are doing.

Interest and pressure groups

These groups are very wide and varied. One of the best known examples of a pressure group is *Greenpeace*. This group is constantly applying pressure to businesses to make them operate in a more environmentally conscious manner.

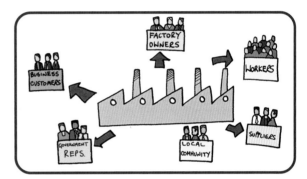

There are many different stakeholders in a business

Evaluation

1 You will need to be able to explain in detail why a business may have chosen to follow a particular objective at that stage of its development. You wil also need to be able to comment on how the pursuit of different objectives is likely to change as other facors, often beyond the control of a business, also change.

2 You will need to consider the reasons why a stakeholder may have an interest in the business. You will also need to be aware, and be able to explain why, stakeholders in the same business may have conflicting interests. For instance, workers may want large pay increases but shareholders may want to keep costs down so that the business makes more profit and is able to pay bigger dividends.

Activity

Activity 3: True or false – Objectives and stakeholders

Tick one box to indicate if the statement is true or false.

Statement	True ✔	False ✔
Stakeholders own the business		
Objectives change with time		
All businesses have stakeholders		
Stakeholders can have different interests		
The objective of profit is followed by all businesses		
All businesses have the same stakeholders		
Objectives can be in conflict		
Stakeholders can be in conflict		
All businesses follow the same objectives		
Stakeholders can influence business activity		

Activity

Activity 4: Research – Stakeholders

Using your school or college as an example of a business resource, complete the table below detailing the stakeholders and their interest in the school/college. Think of as many different stakeholders as you can.

Name of stakeholder	Reason for interest in school/college

Examination questions

1 Jason Lee works for Colliers plc, which makes and sells chocolate. His friend, Alison Stone, works in the Education Department of Marston Borough Council.

  a State which person works in the public sector and which in the private sector? Write your answers in the box below. (2 marks)

Sector	Name of worker
Public sector	
Private sector	

  b State two possible objectives for Colliers plc and two possible objectives for Marston Education Department. (4 marks)

  c Explain how and why the objectives of a business may change over time. (6 marks)

2 a Explain what is meant by a 'stakeholder'. (2 marks)

  b Suggest three possible stakeholders in Colliers plc and explain why they may have an interest in the business. (9 marks)

Advice on how to answer the questions

1 a In this question you need to think which sectors of the economy employ Alison and Colin.

  b Remember that in this question there is a total of four objectives. Make sure you are clear on which objectives are appropriate for which organisation: two in the public sector and two in the private sector.

  c This is a longer question (6 marks) in which you must explain how the objectives of a business change and why they change. The question says 'over time'. You can, for instance, begin your answer describing a business that is just starting up and explain how it then develops. With 6 marks available, try to include three different objectives and explain how and why the objectives change in a business.

2 a You need to give a definition of 'stakeholder'.

  b Here you must apply the idea of a stakeholder to a plc. The question tells you to 'suggest', and then to explain why each of the stakeholders has an interest in the business.

Key facts

- Different types of business will have different objectives.
- Business objectives will vary according to the business and the situation it finds itself in.
- Objectives will change as the business develops.
- Objectives can be in conflict.
- Each business will have a large number of different stakeholders.
- The reason why stakeholders are interested in a business will differ.
- Stakeholders may have conflicting interests in business.

Key Terms

Make sure you can explain each of the following Key Terms

Business objectives Business objectives are what the business is trying to achieve. Examples are profit, growth, survival and providing a service. Objectives vary from business to business and will change with time.

Mission statement A mission statement is a brief summary of the main objectives a business or organisation has.

Satisficing This means that a business will make enough profit to enable it to meet its needs, and not make as much profit as possible.

Dividend A payment made to shareholders from the profits made by a private or public limited company.

Market share This is the amount of a market that a business controls. It is measured as a percentage.

Private sector The part of business activity owned by private individuals. This is the greater part of business activity and includes sole proprietors, partnerships and private and public limited companies.

Public sector The part of business activity controlled by local and central government. including health, education, fire service, police, and the Post Office.

Public corporation An organisation owned by national government

Stakeholders An individual or group of people who have an interest in a business, including workers, customers, owners and the local community.

Organisation, growth and location of business

Learning Outcomes

By studying this unit you will be able to:

- **Explain how business activity may be classified in different ways**
- **Explain the basic differences between unincorporated and incorporated businesses and recommend which type may be suitable for a particular business**
- **Recognise and explain why some businesses operate with unlimited liability**
- **Explain the basic advantages and disadvantages of each type of business organisation**
- **Discuss the appropriateness of a form of business organisation for the size and type of business activity**
- **Discuss why businesses may need to change the way in which they are organised**
- **Identify and discuss ways in which businesses can grow in size**
- **Identify factors that affect the location of a business**
- **Recognise and explain reasons why a business may choose a particular location.**

Activity

Activity 1: Research – Business activity in a local area

The town centre map of Bowton shown in Figure 1 below was used in a GCSE Business Studies examination as the stimulus material for a number of different questions. The map shows some of the businesses trading in the imaginary town of Bowton.

Your task is to:

1 Draw a map, similar in style to the one for Bowton, of a shopping centre, town centre or area where there are a number of businesses and shops with which you are familiar.

2 Mark on the map the trading names of the different businesses.

3 Find out, by using the internet or by asking, the name of the business or person who actually owns the business.

4 Draw up a table, similar to the one in Figure 2, which compares the trading name of the business with the name of the person or firm that actually owns the business.

5 Insert information in the third column of the table showing the type of business activity in which each business is involved.

6 Complete the table by showing in which sector of the economy the business is trading.

7 Use the last column to identify if the business has limited or unlimited liability.

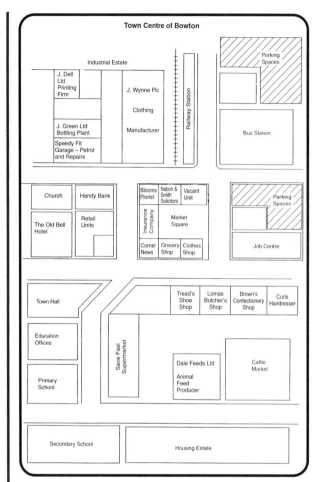

Figure 1 Map of Town Centre of Bowton

Primark owned by Associated British Foods – trading activities include food manufacture and retailing

B & Q owned by Kingfisher plc

Trading name of business	Name of person or business owning the business	Trading activity	Sector of the economy	Limited or unlimited

Figure 2 Businesses in (Insert the name of the area you have chosen)

Argos owned by the Home Retail Group

Classifying business into different types

Business activity can be classified in a number of different ways according to:

- the **sector of the economy** in which it is operating.

A farm is a primary activity

A production line is a secondary activity

A restaurant is a tertiary activity

- whether the activity takes place in the **public sector** or **private sector**.

A supermarket is a private sector activity

A hospital is a public sector activity

- the **type of business organisation and ownership**:
  - There are four basic forms of business ownership in the private sector. These forms of ownership will either be **incorporated** (see Unit 2.3.5) or **unincorporated** (see Unit 2.3.4) businesses.
  - Those businesses that trade in the public sector will usually be controlled and financed by national or local government.
  - **Co-operatives** are those business or trading organisations that are owned and operated by the people who work in the business. For instance, many farmers are part of a producer co-operative. A number of independent farmers get together so that they can sell their milk to dairies as though they are one business. By doing this, rather than working independently, they may get a better price for their milk.

Unincorporated businesses

There are two basic types of unincorporated business – **sole proprietors** and **partnerships**.

Unincorporated business

Sole proprietors
E.g. Allen's
Newsagents

Partnership
E.g. Smith and Jones,
Dentists

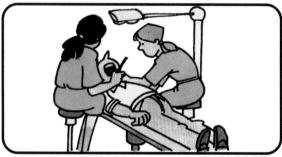

Figure 3 Types of unincorporated business.

These types of businesses have the following features:

Feature	Explanation
Unlimited liability	The owners of the business are personally liable for any debts which the business may have. This means that their personal possessions – TV, DVD, car – may have to be sold to raise finance or private wealth to pay off the debts of the business, even though these items have nothing to do with running the business.
Tax on profits	Income tax is paid on the profits that the business may make.
Continuity	The business, in its present form, ceases on the death of one of the owners.
Financial information	Remains private to the owners of the business.
Bankruptcy	This situation occurs when the business is unable to pay its debts.

Further information on these forms of business is given in Unit 2.3.4.

Incorporated businesses

There are two basic types of incorporated business – **private limited companies** and **public limited companies**.

Incorporated business

Private Limited
Company
E.g. Arcadia – owner
of Dorothy Perkins;
Burtons; Miss Selfridge;
Wallis; Top Shop

Public Limited
Company
E.g. Next plc

Figure 4 Types of incorporated business

These types of businesses have the following features:

Feature	Explanation
Limited liability	The liability of the owners of the business, the shareholders, to pay off its debts is limited to the amount of money that they have invested in the business when buying the shares.
Separate legal entity	The business has a separate legal identity from its owners. It can start legal action against another business or individual in order to protect itself. Other businesses and individuals have the right to take legal action against the business.
Tax on profits	Corporation Tax is paid on any profits that the business may make.
Finance	Finance can be raised through the sale and issue of shares.
Financial information	Some financial information is available to shareholders and the general public if they request to see it.
Insolvency	This situation occurs when the business is unable to pay its debts.

Further information on these forms of business is shown in Unit 2.3.5.

Evaluation point

1 The major advantage of unincorporated types of business is that they are easy to set up and many businesses in the United Kingdom trade as unincorporated businesses. However, this type of business organisation is not always the most suitable for each different business. Recognising when to change to an incorporated form of business ownership can be a difficult decision, but is one which will offer more protection to the owner(s) of the business.

2 The main reasons why some businesses do not convert to an incorporated form of business are usually cost and a fear of a possible loss of control. You will need to be able to explain the circumstances when it may be advantageous to become incorporated.

Activity

Activity 2: Presentation – Unincorporated businesses

Prepare a presentation outlining the advantages and disadvantages of the incorporated form of business when compared with the unincorporated form of business.

Are all businesses successful?

What do entrepreneurs do?

An **entrepreneur** is someone who recognises a business opportunity and who is prepared to take a risk in setting up a business to make the most of the opportunity. Not all business opportunities turn out to be successful. There is always a risk involved.

Activity

Activity 3: Comparison Alley – Sole proprietor and partnership

Below is a 'comparison alley' for the unincorporated form of business ownership. Prepare a similar diagram for the incorporated form of business ownership.

SOLE PROPRIETOR
Differences
- Owner has complete control
- Owner keeps all the profits
- Owner may work long hours
- Owner may not have all the necessary skills

  Similarities
  - Unlimited liability
   - Financial privacy
    - Easy to set up
     - No shares
      - Possible shortage of capital
       - Unincorporated

        PARTNERSHIP
        Differences
        - Partners may have a variety of skills
        - Partners share responsibilities
        - Partners share profits
        - Partners may mean there is more money to invest in the business
        - Partners may not always agree
        - Minimum of 2 partners with no upper limit on the number of partners.

Richard Branson Entrepreneur and founder of 'Virgin'

One of the best known entrepreneurs in the United Kingdom is Richard Branson.

The 'Virgin' name is well known in the United Kingdom and abroad. However, when new Virgin businesses start, there is no guarantee that they are going to be successful. Some examples of successful business activities using the 'Virgin' brand include Virgic Atlantic, Virgin Express, Virgin Mobile and Virgin Trains.

Reasons why some businesses fail

Running a business can be a challenging and time-consuming activity. It can also be a very profitable experience for the owner or owners. However, not all businesses are successful and they can fail for a variety of reasons. Some of the possible reasons are shown below:

● **poor management**

Managers need to spend some time at work

● **no demand for product or service**

Businesses must recognise the needs of customers

● **business is located in the wrong place**

Few people will think of buying paint from a theme park

● **poor cash flow**

Little money will be received from sales of fireworks in February

- costs of running the business are too high

A second-hand van will be much cheaper to run

- too much competition

Too many businesses selling the same product

- poor quality goods or services

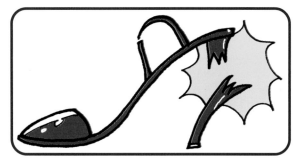

Shoes must be fit for the job

The growth of businesses

Businesses grow in three main ways:

- **Merging with another business.** A **merger** takes place when two or more businesses agree to join together to become one larger business.

- insufficient profit made on goods or services sold

Prices charged must cover the cost of buying the goods

- unfavourable exchange rate between the pound and other currencies.

Holiday companies may find it difficult to sell holidays

- **Taking over another business.** A **take-over** occurs when one business buys control of another. This is achieved by buying enough shares in the firm to be able to outvote other shareholders.

- **By internal expansion.** This is when the business grows by increasing its production, perhaps by building new plant or new shops.

Activity

Activity 4: Missing Terms – Success and growth of business

Use the words below to help you fill in the gaps in the following paragraph.

- driving and responding
- cheaply
- companies
- abroad
- spending power
- brand
- identifying opportunities
- consumer tastes
- high quality
- goods and services

Not all businesses are successful. Some businesses are particularly successful and grow into large_____offering a wide range of_____sold under well-known _____names. However, even successful businesses can encounter problems. Competition from_____; changing_____; fall in consumer_____are all examples of factors that can affect the growth and success of a business. On the other hand, some businesses are extremely good at_____for growth. This will include buying up other businesses relatively_____; offering a consistently_____of product or service. For a business to be really successful, it must be capable of both_____to change and adjusting the way it operates during difficult times.

Types of integration

There are several different types of integration. Each different type will have different advantages and disadvantages. The main reasons which bring about merger or takeover, regardless of the type of integration, will be the desire of the

Figure 4 Types of integration

Type of Integration	Explanation	Advantages	Disadvantages
Horizontal	Occurs between businesses in the same industry at the same stage of production	● Allows economies of large-scale production to be achieved	● Reduced choice ● May lead to a monopoly
Backwards vertical	A business takes over or merges with a supplier	● Control over supply of components or raw materials	● May lead to a reduction in the variety of goods available for consumers or other businesses
Forwards vertical	A business takes over or merges with another business which provides an outlet for the goods and services produced	● Control over sales outlets ● Possibly improve job security for workers	● May lead to higher prices and/or reduced choice
Diversification Sometimes referred to as **Conglomerate**	Merger or takeover of another business involved in an unrelated business activity	● Spreads risk ● Reduces dependency on one product or service area	● No understanding of the new business activity ● May lead to dis-economies of scale

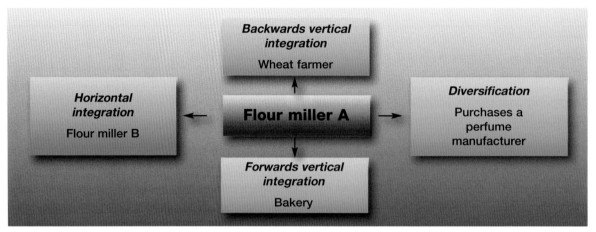

Figure 5 Type of integration for a flour miller

businesses starting the merger or takeover process to achieve growth.
Figure 4 gives more information.

Figure 5 shows different ways in which a flour milling firm may grow.

Activity

Activity 5: Matching Terms – Integration

This following activity is based on the business of a flour miller. Match the correct advantage with the type of integration.

Advantage:

1 The flour miller makes sure that he has a customer for the flour.

2 The flour miller produces a different kind of product so that risk is spread.

3 The flour miller makes sure there is a supply of raw materials.

4 Production of flour can take place in a bigger flour mill, leading to economies of large-scale production.

Type of integration	Advantage
a) Backwards vertical integration	
b) Forwards vertical integration	
c) Horizontal integration	
d) Diversification	

Location of business

Is location important?

The decision where to locate is one of the most important decisions a business takes. Make the right decision, and the business may flourish and become very successful. Make the wrong decision, and the business may find it very difficult to succeed. Some examples of businesses choosing locations for different reasons are given below.

Cargill Foods is a multi-national company. It has a factory in Liverpool which processes agricultural commodities, such as soya, that are imported from several countries. It is based on the docks in Liverpool. The soya arrives by ship and can be unloaded directly into the factory for processing. If the factory were located away from the docks it would have to be loaded on to lorries, transported and then unloaded. This would be very expensive. For Cargill it is very important that it is located at the port.

Burberry produces expensive, upmarket clothes – it has a Royal Warrant, which means that it has sold goods to the Royal Family. The clothes used to be produced in Wales. This factory was closed and production now takes place in China. Burberry said it had decided to move the production because the costs of producing in the UK were higher than almost anywhere else in the world.

Unit 3.5.5 deals with globalisation. One of the features of globalisation is that some businesses which traditionally have operated in the UK, decide to move production abroad. The most common reason for this is because wages are lower in other countries and so the business can reduce its costs. Location is important, but instead of considering different sites in one country, many businesses are now considering sites in different countries.

Direct Accident Management Limited (DAM Ltd) is based in offices on a small industrial estate in the town of Ormskirk. It helps clients with insurance claims when they have been in an accident. It communicates with clients and solicitors, who may represent the clients, mainly by telephone, fax and email. It could locate in offices in any town; there is no reason why Ormskirk is better than anywhere else.

For some businesses though, like DAM Ltd, location is less important. When a business can locate anywhere it is called **'footloose'**. Developments in ICT have increased the numbers of businesses which are footloose. Many service businesses that sell to customers all over the UK, or all over a region, are footloose.

The factors affecting the location of business

There are a large number of factors which can have an influence on the location of business activity. It is rarely one factor which affects the decision to locate in a particular area but often a combination of factors.

Some of the location factors covered in this unit will have little or no influence on the location decision that a particular business makes, while others will have a significant influence. Much will depend on the type of business activity. For instance, a bakery producing bread and cakes will usually need to be located near to the market it is serving. It can be difficult to transport fresh cream cakes long distances.

Fresh cream cakes do not travel well in warm weather

On the other hand, a business producing clothing will probably need good access to the road network so that it can deliver to its customers, who may be located in many different parts of the country.

The wrong way to decide where to locate

The right way to decide where to locate

Some businesses need good road access

Government and location

Some of the ways the government influences location decisions are described below.

Regional Development Agencies (RDAs)

Nine Regional Development Agencies operate in England. Their work is to encourage business development in the area that they represent so that more jobs are created and so that the businesses then become better and more competitive. They do this in the following ways.

Giving grants to encourage inward investment

Inward investment is when foreign-owned businesses decide to set up in the UK. Some major examples in the UK include Toyota, which opened a factory in Derby, and Nissan's factory in Sunderland. By giving a grant, the RDA reduces the cost to the business of setting up. Most of the grants are given for locating large manufacturing plants. These plants will provide jobs and buy materials and services from other businesses in the area. Other new businesses may be attracted to the area as it becomes richer (see also Unit 3.5.6).

Grants for small business start-ups

These grants are designed to help people who want to start a business, often for the first time. The RDAs will also help by giving advice.

Organising training

The RDA will pay training companies to deliver courses. The aim of this is to improve the skills of the people who work in the area.

Businesses need skilled people. By improving skills, the RDA will help existing businesses to get the labour they need and will encourage new firms into the area, who will be confident that they will get the skilled labour they need.

Improving the infrastructure

The infrastructure of an area means the roads, railways and airports. Transport is really important for businesses, so if the infrastructure is improved, it will encourage more businesses to locate in that area.

Local government

Local councils often encourages businesses to locate in their area. This will create jobs and make the area more prosperous. Three ways in which business is encouraged to locate in an area are as follows.

Giving grants

As with the grants given by the RDAs, this helps to reduce the costs to businesses of setting up. Sometimes a business locating to an area may be given assistance with paying its **uniform business rates**.

Promoting the area

This might be done by advertisements on websites, in newspapers or at conferences. Sometimes they pay for events such as big sporting events, which will bring people to the area and will result in some good publicity.

By creating industrial estates or technology parks

Factories and offices are built ready for new businesses to move into. This makes it quick and easy for the new business to set up and so attracts them to the area. They can be built on both **greenfield** and **brownfield sites**. See Activity 6 on page 137.

Other examples of factors affecting location

Availability of and access to raw materials

The costs of transporting some raw materials to a factory for processing can be very high. Businesses that depend on a particular raw material may choose to locate near to where it is available to help reduce transportation costs.

The United Kingdom imports large quantities of crude oil from the Middle East for processing in oil refineries. The crude oil is brought to the UK by supertanker. Oil refineries, like the one at Milford Haven in Wales, are located near to sea ports capable of handling very large ships because it is expensive to transport large quantities of oil inland.

The cost of the location

This is a very important consideration. The price of land and/or buildings can vary significantly in different areas of the United Kingdom. The amount of work needed to prepare the site will also be a factor.

The cost of the location will have to be paid for through the prices charged for the goods or services supplied to the customer. An expensive location might result in high prices for finished goods or services.

Land in the south-east of England tends to be a much more expensive location than mid-Wales or the north of Scotland. One reason may be the fact that the south-east of England has a high-density population and land is in short supply.

Access to and nearness to markets

Some businesses like or need to be near to the markets that they serve. This mainly affects service industries as people are often not prepared to travel long distances to obtain the things they need.

Supermarkets are located near to the centres of population that they serve. How many of you live within three miles of a reasonably large supermarket?

Availability of labour

The level of unemployment can vary from region to region of the UK. In rural areas or where traditional industries such as coal mining, shipbuilding and textiles no longer exist, labour is usually widely available.

In other areas, workers with particular skills might be in short supply. This has a significant effect on the decision about where to locate, as businesses will need to recruit labour locally.

Devon and Cornwall usually have a plentiful supply of labour during the winter. This is known as seasonal unemployment. In the summer, when the holiday season is in full swing, there can be shortages of labour as the demand for workers is high.

Climate and physical geography

Some areas of the country may be more suited to particular types of business activities than others. The location of agricultural activities is influenced by both climate and physical geography. Large manufacturing facilities like steel works need reasonably flat sites.

Northern Scotland tends to be hilly and the land is not suited to growing cereals, whereas East Anglia is much flatter and is suited to growing cereal crops.

Transport and infrastructure

Some areas of the country are better served by motorways, main roads and railways than other areas. The ease with which businesses

Activity

Activity 6: Research – Government and location

The information below is taken from the website of Cheshire County Council. It is an advertisement for businesses about a location.

Radnor Park Industrial Estate, Congleton

Description

Radnor Park is a well-established industrial estate which lies approximately one and a half miles west of Congleton town centre and benefits from the convenient access to the region's main trunk roads and Junction 17 of the M6.

Location

Leave the M6 at Junction 17 and take the A534 towards Congleton. Continue on the A534 to the junction with the A34. Turn left towards Congleton town centre and immediately left again on to the A54 Holmes Chapel Road. Take the first turning on the right on to Back Lane. Take the third road on the right on to First Avenue.

Major Occupiers

Vanton Pumps Ltd, Hans Lingl (UK) Ltd, Bathgate Silica Sands, Steelhouse Metals Ltd, Copeland & Craddock Ltd

Nearest Town:	Congleton	**Website:**	
Distance to Airport:	Manchester Airport – 20 miles	**Nearest Train station:**	Congleton – 2 miles
Distance to Motorway:	Junction 17, M6 6 miles	**Financial Assistance:**	Local Authority Support, Contact SECE – 01260 285202
Broadband:	ADSL Enabled Exchange	**Planning Uses:**	B1; B2; B8

Figure 6 Advert from Cheshire County Council website

Read the advertisement in Figure 6.

a List the key information in the advert which is designed to attract businesses to locate at this location.

b State and explain two ways in which Cheshire County Council is trying to encourage businesses to locate at Radnor Park Industrial Estate in Congleton.

c Using information available over the internet, look for similar adverts from local or county councils. When searching try *'business locations in'* followed by the name of your local town or county council. Compare what is offered to businesses at a site in your area with what is offered at Radnor Park Industrial Estate in Congleton.

can gain access to the transport system will have a significant influence on where to locate the business. This is particularly important if goods have to be moved great distances to the market.

Some business may also depend on other local businesses to provide goods and services. Areas with a low density of population – for example, mid-Wales – are not well served by motorways and railways. Car manufacturing in the West Midlands is at the centre of the UK's motoring network. It has attracted many other businesses, which make component parts for the car industry.

Tradition

Well-established businesses or industries are often located in particular areas of the country, for no obvious reason. Over time the business or industry may become one of the main employers in a particular area. Many of these traditional industries now no longer employ as many people as they once did.

Although shoes are manufactured at many places throughout the United Kingdom, Northampton was recognised as the centre of the UK's shoe industry. The nickname of the local football team – Northampton Town – is 'The Cobblers', reflecting the town's close association with the boot and shoe industry.

Type or nature of the product or service

Some products or services are very specialised and can only be undertaken in certain locations. Businesses providing these services may have relatively little choice over where they are located.

Shipbuilding is always to be found in coastal or river locations because of the need to access the sea when launching the finished product.

Activity

Activity 7: Presentation – Retail location factors

Prepare a presentation by:

a Preparing a sketch map for an out-of-town retail park near to where you live, or with which you are familiar. Mark on the map the main roads and nearby centres of population.

b Stating and explaining the reasons why so many retail parks are being developed on the edge of towns and cities.

c Explaining the advantages and disadvantages of locating shops in a town or city centre.

Evaluation point

3 Think carefully about the way in which location factors may change as the nature of business activity changes. Factors that may have affected the location of a business 20 years ago may no longer be relevant today.

4 Why is local and national government so keen to help businesses locate to particular areas? There must be some reasons. Consider what those reasons might be and why so much money is spent attracting business to a particular location.

Activity

Activity 8: Explanation and presentation – Factors affecting location

This activity is based on a question that appeared in an OCR examination paper and is designed to make you think about the factors which might affect the location of a garage business in the imaginary town of Marston.

Read the information in conjunction with the map of Marston and use your knowledge of the factors which affect the location of a business to answer the questions that follow.

John Taylor is thinking of opening a new garage business in Marston. He intends to sell petrol, provide car maintenance and fit car alarms. He is considering two possible sites for the location of the garage. They are marked A and B on the map below. Both sites have suitable premises for the business he is considering opening.

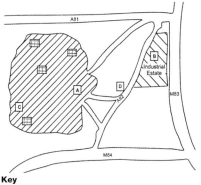

Key

- A – Available site with garage premises
- B – Available site with garage premises
- C – Car alarm specialist fitting business
- D – Existing garage – petrol retail and shop
- (grid symbol) – Existing garages – petrol retail and maintenance/repair services
- (hatched symbol) – Marston (population: 46 000)

1 State and explain two advantages of locating the garage business at Site A.

2 State and explain two disadvantages of locating the garage business at Site B.

3 Explain what other information John might need before making a final decision on the location of his garage business.

4 Explain how John's business might benefit if the town of Marston grows in size.

5 Recommend to John location A or B for the garage business.

6 Produce a leaflet for distribution to houses in Marston advertising the new garage. Do not forget to include a location map and information on some of the services which John's garage might provide.

Examination questions

1 a What do the letters plc stand for?   (1 mark)

   b The following are features of public limited companies and sole proprietors. Place them under the correct heading.

      i   able to sell shares to raise finance

      ii   owned by one person

      ii   the owner has unlimited liability

      iv   the business has separate legal identity from its owners.   (4 marks)

Features of a Public Limited Company	Features of a sole proprietor

   c Some retail businesses are small independent sole proprietors. Other retailers are large public limited companies. Suggest why both forms of business organisation exist in the retail trade.
                                                                                             (7 marks)

2 Nicole and Colin decided to open a sandwich business by purchasing new premises.

   Below are two factors which Nicole and Colin should take into consideration when deciding on their choice of location.

   Competition   Wealth of area

   Explain how each factor might affect their decision.   (4 marks)

3 Dovetail, a medium-sized furniture manufacturer and retailer, has recently moved premises, locating to a number of large cities.

   a What benefit would locating near to large cities bring to Dovetail Ltd?   (3 marks)

   b Another factor which attracted the business to some locations is that they are in an area which receives Regional Development Agency support. Explain one advantage and one disadvantage of locating in an an area which receives Regional Development Agency support.   (4 marks)

Advice on how to answer the questions

1 a This is a simple definition which requires you to write out what the three letters stand for.

   b This question requires you to select two features which are appropriate to a public limited company and two features which are appropriate to a sole proprietor. Each feature can only be used once.

   c A more detailed response is required in order to answer this question. You will need to provide an answer which relates information to the retail trade and gives reasons why both forms of business organisation exist in the retail trade. Any examples which you can provide will help with your explanation.

2 To answer this question successfully you will need to provide a detailed explanation of how each of the two factors listed in the question has an effect on the location of a business. You should try to develop your answer by providing an example which illustrates why each of the two factors affecting location is important.

3 a This question requires you to consider why locating near to a large city is of relevance to a company manufacturing and retailing furniture. You will need to consider whether there are any different locational factors which are likely to affect both the manufacturing and retailing sides of the business.

  b Before you can answer this question you will need to be certain that you know the types of Regional Development Agency support *available*. The question requires you to provide an advantage and a disadvantage for a company like Dovetail Ltd of locating business activity with the aid of Regional Development Agency support. The use of examples will help to improve your answer so that you gain all 4 marks.

Key facts

Organisation:

- All businesses must operate as one of the four main forms of business organisation.
- Setting up a business as a sole proprietor is very simple.
- Some of the disadvantages of the sole proprietor form of business organisation can be overcome by taking a partner.
- Setting up as an incorporated form of business can be expensive.

Growth:

- There are advantages and disadvantages of each type of business organisation. Firms can grow through mergers, take-overs or internal expansion.

Location:

- There are a large number of location factors.
- Not all location factors will affect every type of business.
- Some types of business are not affected by location factors.
- Consider how the factors affecting location may change as the business changes and develops.

Key Terms

Make sure you can explain each of the following Key Terms

Incorporated A form of business organisation which is a separate legal entity. It has limited liability and is owned by shareholders.

Unincorporated A type of business organisation which has unlimited liability.

Co-operatives Trading organisations where a number of independent producers work together and trade as though they are a single larger business.

Sole proprietor Sometimes known as a sole trader. One person owns the business.

Partnership A form of unincorporated business organisation which is owned by more than one person.

Unlimited liability Owners of the business are liable for its debts.

Bankruptcy Something that affects individuals and unincorporated businesses when liabilities are greater than assets.

Private limited company A business owned by shareholders. It is normally identified by the word 'Limited' or 'Ltd' somewhere in the name of the business.

Public limited company (plc) A business owned by shareholders. Shares in the business can be bought and sold without restriction. The business must use the words public limited company or plc somewhere in the name of the business.

Limited liability The owner of a business does not risk losing personal possessions in order to pay off the debts of the business.

Insolvency A limited liability company is said to be insolvent when liabilities are greater than assets.

Entrepreneur A person who sees a business opportunity and who accepts the risks involved in running a business.

Merger Two or more businesses join together to make one larger business.

Take-over One business buys control of another.

Horizontal Merger or takeover of another business involved in the same industry at the same stage of production.

Vertical Merger or takeover of another business involved in the same industry at a different stage of production. The merger or takeover can be backwards or forwards.

Diversification A process of spreading risks by reducing dependence on one particular product or service.

Conglomerate Merger or takeover of another business which is involved in a totally different business activity.

Footloose A business is able to locate anywhere it chooses.

Uniform business rates A type of tax paid by businesses to cover the cost of providing local services.

Grants Payment of money for a specific purpose, which does not usually have to be paid back. Grants may be available from the EU, central government or local authorities to help businesses improve employment opportunities.

Infrastructure The name given to basic services needed by a business in order for it to operate effectively. Such things as roads, power supplies, telephones and water supplies would be included under this heading.

Greenfield site Industrial or commercial development in an area that has previously not been built on.

Brownfield site Industrial or commercial development that was previously derelict or occupied by another industrial activity.

Sole proprietors and partnerships

Learning Outcomes

By studying this unit you will be able to:

- **Explain the basic structure and key features of the sole proprietor and partnership forms of business organisation**
- **Explain the advantages and disadvantages of the sole proprietor and partnership forms of business organisation**
- **Explain and apply the principle of 'unlimited liability'**
- **Recommend a form of business organisation for a business**
- **Discuss and explain why it is beneficial for a partnership to draw up a deed of partnership.**

Introduction

It is almost impossible to estimate the number of businesses in the United Kingdom that are operating as **sole proprietors** but there must be a lot of them. This is mainly because they are very easy to set up and particularly suited for new businesses. In addition, many self-employed people do not actually realise that they are operating as sole proprietors.

Partnerships, on the other hand, are a more formal form of business organisation and, whilst not as numerous as sole traders in the United Kingdom, are a very common form of business organisation.

This unit looks at the key features, advantages and disadvantages of the two most common forms of business organisation in the United Kingdom.

Sole proprietors

There are a very large number of **sole proprietor** businesses in the United Kingdom. Sole proprietors are also known as 'sole traders' because there is just one person who owns the business. However, although the business is *owned* by one person, it does not stop it from employing other people to work in the business.

Sole traders can be found in many different types of business activity

Advantages of the sole proprietor form of business organisation

There would not be so many sole proprietor businesses in the United Kingdom if there were not some important advantages in this form of business organisation.

The main reasons for this large number of sole proprietors are shown in Figure 1.

Promotional 'flyer' advertising the services of a sole trader

Figure 1 Advantages of sole proprietors

Suitability	It is a form of business organisation that is suited to a wide variety of different types of business. Many new and small businesses find it a suitable form of business organisation.
Set up	It is an extremely easy and cheap type of business organisation to set up with very few forms which need to be completed.
Capital	Some sole proprietor business can be set up with very little **start up capital**.
Control	The owner is in complete control of the business and does not need to obtain the agreement of other people when making business decisions.
Financial information	All the financial information about the business is private. No information has to be provided to the general public or other businesses.
Ownership	The owner is able to keep all the profit that the business makes.

Disadvantages of the sole-proprietor business organisation

As with most things, there can also be some disadvantages. Operating as a sole proprietor business does have some problems. The main problems which sole proprietor businesses face are shown in Figure 2.

Figure 2 Disadvantages of the sole proprietor business organisation

Unlimited liability	This can be a real problem if the business is not doing well. The owner of the business runs the risk of losing his/her personal possessions to pay off the debts of the business if it fails. Any losses that the business makes will have to be met by the owner of the business. There is nobody else with whom to share the losses.
Shortage of capital	Some sole proprietors may find it difficult to operate or grow in size because they do not have enough capital. Some small businesses can find it difficult to obtain bank loans because providing a loan represents a significant risk to the lender.
Illness	If the owner of the business is ill, there may be no one else who can run the business.
Hours of work	Some sole proprietors work long hours in order to make the business successful.
Continuity	If the owner of the business wishes to sell the business, there is no guarantee that a buyer will be found. Equally, if the owner dies, the business effectively also ceases to exist.
Shortage of skills	It is often not possible for the owner of the business to be skilled in all operational areas of the business. As a result, specialist workers may have to be employed but there may not be enough work for them.
Economies of large-scale production	Because sole-proprietor businesses tend to be small, there is limited opportunity for the business to gain financial advantages from large-scale production

One person cannot do all the jobs

Partnerships

This form of business organisation is very common in certain sections of the economy. The doctor and dentist that you attend are probably businesses operating as a partnership.

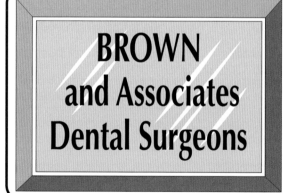

An example of a business trading as a partnership

The names of the partners that own the business are often shown on invoices, as in the example below.

Name of business trading as a partnership

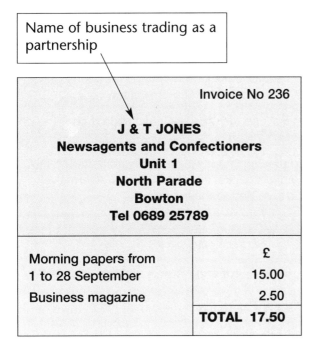

Invoice No 236	
J & T JONES **Newsagents and Confectioners** **Unit 1** **North Parade** **Bowton** **Tel 0689 25789**	
Morning papers from 1 to 28 September	£ 15.00
Business magazine	2.50
TOTAL 17.50	

Partnerships are often the preferred type of business organisation for veterinary surgeons, solicitors, dentists, and accountants, although many other businesses can be set up as partnerships.

There are very strict rules controlling the creation of partnerships. There can be a minimum of 2 and a maximum of 20 partners, although not all the partners may have an equal share of the business. This form of business organisation has many of the advantages, and avoids some of the disadvantages, of the sole-proprietor form of business organisation.

Specialist skills	Each partner may have a different specialist skill that can be used by the business – for example, a small building business may be owned by three partners. One partner may be skilled in electrical work, another in bricklaying and another in plumbing.
Illness	The work of the business can be shared and, in the event of illness of one of the partners, the business should not experience a particular problem.
Set up	It is easy and cheap to set up.
Financial information	Financial information about the business remains confidential to the partners.
Ownership	If extra skills or capital are needed in the business it is quite easy to admit another partner to the business. Some partners may not wish to take an active part in the running of the business but are happy just to contribute capital to it. These partners are known as a **silent** or **sleeping partner**.

Advantages of the partnership form of business organisation

Figure 3 Advantages of partnerships

Capital	Because there are more people who own the business, more capital can be introduced into the business to help it operate or grow in size.

Each partner in the business is a specialist

Figure 4 The main disadvantages of partnerships

Profit	This has to be shared between the partners.
Unlimited liability	Partnerships with unlimited liability put the personal possessions of the partners at risk in the event of the failure of the business.
Disagreements	The partners may not always agree how the business should be operated.
Shortage of capital	The ability of the partnership to raise finance is generally restricted to the existing partners introducing more capital into the business. Alternatively, new partners may have to be admitted to the business.

Disadvantages of the partnership form of business organisation

As with sole proprietors, partnerships do have some disadvantages. The main problems are shown in Figure 4.

Deed of partnership

Because a partnership is a more complicated form of business ownership than a sole proprietor, most partnerships draw up a **deed of partnership**. If there is no deed of partnership, the law states that each partner is equal regardless of the amount of capital that they have contributed. The deed is a legally binding agreement, which:

● provides information on the way in which the business operates.

● states how profits and losses will be shared amongst the partners.

● details how much capital each partner has contributed to the business. This is important as partners do not need to provide an equal amount of capital.

Deed of Partnership

between Anthony Brown of 12 Corden Street, James Taft of 52 Porter Drive and John Davey of 16 Copley Road all of the town of Midchester.

Trading name of the business: JPJ Computer Services. The business will sell and repair computer equipment.

Each partner agrees to provide the sum of £10 000 and will share the profits or losses of the business equally.

The responsibilities of each partner are as follows:

A Brown – Repairs to equipment. Technical support to customers.

J Taft – Sales of new computer equipment.

J Davey – Maintaining financial records and accounts.

Signed   *A Brown*

J. Taft.   *J. Davey*

Date 11th July 2008

Figure 5 Extract from a deed of partnership

Limited liability partnerships

You may have seen the letters **LLP** after the name of some businesses. This is because a recent change in the law now allows partnerships to operate as 'limited liability partnerships'. Many solicitors are choosing to operate this type of business organisation.

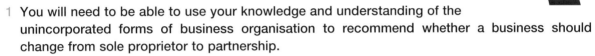

Evaluation point

1 You will need to be able to use your knowledge and understanding of the unincorporated forms of business organisation to recommend whether a business should change from sole proprietor to partnership.

2 You will also need to consider what might happen if one of the partners of a business wishes to leave the partnership. Consider what might happen to that part of the business which that partner owns. Will it be sold to a new partner or might the deed of partnership require the partner who is leaving to offer his part of the business to the other partners?

Activity

Activity 1: Research – Drawing up a deed of partnership

a Study Figure 5 carefully. Write down any other information which you think should be included in the deed of partnership.

b Think of a business activity which you might eventually like to own and operate.

  i Working with a group of two or three other people, draw up a deed of partnership similar in outline to the one in Figure 5, detailing the responsibilities of each partner and how the business is to operate. You will need to think carefully about what you want to include in your deed of partnership in case you have a disagreement with your partners. Such things as working hours, partners' responsibilities and wages may need to be included. Consider carefully what else you would want to include if you were going into business.

  ii Explain the reasons why you have included each key item in the deed of partnership.

Activity

Activity 2: True or false – Sole proprietors and partnerships

Tick one box in the table below to indicate if the statement is true or false.

Statement	True ✔	False ✔
A partnership has shareholders		
A partnership usually has between 2 and 20 partners		
The deed of partnership usually states how profits will be shared amongst the partners		
Sole proprietors find it easy to borrow money from a bank		
One disadvantage of a sole-proprietor business is that it will have unlimited liability		
At least one partner has unlimited liability for any debts that the business might have should it be declared bankrupt		
A sole proprietor is owned by more than one person		
Partners often use their own savings to set up the business		
A sole proprietor cannot employ anyone		
Partners cannot employ people to work for them		

Activity

Activity 3: Presentation – Unincorporated business

Prepare a presentation outlining the key features of both the sole proprietor and partnership forms of unincorporated business organisation.

Activity

Activity 4: Missing Terms – Sole proprietors and partnerships

Use the bold words below to help you fill in the gaps in the following paragraph.

- **bankrupt**
- **sole**
- **small**
- **partnerships**
- **unlimited**
- **unincorporated**
- **disadvantage**
- **medium**

The _____form of business ownership is very popular in the UK. There are a very large number of _____and _____sized businesses which are operating as _____Proprietors and _____. One of the reasons for this is the ease with which these types of business ownership can be set up. However, a major _____is _____liability where the owners of the business are responsible for the debts of the business should it become _____.

Examination questions

a Explain how a sole proprietor might finance the purchase of a shop and its fittings.　(4 marks)

b Dave Smith is a sole proprietor. Complete the table below by providing answers to the questions in the 'Feature' column.　(4 marks)

Feature	Answer
Number of owners?	
Who provides the capital?	
Who controls the business?	
Who receives the profits?	

c Explain the meaning of unlimited liability.　(2 marks)

d Using the following headings, explain how a sole proprietor business employing several people might be organised:

　– control and management

　– distribution of profits　(6 marks)

e Many small businesses fail very quickly. Explain three possible reasons for a small business failing.　(6 marks)

Advice on how to answer the questions

a This question requires you to think carefully about the types of finance that are available to sole proprietors. Not all types of finance will be available. You will then need to think about which types of finance are appropriate for the purchase of shop fittings such as shelves and display cabinets. You will need to explain *why* these types of finance are appropriate.

b To answer this question you to need to provide a range of basic facts about the key features of the sole proprietor form of business organisation.

c A clear and detailed explanation of what the term 'unlimited liability' means is needed to answer this question successfully. The use of examples will help improve your explanation.

d Specific information about 'control and management' and 'distribution of profits' in sole proprietor organisations needs to be provided in order to answer this question.

e You will need to think carefully about the reasons why some business fail and eventually go out of business. There are many reasons. You need to think about whether the reasons are particularly relevant to small businesses. Remember to give an explanation for each of the three reasons.

Key facts

- There are two different types of unincorporated business organisation.
- Some businesses are ideal for a particular type of business organisation.
- There are advantages and disadvantages of different types of business organisation.
- A deed of partnership will give details how the partnership is to operate its business.

Key Terms

Make sure you can explain each of the following Key Terms

Sole proprietor Unincorporated business owned by one person. Also known as a 'sole trader'.

Start up capital Money needed to start up a new business. It is usually provided by the owner of the business.

Economies of large scale production These occur when the scale of business activity increases, resulting in a reduction in the average costs of production.

Silent or sleeping partner A person who has invested capital into a business but who does not take an active part in the running of the business.

Deed of partnership   A legal agreement drawn up between the partners of the business stating the responsibilities of partners – for instance, how profits and losses are to be shared; how the business is to operate.

LLP A limited liability partnership. This is a new form of business organisation which trades as a partnership but with limited liability.

Private and public limited companies

Introduction

There are a large number of private and public limited companies in Great Britain and you will have done business with a great number of them. The bus company which brought you to school, the cinema you visited recently, the fast food restaurant where you bought a burger, or the supermarket where your family does its shopping are probably all examples of businesses that are trading as private or public limited companies.

Figure 1 Number of private and public limited companies registered in Great Britain

Type of business organisation	Number of companies	
	2000	2008
Public limited company	15,181	11,905
Private limited company	1,619,500	2,700,851

Source: Companies House

There are probably many reasons for the change in number of registered companies between 2000 and 2008 shown in Figure 1. Some of these reasons might include:

- Merger or takeover activity eliminating competition

- Companies going out of business

- New companies starting

- Existing businesses converting from unincorporated to incorporated status

- Transferring the registration of the company to another country.

Operating as an incorporated business is obviously very popular. This unit looks at some of the possible reasons why this may be the case and also some of the reasons why it may not be such a good idea.

Finding out the type of business organisation

All private and public limited companies must let customers know what type of business organisation they are trading as. This information is sometimes written on receipts, company headed paper or other documentation.

Private limited companies must have the word 'Limited' or 'Ltd' somewhere in their title, and public limited companies must have the letters 'plc' or words 'public limited company' in their title.

This type of information tells customers and suppliers that they are trading with:
- an incorporated organisation

- owned by shareholders

- which has limited liability. In other words, the owners of the business (shareholders) will not be personally responsible for any debts that the business might have.

There are many reasons why both of these forms of business organisation exist in the United Kingdom. There are, however, important differences between each of these two forms of business organisation.

Incorporation

Incorporation is a complicated and sometimes costly legal process which private and public limited companies must go through before they can begin to trade. Once all the requirements of the process have been met, the **Registrar of Companies** will issue a **Certificate of Incorporation**.

Board of directors

Both private and public limited companies must have a **board of directors**. Directors are people who are elected by shareholders at the company's **annual general meeting** (AGM), to make important decisions and run the company on their behalf. Some directors may hold a specific responsibility for one part of the work of the company. One of the directors is responsible for the way in which the board of directors operates and will have been elected as the **chair of the board of directors**. Another director may take on responsibility for the overall running of the company and act as **managing director**.

Activity

Activity 1: Research – Company organisation

Visit the websites of several large private limited or public limited companies.

a Print off a copy of the name of the business making sure that the terms 'Limited' or 'Ltd' or 'PLC' are showing somewhere in the name of the business.

b Identify, on the information you have printed off, the names of the:

   i   Chair of the Board of Directors

   ii Managing Director

   iii Directors and the responsibilities which they hold

   iv date of the last or next Annual General Meeting.

A typical organisation chart for of a large public limited company is shown in Figure 2. Figure 2 also shows the roles and responsibilities of each of the key groups involved in the running of a public limited company.

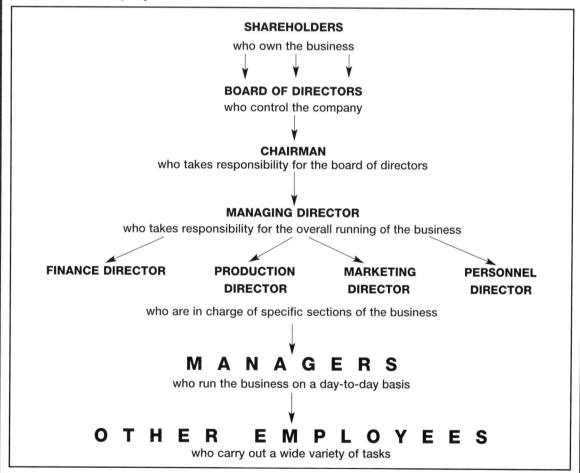

Figure 2 Organisation chart for a typical public limited company

In a small business there may be very few directors, and it is not uncommon in a family business to find a husband and wife as the only two directors. This means that they may have to take on responsibility for more than one role.

Private limited companies

Features and advantages

We have already discovered that one of the main advantages of this form of business organisation is limited liability and that the business must have the word 'Limited' or 'Ltd' somewhere in its title. This major advantage of limited liability is the reason why there are so many private limited companies registered in the United Kingdom.

There are other advantages as shown in Figure 3.

Figure 3 Advantages to private limited companies

Shares	These can be issued to investors in exchange for money as a means of raising **capital**.
Legal identity	The business is separate from its owners. It can take legal action against other persons or companies and be the subject of legal action against it.
Continuity	Subject to agreement by the shareholders the business can be sold. Equally, each individual shareholder is free to sell the shares he or she owns to other people or businesses. In the event of the death of a shareholder, the business will be unaffected and will continue to trade normally.
Directors	There are usually a minimum of two directors. In certain circumstances it may be possible to have just one director. There is no upper limit on the number of directors. Much will depend on the size of the business. If there are too many directors it may be difficult to run the business efficiently.

Disadvantages

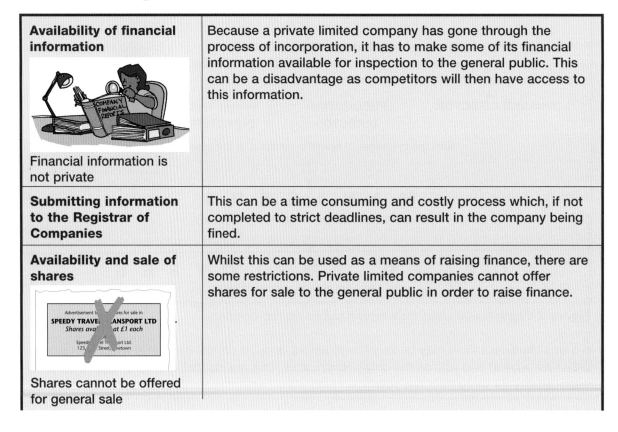

Availability of financial information Financial information is not private	Because a private limited company has gone through the process of incorporation, it has to make some of its financial information available for inspection to the general public. This can be a disadvantage as competitors will then have access to this information.
Submitting information to the Registrar of Companies	This can be a time consuming and costly process which, if not completed to strict deadlines, can result in the company being fined.
Availability and sale of shares Shares cannot be offered for general sale	Whilst this can be used as a means of raising finance, there are some restrictions. Private limited companies cannot offer shares for sale to the general public in order to raise finance.

Lack of capital	If the business wishes to expand it may find that the existing shareholders are unable to provide more capital. Because shares cannot be sold to the general public, it may also be difficult to find new shareholders who are willing to invest money in the business.
 Private limited companies can be short of capital	
Dividends	Shareholders will probably expect a share of the profits in the form of dividends. This can be a drain on the company's assets if the directors decide to pay a dividend. If no dividend is paid, shareholders become unhappy with the way in which the company is being run.
 Most shareholders will expect a dividend to be paid	

Activity

Activity 2: Zone Activity – Features of shares and dividends

Each of the following phrases below relates to either shares or dividends. Using the table outline below, place each phrase in the appropriate column.

- gives the owner voting rights
- issued as a way of raising finance for the business
- a payment made to shareholders
- the amount paid can vary from year to year depending on the success of the business
- the value can go up or down on a daily basis
- allows the owner to attend the AGM of the company
- gives the owner part ownership of the business
- is usually paid twice a year
- may not be paid each year

Dividend	Share

Public limited companies

There are a large number of public limited companies registered in the United Kingdom. A look at the share pages of most newspapers will give the names of just a few of the public limited companies that trade their shares on the London Stock Exchange.

Many are household names, such as those illustrated below, and will be well known to you. Many of the others you will have never heard of.

Shares

One of the most important features of this type of company organisation is the ability to trade shares freely on the Stock Exchange.

The sale of shares is an extremely important method of raising finance or capital and is thus one of the most important advantages of this form of business organisation.

There are other important features of this form of business organisation:

- For a company to become a public limited company, it must have an **issued share capital** in excess of £50,000.

- It will usually pay part of its profits to shareholders in the form of dividends.

Shareholders

Private individuals usually only own a small percentage of most public limited companies. This is because they cannot afford to buy large numbers of shares – they are therefore known as **'minority shareholders'**.

Major shareholders like banks and investment companies will own a large number of shares – they are also known as **'institutional investors'** and will have much greater influence on the way in which the company is operated.

The value of a share of a public limited company can change for a number of reasons. Usually they will increase in value if the Stock Market thinks:

- that the prospects of the company are good

- there is the possibility of a takeover bid

- the economy is doing well

- the asset value of the business is increasing.

They can also fall in value for the opposite reasons.

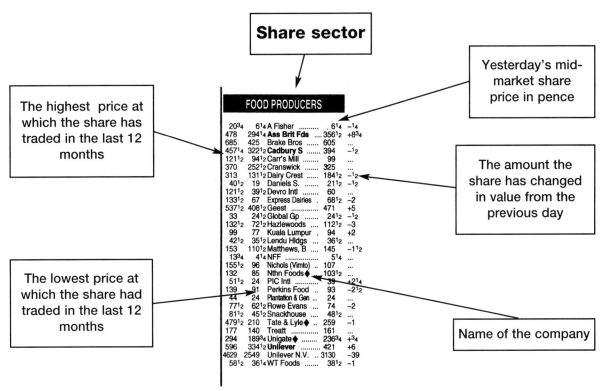

Figure 3 Extract from *The Times* newspaper share page

Activity

Activity 3: Research – Tracking the share price of a company

1 Using a newspaper that publishes share prices, or by using the internet, choose six companies in which you are interested, or with which you are familiar, and follow the way in which the share price of the companies changes over a period of time. Present the information in the form of a graph.

2 Look for possible reasons why the price of the shares may have gone up or down on a particular day and present a summary of the information you find.

Evaluation

1 You will need to be able to use your knowledge and understanding of the incorporated forms of business organisation to recommend whether a business should change from a private limited company to a public limited company.

2 You will need to consider, and explain, why so many large companies choose to become plcs.

3 Some businesses that have become plcs decided that this is the wrong form of business organisation and have returned to being private limited companies. You will need to consider why this may have happened.

Other features and advantages

We have already seen that one of the main advantages of this form of business organisation is limited liability, where shareholders can invest money in the business without running the risk of personal bankruptcy.

There are other advantages which affect public limited companies. These are:

- the ability to raise large sums of finance by offering shares for sale. The vast majority of capital raised by public limited companies is by this method

- the relative ease with which additional funds can be raised from other sources to help finance expansion plans.

Other features and disadvantages

Although there are a large number of public limited companies in the United Kingdom, there are a number of disadvantages of this form of business organisation.

- **Cost of setting up.** It is a complicated and expensive process to set up a public limited company or convert from one of the other forms of business organisation.

- **Financial information.** The general public is allowed to request a copy of the company's accounts. This is usually made available in the form of an annual report, which is usually sent to all shareholders and published on the company's website

The cost of becoming a plc is high

- **Dividends.** Shareholders will expect the company to perform well. They will usually expect a share of the profits paid in the form of dividends.

- **Takeover.** Because the shares in the company can be easily traded on the Stock Exchange it is possible for other companies to buy up large quantities of a company's shares. An offer may then be made to shareholders to buy their shares and, if sufficient agree, ownership of the company will change.

- **Shareholders** own the company but, unless they have a large number of shares, they will have very little say in the way in which the company is run.

Shares in another company are easy to buy

Activity

Activity 4: Zone Activity – Identifying features of limited companies

The following list shows some features of private limited companies and plcs. Some features are common to both forms of business organisation. Place a tick ✔ in the column to which the feature applies.

Feature	Limited company	PLC	Both private limited companies and PLCs
Able to sell shares on the Stock Exchange to raise capital			
Can have any number of shareholders			
Managing director runs the business			
Chair of the board of directors is responsible for managing the directors			
Must make financial information available to the general public			
Has a board of directors			
Limited liability			
Must have a share capital in excess of £50,000			
Name of business must show that it is an incorporated business			
The business has to go through a process of Incorporation			
Financial information available to the public			
Dividends paid to shareholders			
Must hold an AGM			
Any number of directors			

Activity

Activity 5: Explanation – Using share finance to raise funds

Weir and Russell plc wishes to raise additional finance for an expansion programme. The company intends to raise the additional finance through the sale of shares to interested investors.

a Explain, with examples, the problems which the business might face in:

  i attracting sufficient investors to buy the shares

  ii the future, with an increased number of shares in circulation.

b Compare the benefits and disadvantages of raising funds thorough a share sale in comparison to a loan.

Examination questions

a Gerald Marsh and his wife are concerned about their farm's future as a partnership and are thinking of forming a private limited company.

  i Explain why Gerald Marsh and his wife may wish to change the business from a partnership to a private limited company. (4 marks)

  ii Explain how the owners of the partnership will be affected if a private limited company were formed. (4 marks)

b Many retailers of chocolates are small, independent sole proprietors, while the companies that manufacture chocolates are usually large public limited companies. Are these appropriate forms of ownership for these different businesses? Give reasons for your answers. (7 marks)

Advice on how to answer the questions

a i You will need to provide reasons explaining the advantages of changing the business to a private limited company. Your answer will be improved if you explain why and how the change to private limited company overcomes some of the disadvantages of the partnership form of business organisation.

  ii This question requires you to provide an answer which concentrates on who owns the business and the way in which these owners will be affected by the change of company organisation.

b To answer this question successfully you will need to consider and explain why there are so many sole proprietor type businesses which are reasonably small in size. You should also consider the advantages of this particular form of business organisation. An explanation of why the plc form of business organisation is particularly suited to very large businesses will also be required.

Key facts

- There are two different types of incorporated business organisation.
- Some businesses are ideal for a particular type of business organisation.
- There are advantages and disadvantages of different types of business organisation.
- Raising capital through the sale of shares is a key feature of a public limited company.

Key Terms

Make sure you can explain each of the following Key Terms

Incorporation The process of becoming a limited liability company.

Registrar of Companies Person responsible in the United Kingdom for maintaining records relating to the activities of private and public limited companies.

Certificate of Incorporation Legal document issued by the Registrar of Companies allowing a business to trade as a limited liability business.

Board of directors People usually elected by shareholders to represent their interests and make important decisions on how the company is to be operated.

Annual General Meeting (AGM) A yearly meeting of shareholders, which, amongst other things, will elect directors to the board and confirm the amount of dividend to be paid.

Chair of the board of directors The person who takes responsibility for managing the board of directors.

Managing director The person responsible for putting into action the decisions made by the board of directors.

Capital Money usually raised through the sale of shares to investors.

Issued share capital The amount of share capital issued to investors.

Minority shareholders Private individuals who may only own a small percentage of the shares of a company.

Major shareholders These are shareholders who will probably own a large percentage of the shares issued by a company.

Institutional investors Banks and investment companies, which may invest money on behalf of themselves or private individuals. They will probably own a large percentage of the shares of a company.

Other types of business organisation

Learning Outcomes

By studying this unit you will be able to:

- Understand and explain the terminology, advantages and disadvantages relating to other forms of business organisation
- Explain the principle of franchising and be able to recommend its suitability for particular types of business
- Explain why businesses may choose to operate as multinational companies
- Recognise and explain the role that public sector organisations play in the economy of the United Kingdom and how they differ from private sector organisations.

Introduction

In the previous two units we have seen how businesses in the private sector are organised into one of four basic forms of business.

We have also seen that the way in which a business chooses to organise itself can depend on a variety of factors, with each form of business organisation having clear advantages and disadvantages.

This unit looks at some other different ways in which businesses can operate.

Franchises

A **franchise** is **not** a form of business organisation but a type of marketing arrangement. In recent years, setting up and operating a business as a franchise has become a very common form of business model. Franchises are available in most sectors of business activity. More information on franchises can be found in Unit 1.3.3.

A business operating as a franchise can be organised into any one of the four main forms of business organisation.

What is a franchise?

Franchise opportunities exist where an already established business (the **franchisor**) offers for sale to other businesses or individuals (the **franchisee**) the right to use its products, services and logos – usually in a defined area.

Franchises are not cheap to buy. Usually, a considerable initial payment is required and a percentage of the sales revenue of the business, known as a **royalty**, has to be paid on an annual basis in addition to the initial fee.

Figure 1 Advantages and disadvantages of a franchise

Advantages of franchises	Disadvantages of franchises
A designated area of operation, with no competition from other franchises made available from the same company.	All supplies must usually be purchased from the franchisor at the price which they determine.
A tried and tested business idea.	A large amount of initial capital may be required.
Logos and products which are usually already established in the market.	Annual royalty payment based on profit or sales revenue may be required.
National advertising and promotion campaigns may be paid for by the franchisor.	The owner of the business may not have total control over the way in which the business operates.
Training and advice on how to run the business.	The business may not make enough profit to help cover the cost of the initial payment.
Reduced risk of business failure.	Losses have to be paid for by the franchisee.

Some of the businesses that offer franchises are shown below.

Multinational companies

With the increasing **globalisation** of the world economy, there has been a significant increase in the growth in the number, size and type of **multinational companies** around the world.

Multinational companies are usually very large companies that may have a head office based in one country but manufacturing or service facilities in other countries. The number of multinational companies is increasing on a yearly basis mainly as a result of the globalisation of the world economy. This is happening on a worldwide basis but particularly in Europe as business activity in European countries becomes more and more closely integrated. Some examples of well-known multinational companies are shown overleaf.

Activity

Activity 1: Research and presentation – Franchises

The internet has a lot of pages of information about franchises. Using the internet:

1 Find out some information about a franchise which interests you.

2 Prepare a presentation detailing:

   a the product or service being offered

   b the advantages and disadvantages of entering into that franchise arrangement.

3 Include in your presentation the cost of purchasing the franchise and the royalty arrangements.

The American company Proctor and Gamble and the Swiss company Nestlé Group are both very large and well-known multinational companies with manufacturing facilities located in a large number of countries in all five continents. The product range of well-known branded goods produced by both companies is enormous.

Activity

Activity 2: Research and presentation – Multinational companies

1 Visit the website of Proctor and Gamble or the Nestlé Group and find out the size of the company's operations based in the United Kingdom.

2 Prepare a presentation detailing the range of products which the company manufactures in the United Kingdom.

3 Identify other relevant information such as the value of the products produced; the number of employees; the number and location of production sites.

Advantages for multinational companies

There are a number of reasons why multinational companies exist:

- Manufacturing bases can be spread around the world nearer to the markets they serve.

- Economies of large-scale production can be obtained.

- Production may be located in countries where production costs are lower.

Disadvantages of multinational companies

Operating as a multinational company is not without its problems. The main problems are:

- Communication problems caused by being located in different countries.

- The high cost of transporting goods between countries.

- Coping with the differing legal requirements of different countries.

- Fluctuating exchange rates for different currencies.

Activity

Activity 3: Explanation – Multinational companies

1 Name four other multinational companies and list the types of products and services that these businesses make available.

2 Explain why so many large public limited companies choose to operate as multinational companies.

3 Outline the advantages of allowing companies owned by a multinational company to continue to trade under different names.

Public corporations

Public corporations are limited liability business activities in the **public sector** of the economy, which provide a range of goods and services. They are owned and controlled by national or local government.

The number of **public corporations** in the United Kingdom has decreased significantly in recent years. Today there are very few public corporations remaining. The BBC (the British Broadcasting Corporation) is one example. It is funded through the TV Licence Fee. Another is the Post Office but its future as a public corporation has been the subject of debate in Parliament and consideration has been given to transferring it to the private sector. It obtains its finance through the charges it makes for the services provided. Any surplus money goes to the government.

In 2008 some banks in the UK which had got into financial difficulties were taken over by the Government. The long-term future of these banks is uncertain.

Evaluation point

1   Be prepared to explain why and how business is constantly changing and the way it responds to the needs of the market and pressure from competitors.

2   Consider why there are so many different ways in which business activity is organised. Be prepared to explain why and how that type of business organisation is appropriate.

3   Few large businesses trade or operate in just one country. Increasing the scale of production is an important part of helping to reduce costs – and this, in many cases, can only be achieved by operating in more than one country.

Activity

Activity 4: Zone Activity – Franchises, multinational companies and public corporations

The following table shows some features of franchises, multinational companies and public corporations. Place a tick in the column(s) to which the feature applies.

Feature	Franchise	Multinational company	Public corporation
Owned by the government			
Owned by shareholders or individuals			
May pay dividends			
Must pay a royalty			
Located around the world			
Taxation used to provide some funding			
Profit is probably an objective			
Involved in large-scale production			
May be non-profit making			
Operates in a defined area			

Activity

Activity 5: True or false – Franchises, Multinational companies and public corporations

Tick one box to indicate whether the statement is true or false.

Statement	True ✔	False ✔
Franchises can trade as any one of the four main types of business organisation.		
Multinational companies usually operate as limited companies.		
Franchises are a form of marketing arrangement for a product or service.		
Public corporations are owned by the government.		
Multinational companies usually have bases located in several countries.		
The taxpayer funds any loss made by a public corporation.		
Multinational companies produce goods in one country and export the products to customers around the world.		
Public corporations always make a profit.		
A franchise is usually allowed to operate a business in a defined geographical area.		
A royalty payment may be made by a franchise.		

Examination questions

Question 1

a State four features of a franchise.   (4 marks)

b Jason is thinking of opening a new shop selling sweets and chocolates. Should he open the shop as a franchise or as an independent shop? Discuss the advantages of each option and give reasons for your answers.   (8 marks)

Question 2

a Explain one way in which the aims of a public sector enterprise such as the BBC are different from those of a private sector organisation such as Next plc.   (2 marks)

b Explain why public corporations continue to exist in the United Kingdom economy. Give examples to support your explanation.   (4 marks)

Advice on how to answer the questions

Question 1

a This question requires four simple facts about franchises. No explanations are needed.

b To answer this question successfully, you will need to make a recommendation based on the evidence you provide. This evidence will need to consider the advantages and disadvantages of both operating as an independent shop and as a franchise selling the products of an already established chocolate business.

Question 2

a This question requires you to consider how the aims of public and private sector organisations differ. You are then required to answer, by providing a detailed explanation of one factor, within the context given, why these two organisations will have differing aims.

b Your answer will need to consider why national government continues to be responsible for some business activity. Current examples of public corporations will be needed to support your example – there are now very few public corporations.

Key facts

- Businesses can operate in many different forms.
- It is unusual for the way in which a business is organised and managed to remain the same year after year.
- Some businesses are extremely large with activities all over the world.
- Multi-national companies may find they are able to reduce costs by taking advantage of lower production costs by concentrating production in one manufacturing facility located in one country.

Key Terms

Make sure you can explain each of the following Key Terms

Franchise A marketing arrangement that allows another business to trade in the same style as an existing business.

Franchisor The name given to the person or business who offers to franchise to other businesses its trading methods, products and business logos.

Franchisee The name given to a business or person buying a franchise.

Royalty A payment made to the franchisor based on the sales revenue of the franchise.

Globalisation The worldwide interdependence of business activity.

Multinational company A company with facilities in several different countries.

Public sector Business activity which is owned and funded by local or national government.

Public corporation An organisation which is owned by national government.

Unit 2.4.1

Employment and retention

By studying this unit you will be able to:

- **Explain the different stages in the process of recruitment and selection**
- **Discuss the importance of job descriptions and person specifications**
- **Recommend when to use different types of media when advertising for new staff**
- **Discuss the advantages and disadvantages of different sources of information about applicants for jobs**
- **Recommend when to use the different selection methods that can be used.**

Introduction

Read the following two case studies and then answer the questions in Activities 1 and 2.

Trouble At Mill

Mill Estate Agents runs a chain of estate agencies in the east of England. One of its branches was particularly successful. The manager of the office, Graham Smith, consulted well with his workers. There was a good team spirit amongst the workers and they worked very hard. When Graham was promoted, a new manager, Catherine Moss, was appointed. She was very bossy. Workers felt demotivated. The profits made by the office fell. Catherine moved on to another firm after nine months. The human resources manager for Mill Estate Agents said, 'We got it wrong when we appointed Catherine. In the interview, Catherine came across well, she spoke about how well she had dealt with staff in her previous job and how she had been able to create a good team spirit. We thought that she would be like Graham, but she did not have the right skills to get the best out of the staff in the office. We changed our method of recruitment when we appointed a new manager to succeed Catherine'.

Hiring the wrong people is draining business

A survey of human resource managers by the SHL Group (a business that assesses workers) found that, on average, recruiting a new member of staff costs £2,000. The survey also found that half of all the people that are recruited do not work successfully for the firm – they cannot do the job properly or they leave in a short period of time. Large organisations may need to recruit as many as 1,000 people each year.

Source: http://www.onrec.com

Activity

Activity 1: Explanation – The importance of recruitment and selection

ABC plc sells in a very competitive market where costs and prices are very important. It recruits 1,000 staff each year.

a Calculate the cost to ABC plc of recruiting 1,000 new staff at a cost of £2,000 per person.

b Using your answer to part a) calculate how much of the money ABC plc spends on recruitment is wasted. Remember that half of the staff it recruits will not work well for the firm.

c ABC plc works in a very competitive global market where costs and prices are very important. Explain why recruitment is important to ABC plc.

Activity

Activity 2: Missing words – The importance of recruitment and selection

Use the words given below to complete the paragraph about the importance of recruitment and selection.

- expensive
- workers
- profits
- success
- wasted
- interviews
- methods
- selection

The importance of recruitment and selection

Recruitment and _____ are very important to businesses. The _____ in a business make it successful or not. Recruiting new staff is _____. If good staff are not recruited by firms, money spent on the recruitment process is _____. Also the productivity and the _____ of the firm may fall. For this reason, getting the recruitment and selection _____ correct are important. _____ are one way of finding out about people but they can give the wrong impression. Many firms now plan their recruitment and selection very carefully – employing good workers can be the difference between _____ and failure for a business.

The recruitment and selection process

In larger organisations recruitment and **selection** is usually one of the jobs of the **personnel** or **human resources department**. In smaller businesses, the owner, or one of the partners, may have to do it. Figure 1 below shows the three main stages that are part of a planned system of recruitment and selection:

1 Needs analysis

2 Advertising the post

3 Selecting from the applicants

Figure 1 The stages of recruitment

Needs analysis

The main decisions that an organisation may have to make as part of its **needs analysis** are:

- how many workers it will need to employ, how many will need to be full-time employees, how many part-time

- what kind of staff will be needed – what qualities and skills the workers will need

- when the workers will be needed – the times in the week when they must work, and when their employment should start.

There are two documents that are very useful to a business when planning the recruitment of new workers:

- A **job description** lists the duties and the responsibilities the worker must perform. Figure 2 shows the job description for an administrator employed by Marston Children's Services Department.

- A **person specification** states the knowledge, qualifications, experience, personal qualities and skills the worker will need in order to do the job. Figure 3 shows the person specification for the administrator. It shows how the person specification can be used to plan the methods of selection to get the information needed, in order to judge who is the right person to employ.

Marston Children's Services Department Job Description

Post: Administrator, Functional Skills Project

Grade: 4

Responsible to: 14 – 19 Development Officer

Job purpose: To manage the accounts of the project and to provide administrative assistance support.

Main duties

1 To ensure that the accounts are up to date and readily available.

2 To assist the 14 – 19 Development Officer in the preparation and presentation of reports.

3 To establish good working relationships with the partners in the project.

4 To carry out other duties that it would be reasonable to ask for.

Figure 2 Sample job description

Marston Children's Services Department Administrator, Functional Skills Project – Person Specification		
Personal attributes required	*Essential/desirable*	*Method of assessment*
Qualifications Educated to Level 3 of the National Framework of Qualifications – A levels or Diploma	E	AF
Experience Managing accounts Taking minutes at meetings General administrative work	E D E	AF/I AF/I AF/I
Knowledge/skills/abilities Good interpersonal and communications skills, both spoken and written Ability to work as part of a team Knowledge of managing budgets Computer literacy – setting up and using spreadsheets, databases, word processing and presentation packages	E E E E	AF/R/I R/I AF/R/T AF/R/T
Special requirements Current driving licence Able to work unsociable hours Flexible and adaptable	E D E	AF I R/I
Methods of assessment: AF (Application Form), R (Reference), I (Interview), T (Test)		

Figure 3 Sample person specification

Activity

Activity 3: Explanation – Job descriptions and person specifications

Draw up a job description and a person specification for the following:

i A teacher of business studies

OR

ii A job that you have done – the work experience or part-time employment that you have done.

OR

iii A job that a relative or friend does.

Advertising the post

Examples of advertising media

Activity

Activity 4 – Explanation – Criticising a job vacancy advertisement

Look at the following advertisement. Explain why it is not very good.

Ingham's Catering Ltd
Clerical Assistant required

Start as soon as possible

Contact: John Meeks

Designing an advertisement for a job

The advertisement for the job advertised in Activity 4 does not give potential applicants for the job enough information. If people apply who don't have the necessary qualifications, skills and experience it will waste their time – as well as that of workers at Ingham's, who will have to read the applications and write back to these applicants to tell them that they haven't got the job. It is important that a job advertisement contains information that will encourage people with appropriate skills and experience to apply. It must tell potential applicants how to apply. The design of the advertisement will also be important in order to catch the attention of the reader.

Some of the information that may be included in a job advertisement includes:

- duties
- qualifications needed
- experience needed
- salary details

- description of work
- hours
- place of work
- training opportunities
- future prospects.
- contact address
- details of how to apply for the job.

Activity

Activity 5: Explanation – Advertising a vacant post

Embassy Caravans makes folding trailer tents. The business was set up in 1953. It now needs to recruit a production worker to work in the factory making the tents. All production workers need to be able to do some woodwork, welding and sewing of materials. The basic pay will be between £16,000 and £20,000 per year, depending on experience. Overtime is available when the factory is busy. The address is Unit 10, Industrial Estate, Ormkskirk L31 5XY. The telephone number is 01695 558899. Applicants will be expected to telephone for a discussion about the job and to ask for an application form.

1 Draw up an advertisement for this post. You should use some of the information provided but you do not have to use it all. The advertisement will go in the local newspaper, which charges according to the number of words – so keep the number of words to a minimum.

2 Explain why the firm would ask people to telephone for a discussion about the job before sending out an application form.

3 Write a short explanation as to why you have included each piece of information in the advertisement.

If possible, use a computer to create the advertisement.

Internal or external recruitment

Internal recruitment is when a job is filled by someone who already works in the organisation. The job may be advertised on a notice-board, in a company (in-house) magazine for the workers or by emailing the details to all workers who might be interested in, or able to do, the job. The advantages of internal recruitment are:

- it is often cheaper to advertise internally rather than externally
- it may be quicker to recruit someone who is already employed within the organisation
- the person appointed will already know about the organisation, its aims and objectives and its ways of doing things
- the organisation can be confident, because the person appointed will be known well, that the person appointed will be suitable
- it can be good for the morale of the workforce to give opportunities for promotion.

External recruitment is when the organisation fills a post with someone from outside the organisation. It will be appropriate when:

- there is no one in the organisation who would be able to do the job
- someone with new ideas is required
- it would cause unpleasantness between workers if the one of them was promoted.
- more workers are needed than the business currently employs.

Evaluation point

When management posts become available in an organisation, the managers may have to decide whether to recruit staff internally or externally. Their decision often depends on how the business is doing. If it is doing well and the managers know there is someone on the staff who is capable of being promoted, they may want to recruit internally. It may be good for staff morale if they see workers in the business being promoted. However, it may also cause problems if those who apply and do not get promoted are upset by the decision. If the business is not doing very well or the managers just think it is time for change, it will be necessary to bring in new people from outside to bring new ideas to the organisation and to prevent it becoming complacent. The risk then is that workers already employed feel that their work is not being valued.

Activity

Activity 6: Explanation – Internal and external recruitment

For each case below, state whether you would recommend the use of internal or external recruitment. Give reasons for your choice. What problems, if any, may the firm have to deal with as a result of your recommendation?

a The local council needs to appoint someone to cover for the office manager while she is on maternity leave. She is expected to be on leave for six months.

b Computec Ltd assembles computers. Its production of computers has increased by 20 per cent in the past year and is expected to rise by a further 15 per cent in the coming year. It needs to employ one more technician to add to the eight technicians that it already employs to assemble computers.

Deciding where to advertise

When a business advertises a job it needs to think about a number of things:

● the type of worker required

● the number of workers needed

● the location of the work

● the size of the firm

● the amount of money the organisation has available to spend on advertising for workers.

Table 1 gives a list of the media that can be used to advertise a post externally. It also gives examples of when each of the media might be right to use.

Activity

Activity 7: Research activity – Media used in recruitment

Conduct research about job advertisements in different media and then write a report to summarise your findings. Consider the types of jobs advertised, the style of the advertisements and the costs of the advertisements. You could compare, for example, advertisements in national and local newspapers, in specialist publications like The *Times Educational Supplement* (TES) or on different websites. Collect advertisements from printed publications or use the internet. For example, www.jobs.telegraph.co.uk gives you information about advertising in the newspaper or on *The Daily Telegraph* jobs website. If you use 'Products' it will then lead you to the costs of advertising (see 'paper' and 'online' rate cards).

Media	Description	Job examples
Local newspaper	These usually contain a jobs section that local people would know to look in. It is not usually expensive to advertise in these.	Local newspapers are useful when an organisation knows that there will be people in the local community who will be able and available to do the work. Posts for hairdressers and clerical assisstants are often advertised in this way.
National newspaper	These may have sections or even supplements for advertising jobs. It is usually more expensive to advertise in national rather than local newspapers.	National newspapers are often used when recruiting skilled workers for whom there may be a shortage in the local community or for recruiting senior personnel. They will attract people from all over the country.
Specialist magazines (for example The Times Educational Supplement, The Lancet (for doctors)	These will include specialist articles that interest particular types of workers.	Specialist magazines are often used for recruiting highly skilled specialists such as personnnel officers, engineers and scientists.
Job Centres	These are centres run by the government. They display advertisements as well as mentioning posts to unemployed people that they know would be suitable. It is free to advertise through these.	These are often used for semi-skilled and unskilled workers such as building site labourers, supermarket shelf-stackers and cleaners.
The internet	There are different kinds of websites that organisations can use, including sites that advertise a range of jobs or the organsation's own site. It is fairly cheap to use these sites.	Useful for attracting people with computer skills, but now used widely for a lot of different jobs.
Word of mouth	This is when people in an organisation with a vacancy mention it to other people that they know.	Word of mouth is very commonly used. A friend may mention a vacancy; a consultant or adviser may alert someone they have worked with to an opportunity.

Figure 4 Media used to advertise jobs

Activity

Activity 8: Explanation – Recommending media to use in recruitment

Recommend suitable media to use to advertise the jobs given below. In each case give reasons for your recommendations. Note that there may be no single correct answer; you may want to recommend more than one medium.

a Bowton Hospital wishes to appoint a doctor who is a cancer specialist.

b A large, multinational sports clothing firm needs to employ an experienced sales manager to head its European section.

c The supermarket in Marston needs to appoint three part-time check-out staff.

Sixty words per minute? More like sixty mistakes a minute!

Figure 5 discusses the advantages and disadvantages of different sources of information about applicants.

Selecting from the applicants

An organisation needs to find out information about the people who apply for the job. Often they will use more than one method for this. Often the selection process can be divided into two stages. First, the organisation may want to draw up a shortlist of applicants. It may use letters of application, application forms, CVs, and references to get a first impression. Those shortlisted are those applicants who will be invited to the next stage of the selection process. At this stage, sometimes called the 'final stage of selection', it might be enough just to interview the candidate. However, other methods such as tests, group activities and presentations are often used for jobs that require a lot of skill. Of course, the information that had been used for shortlisting may be used again at this stage.

Evaluation

Selecting who to employ from a number of applicants can be really tricky. One of the main problems is assessing how good the information is that has been gathered about each applicant. Sometimes people tell lies about what they have done, perhaps on their CV, or in a letter of application, or during an interview. Sometimes, employers will give good references to a person because they no longer want to employ that person and they hope that they will get a new job. For this reason, organisations often use more than one source of information and try to build up a true picture of what the person is capable of by piecing the information together. Even so, it often comes down to the gut instinct of the people doing the recruiting about whom they should employ.

Method	Description	Advantages
Letter of application	Letter written by applicant explaining why they belive that they are suitable for the post.	Shows a person's communication skills.
Application form	Applicants provide information in answer to questions on a form.	The firm can make sure that all applicants supply the same information so that it is easy to make comparisons.
CV (Curriculum Vitae)	The applicant writes down personal details such as their address, qualifications, employment history and names of referees.	Shows the ability of the applicant to organise information. Easy to see essential details at a glance.
References	Someone who knows the applicant well describes the personal qualities of the applicant, what work they did and how well they did it, their attendance and punctuality records and any other information that may be relevant to the post.	References can be very honest assessments that can recommend whether someone should be appointed or not. Sometimes, though, firms give employees good references because they want them to leave!
Interviews	The applicant meets people from the firm for a discussion. Often the people making the appointment ask all the candidates for the job the same series of questions and then compare the answers that they give. Sometimes the candidates may be interviewed as a group.	The employer sees the candidates and can judge how well they present themselves and communicate and how well they are likely to get on with other workers. Group interviews are very useful for seeing how people might get on in a team.
Psychometric tests	The applicant answers a series of questions, usually multiple choice, about themselves, what they like and dislike.	The test produces a profile or description of the personality of the applicant. Matched against the person specification, this can be useful information.
Presentations	The applicant is asked to give a talk to the employer on a given subject.	This will show up the personal qualities of the applicant. It may also be an opportunity for the applicant to put forward their ideas about the job.
Tests	The applicant may be given a pencil and paper test or a practical test.	These tests give very specific information, such as how good the applicant is at mathematics, typing or using equipment.

Figure 5 Sources of information about applicants

Activity

Activity 9: Role play – Interviews

a Plan an interview for a job. Choose either the Administrator for the Functional Skills Project shown in Figures 2 and 3 or the job that you wrote about in Activity 3. Using the information in the job description and the person specification, write down some questions that you would ask.

b Carry out the interview. One of the people in the class will need to volunteer to be the applicant.

c Discuss what was good about the interview and what could have been better. For example, what information did you get that you needed? What further information do you need to make a decision about whether the person would be suitable or not? How would you change the interview? What other sources of information would you use?

Activity

Activity 10: Explanation – Sources of information about job applicants

For each of the situations described below, recommend how the organisation should get information about applicants for the job. You may recommend more than one source. Give reasons for your recommendations. Each of the organisations expects to receive a large number of applicants for the jobs.

a Homesafe Insurance plc requires experienced clerks able to use spreadsheets to keep financial data, word processing for writing letters and Microsoft PowerPoint for creating presentations.

b Bowton Borough Council requires five road sweepers for the summer period when the town is busy.

c Abbey Homes Ltd builds and sells houses in most regions in the UK. Sales have been poor for the past two years compared with other house builders. The firm needs a marketing director with responsibility for sales throughout the country.

Activity

Activity 11: Flow chart – The process of recruitment and selection

Complete the flow chart by putting the terms about recruitment and selection next to the appropriate stage in the process. One has been done for you.

Stage	Terms
Needs analysis ↓	
Advertising the post ↓	
Shortlisting ↓	
Final stage of selection	Interviews

- interviews
- CV
- job centre
- application form
- job description
- specialist magazine
- psychometric tests
- national newspaper
- tests
- word of mouth
- letter of application
- references
- local newspaper
- presentations
- person specification
- website

Recruitment agencies

The use of **recruitment agencies** has increased dramatically in the UK in recent years. These agencies will do a lot of the work involved in recruiting and selecting staff. For example, if a firm wants to appoint a new sales manager it may discuss its needs with a recruitment agency. The agency will draw up a job description and a person specification in consultation with the firm. It will then advertise the post and receive applications from interested people. From these applications, it may recommend a small number of people it thinks are most suitable for the job. The firm may then interview the people recommended before finally deciding which one to appoint. Using a recruitment agency saves time and money. The recruitment agency is a specialist organisation and will know best about how and where to advertise the post, as well as what kind of information will be needed about the applicants in order to decide which of them to employ.

Employment agencies

These agencies keep lists of people who are willing to do certain kinds of work – for example, lists of receptionists or office typists. A firm may ask the agency to provide a worker for a short period of time. The firm pays the wage of the worker and the employment agency also receives a payment. Sometimes, if the worker is good, the firm will offer the temporary worker a full-time post. This is a good way of recruiting staff because it gives the firm a chance to get to know how good the person is. However, the agency may then ask for an extra fee for introducing the worker to the firm – it had recruited the person in the first place! This fee can be quite a lot of money.

Examination questions

1 Danielle Smith runs the BWHF franchise. The franchise sells bottled water to organisations in the Bowton area. She needs to recruit a worker to help with the delivery of the water and to act as a sales person.

a The table below is a list of ideas Danielle has about the job and the person. Tick next to each statement to indicate whether the idea should be included in a job description or a person specification. The first statement has been ticked for you.

Danielle's ideas about the job and the person.

Idea	Job description	Person specification
The person must deliver water to the customers.	✔	
The person must have a clean driving licence.		
The person has to have good communication skills.		
The person will have to find new customers.		
The person will be punctual and reliable.		
The person will be responsible to Danielle.		
The person will need to look smart.		

(6 marks)

b Using the information provided by the applicants on their application forms and CVs, Danielle produced a shortlist of four final candidates. Recommend two methods of selection that she should use to choose which of the four shortlisted candidates to employ. Give reasons for each of your recommendations. (6 marks)

2 Peter and Rosie own Pete's Pantry, a sandwich bar. They need to employ a manager to run it. Recommend a process of recruitment and selection that should lead to the appointment of a suitable person. Justify your answer. (12 marks)

Advice on how to answer the questions

Question 1

a Ask yourself whether the statements given describe what the worker will have to do, in which case it should be in the job description; or whether they describe what kind of qualifications and qualities the person will need to have to do the job, in which case the statement will go in the person specification.

b Danielle is looking for a driver and sales person. Think about the qualifications and skills the person will need to do this job successfully and then think how she can find this out. Refer to Figure 5 in this unit to remind yourself about the different sources of information that can be used. Select the sources you think should be used, then state the kind of information that it will provide that will be relevant to the job.

Question 2

To answer this question you need to write about all the stages of recruitment and selection. The key thing is to apply what you know to the specific context – the job is a manager in a small business. Think about the job and the type of person needed. Write about how it should be advertised and what sources of information will provide the type of information Peter and Rosie require to appoint the right person.

Key facts

- Workers are very important to businesses. They are often the most important resource employed.
- Although expensive, it is often worth taking time and trouble over recruitment.
- Needs analysis helps the firm to be absolutely sure about what kind of person they need to recruit and what that person will do.
- It is important to advertise the job correctly so that the firm gets applications from people who can and who are willing to do the job.
- When selecting who to employ from a number of applicants, firms often use more than one source of information about them.
- Sometimes firms can save time and money by employing recruitment agencies to recruit and select staff on their behalf.
- Sometimes firms prefer to employ temporary staff from employment agencies rather than take on full-time workers.

Key Terms

Make sure you can explain each of the following Key Terms

Selection The process of choosing between applicants for a job.

Personnel or human resources department The department in a business that deals with the recruitment and selection of workers, with pay and other employment matters.

Needs analysis How an organisation decides how many and what type of workers it should employ.

Job description This lists the main duties or tasks or responsibilities of a worker.

Person specification This lists the qualities, qualifications and knowledge that a person should have to do a particular job.

Internal recruitment This is when a job vacancy is filled by employing someone who is already an employee of the business.

External recruitment This is when a job vacancy is filled by employing someone from outside the business.

Recruitment agency A specialist agency that carries out all the tasks involved in recruitment and selection of workers on behalf of an organisation.

Employment agency An agency that has workers readily available for business hire, usually for a short period of time.

Motivation

Learning Outcomes

By studying this unit you will be able to:

- **Explain why people work and what benefits they can get from it**
- **Explain the different methods of pay that can be used to motivate workers**
- **Perform calculations connected with the different methods of pay**
- **Recommend when different methods of pay are appropriate**
- **Explain the different non-pay methods that can be used to motivate workers**
- **Recommend when different non-pay methods of motivation are appropriate.**

Introduction

Why do people work? It seems obvious! People work to earn money. But is that the full story?

Neave Patel works as a shop assistant for Boots the Chemist in Marston. Her friend, Joseph Hardman, works as a sales assistant in the charity shop next door. Neave is paid for the number of hours that she works and is given a discount on any goods that she buys from the shop. She has also been given some shares in the company. Neave's husband is very well paid. They live in a large house and have everything that they want. Neave says that she works because she likes to meet people and that she would be bored if she stayed at home all day.

Joseph is a volunteer. He does not get any pay for the work that he does. Joseph works, but not for money. His wife earns enough for them to live reasonably well. Joseph believes that it is important to make a contribution in life – he wants to do some good for other people. He is the manager of the shop and enjoys the respect he is given by people he works with and the customers who come into the shop.

These examples show that there may be more to why people work than just money. The different reasons or motivations that people have for working are important – managers must be aware of these so that they know how to motivate workers.

Maslow's Hierarchy of Needs

Many writers have been interested in finding out why people work. Abraham Maslow said that people have a **hierarchy of needs**. The **needs** are explained below. Physiological needs are the basic needs; self-actualisation is the highest need.

- **Physiological needs** – These are the basic needs that all humans must satisfy in order to stay alive: the need to eat and drink, the need for shelter and clothing.

- **Safety** – the need to feel safe from physical danger that might put you at risk of injury or death.

- **Social needs** – the need to be with other people, to get on with them, to have fun and to work in groups.

- **Self-esteem** – the need to feel that other people value what you are and what you do.

- **Self-actualisation** – the need to feel that you have been able to use the talents that you have to achieve your potential.

The pyramid below is one way of showing the different needs. It also gives examples of the different kinds of needs and how these could be satisfied at work.

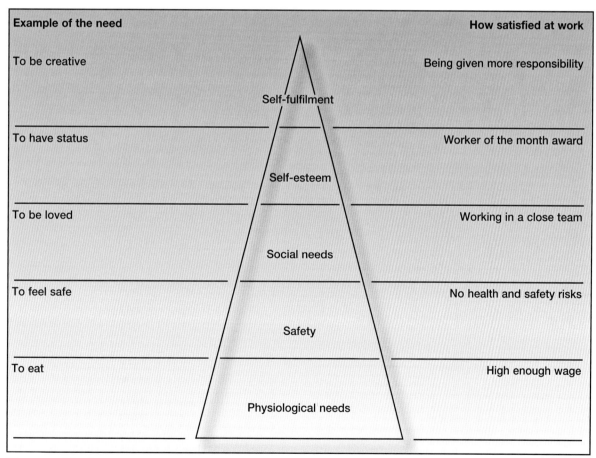

Figure 1 Maslow's Hierarchy of Needs

Activity

Activity 1: Missing words – Maslow's Hierarchy of Needs

Copy out the diagram of Maslow's Hierarchy of Needs. Complete the left-hand side of the diagram by using the words typed in bold below to give more examples of each type of need.

- **Friendship** – the need to have other people to get on well with
- **Recognition** – a desire to have other people acknowledge the work that we do, to pat us on the back
- **Drink** – a means of satisfying the physical need for liquid
- **Achievement** – the desire to do things, to reach goals
- **Respect** – the need to be appreciated by others
- **Control** – the feeling of being in charge of what happens
- **Fellowship** – the need to belong to a group

Activity

Activity 2: Research activity – Why people work

1 Prepare some questions to ask people why they work – relatives, neighbours or colleagues at work or school may be willing to help.

2 You should try to interview three different types of workers. Write down their answers.

3 Prepare for a discussion with other pupils in your class about why people work. Write down the main reasons that people have told you. Note any differences between the work they do, how much responsibility they have, what qualifications they needed to get the job, Try also to say which of the hierarchy of needs they say are important – remember work may satisfy more than one need.

4 Take part in a group discussion in class about what motivates workers. As a group, try to list in order of importance the needs that work meets for workers.

The importance of motivation at work

Motivating workers is about encouraging them to work hard and to work well. All organisations, whether in the private or the public sector, have objectives. If workers are working well then the organisation has a good chance of achieving its objectives. Workers who are working well are said to have 'high productivity'. The importance of **motivation** and **productivity** is shown in the two examples below:

- Anselm's Pies introduced new measures to motivate workers five years ago. The result has been that the firm has increased the number of pies it makes and sells, increasing its profit. Also, the cost of producing pies has fallen. The firm has been able to reduce the price it charges for some of the pies that it sells and has still increased its profits. A local competitor closed down six months ago.

● Marston Council introduced new motivational schemes for all its office employees. The council found that as a result work was done more quickly and fewer mistakes were made. The number of complaints that the council has to deal with has fallen.

How to motivate workers

In the remainder of this unit we look at how firms can motivate workers. Greed and fear are said to be the two great motivators. However, there are many other ways in which workers may be motivated and the evidence from business is that non-pay methods of motivation, as well as pay methods, are very important.

Pay and motivation

Pay advice slips

A pay slip shows the amount of **pay** that a person receives and any deductions taken from that pay. A pay slip usually covers the period of a week or a month. **Gross pay** is the total income that a person receives before any deductions are made. **Net pay** is the amount that the person receives after **deductions** have been taken off. The main deductions are for **income tax**, **National Insurance** and **pension contributions** (also known as 'superannuation'). A pay slip will also show any **expenses** paid to the worker. For example, some workers use their own cars for their work and will usually be able to claim for the mileage they do.

Figure 2 below shows some of the methods of pay that are used.

Figure 2 Methods of pay

Method	Description	Comments
Time rate	The worker is paid a set sum of money for each hour worked.	The worker may need to clock on and off to measure the hours worked. The system encourages workers to work a set number of hours but gives no reward for the quality of work done.
Overtime pay	The time rate may be increased to persuade the worker to work extra hours above the normal working day or week. Overtime may be paid at time and a quarter or time and a half.	It costs the firm more money but this may be covered by extra sales that the firm makes.
Salary	The firm agrees to pay the worker an amount of money for the year. This is divided by 12 and paid out monthly. The worker will not usually be paid for any extra hours that they work. However, they may receive extra money for reaching targets.	Salaries are often used to pay professional workers who have some kind of duty or responsibility for the people they serve and where it is difficult to measure what they produce – teachers and social workers, for example. However, there may be no incentive for the workers to work hard without some kind of additional reward.

Piece rate	This method of pay may be used where the work of individual workers can be measured. The worker is paid a sum of money for each item they complete. The more items the worker produces, the more pay they receive.	Piece rates motivate people to produce a lot. However, workers may rush their work which can lead to waste, higher costs, poorer quality and harm to the reputation of the business.
Commission	This is paid to workers who sell goods or services. The amount to be paid is usually calculated as a percentage of the value of the goods or services the worker sells.	This is a good motivator where the sales of workers can be measured. Sometimes sales people can become too pushy and can put off customers.
Bonus	This is an extra lump sum that may be paid to an individual or a group of workers when they reach a target level of production.	The target level of production needs to be realistic. If it is too high, workers may decide that it is not worth the effort to achieve.
Profit-sharing	The worker may be paid a share of any profits that the firm makes. It may be used to reward senior managers or where the individual contribution of workers cannot be measured.	The more successful that the business is in terms of profits, the more the worker receives. The problem may be that some workers may not deserve the payment if it is given to all workers in the business.
Fringe benefits or perks	The firm may give the worker non-money rewards. Examples of these include a company car, non-contributory pension scheme, luncheon vouchers and free health insurance.	It costs employers less to give workers fringe benefits than to give them extra income. If a person is given something worth £100, that is all that it costs the business. To give the worker an increase in take-home pay equal to £100 would cost more. If the worker was paying tax at 40% of any extra income they earn, it would cost the business £140 to give the worker take-home pay of £100.

Evaluation point

The method of pay that is appropriate for motivating workers will depend upon the work that the workers do and the type of business that they work in. Commission is often used with sales workers and piece rates are used with production workers. Profit-sharing may be useful when the individual contribution of workers cannot be worked out.

Activity

Activity 3: True or false – Pay and motivation

Place a tick next to each of the statements about pay methods of motivation to indicate whether they are true or false.

Statement	True ✔	False ✔
A bonus may be paid to a worker for achieving a target level of sales or a target level of output.		
Overtime is money taken off a person's wage when they have spent longer than they should in doing a job.		
Time rate is when a worker is paid for each hour that they have worked.		
A piece rate is usually paid to sales people to motivate them to sell more.		
Commission is usually calculated as a percentage of the value of the sales that the worker makes.		
A fringe benefit is a free haircut given to an employee for good work.		
Profit-sharing is a good way of motivating workers whose individual contribution cannot be measured.		
Workers who are paid a salary are given an amount of money for a year's work. A certain amount is paid each month.		

Activity

Activity 4: Calculations – Methods of pay

For each of the following state:

● the method or methods of pay being used to reward each of the following workers
● the amount of pay that they would receive.

1 Angus Deade receives £6 per hour and works a 35-hour week. In May, he worked four weeks. He also worked 12 hours overtime at time and a half.

2 Elsie MacIntosh receives £8 per hour and a commission of 10 per cent of sales. Last week she worked 40 hours and sold £600 worth of goods.

3 Alastair Munro is the managing director of a firm. He receives £80,000 per year. He is also paid 2 per cent of any profit that the company makes. In the last year the company made £2 million in profit. He has a company car and is given free health insurance.

4 Wasim Ikram earns a basic salary of £30,000 per year. In October he received a bonus of £1,500 when the output of the production department that he manages was 25 per cent greater than the target level.

5 Morag MacTavish knits woollen jumpers. She receives £15 for each one produced. In April she knitted 20 jumpers.

Non-pay methods of motivation

The methods of pay described in the previous section are examples of motivating people by satisfying their need for money. This section looks at methods of motivating workers that do not involve pay.

Fear

Using fear as a motivator involves threats such as being told off or being sacked. As pupils you may be able to relate to this. You may do your school work because you fear being told off by the teacher or by your parent or guardian. You may fear being put in detention, having to write lines or being 'grounded' at home. A lot of evidence from business shows that fear is not a good motivator in the long run. Adults who feel threatened or intimidated at work often decide to change jobs, or they involve the trade union. Intimidation makes workers resent their bosses. Even if they stay in the job, the workers may not contribute willingly to the business by, for example, suggesting improvements or by doing a bit extra work out of goodwill. However, that does not mean to say that it is not sometimes right to use fear!

Job rotation

This involves workers performing different jobs during the day, week or month. It stops them getting bored by doing the same work day after day. This is often done with workers who work on a production line, where jobs tend to be simple and do not require a lot of skill. This makes it easy to switch the workers around. However, it also means that they may just move from one uninteresting job to another.

Job enlargement

This involves giving the worker some different tasks to do. A packer in a food factory may be asked to label boxes and move the stock to the warehouse. The worker does not have any extra responsibility but does have some variety in the work that they do.

Job enrichment

This involves giving the worker more responsibility. A production line worker may be given responsibility for checking the quality of the goods being made and writing a report to suggest improvements. Where job enrichment is involved, the worker is often given training to improve their skills so that they can deal with the extra responsibility.

Team-working and team-building

Workers may be put in teams according to the abilities that they have. Each person in a team has a particular task or type of work that they are responsible for. People often enjoy working in teams and do not want to be seen to let the group down by not performing well.

Sometimes groups of workers will be given responsibility for what they do. They will be free to choose how to make the product, when they will work, who will complete which tasks and so on. The workers may be more motivated because they feel in charge of what they do. When this happens the workers are said to have been **empowered**. Sometimes, but not always, the group may share a bonus for reaching targets. Empowerment is not only for groups of workers; individuals may be given freedom about how to complete a task.

One part of team-building is deciding which workers to put together in a team so that the team has the mix of skills and qualities necessary to make it work well. Another side is motivating people to get on well and feel a responsibility towards the group. This may be done in different ways:

- Some organisations have social events and activities. Many organisations have social clubs and works sports teams. These bring workers together outside work.

- An organisation may send workers on team-building courses. Outdoor pursuit activities are commonly used for this purpose. The workers are put in teams to take part in activities such as backpacking, rock-climbing and raft-building. While the activities are often fun, they also challenge people, both as individuals and as groups, to do things that may be dangerous or require initiative. Workers often see their colleagues in a different light as a result of this and may appreciate their qualities more than they did before.

Award schemes

An 'employee of the month' award is an example of an award scheme. The work of a worker is recognised in some way, perhaps by being given a certificate or having his or her name added to a list of employees of the month. These schemes can meet the need of the worker for self-esteem.

Promotion

Giving promotion to a worker is a way of giving recognition to their achievements and this may motivate them to continue to work hard. The possibility of gaining promotion also encourages workers.

Leadership

Leadership is about motivating others so that they perform well and contribute towards the objectives of the organisation. Some leaders motivate by inspiring people; others may bully and threaten. Leadership styles can be put under three headings – see Figure 3.

Figure 3 Leadership styles

Autocratic leadership	This is when the leader makes all the decisions and expects the workers beneath him/her to carry out his/her orders. There will be little or no discussion with the workers about the work – workers are simply expected to obey workers.
Laissez-faire leadership	The French term '*laissez-faire*' means 'leave to do'. The leader will decide the main objectives of the organisation but the workers are given the responsibility for deciding how they are to achieve the objectives.
Democratic leadership	This is when the workers are allowed to discuss plans with the leader and to influence decisions about what to do and how to do it.

Evaluation point

The style of leadership that is appropriate for a business will depend on what the organisation makes, how able and motivated the workers are, how well the business is performing at present, and what problems the organisation faces and how urgently they must be solved. A business that is not doing well may need a dictator to give it a strong sense of direction. A creative business, such as design work, may work better if there is a democratic style of leadership that encourages workers to develop their own ideas and contribute them to discussions about what the business should do. Different leadership styles may be used along with some of the other methods of motivating workers that have been discussed.

The environment

The conditions in which people work affect how well they perform. Conditions that are safe, warm, light and comfortable are more likely to motivate workers than dangerous, cold, dark and uncomfortable conditions. Open-plan offices, music and staff rest areas are other examples of changes to the environment that may help to motivate workers.

Activity

Activity 5: Matching terms – Non-pay methods of motivation

Match the advantage of the non-pay methods of production to the name of the method.

Advantage of the non-pay method		Method
1 This is good for the self-esteem of the worker because their efforts are officially recognised.		a Job rotation
2 This may give clear orders to workers so that they are certain about what they must do.		b Award Scheme
3 When workers are safe and their work area is clean and pleasant they feel comfortable and so may work hard.		c Autocratic leadership
4 Workers do something different each week or month so they have variety in their work, which stops them getting bored.		d Democratic leadership
5 People like working with others to achieve things and they work well so that they do not let their colleagues down.		e Team-working
6 This involves the workers in decision-making so that they feel valued and feel that they have some control over their work.		f Environment

Activity

Activity 6: Explanation – Methods of motivation

State the method of motivation being used in each of the following cases:

1 Software designers have been asked to work together to identify the kind of software that schools are likely to need in five years' time and then to write it.

2 Marston Football Club are at the bottom of the league. The players lack confidence and are dispirited by the poor performance. A new manager has been appointed. He has introduced extra training and has told the players that he will transfer anyone who fails to attend these sessions.

3 The workers at a chocolate factory have been asked to do different jobs on different days of the week. One day they may be involved in packing the chocolates, another day they may unpack and move the raw materials to the production line. All the work is considered to have the same level of responsibility.

4 John is a doorman at the Empire Theatre. He has been given the additional responsibility of meeting and greeting 'celebrity' visitors to the theatre and escorting them to the special hospitality facilities.

5 City High School has built a new English block to replace the mobile huts previously used. The building is light and airy. Teachers have started to play music in some lessons.

Examination questions

Question 1

a Mark Seddon was employed as an engineer for Airight Ltd. He fitted and maintained the air conditioning systems that Airight Ltd sold. Figure 4 below shows Mark's wage slip for the week ending 12 May 2009.

Employee: Mark Seddon		Employee: Number 26	
Week No: 2		Week ending: 12 May 2009	
Pay	£	*Deductions*	£
Basic Pay		Income Tax	84
Overtime Pay	72	National Insurance	36
Gross Pay	492	Pension Contribution	20
		Total Deductions	140
Net Pay	352		

Figure 4 Wage slip for Mark Seddon – week ending 12 May 2009

i   Calculate the basic pay that Mark earned in the week ending 12 May 2009. Show your working. (2 marks)

ii Mark worked four hours overtime in the week ending 12 May. Calculate the amount he was paid for each hour of overtime. Show your working. (2 marks)

iii Mark is usually paid a basic rate of £12 for each hour that he works. Explain why Airight Ltd pays a higher amount for each hour of overtime that he works. (2 marks)

iv Some air conditioning firms pay engineers such as Mark Seddon a piece rate for each unit that they fit. Airight Ltd does not pay piece rates. From the list of statements below tick against the three disadvantages to Airight Ltd of paying piece rates to air conditioning engineers. (3 marks)

Statement	Tick the three statements that are disadvantages of paying piece rates to air conditioning engineers
The engineers will concentrate better on their work to get more done.	
The engineers may rush their work leading to poorer quality.	
Airight Ltd will fit more air conditioning units in the same amount of time.	
Airight Ltd could get a reputation for poor workmanship.	
Airight Ltd would need to employ people to check the quality of the work done by its engineers to reduce mistakes.	
Engineers would need more training.	

b Mark was paid overtime as an incentive. Airight Ltd is considering paying a piece rate instead of overtime to motivate its engineers. Discussing both methods of motivation, recommend the most appropriate method to motivate engineers such as Mark. (10 marks)

Question 2

Danielle Smith runs the BWHF franchise. The franchise sells bottled water to organisations in the Bowton area. She has recruited a worker to deliver the water and also to act as a sales person. Recommend two ways in which Danielle should motivate this worker. Give reasons for your recommendations. (6 marks)

Advice on how to answer the questions

Question 1

a The first three parts of the question i), ii) and iii) are calculation questions. These always have the instruction 'Show your working'. This is so that if a candidate makes a mistake doing the calculation, he or she might still get a mark if the method they used was a correct one.

b This is an evaluation in which you need to make a decision. Show that you know what overtime is and what piece rates are, and the advantages and disadvantages of each method. To get the maximum marks you will need to justify your reason in terms of what the business does. This might be connected with its reputation and the effect on sales or its costs and the effects on prices. One strategy is to make an 'It depends' statement. For example, deciding which one is appropriate may depend on whether reputation or prices are more important in terms of making sales.

Question 2

The worker in the question has two parts to his job – he or she delivers water and also finds customers as a sales person. Think how the worker might be encouraged to do each part of the work well. What will encourage him/her to deliver as many bottles of water as possible in the time available? What will encourage him/her to sell as much as possible? You may use pay or non-pay methods in your answer. There is no single right or wrong answer; you need to argue the case for what you recommend.

Key facts

- There are many different reasons why people work.
- People have different kinds of needs that can be satisfied through work.
- Pay is an important motivator because it provides the money people need to buy the goods and services they need.
- Different methods of pay are used to motivate different kinds of workers. For example, commission is good for sales people, while piece rates may motivate production workers.
- People can be motivated in many ways besides paying them money.
- The non-pay methods of motivation used should meet the needs of the people they are intended to motivate.

Key Terms

Make sure you can explain each of the following Key Terms

Maslow's Hierarchy of Needs A theory that can be used to explain what motivates workers.

Needs The human wants and desires that work can help to satisfy.

Motivation The encouragement given to workers to work hard and to work well.

Productivity The measure of how well workers are working. It is usually measured by the amount they produce or the average costs of production of what they make.

Pay The money reward given to workers.

Gross pay Pay before any deductions.

Net pay Pay after deductions.

Deductions Money taken off a person's gross pay for income tax, National Insurance contributions and pension contributions.

Income tax A tax paid out of a person's income.

National Insurance contributions Money paid out of a person's wage or salary to pay for things such as the state pension, and unemployment payment and sick pay if these are needed.

Pension contributions Money paid out of a person's wage or salary to provide a pension when they retire. This is extra to the National Insurance contributions, which provides the state pension.

Expenses Money paid to workers to pay them back for any money that they have spent doing work for the business. Expenses may include travel expenses.

Non-pay motivators Methods of motivating workers that do not involve the payment of money as a reward. They meet needs in Maslow's Hierarchy of Needs other than basic or physiological needs.

Empowered When workers feel that they have responsibility and are motivated because of this.

Training

Introduction

The two case studies below are of two very different businesses. One, Avon, is a large multi-national company manufacturing and retailing cosmetics; the other, Ashfield, is a small textiles manufacturing company. The message, though, is the same – training staff can bring important benefits to the business.

Avon Calling!

Avon is a large company which manufactures and sells cosmetics across the world. It has sales of over £250 million per year. It is famous for its Avon Ladies, who are part-time, door-to-door sales staff.

In the early 2000s it decided to improve its training. Managers were asked to become 'coaches', working with staff to identify all their development needs, which might include job training or learning subjects that have nothing to do with the job. In its learning resource centre, built at a huge cost, employees can find out more about courses or take workshops. (One that teaches the kinds of mathematics you will learn in school is called Maths is Magical – but you probably know that about maths already!)

After six years, the result is that the workers have greater job satisfaction, are willing to contribute more to the business and stay longer. Avon is developing its own workers and can offer them new and more challenging jobs because of their improved skills.

Source: Adapted from www.trainingreference.co.uk

Why training is good for business

Five years ago, textiles manufacturer Ashfield embarked on a training drive to boost business. Most shop-floor workers at the small Leicester-based company are of Indian origin and speak Hindi, Gujarati or Punjabi. So the company, which specialises in making clothing for businesses, introduced English classes that employees could attend after work. As language skills improved, managing director, Ayub Mahomed, decided that the firm should go further by encouraging staff to do more training. In three years, 16 out of Ashfield's 26 employees have gained NVQs in performing manufacturing.

Productivity rose by one third and staff became far more confident and willing to share ideas, according to Mahomed. 'People are more aware of the environment they work in,' he says. 'We make sure that machines are looked after and that the information we use is correct.'

Source: Adapted from Londoncareers.net

Activity

Activity 1: Explanation – The benefits of training

Read the two case studies.

1 Write down what kinds of training the workers have received.

2 Write down any benefits that the workers have gained from the training.

3 Write down any benefits that the businesses have gained from the training.

4 Training costs money. Explain why it might have helped these firms to increase their profits.

Training and the global economy

The two case studies above show how important training is to individuals and firms:

- For the individual it can help them to find a job, to do their job better, to gain promotion and to feel that they are improving themselves.

- For businesses, training is leading to better skilled and better motivated workers who want to stay with the firm and to increased productivity – which lowers costs, increasing competitiveness and profits.

It is also important for the economy. More and more UK businesses must compete with firms from around the world. Unit 3.5.5 discusses 'Globalisation' and the rise of countries such as China and India, whose businesses can produce many goods and services very cheaply. UK firms know that they must have very highly educated and trained workers to produce 'high tech' goods and services in industries such as motor manufacturing and pharmaceuticals. Education and training are vital for us all. The UK must be a high skilled economy if its businesses are to compete and if its people are to maintain their high standard of living.

Evaluation

Training can be very expensive. When a business is not doing well it may decide to save money by cutting back on training and this may help it to survive by not making a loss. However, this may not be a good thing because training helps to improve workers and this may help the business to compete. This is really important in a market that is very competitive. It is very important for UK businesses in general because of the increased competition from abroad.

Training needs

Training is about developing the knowledge, skills and abilities of workers. Different kinds of workers need training for different reasons. Some of these are suggested below:

- **Technical skills** Workers may need to learn the skills needed to use a machine or to upgrade their skills to deal with new machines.

- **Personal skills** Workers may need to develop personal skills such as communication skills because these are needed in the work that they have to do.

- **Management skills** A worker may have been given a promotion or may be seeking promotion. He or she will have to learn the skills needed to manage other people, control budgets, solve problems and so on.

- **New workers** These will need **induction training** to introduce them to the organisation that they will work in.

- **Group working** Workers may need training about how to work together well, how to get the best out of each other.

- **Knowledge of new products** Workers may need to be told about new products that they have to sell so that they know what information customers will require.

- **Flexibility** A firm may want to provide workers with a range of different skills so that they can do different jobs.

- **Retraining** The job that a person did may no longer exist, perhaps because a machine does it instead. This person will need to develop new skills if he or she is to find employment.

- **Personal development** This is about developing the person in ways that may not be connected directly to work. This can raise the worker's self-esteem, their ambitions and their motivation.

Activity

Activity 2: Matching terms – Training needs

The left-hand column below gives business situations where people need training. Match the situation to the different training needs given in the right-hand column.

Situation	Training need
Annabel's, a hairdressing salon, has taken on a young trainee, Colin Wynne. Colin starts work next week. He needs to be told about the business, how he is paid, what he can do at lunch-time and other basic, practical matters.	New products
Catherine Schoey, who runs Annabel's Hairdressing Salon, wants to expand the business to offer a range of beauty treatments. She needs to develop her own skills for running a business before this can be done.	Personal development
Ian Daly has been a machine operator at Lathom's Paints for 15 years. New machinery has been developed to do the work he did. The firm does not want to make him redundant. It has sent him on a training course to learn how to work in the warehouse.	Management skills

Elegant Conservatories employs three window fitters. It is sending them on a basic electrician training course. They will be able to fit plugs and lights instead of having to call in a fully qualified electrician.	Induction training
TechWorld Ltd provides training each week on the new computers and games consoles that it sells.	Flexibility
Exton Engineering Ltd provides an opportunity for all its employees to study courses that interest them such as GCSE Spanish and guitar lessons.	Retraining

More about induction

Induction is for new workers. The purpose of induction is not to teach a new worker how to do the job, it is to help the employee to settle in. At B&Q, the DIY retailer, new employees are sent to the B&Q University (its training centre). Here they follow a course about the history and aims of the business, the rules of the company and health and safety considerations. Staff also find out about how they are paid, opportunities for promotion, and so on. Smaller businesses also cover these things but are more likely to do them in the factory or offices that the employee will work in. They may give the worker a tour of the works and introduce them to the other workers. Employees are made to feel welcome. It helps the firm, because new employees will know what the business is trying to achieve and they will have a good impression of the business and will want to do well.

Types of training

There are two main types of training: **on-the-job** and **off-the-job**. Details of the types of training are shown in Figure 1.

On-the-job training

The training is done in the place where the worker works. Either:

- the trainee does a job and is given help by someone more experienced

or

- the trainee will shadow another worker, learning the job by watching what they are doing and asking questions.

Advantages	Disadvantages
• Trainee is given individual training • Cheaper – no travel or accomodation costs • Worker still produces while training • Trained in the ways of the firm	• Trainee may not produce as much as they would when working • Trainer may need to leave his or her work to help the trainee • The quality of the work may not be very good if a trainee does it. This could lead to wasted resources and/or a poor reputation for quality • Not suitable for groups of workers

Off-the-job training	
The worker will do the training away from where they work. Either: ● the trainee will go to a different site, perhaps a college or a special training centre or ● the trainee goes to another part of the site where they work, perhaps to a lecture room or resource centre.	
Advantages	**Disadvantages**
● Experts may provide training ● Trainee can use specially designed training equipment ● Workers often enjoy the change of environment	● Usually more expensive because of fees, travel and accommodation costs

Figure 1 Types of training

More about on-the-job training and coaching

In recent years, **coaching** has become very important in many businesses. Coaching takes place when one worker (the coach) works with another (the coachee) in the work place. The purpose is to develop the skills and abilities of the coachee. The coach may watch the coachee work and then make suggestions about how the coachee might improve. Sometimes, the coach does not give suggestions but simply asks questions to make the coachee think through for

On-the-job training is done while the person is doing their job

Workers may need to improve personal skills

themselves how to improve. Coaching can be like 'peer assessments' which you may do in school. Another pupil marks your work and then makes suggestions about how you can improve. There is a lot of evidence that coaching works very well. It does not just help the coachee – coaches can also learn a lot because it makes them think about different ways of doing the job and improves their skills in managing and guiding others.

More about off-the-job training

There are several different forms of off-the-job training:

Figure 2 Forms of off-the-job training

Lectures	These are good for telling people about things, for giving information. They are not good for developing skills.
Demonstrations	The trainee watches someone show them how to do a job. These are good because you learn from an expert. It is often necessary to practise the work after the demonstration in order to develop the skills.
Role-play or simulation	The worker experiences a situation as if it were a real work situation. The trainee practises the skills or practises how they would deal with the situation.
Team-building	A group performs tasks together in order to develop. It helps them to learn how to work best in teams and to appreciate the different qualities that other people have. The tasks might be connected to the work that the people do but often they are not. Non-work connected tasks can include outdoor activities such as climbing and raft-building, or they may be problem-solving activities.

Activity

Activity 3: Explanation – Recommending methods of motivation

Recommend the method or methods (more than one method may be appropriate) of training that would be suitable for each of the situations below. State whether the training should be on-the-job, or off-the-job, and the type of training that should be given. Justify your recommendations fully.

1 Direct Bank needs to employ ten new workers at its call centre. The workers need to be able answer calls correctly and use the computer software designed specifically for Direct Bank.

2 Braswell Insurance wishes to improve the word processing skills of five clerical officers that it employs.

3 Plumbs Garden Centre wishes to train one of its drivers to be able to feed and prune plants when there is no other work for him to do.

4 Johnston Clothing Ltd wishes to train its supervisors to be able to deal with problems brought to them by staff. The problems may be minor or major issues. Some of the major issues that have occurred in the past have concerned bullying, racial discrimination and health and safety problems. There have been some heated arguments and unpleasant scenes.

5 Annabel's, a hairdresser, has taken on a young trainee. He needs to learn different skills – from washing and drying hair to cutting and perming.

6 Annabel, who runs the salon, wants to expand the business to offer a range of beauty treatments. She needs to develop her own skills before this can be done. Annabel will also have to deal with more staff, advertise more and purchase more stock.

Staff appraisal

Many organisations have staff **appraisal** schemes. At least once each year, an employee (the appraisee) will meet with his or her boss (the appraiser). Together they will discuss the performance of the employee. Many organisations set targets for their workers. For example, a salesperson might be set a sales target. If the worker reaches the target, he or she may be given extra money – **performance-related pay**. New targets will be set for the next year. Sometimes a programme of training and development is agreed. This programme may be designed to help the worker to improve their performance or to help them to get promotion.

Evaluation

In some firms workers fear their appraisal whilst in others they look forward to it enthusiastically. How workers feel about appraisal will depend on the approach the firm takes and on the motivation of the individual worker. Many firms use appraisal to encourage workers to better things and help them to do this by offering appropriate training. This kind of appraisal is not just about the needs of the firm, it is about the development of the worker as well. It is these firms that are most likely to get enthusiasm from their workers. For others firms, appraisal may only be about checking up on whether or not targets have been met, which can trigger a reward or perhaps cause increased stress in a worker who is struggling to perform well but does not feel supported.

Investors In People (IIP)

The **Investors in People** award is a quality assurance scheme for organisations who provide structured opportunities for staff development. The organisation sets out its goals and targets in a plan. Staff training will be needed to achieve these. The whole programme must be properly evaluated. If the planning, implementation and evaluation of the programme meet the criteria, the organisation can be awarded IIP status. It can then display the IIP plaque in its premises and display the symbol on its letterheads.

Activity

Activity 4: Role play – Appraisal and coaching activity

Work with a classmate. Your classmate will be your coach. You can return the favour for him or her.

a Write an answer to one of the Examination Questions at the end of the unit (or a different question set by your teacher). Now get your classmate to mark your work. He or she should write down (i) what is good about the work and (ii) how the work might be improved. The 'Advice on how to answer the questions' will help when deciding what mark to give.

b Spend a little time thinking about the work that you have done in business studies so far. Write down

i what you have been good at and why you think you have done this work well

ii what you have found difficult and why you have found it difficult.

c Now have a discussion with your classmate. Share the answer you wrote to b. Between you, try to come up with ideas about how you can improve. Sometimes this might simply be to concentrate more in class, or to do homework on time. Other targets might be to revise a certain topic by a certain date. Others might be about how to answer questions better – for example, by making sure you give reasons for recommendations, writing more advantages or disadvantages or explaining your points in more detail.

Lifelong learning

Many older people that you know will have done the same job all their life. After school, they might have completed an apprenticeship or been to college and gained qualifications. From this, they might have started in a job which they still do – perhaps for the same firm, perhaps for a different one. For you, it is more likely that you will need to change careers several times during your lifetime. This means that you will need to keep learning new skills or developing the skills that you already have. The government has been encouraging workers to learn throughout their lives: **lifelong learning**. There is now a national framework of qualifications, which includes different kinds of qualifications suited to different people. There are five 'levels' of qualifications and there are academic qualifications and vocational qualifications for different occupations. Training organisations that receive government support must offer courses that lead to qualifications in the framework. There are three kinds of qualifications:

- **Academic qualifications**. These include GCSEs, AS and A levels and university degrees. These are intended to develop general knowledge and skills.

- **General vocational qualifications**. These include 'applied' A levels and GCSEs, BTEC, Diplomas, HNDs and vocational degrees, which develop general knowledge and skills for a particular area of work. Functional skills in Mathematics, English and ICT are to test a person's ability to use skills independently, in their private and in their working lives.

- **Vocational qualifications**. These qualifications show that a person is able to do specific tasks related to a particular occupation, for example, as a hairdresser, a plumber or as a clerical officer. Many of these qualifications are NVQs (National Vocational Qualifications).

One type of qualification is not better than another. They serve different purposes and they suit different types of people. Some people will be more suited to doing vocational courses, others to academic work.

Activity

Activity 5: Research activity – Career planning

Investigate an occupation that you are interested in. Find out the qualifications that you will need to do the job. Your careers library and the internet will be good sources of information. Develop a plan to say how you will gain those qualifications. Write up your findings and your plan as a personal action plan. Note that you may need to gain both academic and vocational qualifications as part of the plan.

Examination questions

1 Dream Days Ltd is a travel firm that sells special event trips and holidays.
  a It must train new cabin crew staff about what to do in an emergency. Recommend whether Dream Days Ltd should use on-the-job or off-the-job training for this. Give reasons for your answer.   (4 marks)
  b Dream Days Ltd is concerned that some of its cabin crew do not deal with complaining passengers very well. Recommend a method of training that would improve the personal skills of the cabin crew. Give reasons for your answer.   (4 marks)
  c Dream Days Ltd provides induction for all new workers. Explain how both the workers and Dream Days Ltd will benefit as a result of the induction course.   (4 marks)
2 Schuker Engineering Ltd makes parts for motor car engines. It has faced increasing competition from abroad in recent years. There has been a short-term fall in sales of car engines, generally caused by an international recession. Schuker Engineering Ltd is considering cutting its costs to maintain profits by reducing the amount of training it provides for its engineers. Explain whether or not Schuker Engineering Ltd should reduce its training.   (6 marks)

Advice on how to answer the questions

1 a Think about the type of training that is needed. Would it be safer to give on-the-job training or off-the-job training? Explain your answer fully.
  b Think about the type of skills that the cabin crew need. How could they learn these skills? Would they need to see someone demonstrating the skills? Would they need to practise the skills? Would it be useful to give them feedback on how they deal with customers? There is no one correct answer here – make a decision and justify it.
  c Think about the things that the new employer will learn. How will he or she feel if they are given good induction training? How might this affect the way they work and why?
2 There is no correct answer to this. Think about the difference between the short-term needs of the business and what it must do in the long term to succeed. As with many evaluation questions, one answer would be to say what the decision will depend upon.

Key facts

- Training costs money.
- There are different types of training needs.
- Training can improve the performance of workers and of the business.
- It may take place on or off-the-job. There are different types of each.
- Staff appraisal is now a very important way in which businesses decide the training that workers should receive.
- The Investors In People award recognises organisations that provide structured development opportunities for their workers.

Key Terms

Make sure you can explain each of the following Key Terms

Induction training Special training to introduce a new worker to the business, place of work and their fellow workers.

On-the-job training Occurs at the place of work and while the worker is doing their job.

Off-the-job training Occurs when the worker is not doing their job. It may still be at the place of work, or the employee may be sent somewhere else for the training.

Coaching When one worker supports another to develop that person's knowledge and skills.

Appraisal When a line manager assesses the work of somebody he or she is responsible for. They may discuss targets for the worker to achieve and training that is needed.

Performance related pay. Any way of paying workers that rewards them for how much they produce or how well they work.

Lifelong learning The idea that workers will need to keep learning different skills during their working lives.

Investors in People (IIP) A scheme by which the quality of staff training and development in a business can be recognised by an outside organisation.

Employment law and trade unions

Learning Outcomes

By studying this unit you will be able to:

● **Explain different laws that exist to protect workers**

● **Explain how workers can take legal action against employers through employment tribunals**

● **Discuss how health and safety at work legislation protects workers and what the consequences are for employers who fail to obey the legislation**

● **Explain how trade unions can help their members and discuss what will influence how successful they are**

● **Discuss the benefits of single union agreements between employers and workers.**

Introduction

Sometimes workers need support. In the two cases below, support comes from the trade union and from the law. But passing a law does not necessarily solve a problem. This unit examines some of the laws that have been passed to protect workers. It also looks at how trade unions can help workers – and not just by organising strikes for more pay.

Sea warning over strike action

SWANSEA Coastguard station will be shut this evening for two of the busiest days of the year as part of a nationwide strike.

Operations will be transferred to Milford Haven – but distress calls and rescue and search operations will be carried out as normal.

The two-day walkout, which is due to finish on Monday at 8 pm, is the latest installment of a long dispute over pay.

PCS (Public and Commercial Services Union), which represent coastguards, said some of its members' salaries were barely above the minimum wage.

Source: www.thisissouthwales.co.uk, 23 August 2008

Thirty years on, the battle for equal pay is still being lost.

IN THE past few weeks a local authority was reported as facing a £50 million bill after losing a sex discrimination claim involving 3,000 women employees over the overtime and bonuses paid to male workers. A young waitress was awarded £124,000 for sex discrimination and unfair dismissal after suffering a campaign of harassment by a chef, and a former beauty queen hired for a sales job because of her good looks – then fired when she became pregnant – was in line for £42,000 after a tribunal ruled she was unfairly dismissed.

In the 30 years since the Sex Discrimination Act came into force there have been many positive changes for women in the workplace. But some problems stubbornly persist.

Source: The Times, 4 April 2006

However, whether there is a problem or not is not always clear. Opinions are important. Think about the following, which was taken from a blog on the Sun Online website.

"I don't mind equal pay for women when they can do an equal amount of work. Being in the Military I saw far too many female soldiers who could not even carry their own tool boxes without a man having to help. They were supposed to be equal and yet they carried less weight on runs and got extra time! There was nothing equal about it. Men do more work and should be paid more, we don't get pregnant and have months off, we certainly don't retire as early as women are allowed. So why should they get equal pay. "

Source: Blog on the Sun Online website 26 June 2008

Employment tribunals

Employment tribunals are courts of law, and deal with most of the laws relating to

"What were you saying about equality?"

Activity 1: Debate/research – Discrimination

'Women should be treated as equals with men in the workplace.'

a Decide whether you agree or disagree with this statement. In groups, use the internet to research the arguments to support your view. You may use newspaper websites to find examples of cases that have been taken to court.

b Conduct the debate. Remember to have a vote at the end of the debate.

Workers can get a dispute settled in an employment tribunal

employment mentioned in Figure 1 – as well as some others including regulations dealing with data protection and asbestos. If a worker sues an employer the tribunal will hear evidence for both sides. The tribunal then makes a decision. If the employer is found to be at fault, the firm can be made to pay compensation. If a worker has been dismissed unfairly, the tribunal may order that he or she be reinstated. The firm may also be fined for breaking the law. Another consequence is that the firm may receive some bad publicity if the problem is covered in the newspapers.

Health and safety issues may be dealt with in the civil courts, which deal with disputes between two individuals. The Health and Safety Executive employs inspectors who visit places of work. They inspect the premises to check that they meet the health and safety regulations. Legal action can be taken against employers who breach the regulations. The court can order the employer to pay compensation and can impose fines. A worker can also take their employer to court to get compensation if they have been injured because the employer did not obey health and safety rules.

An employer has the right to dismiss or sack an employee if they cannot do the job properly, or if they behave badly in some way – known as 'misconduct'. Very serious bad behaviour – for example, theft or being drunk at work – is known as 'gross misconduct'.

Employment laws

Figure 1 summarises some of the main laws that exist to protect workers. The laws described are designed to protect the worker from bad employers, but also to protect employers too.

Figure 1 Employment laws

Name of the law	Main points
Equal Pay Act 1970	This law was introduced to make sure that women are paid the same as men when they do similar work.
Race Relations Act 1976	This law was introduced to stop people of one race, colour, nationality or ethnic origin being treated differently from those of other origins. Direct discrimination is when one worker gets better treatment than another does – perhaps being given promotion when another employee is actually better qualified. There are some exceptions to the law – for example, if, for some reason, the job must be carried out by someone of a particular race, such as a waiter in a Chinese restaurant.
Sex Discrimination Act 1975	This law was introduced to stop males or females being treated differently from members of the opposite sex. A job advertisement that says the job is for a woman would be breaking the law. There are some exceptions – for example, if, for some reason, the job must be carried out by someone of a particular sex (such as a female PE teacher who would need to deal with female pupils in the changing room).

Health and Safety at Work Act 1974	The law makes it the responsibility of the employer to protect worker from dangers in the workplace. Responsibilities include providing safety equipment, washing facilities and toilets, and adequate breaks.
Minimum Wage Legislation	This was introduced to stop workers being exploited by employers. It applies to people over the age of 18. For people in the age range 18–21 the minimum hourly wage rate is less than for those aged 22 years and over. There are some exceptions to the legislation, including au pairs and members of the armed forces. The rate is reviewed, and usually increased, each year.
Employment Rights Act 1996	The firm does not need to give a worker a written contract of employment but it must give a 'statement of particulars' within eight weeks of starting work. This states the job title, the hours the person must work, details of the job, the pay, when the worker will be paid, what deductions will be taken from pay, how much notice must be given to end the contract and any disciplinary rules that apply to the employee.
Disability Discrimination Act 1995	The Act is designed to give equal opportunities to disabled people. Employers cannot discriminate against disabled people when recruiting staff. They are expected to make reasonable changes to premises to permit access and mobility around them. They have to provide appropriate equipment so that disabled people can work.

Activity

Activity 2: Employment laws – Matching terms

The left-hand column gives cases that have been heard by an employment tribunal. Match each one with the employment law that has, or may have, been broken.

Case	Employment Law
a Jessica Starmer, 26, claims that the company's 'family-unfriendly working practices' were reinforcing its male-dominated ethos, and would force her to resign from the job she loves. Ms Starmer, from Wareham, Dorset, wants to halve her hours to allow her to share the care of her one-year-old daughter Beth with her husband Simon, who is also a BA pilot. *Source:* Times Online *10 January 2005*	Minimum wage legislation
b Macclesfield County Court heard evidence that Clingfoil, a packaging company, had failed to show a duty of care to a member of staff caught unloading a box of offcuts by balancing seven feet up with one foot on a ladder and the other on a fork of his forklift truck. *Source: Adapted from the* Daily Telegraph *6 June 2006*	Sex discrimination law

c An advert by the Arnolfini Art Gallery in Bristol for the position of curator's assistant at a racism exhibition appeared earlier in the year. The Gallery claimed it was trying to employ more people from under-represented groups. Only African, Asian and Caribbean curators based in England can be appointed. *Source: Adapted from the BBC website*	Health and safety at work
d Earlier this month it was discovered that staff working at London's Hard Rock Cafe were paid a basic wage of £2.06, made up to the minimum wage with tips. *Source: Guardian.co.uk 31 July 2008*	Race relations law
e The threat of a multi-million pound compensation bill is hanging over Birmingham City Council. Several hundred female council workers, including school cooks, cleaners and care assistants, are now seeking redress, alleging they are being treated unfairly because, unlike male manual workers, they do not qualify for hefty bonuses. *Source: Adapted from the* Birmingham Post *– 10 October 2006*	Disability discrimination
f Blind woman Sue Williams, a highly qualified IT specialist, got a job with the J Walter Thomson advertising agency. The tasks she was asked to do were not challenging for a person of her intellect and industry.	Equal pay law

Activity

Activity 3: Employment laws – Research activity

Choose one of the employment laws. Using the internet, research a current case where one of the employment laws may have been broken. Prepare a brief presentation to explain the case to your class.

Health and safety at work

There are a number of laws that deal with health and safety at work besides the 1974 Act mentioned in Figure 1. These laws have helped to make firms more health and safety conscious. All organisations must now have a written health and safety policy. Employees must receive adequate health and safety training. Health and safety issues must be communicated to workers through posters, on notice-boards, in training and so on.

The minimum wage debate

The minimum wage was introduced to stop businesses from exploiting workers by not paying them very much. It has achieved this for some workers. There are still some businesses that employ illegal immigrants and often these are paid at below the national minimum wage – these businesses are behaving in an illegal and unethical manner (see Unit 3.5.2 on Ethics). For many businesses, the introduction of the minimum wage has had no effect – they already paid

Activity

Activity 4: Health and safety in the office

Find the health and safety problems in the cartoon.

their workers above the minimum wage. For others, it has meant a fall in profits as their costs have risen. In some cases, businesses have been forced to close down because they can no longer compete. Others have decided to cut costs by using machines rather than workers. Unemployment has been the result for some workers.

Activity

Activity 5: Research – The minimum wage

a Using the internet, find out the current national minimum wage. Remember there are different rates for different age groups. (Google 'national minimum wage' and you will get a range of interesting websites to look at.)

b Using the internet, research a current case where an employer may be paying a worker less than the national minimum wage. Write a brief account of the case.

Evaluation point

The minimum wage has protected some workers from greedy and unkind employers who would have paid their workers much less if they could have done so. However, some firms have had to lay off workers because they could not afford to pay them the national minimum wage. This has happened in markets where there is a lot of competition from abroad, particularly when the competitors are in countries where there is no minimum wage, or it is much lower than in the UK. This makes it possible to provide the same goods or provide the same service at a much lower cost and price.

STATEMENT OF PARTICULARS

XYZ LTD, Grove Street, Bowton.

BL2 3FF

Employee _____

Place of work _____

Job title _____

Start date for employment _____

Hours of work _____

Pay _____

When paid _____

Probationary period _____ weeks

Pension rights*

Holiday entitlement*

Sick Pay*

Grievance and Disciplinary procedure – see separate document

Termination of employment – Each party to give 14 days notice.

*See Handbook for Employees for further details.

Contract of employment – the statement of particulars

When a person starts to work for a business, a contract has been made. This is because the business has offered work and the person has accepted this offer. The statement of particulars is a written statement of the agreement that exists. It must be given to the worker within two months of the worker starting employment. The statement covers information about the job title, when employment began, hours of work, pay, holidays entitlement and how much notice must be given for terminating employment.

Activity

Activity 6: Writing a statement of particulars

Suppose that you own a local newsagent's shop. Draw up a statement of particulars for a shop assistant who you have appointed to a full-time post. Use the example above of a statement of particulars to help you.

Redundancy

When a worker's employment is ended because the work they do is no longer needed by a firm it is called **redundancy**. The main reasons why a worker may not be needed are:

- the firm has started to use machines instead of labour

- the firm is producing less, so does not need as many workers

- the firm has gone out of business, so does not need any workers.

The law gives protection to workers who are made redundant. If they have worked for their employer for at least two years, the employer must pay them 'redundancy money' as compensation for losing their job. The law states the minimum that must be paid. Some employers pay more than the minimum. The firm may ask for voluntary redundancies. People may choose to be made redundant, perhaps because the redundancy money is good, because they are nearing retirement or because they want a change.

Trade unions

Examples of **trade unions** are the National Union of Teachers and Unison, which represents workers in public sector organisations. Trade unions set out to do two main jobs:

- **To act as a pressure group:** A pressure group is an organisation that seeks to influence government to make laws that are in the interests of its members. A trade union, asking government to limit working hours more strictly, would be acting as a pressure group.

- **To protect the interests of its members:** Unions help workers with all kinds of matters. These include:

  - working conditions

  - hours

  - redundancy

  - unfair dismissal

  - safety at work

  - race and sex discrimination

  - pay

  - holiday entitlement.

Benefits of union membership

Unions are able to help workers with these kinds of matters because:

- They have strength in numbers. The actions of a large group of workers will have more influence on employers than the actions of an individual.

- They can give expert advice and support. Unions employ specialists such as solicitors. These will be able to give workers expert advice about the rights the workers have and what to do in a dispute.

- They have the money to help to pay for expensive court cases.

- They will have trained negotiators who know how to deal with the employers.

Figure 2 The main forms of industrial action

Strike	Nearly all workers have the right to withdraw their labour. Sometimes a strike can be by selected workers who have key jobs. If their work is not done, the whole of the production may have to stop. A strike involving all the workers is known as an 'all out strike'. It may be for one day or until the dispute is settled.
Overtime ban	This is when the workers will only work the hours stated in their contract of employment. They will not work any overtime.
Work to rule	This is when the workers will only do what is included in their job description.

Pickets encourage workers to join the strike

Unions can also negotiate benefits for their members. Discounts in some shops and lower rates of interest on loans are examples of these benefits.

Industrial action

This term refers to the action that workers can take to try to achieve what they want in a dispute with the employer. Many disputes are settled before any **industrial action** takes place. The main forms of industrial action are as shown in Figure 2.

Industrial action is designed to benefit the workers. However, it may also have costs for the worker. It will also harm the employer, the customers of the firm and the economy as a whole – see Figure 3.

Single union agreements

In some places of work, several different unions may represent different kinds of workers. Different craft unions may represent different kinds of skilled workers. White-collar

Figure 3 The costs of industrial action

Costs to the workers	1 Lose wages.
	2 May lose bonuses, commission, overtime pay, etc.
	3 If the firm suffers a loss of sales, workers may be laid off or made redundant.
Costs to customers	1 They are not able to buy the products they need.
	2 If the products are raw materials or stock that they sell, they will not be able to produce or sell anything so they lose sales revenue.
Costs to the firm	1 Cannot produce or sell so loses income.
	2 May make less profit.
	3 Customers may take their business to competitors – sometimes permanently.
Costs to the economy	1 People and firms will have less money to spend – businesses will lose sales revenue.
	2 The government will lose tax revenue because people have less income and spend less.
	3 Imports may rise if people buy from abroad rather than from British firms.
	4 Unemployment may rise, increasing the cost of social security benefits.

Activity

Activity 7: Trade unions – Missing terms

Use the terms in the right-hand column to complete the paragraph in the left-hand column.

Paragaph	Terms
Trade unions help their _____. They help them to get fair _____, more _____ and less _____ of work. They also deal with issues such as _____ resulting from _____ discrimination. They have _____when a lot of the workers are in the union. They also employ experts such as _____. If the employers will not do as the unions want, the union can organise a _____ of its members or a _____-_____ or an _____ ban. This disrupts productions but it also costs the _____.	solicitors go-slow pay unfair dismissal hours members strength strike workers sex holidays overtime

Evaluation point

Whether or not a union is successful when it takes strike action for more pay depends on a number of things. Are there a lot of workers involved? Will it cause a lot disruption? Will the employers lose a lot of money? Can the employer afford to give a pay increase (if that is what the dispute is about)? Does the union have enough money to help the striking workers who will not be being paid? Often the trade union and the employers will have taken 'bargaining positions' and may finally settle somewhere in-between.

unions represent office workers. A general union may represent some semi-skilled and unskilled workers. This can make **industrial relations** complicated. In some firms there are **single union agreements**. This means that all the workers agree to be a member of the same union. This can help the workers as well as the employers. The workers benefit because all the workers in the firm will speak with one voice and this may add to their strength. For the firm it is easier to negotiate with one union rather than several of them.

ACAS – Advisory, Conciliation and Arbitration Service

This organisation exists to try to settle disputes between workers and employers. First, it will give advice to both the employer and to the union. Second, it will provide conciliation – it tries to find areas that both sides can agree upon to restart negotiations when they have broken down. Third, it provides arbitration. When the two sides cannot reach an agreement, ACAS appoints an arbitrator who hears the arguments and makes a decision. This person will have to be acceptable to both sides. The union and the employer cannot disobey any decision the arbitrator makes unless they had agreed to 'non-binding arbitration'.

Activity

Activity 8: Challenge activity – Union–management dispute role play

The class should divide into three groups; one representing the employers at Practical Plastics Ltd, one the workers and the third ACAS. Each group should appoint two negotiators.

A dispute has developed between the workers and the management. The background to the dispute is as follows:

Practical Plastics Ltd makes storage boxes for use in the home and in work. It has many competitors. Sales have been only just satisfactory for 18 months – enough for the firm to make a small profit. Workers are unhappy about conditions in the factory. Some of the machinery is old and dangerous and the floor needs repairing in places. They are also unhappy about wages. Two years ago the wage rate was cut by 5 per cent at a time when the firm was making a loss. The employer said that this was necessary to see the firm through a difficult period. Wages were increased by 2 per cent last year. Inflation has run at 3 per cent for the past three years. There are signs that the economy is improving. Exports have risen in the last six months, as have incomes. The firm would like to buy some new machinery.

Each group should prepare its arguments. Also decide what actions you might take to help you to win the dispute. Negotiations should take place between the negotiators of the two groups. One of the ACAS representatives should act as the chairperson. The negotiators may withdraw from the discussions on three occasions to discuss matters with the group they represent. If it is not possible to reach an agreement, the ACAS group should decide what should happen.

Activity

Activity 9: Industrial dispute – research activity

Research an example of an industrial dispute. You might use the internet or a local or national paper for this purpose. If you use the internet, try a website for one of the national newspapers.

Write an account of the dispute including:

● why the dispute was taking place
● what actions both the management and the workers took
● how the dispute was settled – if it was
● what costs there were – to the workers, the firm, the customers and the economy.

Examination questions

Question 1

Olympic is a small firm that manufactures sports clothes.

a Recommend three ways in which Olympic could inform its workers about health and safety matters in the factory. Give a reason for each of your recommendations.   (4 marks)

b State three ways in which employment laws, other than health and safety at work laws, affect the employment of workers.   (3 marks)

Question 2

a Suzanne Hart runs Aunt Sue's bakery shop.

   i State **two** legal requirements she must meet when employing workers.   (4 marks)

   ii The workers that Suzanne employs are not in a trade union. What benefits can workers gain from being in a trade union?   (4 marks)

b Tastybread Bakeries Ltd is a large firm. A single union represents all the workers at Tastybread Bakeries Ltd. Explain the benefits of single union agreements to:

   i the workers   (2 marks)

   ii the management.   (2 marks)

Advice on how to answer the questions

Question 1

a Think of what it is like inside a small factory and how it would be best to tell the workers about health and safety matters. It is likely that they will need something that will remind them every day about some of the dangers. Explain why you have made your recommendation.

b Look again at Figure 1 giving the different types of employment laws.

Question 2

a i Refer to the laws that an employer must obey. ii State four benefits here – no explanation is needed.

b You need to be clear when explaining this. Why is it sometimes better that all the workers in a workplace belong to the one and only union? Why will it be easier for the employer to deal with the single union?

Key facts

- Labour laws deal with relations between workers and employers.
- Many laws are designed to protect the worker from employers who might treat them unfairly in some way.
- The worker can sue the employer if they think they have been unfairly treated.
- Disputes between workers and employers are heard at an employment tribunal. The tribunal can make a guilty employer pay a fine and pay compensation to the worker.
- Trade unions exist to help workers to deal with employers.
- Trade unions increase the power of workers because they represent the views of many people.
- Single union agreements exist in some firms. These simplify industrial relations between the workers and the employers.

Key Terms

Make sure you can explain each of the following Key Terms

Labour law This term refers to laws that deal with relations between workers and their employers, for example laws such as the Equal Pay Act and the Race Relations Act, which are designed to protect workers.

Employment tribunal A special court of law that deals with disputes between workers and employers.

Contract of employment A legal agreement between the worker and the employer.

Redundancy When employment is ended because the firm no longer needs the work that was done by an employee.

Trade unions Organisations that represent the interests of workers.

Pressure group An organisation that tries to influence the government and Parliament to pass laws in its favour.

Industrial action Actions taken by workers to put pressure on employers to give in to their demands.

Industrial relations The term for the dealings between unions and management.

Single union agreements Where workers and the employers agree that all workers will be represented by only one union.

Advisory Conciliation and Arbitration Service (ACAS) An organisation which helps to settle industrial relation disputes between workers and employers.

Organisation and communication

Learning Outcomes

By studying this unit you will be able to:

- **Explain the importance of communications to businesses**
- **Explain the different types and methods of communication, and give examples of each. Discuss when the different types and methods are appropriate for businesses to use**
- **Explain the different barriers that exist to communication and suggest ways of overcoming them**
- **Evaluate the uses of ICT for businesses**
- **Discuss and explain the importance, need for and types of organisation charts in business.**

Introduction

Whilst **ICT** technology has revolutionised the way we communicate and the way we work, it is interesting that personal contact is still considered by many business people, like Steve Bower, to be essential for business success. This unit looks at **communications** in more detail.

Me and my gadgets: Steve Bower

Steve Bower is the managing director of Seven Communications. Its website describes its business, 'We plan, design and build websites, touch-screen kiosks, information points, on-line stores and intranets for businesses in Stockport (South Manchester) and beyond'.

Steve spends about half of his time out of the office 'usually because I am pitching for business or looking after client needs'. He says that his most useful gadget 'must be my Blackberry, which has enabled me to work and communicate more effectively. It really

has improved the level of customer service I can provide through being able to respond to client requests quicker, whether I am out of the office or even on holiday'. While he admits to the importance of technology, Steve also emphasises the importance of meeting people in person, 'Even though I have been in technological environments all my working life, I prefer to network in person. I know it is revolutionary'.

Source: Adapted from the Manchester Evening News, *29 July 2008*

Good communication is important in many ways to businesses, and some examples of it are given in Figure 1:

What is communication?

Communication is the transmission of a message from a sender to a receiver. Figures

Figure 1 Communication and different kinds of business activity

Kind of business activity	Example of good communication
Marketing	• Effective advertising that informs and/or persuades the customer to buy the product • Market research that achieves good feedback from customers about their needs
Finance	• Clearly explaining a business plan to a bank manager to persuade him or her to give a loan • Communications about income and expenditures so that accurate accounts are kept
People in business	• Getting good information about applicants for a job so that a correct selection can be made • Developing a good understanding of a job so that a person is trained properly
Government and trade	• Businesses must understand government regulations that control business so that they know how to deal with them • Businesses need to make applications for grants of money from government
Production	• Workers discuss quality so that wastage of materials is avoided • Orders for stock are made so that production is not held up by a lack of stock

Activity

Activity 1: Matching terms – The importance of communication in business

Match the kind of business activity given in the first column with the example of communication in the second column.

Kind of business activity	Example of communication
Marketing	A computer-controlled robot is programmed to paint cars on the assembly line.
Finance	A sales representative visits a possible customer.
People in business	Information about new health and safety regulations is posted on a website.
Government and trade	A business sends out a bill to a customer for money that is owed.
Production	An employee is given a telling off for repeatedly being late for work.

Table 1 Examples of how communication is important in business

2 and 3 show **one-way communication** and **two-way communication**.

One-way communication is when the sender sends the message but does not receive a message in return. If an announcement is made over the tannoy at a pop concert you are attending, this is one-way communication because you cannot reply to the message. Another example would be an advertising leaflet pushed through your door. One-way communication is good for giving information.

Two-way communication takes place when the person receiving the message can reply to the sender. Having a conversation is an example of two-way communication. Two-way communication is important because:

- **Feedback** from the receiver makes it clear that the message has been received and understood.

- It is good for generating ideas and coming up with solutions to problems.

Internal and external communications

Internal communications take place between people who work in the same organisation. It may be vertical or horizontal – see Figure 4.

Vertical communication is between people on different layers of the organisation's hierarchy. It can be upward or downward. If a manager talks to workers (subordinates) it is an example of downward vertical communication. If a worker sends an email to his or her boss this is upward vertical communication.

Horizontal communication takes place when two people at the same level within the organisation structure communicate with each other.

External communication takes place between one person in an organisation and someone outside that organisation.

Formal and informal communications

Formal communication takes place when the official means of communicating are used within an organisation. Examples of these are letters, memos, faxes, official meetings and reports.

Informal communication can be just as important as – and sometimes more important than – formal communication. An example of an informal communication is a conversation during a break or at a social event.

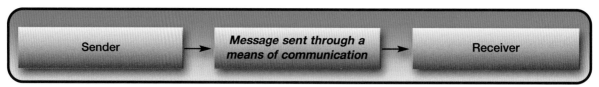

Figure 2 One-way communication

Figure 3 Two-way communication

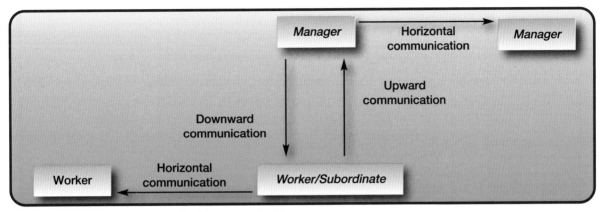

Figure 4 Horizontal and vertical communication

Activity

Activity 2: Types of communication

Table 2 shows some of the communications connected with Bolton Wanderers Football Club. Tick the boxes next to each item to say whether:

1 It is an example of internal or external communication

2 The communication is an example of formal or informal communication

3 The communication is likely to be one-way or two-way.

Table 2

Example of communication	Internal	External	Formal	Informal	One-way	Two-way
The team manager must talk with the directors about buying a new player.						
The ticket office must let the fans know that tickets for the cup final will be on sale from next Monday.						
Club officials talk to the police to agree security arrangements at games.						

The manager needs to discuss tactics with his coaching staff.						
The players complain about the manager's tactics as they get changed after the game.						
The personnel officer needs to write for references about applicants for a job.						
The stadium announcer must tell away supporters that their coaches will meet them in Car Park A after the match.						
The chief groundsman must tell one of his staff to mark the lines more clearly on the pitch.						
The marketing manager discusses an idea with the personnel manager over lunch.						
The marketing department must negotiate prices of replica shirts with a supplier.						

The marketing department must tell customers about the special Christmas gifts on sale in the club shop.						
The ticket office manager must agree a rota with the office workers to make sure there is someone there during all opening hours.						

Methods of communication

Verbal communication

There are several ways in which people can speak to one another: face-to-face discussions (one-to-one or in group meetings), voice-mail, tannoy announcements, on the telephone, on the radio, through presentations or lectures, or using video-conferencing.

Verbal communication	
Advantages	**Disadvantages**
● The person can check that the message has been understood by asking for feedback. ● The person can emphasise points by their tone of voice or their body language.	● If there are a lot of people listening to a message it may not be clear that all have heard or understood it. ● If the receiver of the message does not like what they hear, they may answer back and cause trouble. ● There is no permanent record of the message (unless minutes of what was said are taken, or a recording made). This may be important if a worker is being disciplined.

Figure 5 Advantages and disadvantages of using verbal communication

Written communication

There are many forms of written communications: letters, memos, reports, notices, faxes, e-mails, social networking websites, leaflets, books and so on.

Written communication	
Advantages	**Disadvantages**
● There is a record of the message. ● The receiver can read and reread the message to try to understand it. ● The message can be sent to more than one person at a time – for example, circular letters or advertising flyers. ● A written message can avoid confrontation.	● It is not possible to check immediately that the receiver has understood the message properly. ● The success of the message depends on how clearly it has been written.

Figure 6 Advantages and disadvantages of using written communications

Communication using images

Pictures, posters, diagrams and charts and TV and films are ways of communicating using images.

Communication using images	
Advantages	**Disadvantages**
● People often like looking at images. ● Images can have more imact – remember the saying 'a picture paints a thousand words'!	● As with written communication, it may not be possible to check immediately that the receiver has understood the message properly.

Figure 7 Advantages and disadvantages of using images

Evaluation point

When deciding how to communicate, businesses must consider who they are communicating with, what the purpose of the communication is and what methods of communicating are available and affordable. For example, if a business wishes to advertise to its potential customers, it can use a number of different media. If there are not many customers and they need technical information, it might be appropriate to send a personal representative. If there are a lot of customers for a mass consumer product such as an anti-perspirant deoderant, it might be appropriate to use TV, which can be used to send a persuasive message to a lot of people. If the communication is internal, different methods will be relevant. If there is a need to inform all workers about something, perhaps email will do but if there is a need to talk about problems at work, people may need to meet to have a discussion.

Activity

Activity 3: Explanation – Verbal, written and image communications

1 Write a short description of each of the methods of communication listed below. Note the advantages and disadvantages of each to business:

- telephone
- business letter
- faxes
- posters
- video
- website

2 For each of the cases (i)-(vii) below:

a You should say whether you would use verbal or written communications or use images. You may recommend more than one kind of communication.

b You should also should state what form the communication should take; for example, if you recommend written communication, state whether a letter or memo or fax or other form of written communication should be used.

Give reasons for your recommendations.

i A school with 1,500 pupils wishes to let pupils know that the school will not be open today because of problems with the central heating boiler.

ii A salesperson wishes to demonstrate the advantages of a new computer to a potential customer.

iii A holiday firm wishes to advertise its new brochure for next summer's holidays.

iv A project manager for a construction firm wishes to remind colleagues who work in several different departments located on different sites that there will be a meeting for all concerned later in the week.

v The social committee wants to advertise its summer barbecue to all workers.

vi A manager wishes to find out from workers in her department about an accusation made by a worker that he was racially abused by a colleague.

vii A firm wishes to advertise special offers for all its shareholders.

Barriers to communication

- **Timing.** The message may be sent at the wrong time. For example, a person who is in a rush to leave work for the day may not listen carefully to what his manager has to say to him.

- **Clarity.** The sender may not make the message clear to the receiver. This may be because the sender uses language that the receiver does not understand, or assumes that the receiver knows more than he or she actually does.

- **The attitudes of the sender or the receiver.** The sender may 'talk down' to the receiver so that he or she does like what they hear. The receiver may not trust or respect the sender and so does not take notice of what is said.

- **The wrong method of communication may be used**. An email giving an urgent message will not work if the receiver only checks for new email at the beginning of each week.

- **Feedback is not received or is not appropriate.** The sender may not check with the receiver that they have understood the message. The sender might ask the receivers of a message to give feedback in writing. This would not be suitable if people do not want to put their feelings or ideas down on paper.

● **There is a problem with the means of communication.** Email may not be received if there is a problem with the receiver's computer.

Activity

Activity 4: Explanation – Communication problems

For each of the cases below:

1 Explain why the problem may have arisen.

2 Recommend how you would deal with them.

　i Two workers have had an argument. A friend of one of the workers has said that the other worker has been saying bad things about him. As the manager of the office in which they both work, you do not want any 'bad blood' to affect how they work together.

　ii A manager has sent a page of written instructions to a clerical assistant about how to lay out a report but the assistant does not understand what is required.

　iii Workers are not obeying a safety notice instructing them to wear hard hats at all times. Many of the workers have not seen the notice; others have seen it but have chosen to ignore it.

　iv A school has sent a message home with a pupil asking her parents to get in touch about missing homework. However, the pupil has never passed the message on.

Information and communications technology (ICT)

Work in offices has been revolutionised by information and communications technology. Sefton Education Business Partnership (SEBP) provides a service linking businesses and schools in the Borough of Sefton on Merseyside. The services that it provides include arranging work-experience placements and mock interviews for all the pupils in Sefton schools, providing activities to develop personal skills, co-ordinating industry days and organising teacher placements. ICT is very important to the work of SEBP. Some of the uses that SEBP makes of ICT are described below:

● *Word-processing* for letters, reports and teaching materials.

● *Graphics packages* for putting images into documents such as teaching materials to make them look good.

● *Spreadsheets* for keeping the accounts.

● *Databases* for keeping records of work placements and pupils who use them.

● *Presentation software* for presentations to pupils and to businesses.

● *Email* for communications with schools, business and employees.

● *The internet* for advertising the EBP and for researching data to be used in teaching materials.

● *The intranet* for sharing files within the office.

Mobile phone technology

The speed of change in the world of communications is remarkable, and what has happened with mobile phones in recent years is an excellent example of this. Now these are not just phones for talking and texting on but are also organisers, cameras (still and video), GPS systems for navigation, and music players. They can be used to email and access the internet.

The advantages of using ICT

- The productivity of workers is high. Workers are able to produce more than they could without using ICT, and produce work more quickly.

- The quality of the presentation of the work is better.

- Information can be shared more easily.

- Large amounts of information can be processed very quickly.

- Communications, both internally and externally, may be improved and can be achieved more quickly.

- ICT makes the use of mail-shots of information to large numbers of customers possible at a reasonable cost.

- Computer-controlled telephone systems can be used to phone thousands of numbers with a recorded message.

- Workers have greater freedom about where to work – at home, on holiday, on the train, in the car, etc.

- Businesses can communicate better with their customers.

- Less office space is needed, especially when workers work at home, and this can save the business money.

Disadvantages of using ICT

- Workers need training to use the technology efficiently and this costs money.

- It is expensive to invest in computer technology. It also becomes obsolete (out of date) very quickly and needs replacing.

- Technical problems can occur with the computer. If the problem is on a server, all work may have to stop.

- Workers need to be aware of the health and safety issues related to using computers. They should use anti-glare screens and take regular breaks to prevent eyestrain. Some heavy users of keyboards have experienced repetitive strain injury (RSI) – problems with hand and wrist joints.

- Hackers can (sometimes) steal information and credit card numbers.

Activity

Activity 5: Research activity – ICT in a school

Write a report about the use of ICT in your school. Your report may deal with:

- The work of the administration (the school secretary and the bursar)

- The work of the examinations officer who is responsible for the entry of pupils for examinations

- The work of teachers – creating materials, teaching in class, keeping records, writing reports and so on.

In each case your report should cover:

1 What ICT is used and what it is used for

2 The advantages that the users have found from using ICT

3 The problems that they have using ICT.

You should prepare questions to ask the people who use ICT. To save time and trouble, you may work in groups to prepare the questions. Arrange for one or two members of the group to carry out the interview with one of the workers. You might find it useful to post the answers that you get on the school intranet – then other people in the class can have access to the information as well as pupils in future years.

Write your report. If it is practical, word-process your report.

Government and ICT

Data protection law states that people are entitled to have access to data about themselves that is stored electronically.

Organisations that use ICT must comply with health and safety regulations.

The effect of technology on work

Where people work and the nature of the work that they do has changed significantly with developments in technology.

Working from home

Many workers are now able to work from home. They may have an office in their home containing a computer, telephone and fax machine. They contact clients by telephone or fax or email. Reports can be written on the computer and sent by email to the client or to the employer. Meetings at the offices of the employer may not take place very often – perhaps only when problems arise that require face-to-face discussions to produce solutions. Some businesses are using video-conferencing so that workers do not even have to come to work for meetings. (All this is very good environmentally since it reduces the amount of travel that workers need to do.)

More people work at home

Hours of work

ICT has made it possible for people to work at different times. Work does not need to be done during office hours. However, some workers may find that they work longer because there is no restriction on the time they can work. This may be good if they want to do this and are paid for it, but it may cause stress and harm a person's work–life balance. Figure 8 shows the advantages and disadvantages of working from home.

Working from home	
Advantages	**Disadvantages**
● The worker saves time by not having to travel to work. ● The worker saves money by not having to travel to work. ● The workers have more freedom about how much they work and what hours they work. ● There may be fewer distractions at home than in a busy office environment.	● The worker may not be able to exchange ideas with fellow workers if he or she does not see them very often. ● Some workers need the discipline of clocking on and off at work. ● There may be a lack of space or facilities at home. ● There may be distractions from family and friends. ● The worker may miss the social side of working with other people.

Figure 8 Advantages and disadvantages of working from home

Evaluation point

The way in which we work has changed dramatically in recent years. New technology has made it possible for more work to be done at home. This can save money, increase staff motivation and enable them to work with greater concentration. However, working at home is not always possible or desirable. Where face-to-face contact is needed, working at home may not be successful. Also some businesses need to be located near to their customers – a recruitment specialist could work from home, but it would create a better image for the business and be more convenient for meeting customers if it had an office near to its main customers, say in the centre of a city or town. Many workers now spend some time working at their place of work and some at home.

Activity

Activity 6: Zone activity – Working from home

The following statements are either advantages or disadvantages to business of allowing workers to work at home. Put them under the correct heading in Table 3.

a Workers feel trusted that they will do the work they have to.

b It is not as easy for workers to talk to each other to discuss ideas about a job.

c The worker can concentrate better without the distractions of others at work.

d Workers will need to be trained to use the technology, which costs time and money.

e The technology may be expensive to buy.

f The worker is less stressed because there is no need to travel to work.

g Some workers like the social side of work and may not be as happy working on their own.

h Some workers may find that there are distractions at home from family and friends.

i Time may be wasted if unsupervised workers do not focus or do not understand properly what they need to do.

j The worker feels good because he or she saves the cost of travelling to work.

k The worker can work whatever hours they wish as long as they get the job done, and this can take some stress away.

l Some workers need the discipline of having to start work at certain times and having to be supervised.

Advantages of working at home	Disadvantages of working at home

Table 3

Teleworking and call centres

There has been a growth in teleworking and call centres.

Peter Schonberg works in telesales for Martin Mulligan UK in St Helens. Mulligan's sells bar code equipment. Peter's job is to call firms to ask for their address and telephone number. He records these on a database. The sales team will ring these contacts to try to sell them the bar code equipment. The equipment is stored elsewhere. When a sale is made, the order is passed to the warehouse for the goods to be delivered and installed. The firm saves money because it does not need a lot of sales representatives with company cars who visit clients to arrange deals. Neither does it need expensive sales offices that people visit to view the equipment. In fact, the office is sited in low-rent office space in a run-down part of the town.

John Didds works at Gifts for U call centre in Preston. He answers the telephone all day, recording orders for gifts chosen from the firm's Christmas catalogue. John has never seen any of the gifts that the firm sells, only pictures of them in the catalogue. Orders are entered onto the firm's computer system and will be processed at the warehouse on an industrial estate out of the town. Like Mulligan's, Gifts for U does not require expensive offices. Nor does it need shops on the High Street where rents are high and many shop assistants are required.

Call centre work continues to increase

Technology also allows automated calls. A pre-recorded message is made and telephone equipment is programmed to dial, sometimes hundreds of thousands of numbers.

Activity

Activity 7: Explanation – Working from home

a What do you think are the main advantages of teleworking?

b Why might workers not like working in telesales or call centres?

Organisation charts

Organisation charts can be used to examine how production is organised. They show how responsibilities in an organisation are divided up amongst different departments and people. An example of an organisation chart is shown on the next page.

Explanation of Griffin Engineering Ltd Organisation Chart

Griffin Engineering Ltd makes components for cars. The departments in the business are organised by **function**. This means that each department has a specific job to do. For example, the *purchasing department* will be responsible for buying in the materials which are needed to make the components, the *sales department* will be responsible for finding customers to buy the components and the *personnel department* will carry out all the jobs connected with recruitment, training and relations with the workforce. The *information technology and research departments* have responsibility for helping all the other departments when they need it. For example, the IT manager will give advice to other departments about the kind of hardware and software which the other departments should use.

The organisation of Griffin Engineering Ltd is a **hierarchy** with several **layers**. Employees

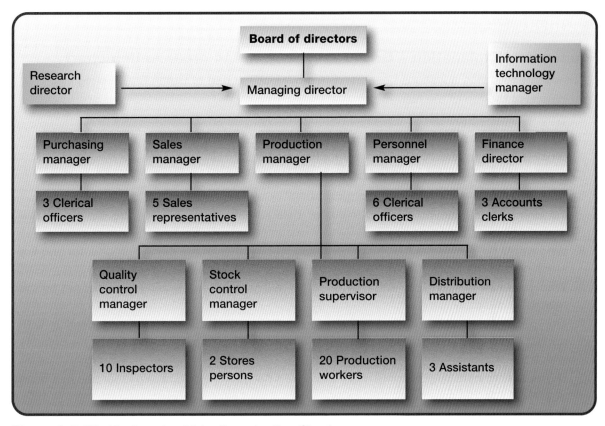

Figure 9 Griffin Engineering Ltd – Organisation Chart

on the higher layers have more responsibility and **authority** than those on the layers below. Authority is the power to make decisions and the right to tell other workers what they have to do. **Accountability** goes with authority. If something goes wrong, the person at fault is the one with responsibility for that function. There is a **chain of command** with those at the top of the hierarchy being able to send instructions to those lower down. The managing director of Griffin Engineering Ltd has more authority than the production manager, who is on a lower layer of the organisation. The managing director could send an order to the quality control manager through the production manager. This would represent the **line of communication** through which the order was made.

The person a worker is responsible to is their **line manager**. The workers for whom someone is responsible are known as their **subordinates**. The number of subordinates for whom a manager is responsible is known as their **span of control**. The sales manager has a span of control of five – he or she is the line manager for the five sales representatives who are his or her subordinates in that department. The line manager will have been **delegated** responsibility by his or her line manager. This means that he or she will have been given authority to make certain decisions and to carry out specific responsibilities. For example, the production manager may have delegated responsibility to the quality control manager for how the quality of production will be monitored. The information technology manager does not have a typical departmental responsibility. He or she is responsible for providing a service, technical support and advice, to all the other departments. Supporting departments across the hierarchy, the manager is a **staff manager**.

Activity

Activity 8: Explanation – Griffin Engineering Ltd organisation chart

Answer the following questions based on the organisation chart of Griffin Engineering Ltd.

1 Who is at the top of the hierarchy?
2 Who is the line manager of the sales representative?
3 Who are the subordinates of the finance director?
4 What is the span of control of the production manager?
5 Give one example of a staff manager.
6 How many layers are there in the organisation?
7 To whom would the production manager delegate responsibility for the stocks of raw materials?
8 Who would be involved in the line of communication between the managing director and the stock control manager?
9 Who would be accountable if the sales of the business did not reach the target set by the managing director?
10 The personnel manager delegates responsibility for advertising jobs and dealing with application forms to a subordinate. Write down which of the following might be benefits which result:

● The subordinate may become more motivated because he or she feels that she has been given a specific area of responsibility.
● The subordinate may feel that the personnel manager is taking advantage of him or her.
● The personnel manager may feel that he or she is losing responsibility and may not be paid as much by the firm.
● The personnel manager may have more time to oversee the work of all the members of the department rather than getting tied down by detailed work.
● The subordinate may improve his or her management skills and this could lead to future promotion.
● The work will be done by a specialist and so the quality of the work should improve.

Benefits of organisation charts

Organisation charts help businesses by showing:

● who is responsible for which functions and tasks

● what a person is accountable for

● which work is delegated to specialists in order to achieve a high quality of work

● to whom a worker is responsible and from whom they must take orders

● lines of communication within the organisation

● how different departments are linked together.

Formal and informal groups

An organisation chart ususally only shows the **formal groups**, such as the departments, which exist in an organisation. **Informal groups** often come into existence in many organisations. These are not set up by the organisation. An informal group could consist of people from different departments who meet together every day to have lunch or who play together in the work's football or hockey team.

Sometimes informal groups are good for the organisation. Workers in one department may share ideas with workers in another department. Their discussion may lead to better ways of doing things. However, informal groups can have a bad effect if people in the groups have negative attitudes to the firm and to work and these de-motivate other workers.

Tall and flat organisations

The height of an organisation chart depends on how many layers there are in it.

Organisation A has a tall structure. It has five layers – many organisations have more layers than this. Organisation B has a flat structure. It has only two layers.

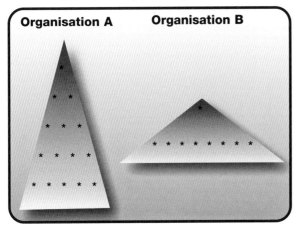

Organisation A   **Organisation B**

Tall and Flat Organisations

Advantages of tall structures

● The lines of communication and the responsibilities of the workers are clear.

● The span of control of managers is likely to be narrower than in flat structures, meaning that he or she does not have too many people to look after.

● There will be plenty of opportunities for workers to gain promotion which will motivate them.

Advantages of flat structures

● Communication from top to bottom will be quicker than in tall structures because there are not as many layers.

● It is likely that fewer mistakes in communications will occur because messages do not have to be passed through so many layers.

● People at the bottom may be encouraged to share ideas with those at the top because they will know who they are and what they are like.

● The wider spans of control of managers will mean that they must delegate work. This will make the workers feel trusted and help to motivate them.

De-layering

This is when one or more of the layers of management are removed from the business.

In the Griffin Engineering Ltd organisation chart in Figure 9, an example of de-layering would be if the managers directly below the production manager were removed – the quality control manager, the stock control manager and the production supervisor. De-layering has the following advantages:

● It saves money since the organisation will no longer need to pay the salaries of the workers it has laid off.

● The responsibilities of those workers who were laid off would need to be delegated to the next layer of workers. If this happens, the workers are said to have been **empowered**. These workers may feel good about having extra responsibility and being trusted by senior managers to make decisions. However, some workers would not be happy to accept the responsibility.

Examination questions

1 Finance Bank plc is a high street bank which operates throughout the UK.

   a From its market research, Finance Bank plc found the following information.

     i Using Figure 10, state the percentage of households which had access to the internet by the end of 2004.   (1 mark)

     ii Analyse the data shown in Figure 10, and advise Finance Bank plc whether it should introduce an on-line banking service.

                                 (5 marks)

   b Finance Bank plc has decided to introduce an on-line banking service. It will be called **e-bank**. The Marketing Director needs to inform new and existing customers about the services which e-bank will provide. She is thinking about using one of the following methods of communication to inform present and new customers about e-bank.

     ● email

     ● leaflets

     ● television advertisements.

     Explain which of the above methods of communication e-bank should use. You should make reference to **each** method of communication in your answer.   (5 marks)

   c The managing director of e-bank is deciding whether to allow its employees to work from home instead of from the office. Figures 11 and 12 show the number of people working from home in the UK and some of the factors e-bank needs to consider before making a decision.

     Using Figures 11 and 12, and any other information, advise the managing director whether she should allow e-bank employees to work from home instead of from the office.

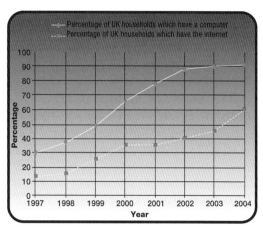

Figure 10 Percentage of households with internet access

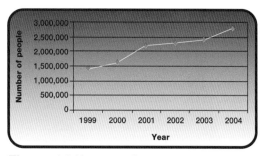

Figure 11 Homeworkers

Factors for consideration

Cost

Motivation of workers

Quantity of work completed

Quality of work completed

Size of premises

Communication

Figure 12 E-bank considerations

2 Ryan and White is a medium-sized business which makes and sells expensive wedding dresses.

    a State **two** methods Ryan and White may use to communicate with its customers. Explain why the methods you have chosen are appropriate for this business.   (4 marks)

    b The list below shows three potential barriers to communication. State the reasons why each factor may be a barrier to communication.

        ● attitude of sender

        ● language used

        ● method used.   (3 marks)

Advice on how to answer the questions

Question 1

a i Read the data carefully to find the answer

  ii To be successful a business will need lots of customers. The data will help you to decide whether or not the bank will get enough customers. Clearly explain your decision and make sure you mention the data in your answer.

b Think about who the bank needs to advertise to (Where will the customers be? Will they have computers, TVs, etc.?). What information will the bank have about possible customers (Will it have their home addresses, their email addresses, etc?) and how much money it can afford to spend? Write about the advantages and disadvantages of each method and then decide which method of communication to use, giving a reason for your decision.

c There is no correct answer to this question. You will need to consider the advantages and disadvantages of letting the workers work at home. Your decision may depend upon the type of work that they do. Do they need to be with other workers to discuss things? Do they need to be managed while they are working?

Question 2

a You need to choose two methods that are appropriate for this kind of business – consider who the customers are and what they want. You must suggest methods that are relevant to a wedding dress business, so think about who the customers are likely to be. Remember also that it is medium-sized and that it sells expensive dresses, as these factors will affect what it can afford to do.

b This is a knowledge question. You need to explain what each barrier means and why it is a barrier to communication; there is no need to relate to a particular business or person. You may write about internal or external communication to explain your answer.

Key facts

- Good communications are essential to business.
- There are many kinds and methods of communication.
- For communication to be effective it is important to choose the appropriate methods of communication.
- There are many barriers to communication.
- Good communications deal with these barriers.
- Information technology has improved the speed and effectiveness of communications in business.
- Developments in technology have led to changes in the nature and location of work.
- There is a lot of business terminology associated with organisation charts.
- Organisation charts can take very different forms depending on the type of business and the objectives that the business is trying to achieve.

Key Terms

Make sure you can explain each of the following Key Terms

Communications The transmission of a message from a sender to a receiver through a means of communication.

Feedback The response made by a person who receives a communication that indicates that they have, or have not, understood the communication.

Internal communications Communications between people employed in the same organisation.

Vertical communications Communications up or down the hierarchy within an organisation.

Horizontal communications Communications between people on the same level of the hierarchy in an organisation.

External communications Communications between people in an organisation and others outside that organisation.

Formal communications Communications that use the official channels of communication within an organisation.

Informal communications Communications that are outside the official channels of communication within an organisation.

Information and communications technology (ICT) The use of technology to facilitate communications.

Organisation chart A diagram which shows how the workers are organised in a business and who is in charge of whom.

Function The specific job that a person or department must do.

Hierarchy This is when a business is organised from the top down, the people higher up the hierarchy having more power than those below them.

Layers The number of levels of authority which there are in a chain of command.

Authority The power that one person has to make decisions and to control what other workers do.

Accountability The responsibility that a person has for a job meaning that he or she will take the blame for what goes wrong as well as the credit for what goes well.

Chain of command The link in the levels of authority from those at the top with the most authority to those at the bottom with the least.

Line of communication The route that a message travels between the sender and the person that it is for.

Line manager This is a person who is directly responsible for other workers in the organisation.

Subordinates The workers that a line manager is responsible for.

Span of control The number of subordinates who report directly to the line manager.

Delegated The process of giving a manager authority to a subordinate to make decisions for which that manager is responsible.

Staff manager A person who supports other departments across the organisation.

PRODUCTION, FINANCE AND THE EXTERNAL BUSINESS ENVIRONMENT

PART 3

Introductory Activity

Learning Outcomes

By studying this unit you will be able to:

- **Explain that globalisation has had an increasing impact on business throughout the world**
- **Explain the main advantages and disadvantages to China and to the UK resulting from the increase in globalisation**
- **Explain that globalisation brings a lot of opportunities for UK businesses.**

The following extracts are taken from a number of different websites. They give an introduction to the study of globalisation.

Dr Martens goes to China

Dr Martens, whose shoes have been worn by Madonna and the Pope, today said it was closing its British factories and moving production to China with the loss of 1,000 jobs.

Source: Guardian.co.uk. 25 February 2002

It is not just Britain that is affected by the development of China.

China: the world's factory floor

National Presto industries in America makes pressure cookers and electric frying pans. Its profits have fallen as a result of competition from China, which now makes high quality goods. The same story is affecting producers all over America.

Source: Adapted from the BBC website

China's share of global output

Cameras: over 50%

Air conditioners: 30%

TV sets: 30%

Washing machines: 25%

Fridges: 20%

Source: Far Eastern Economic Review

It is not just China that is producing goods that used to be made in Britain.

645 jobs lost as Nestlé ships Smarties abroad

Nestlé, the world's largest food and drink company, yesterday announced the loss of 645 jobs at the famous Rowntree chocolate factory in York as it brought to an end 70 years of producing Smarties in the UK.

Smarties, which have been made at the factory in York since 1937, will now be produced in a Nestlé factory in Hamburg. The company is also shifting to Spain the production of the chocolates Dairy Box, and moving the Black Magic line to the Czech Republic.

Source: Guardian.co.uk 21 September 2006

It is not just manufacturing jobs that are being moved abroad.

Lloyds TSB offshores 450

Hundreds of IT jobs could be lost at Lloyds TSB as part of the bank's plans to offshore 450 posts from the UK to India this year, a trade union is warning.

Source: www.silicon.com

Globalisation is influenced by methods of production and costs, especially labour costs.

Manufacturing in Europe has challenges not least in terms of average wage rates. Workers are paid $18/hr in the UK and $36/hr in Germany. This compares with Poland, $2.7/hr; India, $1.12/hr; and China, $0.8/hr.

Source: Adapted from: www.processengineering.co.uk

It is not all bad news for developed countries like the United States of America and the UK.

Globalisation has resulted in a fall in the prices of many goods. The price of TV sets has dropped by 9% and sports equipment by 3% since 1998.

Source: Adapted from the BBC website

There are opportunities abroad for UK business.

UKTI paves the way to China for Ashford-based company

It's a bold and far-reaching step from Kent to China, but it's a step that offers the ideal route to expansion for Ashford-based Integrated Technologies Ltd, or ITL.

This flourishing business, which specialises in contract design, development and manufacture of instruments in use throughout the Life Sciences sector, employs 90 staff and achieves a £14.5 million turnover, forecast to grow to £16 million next year. But its Ashford facility is bursting at the seams with work and the creation of a second centre of expertise in China will enable ITL to develop smoothly and strongly in world markets.

Source: www.uktradeinvest.gov.uk

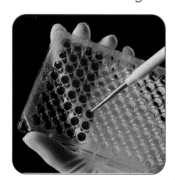

These opportunities are not just in China.

Brazil has a broad and sophisticated industrial base. There is a growing middle class in Brazil who have real spending power and who appreciate high quality products. If a product or service is generally competitive in world markets it is also likely to be so in Brazil.

The UK's top exports to Brazil include:

● Power generation machinery

● Medicinal and pharmaceutical products

● Chemical materials and products

● Plastics in non-primary forms

● Organic chemicals

● Road vehicles

● General industrial machinery and equipment

● Professional scientific instruments.

There are also opportunities for UK companies to help develop the infrastructure needed for the Football World Cup 2014 which will be hosted in Brazil.

Source: www.uktradeinvest.gov.uk

Even sending jobs abroad can be good for Britain.

Sending jobs abroad creates thousands more jobs in the UK

The growing trend for British firms to send jobs overseas has actually helped boost employment in the UK, creating thousands of jobs, according to new research.

Economists at the Globalisation and Economic Policy Centre, from Nottingham University, showed that far from increasing unemployment in the UK, the policy (of moving production abroad) had resulted in the creation of 100,000 extra jobs and an increase of £10bn in company turnover in the UK.

Source: Adapted from:
http://communications.nottingham.ac.uk

And businesses that stay in the UK can still grow and compete.

Bisley Office Furniture, based in Woking, Surrey, is the largest manufacturer of office furniture in the UK. Its product range includes storage systems, multi-drawers, media and card storage units, filing cabinets and cupboards.

The business has around 1,000 employees and a turnover of approximately £70million. About a quarter of this is generated through exports. It is continuing to compete and grow by improving design. Better design work in particular is contributing to creating new markets, developing new products, improving competitiveness, and increasing turnover and profit.

Source: www.designfactfinder.co.uk/

They might not always be UK-owned businesses.

Indian IT services giant Tata Consultancy Services has opened a new Midlands-based innovation centre that will bring the latest thinking and technologies to UK business.

Source: www.ukinvest.gov.uk

Many people in China and other developing countries are benefiting from globalisation.

Living conditions and the consumption of durable goods has increased. For example, owning a car was still a dream to many families years ago. But not today.

Source: http://english.peopledaily.com

Globalisation is not all good news for the people of the developing countries like China.

The story examines the grim working conditions for women who represent 48.5 per cent of the total Chinese population and 45 per cent of the nation's workforce. Forced to live away from their families in company dormitories, many women regularly toil fourteen hours a day, six days a week, earning less than sixty dollars a month.

Source: www.goiam.org

It may not be good for the environment of countries like China – or the world as a whole.

It is now thought that China emits more carbon dioxide than any other country in the world.

Source: Adapted from the BBC website

Activity 1: Listing – Advantages and disadvantages of globalisation

Complete the tables below to weigh up the advantages and disadvantages to China as a developing country and to the UK as a developed country that have resulted from globalisation. List how both consumers and producers have been affected.

Benefits to China	Disadvantages to China

Table 1

Benefits to the UK	Problems for the UK

Table 2

Activity 2: Research activity – Opportunities abroad for UK businesses

Use the website www.uktradeinvest.gov.uk. Choose a country and write a short newspaper article to describe the opportunities for British businesses in that country.

Requirements of the examination – production, finance and the external business environment

Learning Outcomes

By studying this unit you will be able to:

● **Explain the different skills that the examination tests**

● **Explain what you have to do to answer questions that test the different skills**

● **Explain how much you will be expected to write**

● **List the main content of the specification that you will be tested on**

● **Feel confident about what you need to learn to perform well in this examination.**

What is the name of the examination?

The examination is called 'Unit A293: Production, Finance and the External Business Environment'.

What will the exam be like?

● This is a pre-release case study examination. A case study is information about a business situation. 'Pre-release' means that you will be given this information before you sit the examination. Your teacher will probably give it to you months before the examination so that you know what you are preparing for.

● The examination for this unit will last for one hour and thirty minutes.

● There will be a total of 90 marks. The marks will count for 50 per cent of your overall score in Business Studies GCSE.

● There will be three main questions. Each of these will be divided into a number of parts.

● The questions will be based on the case study.

What will the exam test?

The examination tests three skills:

1 **Knowledge.** How well you can define business terms and can explain business ideas. *Example.* You might be asked to define what is meant by the term 'globalisation' or to explain the advantages of competition.

2 **Application.** How well you can use your knowledge to explain a business situation.

Example. You might be asked to explain how a rise in costs may affect the break-even output of a firm

3 **Analysis and evaluation**. This is about weighing up advantages and disadvantages, or pros and cons, in order to make judgements. You may need to suggest how good or bad something is or what a business should do. You might need to recommend what a business should do and then give your reasons why you think this is the right thing to do. *Example.* You could be asked to recommend whether or not a business should move its production to another country. You could be asked to judge if immigration has been good for businesses.

The questions on the examination paper will test different skills. Some will test only knowledge. Those that test application and analysis and evaluation will usually require some knowledge. The marks for the different skills on this paper are:

    Knowledge – 27 marks
    Application – 31 marks
    Analysis and evaluation – 32 marks.

Note that the examination tests your knowledge of terms and business ideas. You should learn these well! However, it has more emphasis on the skills of application and analysis and evaluation than the 'Unit A292: Business and People' examination. You should practise these skills as much as you can before doing this examination.

Something extra about analysis and evaluation questions

Sometimes with evaluation questions it is difficult to come to a definite decision. What you can then do is write that you need more information – and explain what that information is. Also, what is the right answer might depend on certain things – for example, a business may be better moving abroad if it cannot reduce its costs by using more technology. You may find the writing frame below helps to plan an answer for an evaluation question. The example statements in the writing frame are connected with the question below.

Sample question

XYZ Ltd is a manufacturing business based in the south of England. It is in a highly competitive market. It is considering moving its production to China in order to be better able to compete. Recommend whether or not XYZ Ltd should move production to China.

Figure 1 Sample writing frame

Introduction	
Briefly explain the problem.	
Advantages/For/Good Bits	**Disadvantages/Against/Bad bits**

Write down the advantages of something or the reasons for following a course of action.
    For example: *the arguments for producing goods abroad.*
	Write down the disadvantages of something or the reasons for not doing something.
	    For example: *the arguments against producing goods in the UK.*

Conclusion	
Make your decision and explain why you have come to it. Alternatively, say what other information is needed or what the recommendation will depend upon. For example: *XYZ Ltd would be better moving production abroad unless it can introduce new technology that will lower its costs and which would make it more competitive.*	

How difficult will the questions be?

The questions on this examination will vary in difficulty. Some are used to test the F and G candidates, some are there to challenge the A and A* candidates. Some of them can be answered in different ways – a simple answer might gain a grade E or F while a more sophisticated answer might be awarded B or A grade marks.

The people who set the examination spend hours working to make sure that the examination will be a fair test of what you, as a GCSE Business Studies pupil, should be able to do. They are not trying to catch you out. Please remember that the examination is supposed to be *an opportunity for you to show of how good you are at business studies.*

How much should I write

The number of lines that are provided for your answer is a good guide as to how much you should write. If there are ten lines and you only fill two of them, you may not have developed your answer as fully as you should.

Content – the knowledge

There are three main sections to Unit A293: Production, Finance and the External Business Environment.

The first section is called **'Using and managing resources to produce goods and services'**. There are three main parts to this:

● Types of production methods

● Management and control of production

● Production costs.

Job production is one method of production

The second section is called **'Financial information and decision-making'**. There are two main parts to this:

● Sources of finance

● Financial forecasting and analysis.

I did not forecast this!

The third section is called: **'External influences on business activity'**. There are four main parts to this:

● The competitive environment

● Environmental influences and business ethics

● Government and the UK economy

● Globalisation and UK business.

It is unethical to copy, I have the intellectual property rights for this essay

Themes for questions

The list below is designed to give you an idea of the main question themes that come up on this paper. It is not meant to be a comprehensive list. Each of the units in this section of the book has examples of the types of questions that are asked on this examination. When you have finished studying this unit, you should feel confident that you could give an answer to these questions.

● Which method of production should a business use to produce a particular good or service?

● How can a business increase its efficiency?

● What are economies of scale? Why do firms get them? What benefits do they bring?

● What are break-even charts? What use do businesses make of them? What are their limitations?

● When will businesses use the different sources of finance?

● What are cash-flow forecasts? Why are they useful to businesses? What are their limitations?

● What are profits? Why are they important for businesses? What determines how much profit a business will make?

● What are the advantages and disadvantages of competitive markets and monopolies? How can the government control monopolies?

● How can businesses respond to the pressures on the environment? Why should they respond to these pressures? How can the government influence business to protect the environment more?

● What are ethical and unethical business practices (giving examples)?

● How are businesses affected by changes in employment and the incomes of consumers (economic growth and recession)?

● How do changes in interest rates affect businesses?

● How are businesses affected by changes in government spending and taxation?

● Is foreign competition a problem? What can UK businesses do to improve how well they compete against foreign firms?

● Why are education and training so important for UK business?

● Is immigration good or bad for UK businesses?

● What is globalisation? Is globalisation helping UK businesses or is it causing them problems? How can UK businesses compete better? What help can the government give to businesses to improve their competitiveness?

● How do changes in the exchange rate of the pound sterling affect UK business?

● Should the UK join the Eurozone?

● What are the benefits and problems for UK businesses of the country's membership of the European Union?

Unit 3.3.1

Types and control of production

Learning Outcomes

By studying this unit you will be able to:

- **Discuss and explain the process of production**
- **Explain the difference between different types of production methods**
- **Recognise and explain when it is appropriate to use different types of production methods**
- **Discuss production methods and how these may change and develop with the scale of production and the introduction of machinery.**

Introduction

Engels Stationery Ltd produces a variety of goods needed in offices. Its largest selling line is ring-pull files. It competes with a number of other businesses that also produce similar ring-pull files.

To stay competitive, Engels Stationery Ltd must make a number of decisions about the production of the ring-pull files. It must consider the following:

- **The *costs* of production.** It is important to keep the costs of production as low as possible. The lower the cost, the lower the price which Engels can charge for the ring-pull files. If its price is higher than prices charged by competitors, it will lose sales.

- **The *quality* of the ring-pull files.** The ring-pull files must be of good quality. If they are not, customers will not be satisfied with them. Customers may decide not to order any more ring-pull files from Engels Stationery Ltd.

- **The *quantity* of ring-pull files to produce.** Engels Stationery Ltd must make enough ring-pull files to meet the demand for them. If it does not, it will have lost the opportunity to make a profit. Also, customers unable to buy what they want from Engels Stationery Ltd may buy from competitors instead. These customers may continue to buy from the competitors in the future. It is also important for Engels Stationery Ltd not to produce too many ring-pull files. If it produces more than it can sell, it will need to store the ring-pull files and this will cost money.

- **The ring-pull files that customers *want*.** Engels must keep in touch with its customers so that it knows the kinds of ring-pull files which they want. Businesses that do this are 'market-oriented'.

The information in this unit will help to explain how a business like Engels Stationery Ltd may make these decisions.

Producing goods

Producing goods involves a series of activities. This is shown in the table and figure below.

Stage 1	Research what customers want and develop and design products to meet their needs.
Stage 2	Identify the resources (raw materials, components, labour, capital equipment, etc.) needed in the production process to create a finished product or service. It is essential that this process is one that achieves **added value**. This occurs when the revenue earned from sales is greater than the costs involved in producing the product or service.
Stage 3	Obtain feedback from customers. The business may need to change the design of its product in some way, depending upon what customers say.

Figure 1 Stages in producing goods

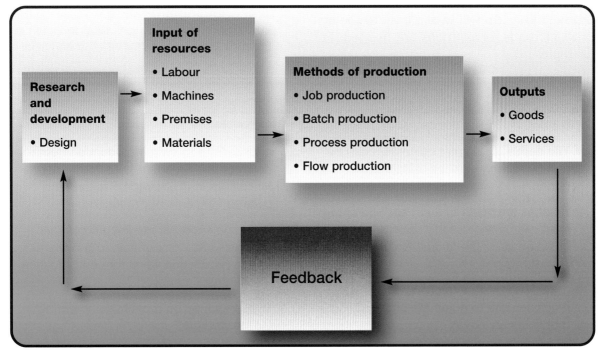

Figure 2 Flow of production

Methods of production

Job production

This method of production involves producing each product individually. For example:

- Eunice Khan is a sculptress. She makes figures out of stone. She works on one sculpture at a time until it is finished.

- Marston Borough Council has paid for a new school to be built. The construction company that is building the school will work on the project until it is finished.

Job production	
Advantages	**Disadvantages**
● Products are usually high quality. ● Products can be made to meet the needs of individual customers. ● Workers often get more satisfaction from working on something until it is finished.	● Costs of production will be high. ● Labour costs may be high because job production often requires skilled labour.

Figure 3 Advantages and disadvantages of job production

Batch production

This method of production involves producing one type of a product for a while, then changing production to another type of product. The firm will switch back to the first product made when more are needed. For example:

● Bakers use **batch production**. They may bake a batch of one kind of bread and then switch production to make a batch of a different kind of bread.

● Some clothing manufactures use batch production, switching production between different sizes and styles of clothing.

Batch production	
Advantages	**Disadvantages**
● The needs of different customers can be met by making batches of different goods. ● Batches are made to meet specific orders from customers and this may reduce costs because the goods may not need storing. ● It may be possible to use specialist machines and to automate production so that costs are saved.	● It takes time to switch production from a batch of one product to a different batch. Machinery may need to be re-set. This adds to the costs of production. ● It may be necessary to keep stocks of materials and components to be able to switch production when required. Holding stocks costs money. ● The tasks may be repetitive and boring for the workers.

Figure 4 Advantages and disadvantages of batch production

Process production

This method of production involves a series of automated processes which, when applied to a variety of raw materials, results in a large quantity of a finished product. For example:

● BP uses this type of production method to refine crude oil into petrol and other products.

● Rugby Cement also uses this type of process to turn raw materials into cement used in the building industry.

Process production	
Advantages	**Disadvantages**
• Large amounts can be made. • Most processes can be automated to allow production costs to be kept low. • The process is ideally suited to products that have to be of a consistent and very exacting quality.	• It is very expensive to set up a process system of production. • A problem with one part of the production process stops the whole process. Starting up or shutting down production can take a long time.

Figure 5 Advantages and disadvantages of process production

Flow production

This method of production involves an assembly line. One kind of product is made continuously. The goods are mass-produced. For example:

• Ford uses **flow production** to make cars. The cars are assembled on a production line. The cars move along a conveyor belt. Different workers and machines complete different tasks as the car moves along.

• Glass is made using flow production. The raw materials are heated and mixed. The glass is moved on flowing water to be cooled and polished.

Flow production	
Advantages	**Disadvantages**
• Large amounts can be made. • The costs of production for each unit made are low because the firm benefits from economies of large-scale production. • Machinery can be used, helping to keep costs low. • Improvements in technology mean that not all the products need to be the same; variations in design can be programmed into the computer-controlled machines.	• Goods are mass-produced and may not be of good quality. • It is very expensive to set up a production line. • Large stocks of materials may have to be kept to keep the production line supplied, and this may be expensive. • If the production stops at any point on the assembly line (because of a mechanical breakdown or industrial action) there may be a complete shut down of production. • Jobs on an assembly line can be repetitive and boring.

Figure 6 Advantages and disadvantages of flow production

Division of labour and specialisation

One of the major advantages of flow production is that many processes which require a labour input can be broken down into small repetitive tasks. As a result of breaking down the production process into a number of small specialised tasks, the amount of time needed to train a worker to undertake the task may not be very long.

While workers may become very efficient

at doing their job, because of the number of times they complete the task each day, the job can become very boring and workers may become demotivated. However, by allowing workers to specialise in production tasks, productivity can improve.

Evaluation points

1 You will need to be able to explain in detail why businesses are sometimes limited as to the type of manufacturing process they are able to use for the product(s) that they make.

2 You will also need to consider how the different production processes allow businesses to keep control of their costs, and the problems that may occur if the business over-produces products.

Activity

Activity 1: True or False – Types of production

Tick one box to indicate if the statement is true or false.

Statement	True ✔	False ✔
Modern businesses do not use job production.		
Flow production is suited to the manufacture of up-market sports cars.		
It is cheap to set up a production system.		
Flow production is suited to large-scale production.		
Flow production is cheap to set up.		
Low-volume production is suited to both job and flow production.		
Job production does not require skilled labour.		
Flow production does not require a workforce.		
Flow production workers are usually highly skilled.		
Specialisation leads to reduced training times for workers.		
Many dangerous processes are best carried out by automated machinery.		
Specialisation allows jobs to be made more interesting.		
Large-scale production is suited to division of labour.		
Process production is suited to high volumes of high-quality production.		
Added value is achieved when revenue from sales is greater than production costs.		
Supermarket in-store bakeries use the batch production method.		
All businesses will try to introduce flow production.		

Activity

Activity 2: Explanation – Applying technology to production

Kingston Carpets Ltd produces a range of high-quality carpets. The carpets are designed in a design studio by a team of designers. Machinery is used to weave the carpets. The machines need to be reset for each different design of carpet. The machines that are used are operated manually. The business is planning to introduce new technology.

a State two types of technology that Kingston Carpets Ltd could use to design and make the carpets.

b Explain the benefits that the automation of production would bring to Kingston Carpets Ltd.

c Explain the problems that Kingston Carpets Ltd might face when it introduces the new technology.

Activity

Activity 3: Explanation – Types of production

For each of the production activities in the table below:

a Select the appropriate method of production from the following list:

- job
- batch
- process
- flow.

b Give reasons for your recommendations.

c Explain the problems which the business may face from using the method, or methods, of production you have recommended.

Production activity	Method of production	Reason for choice	Possible problems
A small company produces three different models of caravan. Each model requires a different steel frame. Some of the components the company makes are used in each of the three types of caravan.			
A specialist tailor makes made-to-measure suits.			
A specialist sports car manufacturer produces cars to order.			
A multi-national car company produces cars in the UK for export to the rest of Europe.			
A local bakery produces a range of bread and cakes for distribution to shops within a 20-mile radius of the bakery.			

An office furniture manufacturer produces solid-wood office furniture to order.			
A sugar refinery produces hundreds of tons of sugar each day.			
A business produces thousands of bottles of beer each day. The bottles need to be washed, filled, capped and labelled.			
An agricultural chemical company produces hundreds of bags of fertiliser each day.			

Activity

Activity 4: Missing terms – Types of production

Use the words below to help you fill in the gaps in the following paragraph.

- advantages and disadvantages
- type of product
- type of product
- technology
- production process
- volume of production
- another type
- batch
- product disadvantages
- Process

There are several different types of production – Job;_____; _____and Flow. Each _____will usually be appropriate for a particular_____. There are _____for each type of production but it does not necessarily follow that the_____of one type of production can be overcome by changing to_____of production. Much will depend on the_____being produced; the_____; the ease with which_____can be introduced in to the production process.

Examination questions

Carlton Press Ltd prints books.

a Which method of production – job, batch, process or flow – do you think would be most suitable for printing books? Give reasons for your answers. (4 marks)

b The directors of the business are attempting to win printing contracts for high-volume print runs, rather than small limited-edition print contracts. Explain why the directors may be seeking these contracts. (8 marks)

Advice on how to answer the question

In your answer to part (a) you need to relate your choice of method to the fact that Carlton Press will have to print a range of books, and that it may need to reprint some books if they are very popular.

In your answer to part (b) you will need to explain the advantages of large-scale production runs, as well as considering the disadvantages of relying on a smaller number of contracts. Consideration will also need to be given to the problems that machine breakdown may cause.

Key facts

- There are four main methods of production – job, batch, process and flow production.
- Each method of production has its own advantages and disadvantages.
- Automation can be an important part of a manufacturing process.
- Large-scale production creates opportrnities for division of labour.
- Listening to feedback from customers is an important part of the production process.
- Costs, quality, quantity and the wants of customers are important considerations in producing goods.

Key Terms

Make sure you can explain each of the following Key Terms

Added value The process of ensuring sales revenue is greater than the costs of production.

Job production The method of production where products are made individually.

Batch production The method of production where one type of product is made and then production is switched to make a different product.

Process production Usually an automated process suited to the large-scale manufacture of products.

Flow production Production of one product takes place continuously using a production or assembly line. This is sometimes called 'mass production'.

Division of labour The organisation of production into a number of specialised 'simple' repetitive processes.

Specialisation Occurs in production processes where workers specialise in carrying out one or several related, but simple, production tasks.

Quality and productivity

Learning Outcomes

By studying this unit you will be able to:

- **Explain the use and importance of using new technological developments in production**
- **Explain why and how businesses try to improve productivity**
- **Recognise and be able to explain why all businesses strive to produce goods of a consistent quality**
- **Explain different methods of controlling costs and ensuring production systems are as efficient as possible.**

Introduction

Have you ever bought anything, taken it home, got it out of the box and found it does not work and/or has parts missing? Annoying, isn't it? Once you have overcome your initial disappointment you are probably very annoyed and threaten never to buy that make of product again. You are then faced with the problem of taking it back to the shop and either asking for a refund, or a replacement product.

All reputable businesses hate to have dissatisfied customers and go to great lengths to ensure that the products that leave their factories are of a good quality. Reputation is an important marketing tool which some businesses exploit. While keeping a good reputation can be hard work, once a business has got a poor reputation it can be hard to shake off. German-owned car companies Audi, Volkswagen, Mercedes and BMW have all earned a reputation for high-quality products and often use this fact in their advertising.

In this unit we will see how companies attempt to control the quality of the finished product and why and how it can help both to control costs and increase sales.

Technology and manufacturing

Labour is expensive to employ. Throughout history, businesses have tried to replace labour with machines in order to save money and also in an attempt to produce goods both more efficiently and of a consistently high quality. Unfortunately, humans can make mistakes while machines rarely make mistakes. Machines just carry out the job they have been designed to do.

- **Mechanisation.** This is when machinery is used but labour is still required in order to work the machine. A lot of farm work is now mechanised. A combine harvester reduces the number of workers needed to reap and bale a harvest, but it still requires a driver.

- **Automation.** This is when machinery is used and a computer controls it. Many manufacturing processes are now automated. Workers are still employed but only to programme and supervise the work that machines do.

Types of technology

CAD – Computer Aided Design	This involves the use of computers to design products. You may have used a CAD program package in technology lessons. The program package is used to draw the design of the product. Information about the product can be stored on computer. If design problems arise, the designer can ask the computer to suggest solutions.
CAM – Computer Aided Manufacture	This is when the machines used to make the product are controlled by computer.
CIM – Computer Integrated Manufacture	This is where a whole factory is controlled by computer.

Figure 1 Different types of technology

Technology in a production environment

The advantages of technology in a production environment include the following:

- Large amounts can be made. This can lead to economies of large-scale production, meaning that the cost of making each product will fall.

- The **productivity** of workers improves. The output per worker increases and so labour costs fall for each product made.

- The quality of production can be improved because machines are less likely to make mistakes than workers This reduces wastage and so saves money. The improved quality may attract new customers.

- Production can be flexible. Machines can be programmed to produce a variety of products in order to meet the needs of individual customers.

- Repetitive or dangerous jobs can be done by machines rather than by people.

The problems of technology in a production environment are:

- When a firm introduces new technology it may need to make workers redundant if the machines do the work instead of them. The costs of making the workers redundant may be high. There may be problems with the trade unions. They may take industrial action against the redundancies.

- The business may need to recruit new employees with the skills to use the new technology. Often, these workers are in high demand and the business may need to pay them big salaries.

- Some existing employees may need retraining to work with the new machines. This may be expensive.

- Buying and installing the machines can be very expensive. A firm risks a lot of money when it introduces new technology.

Lean production

Another way to save costs is to use lean production. The most important feature of lean production is **JIT** or **Just-In-Time production**. The manufacturer does not keep large stocks of components in a warehouse – this would be expensive. Stocks are ordered from the supplier as and when they are needed, or for delivery on a given date. When they are delivered, they are taken straight to the production line and used immediately.

Lean production can also help improve quality. If there were faults with the stocks, production would come to a halt so it is very important that the supplier makes sure that supplies are of good quality.

The use of technology, coupled with the efficient use of labour and materials through modern stock-control methods, can help a business to improve its **productivity**. This happens when fewer resources are needed to produce more goods.

Quality control

Quality control is important at each stage of the production process. It is much better to find faults early on in the process, and correct them, before spending more time and resources completing a product only to find it is rejected due to a problem that could have been identified much earlier.

Quality control is important for the following reasons:

- If goods are not of a good quality, they may not be able to be sold. The producer has wasted money.

- If poor-quality goods can be sold, it may be as 'seconds'. The producer will have to reduce the price for these and so will lose sales revenue.

- The customer will not be happy if they receive poor-quality goods. They may decide to buy from another supplier in the future.

- Production may be disrupted if the quality of materials produced at an early stage in the process of production is not good enough for them to be used at a later stage.

Total quality management

Many businesses have introduced **Total Quality Management** to replace the traditional method of quality control. The traditional method involved the inspection of completed goods for faults – usually by quality control inspectors. Total Quality Management means that **quality assurance** takes place throughout the production process. Quality control is the responsibility of every worker.

Evaluation point

1 You will need to think about the differing impact that developments in technology can have on different businesses. What is good for one business may not be good for another.

2 Equally, different stakeholders may be affected by technological developments in significantly different ways. Some will want to embrace technological change and others will fight against it. Be prepared to explain why this might be the case.

3 You will also need to consider why some businesses are able to continue to operate in the same way in which they did 30 years ago. Be prepared to explain why these businesses do not adopt new technology and yet continue to thrive.

Activity

Activity 1: Research – Reputation for quality

1 Complete the table below with:

   a the names of five global businesses that have a good reputation for good quality products or services.

   b an explanation of why these businesses appear to have earned this reputation and how they use it to help sell their products.

Name of business with good reputation	Explanation of how reputation is used by the business

2 Complete the table below with:

   a the names of five businesses or products that have gained a reputation for uncertain quality.

   b an explanation of why the business or product may find it difficult to achieve a high level of sales.

Name of business or product with uncertain reputation	Explanation of why reputation may affect sales

3 Complete the table below with:

   a the names of three businesses or products which, at one time, had a reputation for poor quality and which now have a high-standing reputation.

   b an explanation of how this improvement in reputation might have been achieved.

Name of business or achieved product with an improved reputation	Explanation of how improved reputation may have been

Activity

Activity 2: True or false – Quality and production

Tick one box to indicate if the statement is true or false.

Statement	True ✔	False ✔
All processes can be automated.		
Only Japanese companies use JIT.		
The use of JIT does not require large warehouses to hold stock.		
Late delivery of supplies to a production line using JIT can halt production.		
Reputation helps improve sales.		
All workers are involved in TQM.		
Quality control can help cut costs and save money.		
All businesses try to improve productivity.		
The introduction of automated machinery usually means more jobs for workers.		
It is easy to achieve a reputation for good quality.		
The use of technology helps improve productivity of workers.		
Automated machinery usually requires a significant capital commitment.		

Activity

Activity 3: Presentation

Prepare a presentation about your work-experience placement or part-time employment. Your presentation should deal with the following points:

● The name of the business.

● The type(s) of business activity in which the business was involved.

● A description of how production took place or how services were provided. Consider whether it involved job, batch or flow production.

● Describing the jobs people did in the firm and what technology they used. Explain the benefits that the technology brought to the business.

● Describing how quality was checked and how faults or problems were solved.

Activity

Activity 4: Matching terms – Quality and production

Match the term with its definition.

● JIT   ● CAD   ● CAM   ● Productivity   ● TQM

Definition	Term
Production machinery is controlled by computer	
A means of assessing the efficiency with which goods are produced.	
Components arrive at the factory just before they are needed.	
A system of control where all workers take responsibility for the quality of the goods produced.	
A system of designing a product with the aid of a computer.	

Examination questions

Carlton Press Ltd prints books.

a Explain how Carlton Press Ltd might benefit from the increased use of technology in the production process. (4 marks)

b Explain the problems which Carlton Press Ltd and its workforce could experience if it introduces new technology. (6 marks)

Advice on how to answer the question

In Part (a) you will not be expected to know a lot of detail about the kinds of technology that are used in printing books. You need to explain the general points about the automation of the production process and the benefits that the firm would gain.

In Part (b) you need to suggest possible problems that the business may have to deal with when introducing new technology. You will also need to explain how the workforce may respond to the introduction of new technology.

Key facts

- Developments in technology:
  - play an important part in helping to change the way businesses undertake production
  - require employees to have flexible and adaptable skills to cope with new production systems
  - allow businesses to develop new products to bring to the market
  - help to keep costs under control and improve productivity
  - allow processes to be automated, which usually results in better and more consistent quality
  - may present new challenges to overcome for the managers of the business.
- Building a reputation for good quality takes time.
- Losing a reputation for good quality can be achieved very quickly if products and services are not of good quality.
- Carrying out quality control at all stages of a production process helps improve quality and reduce costs associated with wasted materials and time.

Key Terms

Make sure you can explain each of the following Key Terms

Mechanisation Machines, controlled by workers, are introduced into the production process.

Automation Machines, controlled by computer, are introduced into the production process.

Productivity A means of measuring the efficiency with which a business produces goods.

Lean production A production system which helps ensure that waste is kept to a minimum.

Quality assurance A system of ensuring that quality standards are met throughout the production process.

Just-in-time (JIT) Stocks of materials and components are not stored but are used immediately when they arrive at the factory.

Quality Control A system of checking the quality of finished goods.

Total Quality Management The process where all workers are responsible for quality throughout the process of production.

Unit 3.4.1

Revenue, costs and break-even

Learning Outcomes

By studying this unit you will be able to:

- Explain the impact of price change on sales revenue
- Calculate and explain different types of costs which a business has to pay
- Discuss and explain why and how businesses use cost and revenue information
- Explain key terms relating to revenue, costs and break-even
- Calculate break-even and explain its uses and limitations
- Discuss and explain the concepts of 'economies' and 'diseconomies' of large-scale production.

Introduction

As with most things to do with business, there are particular business terms that are used to describe different parts of business activity. This is no different to most other types of activity. We use terms like 'midfield' and 'offside' when talking about football. Most, but not all, people will have some idea what these terms mean and why they are important. Some of the terms used in this unit my be familiar and others not. Recognising what the terms mean and when and how to use them is an important part of understanding the finance of business.

All businesses are keen to keep track of the costs of running the business and the income that they receive from carrying out that business.

A business will make a profit if its income is more than its costs. It will make a loss if its income is less than costs. When a business makes a loss, it will need to borrow money, sell off things it owns to raise money or use up its savings. If a business does not make a profit, eventually it will not survive – lenders will stop providing loans, all of the things it owns will have been sold, or its savings will have been used up. For this reason, the management of costs and revenue is very important.

The contents of this unit will help explain how a business might go about managing costs and revenue.

If revenue is greater than costs, a profit will be made

Sales revenue

Sales revenue is the money a business receives for selling the goods or services it produces. Another name for sales revenue is **sales turnover**. The money a business earns in sales revenue depends on how much it sells and at what price. This can be calculated using a formula:

Sales revenue = Quantity sold x Selling price

Joyce Curry runs a photography business. One part of her business is producing school photographs. She charges £10 for each photograph that she sells. After taking pictures in Marston Primary School she sold 80 pictures. Her total sales revenue from this job was:

Sales revenue = 80 x £10 = £800

Increasing sales revenue

A business may be able to increase its revenue by either:

- changing the price it charges – either raising the price *or* reducing the price

- increasing the amount it sells.

More information is given on this in Unit 3.4.3, which looks at sales revenue in relation to calculating profit.

Raising the price

Raising the price of a product or service may increase sales revenue, but not always. If the quantity sold did not change when a business raised its price, it would increase its sales revenue. Suppose Joyce Curry had charged £11 for the pictures she had taken at Marston Primary School. Assuming she still sold 80 pictures, her sales revenue would be:

Sales revenue = 80 x £11 = £880

However, some parents might have been put off by the higher price and decided not to buy a picture. The number of pictures sold would fall. The amount by which sales revenue would change will depend on the extent of the fall in demand for pictures. If, when Joyce raised the price to £11, she had sold 75 pictures, her sales revenue would now be:

Sales revenue = 75 x £11 = £825

Raising the price has *increased* the sales revenue in this case by £25. However, suppose that when she raised the price to £11, the sales of pictures had fallen to 70. Her sales revenue would now be:

Sales revenue = 70 x £11 = £770

Raising the price has resulted in a *decrease* of £30 in her sales revenue. The effect of a price change, therefore, depends on what happens to the amount sold.

Activity

Activity 1: Calculation – Revenue and average price

The following questions are based on the photography business that Joyce Curry runs.

a Calculate the total sales revenue if Joyce:

   i sells 120 photographs in a school at £10 each

   ii sold 2,000 photographs per month for six months at £10 each.

b In the previous six months the sales revenue she received from selling portraits was £10,000. She sold 200 portraits. Calculate the average price of the portraits she sold.

Activity

Activity 2: Calculation – Sales revenue

Joyce Curry decided to reduce the price of school photographs to £9.

a Calculate her sales revenue if:

   i she still sold 80 pictures.

   ii the amount she sold rose to 100 pictures.

   iii the amount she sold rose to 85 pictures.

b Explain the circumstances when it might not be a good idea for a business such as Joyce's to reduce the price of the product or services that are sold.

Reducing the price

Just as the effect of a rise in price on sales revenue depends on what happens to the amount sold, so too does the effect of a fall in price. What happens to the amount of a product that is bought when its price is changed is known as the '**price elasticity of demand**' of the product.

Deciding when to raise or lower prices

When a business wants to raise or lower prices, in order to increase its sales revenue, it needs to judge what will happen to the amount it sells. This will depend on a number of factors:

Figure 1 Factors affecting sales

The number of competitors	Raising the price will not reduce the amount sold by very much, especially if there are no other businesses selling similar products or services.
What competitors do	If competitors also raise prices, the amount sold is unlikely to fall very much.
Whether the product is a not	If a product is a necessity, people will **necessity or** have to buy it anyway **even** though it may be very expensive.
How much people spend on the product	If the product was already very cheap, people may not be put off buying the product by the higher price.

Activity

Activity 3: Explanation – Changes to sales revenue

Suggest what would happen to sales revenue in each of the following situations. Give reasons for your answers.

a A shopkeeper decided to raise the price of a box of matches from 10p to 12p.

b The world price of oil rose. The Red Lion Service Station, like all other petrol stations, decided to raise the price of its petrol price to cover the costs.

c A supermarket decided to reduce the price of its bread by 20 per cent. Competitors left the price of their bread unchanged.

d Malcolm Collier runs the only gents' hairdresser in Marston. The nearest competitor is in Mencaster, eight miles away. He raises his prices by 50p a haircut.

e The Busy Bee Bus Company raises its prices by 15 per cent. Its competitors raise their prices by 8 per cent on average.

Increasing the amount sold

A business can increase its sales revenue if it can increase the amount it sells. Suppose Joyce Curry were able to sell 90 pictures at Marston Primary School at a price of £10. The calculation of her sales revenue now would be:

Sales revenue = 90 x £10 = £900

As well as reducing the price it charges, a business can increase its sales in a number of ways. Three possibilities are:

● increase advertising

● sell in a greater number of outlets

● increase its product range.

All these are connected to the marketing of the product. You should read the units on marketing to learn more about this.

Evaluation points

1 Changing the price of a product or service is not a simple matter. Much will depend on the type of product or service and the strength of demand for the product. Some businesses that try to increase revenue can get it badly wrong and increase the price but find they generate less sales revenue and end up making a lower profit. Recognising this is an important part of the decision-making process.

2 There are lots of factors that can affect the demand for a product. The demand may also change over time and there are few products that continue to have a consistently high level of demand year after year. Being able to explain the factors that are likely to have an impact on the level of demand is an important part of understanding how the business world operates.

3 Some businesses can have very successful and innovative products which sell in large numbers. However, it is no use selling in large numbers if the cost of manufacturing or providing the product is not controlled. Businesses need to know what it actually costs to produce a product or service and then a decision can be made as to the price to charge.

Business costs

Costs are the payments that a business makes in order to make goods and services.

Wages, cost of materials, rent, telephone bill, interest on loans and transport costs are just some of the costs that businesses must pay. These costs can be classified under two headings: **fixed costs** and **variable costs**.

Fixed costs

These are costs that do not change when the business changes the amount it produces. Rent and business rates are examples of fixed costs. Joyce Curry pays £1,000 per month rent for her shop and studio. This cost will not change in the immediate future even if she sells nothing.

Variable costs

These are costs that *do* change when the business changes the amount it produces. Joyce's variable costs will include buying photographic paper, ink and chemicals. The more she sells, the more she will spend on these items. Variable costs may be calculated as follows:

Total variable costs =
Quantity sold x Variable cost per unit

Joyce Curry pays £3 in variable costs for each picture that she produces. The total variable cost of producing 100 pictures would be:

Total variable cost = 100 x £3 = £300.

Total costs

The **total costs** of a business are found by adding together the total for all its fixed and variable costs. If the the total fixed costs that Joyce pays each month add up to £2100, the total cost of producing 100 pictures would be:

Total cost =
Total fixed costs *plus* Total variable costs

Total cost = £2,100 + £300 = £2,400.

Average costs

The **average cost** of production is the cost for each unit of a product that a business sells. It is calculated by the following formula:

Average cost =
Total cost *divided by* Amount sold

The average cost for Joyce Curry to produce 100 pictures would be:

$$\text{Average costs} = \frac{£2,400}{100} = £24$$

It is important for a business to calculate average cost because it helps to decide what price to charge for the product. If the business wants to make a profit, it will need to set the price higher than the average cost of production. However, sometimes a business will set the price lower than the average cost of production. It might do this because it wants to charge a low price so that it takes customers away from its competitors.

Another reason would be to maintain production when the demand for its product was low. The price is set so that the business can pay the variable costs and some of its fixed costs. The business makes a loss in the **short run**, but when business picks up it will raise its price to make a profit.

Managing costs

It is important for businesses to control costs as lower costs may mean higher profits. Also, a business that can reduce its average costs can lower its prices and still make a profit. The business may be able to attract customers away from its competitors because of its lower prices.

Some of the ways which businesses can reduce average costs are:

Spreading fixed costs	By increasing production, the average cost per unit falls. For example, if a business has fixed costs of £100,000 and it produces 20,000 units of a product, its average cost is £5. If the business can increase production to 25,000 units, the average cost would fall to £4. Spreading fixed costs is achieved by using **fixed assets**, like machinery, premises and vehicles, more fully.
Reducing the amount paid for resources and materials	This could be achieved, for example, by shopping around for lower priced raw materials, or reducing wage costs.
Increasing the efficiency of labour	This may be achieved by improving the motivation of workers or by changing the way in which they work – for example, by switching from job to flow production.
By achieving economies of large-scale production	These cost savings are achieved in the **long run** as the business increases its scale of production, perhaps by moving into a larger factory.

Figure 2 Means of reducing average cost

Activity

Activity 4: Matching terms – Costs and revenue

Match the term with its definition.

● Fixed   ● Variable   ● Average   ● Total   ● Revenue

Definition	Term
The money a business receives from selling goods and services.	
All the costs of producing a particular product or service divided by the number sold.	
All the costs of producing a particular product or service.	
Costs that change as output changes.	
Costs which remain the same, in the short-term, regardless of the level of output.	

Activity

Activity 5: Calculation and presentation – Cost and revenue

1 a Some of the costs that Joyce Curry must pay to run her photography business are stated in the table below. Place a tick under the fixed costs or variable costs heading which you think best describes that cost.

  b Think of four more costs which Joyce may have to pay. Add them to the correct column in the table and place a tick under the appropriate column heading.

Joyce Curry's Costs	Fixed Costs	Variable Costs
Interest payments on a three-year loan		
Cost of photographic paper		
Cost of chemicals used to develop and print		
The rent on her offices		
Bank charges		
Cost of her weekly advertisement in the local newspaper		

2 a Complete the costs table showing the costs of operating Joyce Curry's photography business. She charges, on average, £10 for each picture. Her fixed costs are £2,100 and variable costs are £3 per picture.

Pictures sold	Total sales revenue	Total fixed costs	Total variable costs	Total costs	Profit	Average costs
0	0	2,100	0	2,100		
100	1,000	2,100	300	2,400		
200						
300						
400						
500						
600						
700						
800						
900						
1,000						

b Using the information in the costs table, compare and comment on the average cost of production when Joyce produces 100 pictures with the average cost of producing 1,000 pictures.

c Predict the effect on profits of:

i a rise in variable costs to £5 per unit

ii a fall in variable costs to £2 per unit.

You will need to prepare two more tables to do this!

d Recommend how Joyce could reduce her average costs of production.

3 Prepare a presentation about the production costs for Joyce Curry's photography business and how profits could be affected by changes to costs. Use the questions and the data in the costs table to help you to plan what to include in the presentation. Include data about her production costs. If possible, use a spreadsheet to create the table. Use the spreadsheet to help predict the effects of the rise in the variable costs from £3 per picture to £5 per picture and also a fall in variable costs to £2 per picture.

The scale of production

The **capacity** of a business is the amount that it is set up to produce with the resources that it has at present. Sometimes a business will produce more than its capacity – described as producing 'above capacity'. Sometimes a business produces less than it is capable of producing. It is then said to be producing with 'excess capacity'.

Economies of scale

A firm increases its scale of production when it increases its capacity. When the scale of production increases, it is likely that total production costs will also increase. Investment may be necessary to increase the size of the premises and the equipment available to the business. The investment will raise costs. If a bank loan were to be used to finance the investment, interest charges will rise.

As the scale of production changes, fixed costs may also change. They will be different at each scale of output. The firm will spend more on variable costs as it uses more materials and power. However, the average costs of production may fall. When this happens the firm is said to gain **economies of large-scale production**.

In 2006 Langdale Woollens operated from a small, converted barn in the Lake District. The barn, with the equipment in it, was designed to produce 30 knitted jumpers each week. Thirty jumpers per week is the capacity of the business. In the winter, when sales are lower, the firm makes 20 jumpers. It has an excess capacity of 10. In the summer, production can be pushed to 35 jumpers per week. In these weeks it is producing above its capacity.

In 2008 Langdale Woollens built an extension to its barn and installed some new knitting machines. It is now capable of producing 50 jumpers per week. The capacity of the firm has been increased. The total costs rose from £900 per week in 2007 to £1,000 per week. However, the average cost of production fell. The calculations show what happened:

2007
Average cost per jumper

= £900 (total cost)
   30   (number of jumpers made)

= £30

2008
Average cost per jumper

= £1,000 (total cost)
   50   (number of jumpers made)

= £20

The fall in the average cost of production for a jumper from £30 to £20 is an example of an economy of scale. Average costs have fallen as the firm's scale of production has changed.

Types of economies of scale

There are various types of economies of scale. These are shown in Figure 3:

Technical economies	A business saves on production costs by using better methods and equipment.
Managerial economies	A business can employ specialist managers who improve efficiency.
Financial economies	A business does not have to pay out as much money to raise finance.
Risk-bearing economies	A business has a range of products or services, so is not dependent on one product.
Purchasing economies	A business is given a discount for buying in large quantities.
Marketing economies	A business saves on advertising and transport costs.

Figure 3 Types of economies of scale

Diseconomies of scale

Average costs do not always fall as the scale of production is increased. If they rise, a firm is said to experience **diseconomies** **of scale**. These usually occur because the firm becomes too big to be managed efficiently.

Activity

Activity 6: Matching terms – Types of economy of scale

From the following list, choose an economy of scale that best describes each situation.

- Technical
- Marketing
- Purchasing
- Risk-bearing
- Financial
- Managerial

Situation	Type of economy of scale
Evergreen Treescapes decides to branch out and offer a lawn fertilising and weed-killing service in order to obtain new customers	
Busy Buses Ltd decides to replace its single-decker buses with double-decker buses.	
Jensen Fabrics Ltd is able to negotiate a lower rate of interest on bank loans than its smaller competitors.	
Marks & Spencer plc can afford to employ specialist buyers to negotiate deals with clothing suppliers.	
Holden's supermarket chain decides to open a chain of petrol stations.	
Bowton Brewery Ltd starts to sell food through its public houses.	
Austin Engineering Ltd switches production of its hydraulic equipment to a larger factory using computer-controlled machinery.	
The growth of Home Soon Coaches leads to the employment of more office staff. The office manager decides that this is an opportunity for staff to specialise in specific areas of office work.	
Johnstone's Logistics has reorganised its structure. It now employs a specialist manager for each department rather than having managers responsible for several departments.	
When Munro Toys plc bought Talbot Toys Ltd its production doubled. The amount it spent on advertising rose by 50 per cent.	
The Spice Garden Restaurant extends the size of its restaurant from 50 to 80 seats but only takes on one extra waiter.	

Choosing the scale of production

There are a number of factors that will help determine the size of a business. Each individual will have to consider a range of factors and make a decision whether to try to be large or small

The size of the market

- **A large market** gives opportunities for firms to produce on a large scale and to gain economies of scale. This is true of businesses producing canned food.

- **A small market** is likely to be supplied by small firms. Small shops survive because they provide friendly, convenient service to people in a local community. Sometimes, like electrical shops, they may give advice to customers that larger competitors may not provide.

- **A local market** may be supplied by local small firms. An example is the market for domestic building work – extensions, loft conversions and so on.

- **The markets for services** that require personal attention, like hairdressing and made-to-measure tailoring, are often supplied by small firms.

- Small firms often make **specialist goods**. An example is the manufacture of car body paint-spraying equipment.

The amount of capital needed

Some businesses need a lot of capital. Generating nuclear power requires a massive investment in plant and equipment. Only large businesses can operate this type of business. Where only a small amount of capital is needed, small firms can set up. An accountant needs only an office and office equipment. There are many small accountancy firms, as well as some large ones.

Economies and diseconomies of scale

When increasing the scale of production leads to lower costs, large firms are likely to exist. This is true of car manufacturing. When diseconomies result from increasing the scale of production, firms will prefer not to grow in size and small firms will exist.

The motives of the owners

Many people enjoy running their own business. Growing bigger may mean taking on a partner or becoming a private or public limited company. This would lead to more people sharing control of the business. Many owners prefer to stay in charge and choose not to increase the size of their business.

Co-operation by firms

Small firms sometimes work together to help them to compete against larger firms. An example of this is the voluntary chain, SPAR. Owners of small grocery stores all agree to buy their stock from certain wholesalers. The wholesalers are guaranteed large sales and so give bulk-purchasing discounts. In this way, the grocers can compete with the large supermarkets in terms of price.

Activity

Activity 7: Calculation – Scale of production

Oxford Carpets Ltd produces high-quality carpets. The table below shows the costs of producing carpets using different scales of production. The scale of production is measured by the number of metres of carpet that the firm has the capacity to produce each week.

a Complete the table below

b Explain what happens to the average cost of production as output rises from 1,000 to 5,000.

Scale of production (metres)	Fixed costs £	Variable costs £	Total costs £	Average cost £
1,000	10,000	20,000	30,000	30
2,000	10,000	30,000		
3,000	10,000	38,000		
4,000	18,000	46,000		
5,000	18,000	52,000		

Oxford Carpets Ltd – Costs of production for a range of outputs

Doing sub-contracted work

A large firm may prefer to contract out work to smaller firms so that it does not have to employ as many people. British Gas uses some smaller businesses to fit gas fires and central heating systems and to do maintenance work. One advantage is that British Gas does not need to pay wages to these gas fitters if there is no work for them.

Production costs and pie charts

Pie charts can be used to show a breakdown of production costs. The pie charts in Figure 4 show the breakdown of the selling costs of a pair of jeans which a market stallholder, David Morris, had to pay. The first chart shows his costs in 2004, the second his costs in 2008.

Care must be taken when interpreting pie charts. The segments of each 'pie' show a percentage of the total. In the case of production-cost pie charts, a segment shows the percentage of the total cost of production accounted for by one kind of cost.

In the pie chart for 2004:
● paying the rent on the market stall accounted for 25 per cent of the cost of selling a pair of jeans.

● the total cost of selling a pair of jeans was £10. This means that £2.50 was the amount paid in rent for each pair of jeans sold.

In the pie chart for 2008:
● the percentage paid in rent for the stall was still 25 per cent. However, the total cost of a pair of jeans had risen to £20. This means that the amount paid in rent for each pair of jeans sold was now £5.

Figure 4 Selling costs of one pair of jeans

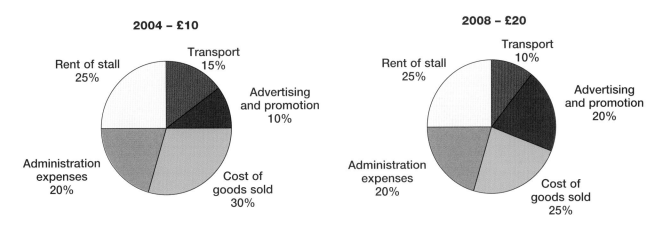

Source: Taken from OCR GCSE Business Studies examination paper

Sometimes the percentage accounted for by one type of cost can decrease, but the actual amount paid rises. This has happened with transport costs. In 2004, transport costs were 15 per cent of total costs. This means that £1.50 was the amount paid to transport each pair of jeans. In 2008, transport costs had fallen to 10 per cent of total costs. The total cost of a pair of jeans had risen to £20 so the amount paid to transport each pair of jeans was now £2.

Break-even

Businesses use information about revenues and costs to calculate the **break-even level of output**. A business breaks even when its costs of production are equal to its sales revenue. This means that the business does not make any profit, nor does it make a loss.

Break-even analysis

Many business use information about costs and sales revenue to forecast profit, loss or break-even levels of output. The information about costs and revenue may be estimated,

from what these have been in the past, or what the business thinks they will be in the future. A **break-even forecast** is usually presented in the form of tables and graphs.

David Adams plans to open a sandwich bar. Figure 5 shows the costs and revenues that David expects for a range of sales from 0 to 1,200 sandwiches per week.

From Figures 5 and 6, we can see that David will make a loss if he sells either 200, 400 or 600 sandwiches per week. If he sells 600 sandwiches, his loss is £100 per week. To avoid making a loss he must sell at least 800 sandwiches per week; this is the break-even level of output, where he does not make a profit nor a loss.

When David sells more than 800 sandwiches he will make a profit. If he sold 1,200 sandwiches he would make £200 profit for the week. The amount by which his actual sales are greater than the level of sales he needs to break even, is known as the **margin of safety**. If David does sell 1,200 sandwiches in a week then his margin of safety is:

Margin of safety =
Actual sales *minus* Break-even sales
= 1,200 *minus* 800 = 400.

Activity

Activity 8: Presentation – Business costs

Magdalen Engineering Ltd produces hydraulic equipment. The table below shows how the breakdown of costs has changed between 2003 and 2008.

The total cost of production in 2003 was £100,000. The total cost of production in 2008 was £200,000.

	2003 Percentage of costs	2008 Percentage of costs
Rent for the factory premises	15	10
Cost of raw materials	15	20
Labour costs	20	20
Marketing costs	5	15
Administration costs	20	15
Other costs	25	20

Prepare a presentation describing the main changes in the costs that have taken place. In your report include pie charts showing the breakdown of costs for each of the years. Use ICT to help you to produce the report. Word-process the report and use a spreadsheet to produce a table of information and to create the pie charts.

Break-even graphs

It is normal for businesses to present break-even figures in the form of a line graph. The graph in Figure 6 shows the break-even forecast for David Adams' sandwich bar.

Uses of break-even analysis

People often prepare a break-even forecast when they are thinking of starting a business. The figures in the forecast will help them to

Sandwiches sold	Sales revenue	Fixed costs	Variable costs	Total costs	Profit (Loss)
0	0	400	0	400	(400)
200	160	400	60	460	(300)
400	320	400	120	520	(200)
600	480	400	180	580	(100)
800	640	400	240	640	0
1,000	800	400	300	700	100
1,200	960	400	360	760	200

Figure 5 The Sandwich Bar – Break-even analysis

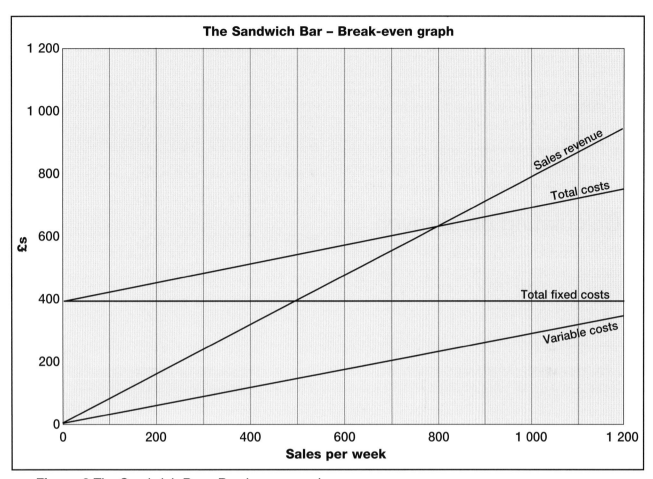

Figure 6 The Sandwich Bar – Break-even graph

plan how much to sell in order to make a profit. If a person needs a loan from a bank, the bank manager will often ask to see a break-even graph as part of the business plan. Break-even information can be used to make judgements about prices and costs. The figures may show a need either to increase the price of the product, to raise revenue, or to reduce the costs. For example, David Adams may decide that a break-even figure of 800 is too high. He might be able to raise prices to increase the sales revenue. Alternatively, he may feel that this is not possible, perhaps because of the competition which he faces. If this were the case, he would have to see if he could cut the costs. Perhaps he could use cheaper ingredients in the sandwiches to achieve this.

Limitations of break-even analysis

Break-even forecasts need to be treated with care. Businesses should remember that:

- forecast figures may turn out to be different

- the figures usually relate to one product

- all output is sold.

The graph in Figure 6 shows that the break-even forecast for the sandwich bar is based on estimates of what price David thinks he will be able to charge in the future and what he thinks his costs might be. Both the price and cost may change for several reasons:

- The number of competitors in the market may change. If another sandwich bar opened in the same area, David may sell less or, to maintain sales, he may need to reduce the price he charges. David would find that he would have to sell more than forecast to break even.

- The cost of ingredients may change. If the cost falls, he will find he does not have to sell as many sandwiches to break even.

Calculating break-even

It *is* possible to calculate the break-even output without constructing a table or drawing a chart. This can be done by using the following formula:

$$\text{Break-even output} = \frac{\text{Total fixed costs}}{\text{Selling price } \textit{minus} \text{ variable costs}}$$

Using the following information, the break-even output would be calculated as follows:

- fixed costs of £10,000 per year

- selling price per unit = £50

- variable cost of each unit = £30.

$$\text{Break-even output} = \frac{\text{£10,000}}{\text{£50 } \textit{minus} \text{ £30}}$$
$$= \frac{\text{£10,000}}{\text{£20}}$$
$$= \text{£500}$$

Evaluation points

1 Before constructing, or using, a break-even graph you will need to make sure that you know the difference between different types of costs, as well as understanding how sales revenue is calculated.

2 Understanding how to interpret the information in a break-even graph is very important, particularly since much of the information in the graph will be made up of forecast or estimated information.

3 You will need to be prepared to comment on the limitations of break-even analysis as a forecasting tool: when it is useful and when it is not.

4 If you need to calculate the break-even level of output consider whether it is worthwhile spending time constructing a graph when the figure can be worked out very quickly using a formula.

Activity

Activity 9: Calculation and presentation – Break-even

Paul Brown runs a driving school. The fixed costs of running the school include the repayment of loans on the cars he owns and administration costs. He calculates these to be £500 per week. The variable costs are the costs of labour and petrol. He calculates these to be £20 per lesson. He charges £30 for each lesson.

1 Use the information above to complete the table below by entering the data into a spreadsheet.

Lessons per week	Sales revenue	Fixed costs	Variable cost	Total costs	Profit/Loss
0					
10					
20					
30					
40					
50					
60					
70					
80					
90					
100					

2 Use the information in the table to draw a break-even graph for the driving school.

Remember that you will need to measure *sales revenue* and *costs* in pounds on the vertical axis and *lessons sold* on the horizontal axis. You will need to plot four lines – fixed costs, variable cost, total costs and sales revenue. It is important to label the axes and the lines clearly.

3 Draw a line on the graph to show the break-even level of output.

4 Using the information in the break-even graph calculate:

a how much profit or loss Paul Brown would make make if he sold:

i 70 lessons in a week

ii 20 lessons in a week.

b Calculate Paul Brown's margin of safety if he sold 90 lessons in a week.

5 Suppose he raised the price of his lessons to £35. Draw a new sales revenue line on the graph to show the effect of this change. What would be the break-even level of output?

6 Suppose that, at the original price of £30 per lesson, Paul Brown was faced with variable costs rising to £25 per lesson. Draw a new graph using a revised spreadsheet to show the effect of this change. What would be the break-even level of output?

7 Word-process a report, including the spreadsheet and graphs, about the break-even analysis for the driving school.

Activity

Activity 10: Calculation – Break-even

Suppose you plan to raise money for a charity by selling home-made biscuits at morning break. The food-technology teacher has said you can cook in his room at lunchtime if you pay £2. This will be your fixed cost of production.

1 Plan how many cakes you will try to sell.

2 Work out the ingredients and materials that you will need to make the biscuits.

3 Calculate the cost of ingredients for each biscuit. This will be your variable cost per biscuit.

4 Using your knowledge of break-even analysis, complete the appropriate table and graph.

5 Using the information in your graph, calculate:

   a how many biscuits you will need to make in order to break even

   b how much profit you will make if you sell all the biscuits.

6 Explain why you may not make as much profit as you predict.

Activity

Activity 11: Calculation – Break-even

The figures below show costs and revenues for a toy manufacturer:

● total fixed costs of producing the toys are £50,000 per year

● *variable costs* per product sold are £2

● the *selling price* of the toys is £6 each.

Using the formula method, work out how many toys the manufacturer must sell to break even.

Examination questions

Question 1

Wanborough Park Hotel has 70 double rooms. Fifty of these rooms, and all the public facilities, are in the main building. The other 20 rooms are in an annexe next door. The annexe is closed during the less busy periods of the year, from November to April.

The following table shows cost and revenue figures for the hotel.

Wanborough Park Hotel – Cost and revenue figures

Fixed costs (daily)	0 – 100 beds available (November – April) 101 – 140 beds available (May – October)	£2,000 £2,100
Variable costs	Per occupant (November – April) Per occupant (May – October)	£20 £15
Revenue	Per occupant (November – April) Per occupant (May – October)	£50 £40

a Explain the difference between fixed and variable costs.   (4 marks)

b Give **two** examples of fixed costs and **two** examples of variable costs which might be appropriate for the hotel industry.   (4 marks)

c Explain why, in this case, fixed costs are not the same regardless of the number of beds.   (4 marks)

d During the period November to April, the hotel has an average of 80 occupants per night. Calculate the profit or loss which it will make each night, on average, during this period. Show your working.   (4 marks)

e During the period May to October, the average occupancy rises to 110 occupants per night. Calculate the profit or loss which it will make each night, on average, during this period. Show your working.   (4 marks)

Question 2

Carlton Press Ltd publishes a Business Studies textbook. It forecasts the following revenues and costs for the book:

The variable costs are £2 per book and the book sells at £5.

Sales of books	Total fixed costs (£)	Total variable costs (£)	Total costs (£)	Total revenue (£)
0	30,000	0	30,000	0
5,000	30,000	10,000	40,000	25,000
10,000	30,000	B	50,000	50,000
15,000	30,000	30,000	C	75,000
20,000	A	40,000	70,000	100,000

a Calculate the missing figures:

  A – The **fixed cost** of producing 20,000 books.   (1 mark)

  B – The **total variable cost** of producing 10,000.   (1 mark)

  C – The **total cost** of producing 15,000 books.   (1 mark)

b Calculate the profit or loss made if 5,000 books were sold. Show your working.   (3 marks)

c Use the information in the table to create a break-even graph. Make sure you calculate the missing figures A, B and C before attempting to draw the graph.   (9 marks)

d Mark on the graph how many books Carlton Press Ltd has to sell to break-even.   (1 mark)

e Give **two** examples of fixed costs and **two** examples of variable costs which Carlton Press Ltd is likely to pay.   (4 marks)

f Explain why Carlton Press Ltd should take care when using a break-even forecast like this.   (4 marks)

Question 3

Jenston Superstores plc operates a large chain of superstores.

a In recent years large retailers like Jenston Superstores plc have increased their share of the market. What are the reasons for their success? (10 marks)

b Superstores have many advantages for shoppers. Why, then, do so many small shops survive? (10 marks)

Advice on how to answer the questions

Question 1

a The command word in this question is 'explain'. You are being tested on your knowledge of the meaning of the two terms. Learn the definitions of the terms and write them down accurately.

b The question is designed to test your ability to apply your knowledge and understanding. You need to think of costs which hotels are likely to have to pay and then, bearing in mind the definitions you have used in answer to part (a), decide whether they are fixed or variable costs.

c You need to read this question carefully. The question is really asking why fixed costs for the summer are more than those for the winter period. What additional fixed costs could the hotel have to pay in the summer when the annexe is open?

d and e The instruction, 'Show your working,' means that marks will be awarded for showing the correct method of calculation (even if you get the answer wrong). Often, there are more marks for the method than for the answer, so make sure you obey the command. Read the figures very carefully – it would be easy to confuse May to October figures with November to April figures. Write the method out neatly and fully – this will help you to avoid mistakes.

Question 2

Parts a and b require you to use your knowledge of the terms – fixed costs, variable costs, total costs and break-even – and apply them so that you perform the correct calculations.

Part c: Take care to draw the graph neatly and accurately. Marks will also be allocated for calculating the three missing figures – A, B and C – and labelling the axes and the lines on the graph

Part d: Make sure that you read the graph at the point which the sales revenue and total costs lines cross and on the correct axis. You could check your answer by using the calculation method to work out the break-even level of output.

Part e: You will need to provide two relevant examples of fixed costs and variable costs that a business like Carlton Press, which publishes books, is likely to have to pay.

Part f: You need to write a clear explanation of the problems of break-even forecasts, mentioning the changes that might occur after the forecasts have been made.

Question 3

This question is about the benefits that large businesses have (economies of scale) and the reasons why small firms still survive. Both parts of the question require that you apply your knowledge of economies of scale and the reasons for the need for small businesses to the case study business. In Part (a) you need to state the advantages that large superstores offer and to explain why these exist. In Part (b) you need to discuss the market needs that small shops can meet.

Key facts

- Businesses earn sales revenues by selling goods and services.
- Businesses must pay costs in order to produce the goods and services they sell.
- The profit a business makes is the difference between its sales revenue and its costs.
- A business may be able to increase its revenue by raising or lowering the price it charges.
- There are different types of costs – fixed, variable, average and total.
- Businesses may gain economies of large-scale production when they increase the scale of their production.
- The scale of production refers to changes in the productive capacity of the business.
- Economies of large-scale production are achieved when the average costs of production fall, even though total costs may rise.
- Diseconomies of scale exist when average costs rise as the scale of production is increased.
- There are several kinds of economies of scale.
- Businesses try to control costs by analysing expenditure on costs.
- Businesses use forecasts of sales revenues, fixed and total costs to analyse the break-even level of output.
- Break-even figures may be presented in a table or on a graph.
- The figures in a break-even calculation may be used to calculate the break-even output and the losses or profits that are made at different levels of output.
- The figures are only forecasts of revenues and costs – actual revenues and costs may differ.

Key Terms

Make sure you can explain each of the following Key Terms

Sales revenue or sales turnover The amount of money that a business receives from selling what it produces or provides.

Price elasticity of demand A measure of the change in the level of demand caused by a change in price

Fixed costs Those costs that do not change as the business changes the amount it produces.

Variable costs Those costs that rise as the business increases production and fall when it reduces production.

Total costs The fixed and variable costs of a particular level of production added together.

Average cost The cost of each unit produced or provided.

Short run A period of time approximately 12 months in length.

Fixed assets Items owned by the business that tend to have a high value. The value of the asset does not normally change on a daily basis and is used in the long term.

Long run A period of time usually in excess of two years.

Capacity The amount that a manufacturing plant is designed to produce.

Above capacity A business is said to be working above capacity when its level of production is more than its capacity.

Excess capacity A business is said to have excess capacity when its level of production is less than its capacity.

Economies of large-scale production These occur when a business increases its scale of production, which leads to a fall in the average costs of production.

Diseconomies of scale When the average cost of production rises as the the scale of production is increased.

Break-even level of output The level of output at which a business neither makes a profit nor a loss.

Break-even forecast A prediction about the break-even level of output based on estimates of future sales revenues and costs.

Margin of safety The amount by which a business' actual output is greater than its break-even output.

Sources of finance

Learning Outcomes

By studying this unit you will be able to:

- **Recognise and explain why businesses need finance**
- **Recognise and explain which sources of finance are available to different types of business**
- **Make decisions about the suitability of different types of finance, explaining how and why the different type of finance is appropriate**
- **Explain the costs of using different types of finance**
- **Explain key terms relating to sources of finance.**

Introduction

Have you ever not had enough money? What have you done about the problem?

It is more than likely these are two questions we have all faced at some time. Usually, we find a solution to the problem, which may or not be ideal, and we sometimes have to make the best of a bad situation.

Businesses experience exactly the same money problems as individuals. Some are more successful at overcoming a lack of money and go on to be very successful. Others, which cannot find suitable sources of money, may fail and go out of business.

Managing money is an important part of business activity, and recognising how to raise money, and the costs involved, is vital for the success of any business.

Activity

Activity 1: Research and presentation – Newly built football grounds

All of the newly built football grounds up and down the country will have required huge amounts of finance to buy the land on which they stand and to build the stadium. These costs will be in addition to the costs involved in buying players and paying wages.

a Use the internet to help you look for different newly built football grounds. Prepare a presentation detailing the names and location of the grounds, together with a possible explanation of where the finance may have come from to build the stadium.

b Investigate the use to which the old ground might have been put, following the move to a new stadium, and how this use might have helped to finance the construction of the new stadium.

c Sales of tickets for football matches are only one source of income for a football club. Investigate and report in your presentation how football clubs generate income from other sources.

d Some of the football grounds may contain the name of a **business sponsor**. In your presentation give the name of the sponsor and explain possible reasons for the sponsor becoming involved in football.

Why do businesses need finance?

All businesses will need finance at some stage in order for them to:

● start up

● grow in size

● buy new machinery and materials

● help with the day-to-day running of the business to help overcome cash-flow problems.

There are many reasons why a business will need finance. Sometimes finance is needed for just a short period of time to help overcome a temporary shortage of funds – for example, when waiting for a customer to pay a large bill. On other occasions, finance may be needed for a much longer period of time – for example, when buying a new building.

In Unit 3.4.3 we will see how important profit is for the finances of most businesses.

Some other reasons and examples why businesses need finance are given below:

Reasons why businesses need finance	Example
Starting up a new business	A person setting up a new business that installs and maintains burglar alarms will need to buy tools, other equipment and probably a van
Internal growth	Buying new manufacturing equipment as a result of increased demand for products
Takeover or acquisition of another company	Lloyds TSB taking over another bank – HBOS (Halifax Bank of Scotland)
Replacing old machinery and equipment	Buying new computer equipment to replace computers that have been in use for several years
Moving to new premises	The business may have outgrown its existing premises or may want to move to a more suitable location
Cash-flow problems	A theme park, which is only open from Easter to October
Research and development	A pharmaceutical company seeking finance to fund the development of a new drug to treat cancer

Figure 1 Reasons why businesses need finance

Types of finance

Finance can be classified into two basic types – **internal** and **external** finance:

Internal finance	External finance
This is finance that comes from within the business.	This is finance that comes from outside the business.
• There is normally no cost to the business as the business is using its own money.	• There is usually some form of cost involved in obtaining external finance. This may be in the form of **interest**, which has to be paid, or giving up some of the ownership of the business to the person or organisation providing the money. For example, the BBC TV programme *Dragons Den* has lots of examples of businesses seeking extra finance in return for part-ownership of the business.
• There is an **'opportunity cost'** involved because once the business has used the money, it cannot use it for another purpose.	
• Figure 3 shows some of the sources of internal finance, and the time periods for which these sources are usually used.	• In some cases, **security**, in the form of an **asset** owned by the business, has to be offered to the provider of the finance. Providing security for a loan means that in the event of the business being unable to pay back the finance, ownership of the asset transfers to the lender; who may then sell it. For example, when buying a property with the help of a mortgage loan, the document detailing the ownership of the property has to be given to the lender of the money. In the event of the borrowed money not being repaid, the lender has the right to sell the property in order to get back the money which was lent.
 Money comes from within the business	• Figure 4 shows some of the sources of finance available to most businesses, and the time periods for which these sources are usually used. 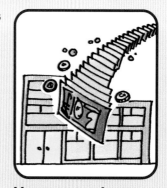 Money comes from outside the business

Figure 2 Differences between internal and external finance

Finance and time

The length of time for which a business needs finance is known as the **time period** – see Figures 3 and 4 below. Business may require finance for different lengths of time. These time periods are usually called the *short, medium* and *long* term.

An indication of the different amounts of time which each time period covers is shown in Figures 3 and 4. Different sources of finance may be used for different time periods. In some cases, the same source of finance may be used to finance an activity over different time periods.

Figure 3 Sources of internal finance

Time period	Short term (Up to 12 months)	Medium term (1 – 3 years)	Long term (3 years or more)
Internal source of finance	Cash in bank	Retained profit Sale of assets	Retained profit Owners' investment

Figure 4 Sources of external finance

Time period	Short term (Up to 12 months)	Medium term (1 – 3 years)	Long term (3 years or more)
External source of finance	Overdraft Trade credit	Bank loan Lease Hire purchase Grants	Bank loan Mortgage Taking a new partner Share issue Lease Hire purchase

Not all sources of finance are available to every business. Some reasons why this is the case are given below:

- Sole proprietors and partnerships (unincorporated businesses) are not able to raise finance by selling shares.

- Limited companies (incorporated businesses) cannot take extra partners in the hope of raising more finance.

- Businesses with a poor financial record are unlikely to find many banks willing to lend money.

- Business activities which are considered to be very risky, or have a poor future, will also find it difficult to raise finance.

Evaluation point

1 Obtaining finance for business development is a serious matter. The business will need to consider carefully the advantages and disadvantages of each source of finance before making a decision on the most suitable source. In some circumstances, a combination of different sources of finance may be appropriate. Not all sources of finance will be available for every business.

2   Most sources of finance represent a long-term commitment for the business. Identifying how economic and business conditions may change in the future is very difficult, but is an important part of the decision-making process when considering obtaining additional finance. Getting it wrong may spell the end for the business but being too cautious may mean that the business is not able to grow and develop in order to compete with its rivals.

Costs and uses of finance

Businesses will need to use finance for a wide variety of reasons. Some of these reasons, together with the costs of the finance, are shown in Figure 5 below. In some cases, the provider of the finance may be taking a risk, in which case the cost of the finance may be much higher or some form of **security** to protect the investment may be required.

Most businesses will find the choice of finance difficult to make

Figure 5 Types, uses and costs of finance

Type of finance		Use of finance	Cost of finance
Overdraft	This is an arrangement with a bank where a business will be able to withdraw more money from its bank account than it actually has. The amount of the overdraft may vary on a daily basis as money is paid into and taken out of the account.	Usually used to help the business overcome a short-term or temporary shortage of funds.	Interest is charged on the daily amount of money that the business owes to the bank.
Trade credit	When a business sells goods it sometimes allows the other business to take the goods away without paying for them immediately. The goods will have to be paid for within an agreed period of time, usually 30 days. Sometimes a longer period of time may be agreed.	This source of finance allows the business buying the goods to sell them on before payment is made to the supplier. This helps businesses that may have a temporary shortage of funds. However, the goods must be paid for even if they do not sell.	The period of credit is usually interest-free.

Type of finance		Use of finance	Cost of finance
Retained profit	Profit that is made by the business but kept back for its own use.	Retained profit may be used to help finance the purchase of many things, which could include equipment, premises and even a research and development programme into new products.	There is no cost involved as the business is using its own money. However, there is an opportunity cost involved, as once the profit has been used it cannot be used for something else – for example, payment of increased dividends to shareholders.
Sale of assets	Selling off, and turning into cash something that the business owns. The assets that are sold may no longer be needed by the business.	This source may be used to help finance the purchase of equipment and/or buildings.	No cost involved other than the opportunity cost of not being able to use the asset again.
Bank loan	An amount of money borrowed from a bank, usually for a stated purpose. In some cases, the bank may want to take a security over an asset in case the money is not repaid. The loan is usually for fixed period of time.	This source may be used to help finance some form of business development or the purchase of new equipment. It may also be used to help a new business start up.	The money that has been borrowed has to be repaid, together with interest.
Lease	A method of obtaining items for a stated period of time. At the end of the lease the items are usually returned to the owner. This source is ideally suited for items that have a relatively short life because of the amount of use, or developments in technology, or where the items are very expensive.	Company cars, lorries, computer equipment, photocopiers and buildings such as industrial units are examples of items obtained through leases. Many shops operate from leased premises.	Monthly or annual payments have to be made for the right to use the equipment. The payment will include an amount for the cost of obtaining the finance to fund the purchase of the leased equipment.
Hire purchase	A system of obtaining items in return for a monthly payment over a given period of time. The items do not become the property of the user until the final payment has been made.	Company cars, lorries and computer equipment are examples of items obtained through hire purchase.	A deposit has to be paid, followed by monthly payments – which may include an interest payment.

Type of finance		Use of finance	Cost of finance
Grants	An amount of money usually made available for a specific purpose by the government and/or local councils.	Factories, costs of training of employees in new skills or the purchase of new equipment can sometimes be financed by grants.	Grants do not usually need repaying. The finance obtained from a grant usually has to be used for a specific purpose.
Owners' investment	The existing owners of the business may invest more money in it.	This source may be used to help pay for a major business development, such as a takeover of another business, or to pay off some long-term debts.	There is no cost involved to the business. The ownership structure of the business may change.
Cash in bank	Money owned by the business and built up over time following successful trading.	This type of finance can be used to help with the day-to-day operation of the business, to purchase assets, or to fund research and development.	There is no cost involved other than an opportunity cost.
Mortgage	A very long-term method of borrowing money which requires some form of security.	The finance is used to help fund the purchase of property. Interest charges tend to be lower than with other sources of finance.	The money that has been borrowed has to be repaid, together with interest.
Taking a new partner	Partnerships can obtain additional finance by selling off part of the business to a new partner.	A new partner may bring new skills to the business. The finance that the partner brings may be used to buy new equipment or premises or to buy another business.	The new partner will have a say in the running of the business and will be entitled to a share of any profits.
Share issue	A source of finance used by limited companies to raise finance in return for a 'share' in the business.	Finance raised from a share issued may be used to fund a major business development, such as a take-over or extension to a factory.	Dividends may have to be paid on the shares, and each share represents part-ownership of the business. Shareholders are entitled to have a say in the running of the company.

Activity

Activity 2: Definitions – Sources of finance

Match the sources of finance in the list below with the definitions.

- hire purchase
- share issue
- leasing
- trade credit
- overdraft
- loan
- retained profit
- sale of assets
- grant
- mortgage

Source of finance definition	Name of finance
A business uses equipment but does not own it until it has made the final payment	
A business borrows a large sum of money to purchase or improve a building	
A bank allows a business to spend more money than there is in its current account	
A business uses equipment but does not own it	
An amount of money which is given to the business to buy something. The money has to be paid back in full	
Money given to a business for a specific purpose. It does not have to be paid back	
Goods are obtained from another business without immediate payment being made	
Money earned by the business but not paid to the owners	
Money received following the sale of capital items owned by the business	
Money obtained by selling part of the business	

Finance for public organisations

Public corporations (see Unit 2.3.6) obtain their finance from different sources. For instance, the BBC receives its money from the sale of television licences and the sale of TV programmes to other countries.

Hospitals and schools, for example, receive most of their finance direct from the government. The money will have come from the taxes that have been collected, for example:

- workers' wages, in the form of income tax
- a bag of crisps, in the form of value added tax (VAT)
- a bottle of perfume, in the form of excise duty and VAT.

Activity

Activity 3: Matching terms and zone activity – Sources of finance

The sources of finance and their definitions in the table below have been mixed up.

a Match the source of finance to its correct definition by writing in the correct letter.

Source of Finance	Incorrect Definition	Correct definition	Advantage	Disadvantage	Use of Finance
Overdraft	**A** Finance obtained to help with the purchase of property				
Share issue	**B** Finance obtained from within the business following successful trading				
Retained profit	**C** The right to use goods, in return for a monthly payment. The goods are not owned by the business				
Trade credit	**D** Finance obtained, usually for a fixed period of time, which has to be paid back				
Hire purchase	**E** Finance obtained for a specific purpose, usually at no cost to the business. The money does not have to be paid back				
Grants	**F** A sum of money that has been borrowed. The amount may vary on a daily basis				
Loan	**G** Part purchase of the business entitles the holder to dividends				
Mortgage	**H** Goods obtained from a supplier, which do not have to be paid for immediately				

Lease	**I** The sale of a part of the business in return for an amount of money				
Taking a new partner	**J** A method of obtaining an asset in return for a series of monthly payments. Ownership of the asset does not transfer until the final payment has been made				

b Select from the list below one example of an advantage and disadvantage for each source of finance. Some advantages and disadvantages can be used more than once.

Advantages:	Disadvantages:
No cost to the business	Interest has to be paid
Lower interest charges	Security required
Immediate use of goods	Finance cannot be used for anything else
Goods sold before they are paid for	Possible loss of control
Large amount of finance in one payment	Limited availability
Finance may be obtained for a variety of purposes	Goods must be paid for even if they are not sold
Only the smallest amount of money needed is borrowed at any one time	Extra payment to cover the cost of finance to allow goods to be used

c In the final column of the table, give an example for a possible use of each source of finance.

Activity

Activity 4: Explanation – Identifying suitable sources of finance

a Identify the most suitable source of finance from the list below for each of the business situations. Some sources of finance may be used more than once. Not all sources of finance need to be used.

- Hire purchase
- Share issue
- Loan
- Mortgage
- Grant
- Lease
- Cash in hand
- Trade credit
- Overdraft

b Give a reason for your choice of finance.

Business situation	Most suitable source of finance	Reason for choice
A small sole-proprietor building business wishing to buy a second-hand lorry		
A family textile business, trading as a private limited company, wishing to invest in some new manufacturing equipment		
The Curzon Veterinary Partnership, which needs to raise finance to help it buy some new premises		
A new business wishing to sell tapes and CDs via the internet		
A new business supplying organic vegetables direct to consumers		
An established hairdresser wishing to open a tanning and nail studio		
An established family-owned fish and chip shop business wishing to take over a rival business		
A nationwide 'coffee shop' business seeking to expand in the north of England		
A ready-mix concrete business, which requires a fleet of new lorries		
A small sole proprietor wishing to buy a second-hand van		
A large public limited company wishing to take over another public limited company		

Activity

Activity 5: True or false – Features of sources of finance

Tick one box to indicate if the statement is true or false.

Statement	True ✔	False ✔
A loan has to be repaid with interest		
Shareholders are part owners of a business		
Banks will always lend a business money		
New partners are usually easy to find		
An overdraft is a cheap way of borrowing money for long-term projects		
A mortgage can be used to buy new machinery and equipment		
Most company cars are leased		
Selling assets is a quick way of raising finance		
All businesses will have some cash in hand		
Opportunity cost requires a payment to be made		

Activity

Activity 6: Calculation – Shares

a Bowton Manufacturing plc is attempting to raise additional finance by offering shares for sale at £1.50 per share. It has 50,000 shares available for sale. Calculate how much money it would raise if it sold:

	Answer
only 10,000 shares	
all of the shares	
50% of the shares it has available for sale.	

b Bowton Manufacturing plc hopes to pay a dividend to all its shareholders. There are 200,000 shares in circulation. Calculate how much money it would pay out if the payment per share (dividend) was:

	Answer
10 pence	
15 pence	
5 pence	

c Bowton Manufacturing plc cannot decide on the size of the dividend to pay. Calculate how much money the business would be able to retain, from a profit of £50,000, if it paid the dividends listed below:

Issued shares = 50,000	Answer
10 pence	
15 pence	
20 pence	

Examination questions

Question 1

a The following are some of the sources of finance which firms use:

 i Shares

 ii Bank loans

 iii Retained profit

 iv Trade credit

 v Hire purchase

Which two of these sources would you recommend to a private limited company to use to pay for new equipment costing £80,000? Give reasons for your choice.   (6 marks)

b Explain why governments give grants to firms to help finance new equipment?   (3 marks)

Question 2

Pleasurewear plc's board of directors has considered the following methods of financing the building of a new clothing factory:

1 Bank overdraft

2 Bank loan

3 Retained profit

a Which method of financing the new factory would you recommend to the board of directors? Give two reasons for your choice. (4 marks)

b Explain why you have rejected the other two methods of finance. In each case give one reason for its rejection. (4 marks)

c Explain why is it important to consider the following before choosing a method of finance:

i the length of time

ii the risk involved (4 marks)

d The opportunity cost of building the new factory is replacement of old machinery in Pleasurewear plc's other two factories in the UK. Explain what is meant by the term 'opportunity cost'. (3 marks)

Advice on how to answer the questions

Question 1

a You will need to choose two sources of finance that are appropriate for a limited company and for the purchase of new equipment. Having made two choices, say why those sources of finance are appropriate.

b This question requires you to explain why governments, in effect, give money away. In order to answer the question it will be necessary for you to explain what a government may expect to get back in return for giving money in the form of a grant.

Question 2

a Choose an appropriate method of finance for building the new factory and say why you think it is appropriate.

b Say why you did not consider the other two methods of finance to be appropriate for the building of the new factory.

c Explain, in detail, why and how these two factors are important when considering obtaining additional finance.

d Explain the meaning of the term 'opportunity cost', preferably using at least one example to illustrate your answer. You should make reference to Pleasurewear plc in your answer.

Key facts

- Finance is vital for all businesses – all businesses will require finance at some stage.
- A shortage of finance may mean that the business will fail.
- Finance may be used for different lengths of time.
- Not all sources of finance are available to all forms of business.
- Internal finance:
  - comes from *within* the business
  - does not normally have to be paid back
  - has no interest charge
  - may have an opportunity cost
  - has no transfer of the business to a new owner.
- External finance:
  - comes from *outside* the business
  - usually has to be paid back
  - usually costs money in the form of dividends or interest
  - can mean a new owner or owners may become involved in the business.
- For most types of finance there is usually a cost involved.
- Some sources of finance are best suited for particular uses.

Key Terms

Make sure you can explain each of the following Key Terms

Business sponsor A business which pays money to another organisation.

Opportunity cost The cost of missing out on something else. This need not be financially related.

Internal finance Finance obtained from within the business.

External finance Finance obtained from outside the business.

Interest An amount of money that has to be paid on borrowed money.

Asset An item of value owned by the business.

Security Something of value which is offered to a lender as a form of guarantee of payment.

Time period The length of time for which the finance is required.

Profit

Learning Outcomes

By studying this unit you will be able to:
- **Explain key terms relating to profit**
- **Calculate different types of profit**
- **Explain why profit is important to most businesses**
- **Use profit figures as a means of comparing business performance.**

Introduction

The burger you bought from the fast food restaurant, or the replica football shirt you had bought as a birthday present, have probably all been sold at a **profit**. The aim of most businesses is to sell the goods and services they provide at a profit.

In its simplest form, profit is the amount of money left over from an activity once the costs of that activity have been paid for. Profit is sometimes used as a measure of how successful a business activity has been.

Not all businesses are successful and make a profit. These businesses which make a loss are unlikely to survive in the long term.

Examples of goods sold at a profit

Activity

Activity 1: Research and presentation – Profit

Use the 'web pages' of a national daily newspaper to research some articles and reports about the profit made by a range of businesses. Prepare a presentation, detailing the profit made by each business. Include in your presentation possible explanations for why the amount of profit made by each business is different.

Sales revenue

Before profit can be calculated, the business will probably need to work out its **sales revenue**. This is calculated by multiplying the number of items sold by the cost of each item.

If you sell 10 handbags for £25 each, the sales revenue (or value of sales) is £250 and can be calculated by using the following formula.

number of goods sold x price = sales revenue
10 x £25 = £250

Some other examples of sales revenue calculations are shown in Figure 1 below:

Figure 1 Examples of sales revenue calculations

Number of items sold	Cost of each item	Sales revenue
100	10p	£10.00
500	65p	£325.00
665	£1	£665.00
TOTAL REVENUE		**£1000.00**

Activity

Activity 2: Calculation – Sales revenue

Shown below is a part of menu from a snack bar.

MENU

Cheese & Pickle Cob **£1.20**   Carton of Milk **60p**

Veggie Burger **95p**   Coffee **60p**

Fresh Fruit **40p**   Small Pasta salad **80p**

Baked Potato   Ice Cream **90p**
with Topping **£1**

Calculate the sales revenue for each item if the snack bar sells:

a 60 baked potatoes with topping

b 100 cheese & pickle cobs

c 200 portions of fresh fruit

d 65 cartons of milk

e 150 veggie burgers

f 62 cups of coffee

g 73 ice creams

h 59 small pasta salads

i 20 cartons of milk and 20 veggie burgers

j 12 cheese and pickle cobs, 10 cups of coffee and 4 cartons of milk

Calculating profit

There are different types and ways of calculating the profit made by a business.

Gross profit is the amount of profit made by a business as a result of buying and selling goods or services, but without paying for any of the day-to-day or other expenses of running the business. For example, if you only paid 15p for each chocolate bar you sold for 25p then you have made a profit of 10p on each bar you sold. This is known as 'gross profit'.

It is calculated by using the following formula:

selling price *minus* the buying price = gross profit
25p – 15p = 10p

This information can also be used to calculate the **profit margin**, which is normally calculated as a percentage. It can be calculated by the following formula:

$$\text{Profit Margin} = \frac{\text{Gross Profit}}{\text{Buying Price}} \times 100$$

$$or \quad \frac{10p}{15p} \times 100 = 66.7\%$$

Where a lot of items have been sold, gross profit can be calculated using the figure for sales revenue. In the example below, the sales revenue has been calculated at £250 and the cost of buying the goods at £150.

- Gross profit it is calculated using the following formula:

gross profit = sales revenue *less* the cost of buying goods that have been sold

$$\text{gross profit} = £250 – £150 = £100$$

Activity

Activity 3: Calculation – Gross profit

Work out the amount of gross profit earned in each of the following examples:

a Weekly sales revenue from CD sales is £15,000. The cost of buying the CDs is £8,000.

b Daily sales of one type of chocolate bar in the school tuck shop are worth £75. The cost to the school is £44.50.

c One of the school bus drivers sells 50 single tickets each morning for 80p each. He estimates the cost of operating the school bus to school is £27.

d The school canteen sells 200 cartons of fruit juice for 45p each. The cost of buying each carton is 28p.

e Last term, the school stationery shop sold 20 electronic calculators for £4.50 each. The cost of buying each calculator is £3.85

Net profit takes into account the profit made as a result of buying and selling goods or services but also makes an allowance for the costs involved in running the business – for example, wages and telephone calls. It can be calculated using the following formula:

Net profit = Gross profit less the costs of running the business

Figure 2 shows how the gross and net profit of a business might be calculated

		£	£
Sales revenue			400,000
less cost of buying goods			160,000
	GROSS PROFIT		240,000
less Expenses	Wages	80,000	
	Energy	10,000	
	Equipment	15,000	
	Advertising	5,000	110,000
	NET PROFIT		130,000

Figure 2 Gross and net profit calculation

Activity

Activity 4: Calculation – Net profit

Calculate the net profit in the following examples by adding up the expenses and subtracting them from the gross profit:

a

Gross profit	£10,000
Electricity	£1,000
Wages	£4,000
Phone	£500
Rent	£2,000
Net profit	

b

Gross profit	£15,000
Advertising	£3,000
Paper for photocopier	£100
Heating	£1,000
Maintenance	£400
Net profit	

c

Gross profit	£10,520
Fuel	£4,000
Wages	£3,000
Annual car tax	£160
Maintenance	£1,260
Net profit	

d

Gross profit	£20,650
Materials	£4,190
Labour	£9,650
Transport	£1,620
Commission	£2,150
Net profit	

e

Gross profit	£26,650
Furniture	£2,250
Labour	£10,000
Energy	£5,630
Rent	£6,155
Net profit	

Comparing profit over time

Calculating and recording the amount of sales revenue and profit provides a means of comparing the financial performance of a company:

● over a period of time

● with its competitiors.

This is an important exercise as the information can also be of use in helping to identify:

● if a business activity is worth doing

● how the financial performance of the business has changed.

The information is likely to be used by:

● the **owners** of the business, such as shareholders

● **employees** of the business, such as managers responsible for running different parts of the business

● **competitiors** who may be interested to see how similar businesses are performing

● **Trade Unions** to see if the business can afford to pay its workers a higher rate of pay.

The amount of profit made in different years is often presented in the form of a table as shown in Figure 3 below:

	2007	2008	2009
Sales revenue (£m)	80	100	120
Gross profit (£m)	20	30	17.5
Net profit (£m)	5	10	5

Figure 3 Sales revenue, gross and net profit from 2007 to 2009

The above information can also be presented in the form of a graph. The line graph below shows the sales revenue, gross and net profit between 2007 and 2009. (See Figure 4.)

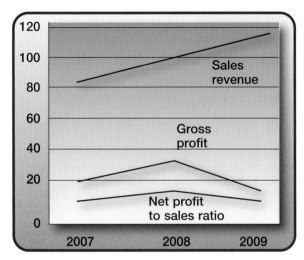

Figure 4 Sales revenue, gross profit and net profit from 2007 to 2009

What affects the amount of profit or loss?

The amount of profit or loss that a business makes can depend on a large number of things. These might include:

● **The type and size of business.** A window cleaner may not have a large value of sales; a public limited company such as Tesco plc, which has many stores and sells a large quantity of goods each day, will make much more profit than the window cleaner.

● **The objectives of the business.** A profit-making business such as KFC wants to make money selling chicken and other

A profit-making business

A non-profit-making business

products. A non-profit making activity, such as a charity like Oxfam, may want to concentrate on raising money rather than making a profit.

- **The demand for the product**. Some products may be popular and sell in large quantities – for example, aerosol deodorants. Other products may no longer be in demand due to changing tastes and fashions – for example, video recorders.

- **The price consumers are willing to pay**. Designer jeans and perfume are often sold at prices much higher than the costs of making them.

The price of products can vary significantly – pens are generally low in price while goods like washing machines can be expensive

- **The way in which the business controls its costs**. Paying workers a low hourly wage rate and using a source of cheaper raw materials helps to keep the cost down. Some businesses deliberately do not do this, preferring to operate 'ethically' by paying a fair rate for the job (see Unit 3.5.2).

- The profit margin or **mark-up** the business is able to use. This is the difference between the price paid for an item and the price at which it is sold.

Price paid by retailer 50p
—
Price paid by customer £1
—
Mark up 50p or 100% profit

Groceries generally have a low profit margin because they sell in large volumes, while other products, that do not sell in large numbers, may have a high profit margin – for example, high-class jewellery. The size of the profit margin or mark-up on a product is very important to a business because of the need to pay for the running costs of the business.

12p per CAN

These will not produce much profit per can

- **The amount of competition**. Where a business has a lot of competitors and is selling an identical product to its competitors, it is not able to sell the product at a price it would like to charge. The business has to accept the price that consumers are willing to pay. (See Unit 3.5.1.)

Too much competition affects profits

- **The cost of setting up a business.** Starting up a new business can be expensive. Some new businesses may find it hard to break into a market and make a profit. There are many reasons for this, a few examples being: customers loyal to existing businesses; difficulty in finding suitable locations; and price cutting.

Activity

Activity 5: Poster – Reasons for profit

Design a poster showing some of the reasons why the profit made by different businesses will be different.

Why do some businesses not want to make a profit?

Most businesses will want to make a profit. However, this is not true of all businesses. Charities, for example, will want to try to raise as much money for the cause which they support. Social or sports clubs will want to raise money to improve facilities for the benefit of their members. Any surplus money that they have will be used to buy new equipment or improve the clubhouse. Many educational establishments like schools and colleges, which operate like a business, do not want to make a profit. Their aim will be to achieve as much income as possible, keep costs down and use any surplus money for the benefit of their employees and the people who are attending the establishment. Think of all the new equipment, buildings, computers and books which your school or college will have bought recently.

Why is profit important to most businesses?

Profit can also be considered as 'a return on an investment', where the owners of a business expect something back in return for investing their money in the business. Profit is also 'a reward for taking a risk'.

Profit is usually paid to the owners of the business in the form of:

- **dividends** to **shareholders** of incorporated businesses (private limited companies and private limited companies)

- **drawings** to the owners of unincorporated businesses (sole proprietors and partnerships).

Profit also has another important function. It can be used to help finance and develop business activity, or buy new equipment and buildings. The profit which is kept by the business is called **retained profit** and it has two real advantages over borrowing money to finance business development:

Evaluation point

1 People who invest in businesses need to be able to judge whether or not they are achieving a good enough profit. To do this, they would need to see if they would have gained more by saving the money rather than by investing it and receiving drawings or dividends. It must also be remembered that the value of the money invested in a business may increase and it may also decrease in value.

2 Comparing the profit achieved by one business with that achieved by other, similar, businesses is important. Sometimes a fall in profit might be because of changes in the economy; for example, demand generally might be low because of a recession (see Unit 3.5.1). In this situation, the profits of other similar businesses will also be falling. A business may just aim to survive the recession and hope to increase profit once it is over.

- it does not have to be paid back, unlike a bank loan or mortgage

- no interest has to be paid, unlike a bank loan or mortgage.

There may, though, be a cost of using profit in this way. This is called **opportunity cost** (see Unit 3.4.2). This is the cost associated with not using the profit for some other activity – for example, paying out profit in the form of dividends to shareholders. Whenever a business or an individual has to decide between alternatives, an opportunity cost is involved in that there is a 'price' to be paid for *not* having something.

For example, if you have £1 to spend and cannot decide between a drink and something to eat but cannot afford both, choosing the drink means that you have had to give up the chance of having something to eat. Therefore, there is a lost opportunity – the cost of which is not having something to eat.

Profit and financial records

Maintaining financial records and calculating profit is important for a business. It needs to know whether an activity is worthwhile and whether it should continue with it. The process of keeping financial records, calculating, checking and comparing profit along with other financial information is called 'accounting'. The document created by accountants, in order to help calculate profit is called a '**trading, profit and loss account**'.

Profit and break-even analysis

The amount of profit which a business might make at a given level of output, when goods or services are sold at a particular price, can be forecast using a technique called **break-even analysis**. This technique is dealt with in more detail in Unit 3.4.1.

Activity

Activity 6: Calculation – Profit

A small firm has annual sales of £600,000 on goods which it has bought for £240,000. Wages and other expenses are £120,000.

1 Using the above information calculate:
  - the gross profit
  - the net profit
  - the profit margin.

2 Explain why it is important for a business to calculate the three different profit figures in question 1.

3 Give three examples of expenses which a business may have to pay.

Activity

Activity 7: Research and presentation – Profit and sales

Prepare a presentation, to be shown to potential investors or shareholders, based on some of the financial information (profit and sales) that a business of your choice makes available on its website. Do not forget to show how the profit and sales figures change from one year to the next. In your presentation, explain briefly what this information tells you about the company.

Activity

Activity 8: True or false – Profit

Tick one box to indicate if the statement is true or false.

Statement	True ✔	False ✔
All goods are sold at a profit.		
Net profit is usually bigger than gross profit.		
Profit is always paid to the owners of the business.		
Expenses of running the business have no affect on profit.		
Retained profit is money kept by the business for its own use.		
The number of items sold multiplied by the selling price equals sales revenue.		
Most charities are non-profit making.		
A profitable business is a well-run business.		
All businesses work on the same profit margin.		
A dividend is payment of profit to the owner of the business.		

Activity

Activity 9: Rearranging sentences – Types of profit

Rearrange the words in the following sentences so that each sentence makes sense.

i   minus net gross equals profit expenses profit

ii business money retained is by the profit kept

iii than a made costs loss are greater when revenue is

iv is expense electricity example an an of

v   sold revenue quantity multiplied equals by price

Activity

Activity 10: Matching pairs – Profit related terms

Complete the sentences below by selecting an appropriate 'ending' from the selection below.

- mark up
- net profit
- to the owners of a business when it makes a profit
- vary from product to product
- source of finance
- by most businesses
- because it can be used to buy new equipment
- loss

Profit is needed by most businesses
Gross profit is larger than
A dividend is paid
Unsuccessful businesses usually make a
Profit margins may
A profit is made
Another name for profit margin is
Profit is a

Examination questions

Read the information below and answer the questions which follow.

	2008 £000	2009 £000
Sales revenue	200	240
Gross profit	40	30
Net profit	15	20

Bowton Garage Ltd – Summary of performance 2008 and 2009

a Explain the factors that might have caused an increase in sales revenue between 2008 and 2009.
(6 marks)

b Calculate the percentage change in:

a gross profit between 2008 and 2009 (3 marks)

b net profit between 2008 and 2009. (3 marks)

c Based on the financial information in the table above, evaluate the performance of the company in 2008 compared to 2009. (6 marks)

Advice on how to answer the questions

a The 'command' word in the question is 'explain'. Therefore you are required to write a detailed response to the question, not just 'Sales revenue has increased'. Rather than listing the things that might affect sales revenue, make sure that you provide detailed information on why the sales revenue of the business has gone up. Your answers should relate to a garage.

b This question is designed to test your numerical abilities. When answering questions like this, start off by writing down the formula and then substitute the figures you are working with into the formula. Do not miss out any steps of the calculation as marks will be available for each step.

c The command word in the question is 'evaluate'. This means that you have to provide a very detailed answer which considers all possible factors. You may need to look at the information from the point of view of both the business and shareholders. Try to determine which of the two sets of financial information is the best, giving reasons for your decision.

Key facts

- Profit is vital for most businesses.
- Loss-making businesses usually go out of business.
- The amount of profit made can be compared with other businesses.
- There are several different types of profit, which are calculated in different ways.
- A number of different stakeholders will be interested in the profit earned by a business.
- Not all businesses have a profit-making objective.
- Costs or expenses of running the business need to be kept as low as possible.

Key Terms

Make sure you can explain each of the following Key Terms

Profit Money left over from sales after all costs have been paid.

Sales revenue The amont of money which a business receives from selling what it produces or provides. It can be calculated by multiplying the quantity of goods sold by the selling price.

Gross profit Sales revenue minus cost of sales.

Profit margin The difference between selling price and the cost of the item. This is sometimes expressed as a percentage.

Net profit Gross profit minus expenses.

Mark-up The amount added to the purchase price of a product to give the selling price. This is sometimes expressed as a percentage.

Return on investment The amount that a person or business receives for providing finance to business.

Reward for taking a risk The financial returns from an acivity in relation to the 'danger or risk' to which a business exposes itself to when undertaking business activity. Better returns are normally expected from activities that have a high degree of risk.

Dividends That part of a company's profit paid out to shareholders of limited companies.

Shareholders Owners of limited companies who have invested money into the business.

Drawings Business profits paid to the owners of a sole proprietor or partnership.

Retained profit Profit which is kept by the business for its own use.

Opportunity cost The cost of having to miss out on an alternative use for the money.

Trading profit and loss account A financial document prepared by accountants which details the costs and revenue of the business in order to calculate the amount of profit.

Break-even analysis A technique for estimating the likley costs, revenues and profit or loss from a business activity.

Cash flow

Learning Outcomes

By studying this unit you will be able to:

- **Explain why businesses need to forecast flows of cash to and from the business**
- **Calculate a cash-flow forecast**
- **Make recommendations about how the business might react to both positive and negative cash flows**
- **Explain why the business may need to make changes to the way in which it is running its business to help it overcome possible shortages of cash**
- **To recognise, explain and solve situations where shortages of cash, which are forecast to go on for several months, may mean that the business is in danger of going out of business**
- **Explain the limitations of a cash-flow forecast**
- **Explain key terms relating to cash-flow forecasting.**

Introduction

We all look forward to birthdays and Christmas, mainly because of the presents we hope to receive on these occasions. On many of these occasions we will receive money as presents and so, probably, twice a year we are likely to be cash rich. If you are unlucky enough to have a birthday very close to Christmas, a lot of your income comes at the same time of year. On the other hand, if your birthday is in June you may have your income more evenly spread out.

As we all know the date of our birthday and Christmas Day, it should be possible for us to plan for anticipated receipts of cash. Some of us are better at planning than others and quickly spend the money we receive. Others may spend the money more cautiously throughout the year.

All businesses will need to plan for the receipt and payment of money. Having too much may mean that it is not being used efficiently. Not having enough may mean that the business is in danger of running out of cash and not being able to pay its bills.

Forecasting the flow of cash to and from the business is a very important part of business planning. This unit looks at how businesses go about this aspect of their work.

What is a forecast?

A forecast is an attempt to predict what could happen in the future, just as the weather forecast attempts to predict what the weather might be like tomorrow, or in a few days' time. Sometimes the forecast is accurate and on other occasions the forecast is only partly accurate. Any forecast will always have a certain amount of uncertainty.

This person was badly prepared as the forecast was incorrect

This person was well prepared as the forecast was correct

Most businesses will try to forecast future events using previous experiences or data which they have collected. This process will help the business to plan for the future.

One of the most important forecasts that a business makes concerns the amount of money which it expects, in the future, to have flowing into (**income**) and out of (**expenditure**) the business. This is called a 'cash-flow forecast'.

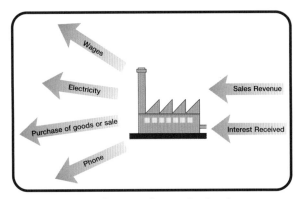

Flow of money into and out of a business

Knowing when a business might have too much or too little money is important so that plans can be made for the future of the business.

In Figure 1, the figure shown as the **balance carried forward** is the difference between the total income (balance brought forward plus income) and the total expenditure.

For the month of January:

Total income = £135,000

This is made up of the balance brought forward (£25,000) plus income (£110,000).

Total expenditure = £75,000

Balance carried forward = Total income *minus* expenditure

Balance carried forward = (£25,000 + £110,000) – £75,000 = £60,000

Any *surplus* money which is left over at the end of one month is carried forward to the start of the next month and is shown as the **balance brought forward**. A sum of £60,000 has been entered for the month of February. The business has a **positive cash flow**.

If total *expenditure* is greater than total income, the balance to be carried forward is a negative figure. There is a *negative* **cash flow** in the cash flow of the business for that month. Negative figures are usually shown in cash-flow forecasts in brackets, e.g. (£10,000).

In business, any financial data written in brackets will usually be negative. In Figure 1, this happened in the month of March and the negative figure has been carried forward to the beginning of April. The business has a *negative* cash flow for the month of March.

For the month of March:

Total income = £85,000
Balance brought forward = £15,000 + income = £70,000

Total expenditure = £95,000

Balance carried forward = Total Income *minus* expenditure

Balance carried forward = (£85,000) – £95,000 = (£10,000)

The balance brought forward is added to the figure for income for that month if it is a positive figure (January to March). If the balance brought forward is a negative figure (April) it is subtracted from the income.

Figure 1 Cash-flow forecast for Bowton Garage Ltd

	Jan £	Feb £	Mar £	April £
Balance brought forward	25,000	60,000	15,000	(10,000)
INCOME: Sales of goods	100,000	80,000	60,000	70,000
Rental income	10,000	10,000	10,000	10,000
TOTAL INCOME	**135,000**	**150,000**	**85,000**	**70,000**
EXPENDITURE: Materials	50,000	80,000	60,000	40,000
Energy costs	5,000	20,000	5,000	5,000
Wages	10,000	20,000	20,000	10,000
Transport	10,000	15,000	10,000	5,000
TOTAL EXPENDITURE	**75,000**	**135,000**	**95,000**	**60,000**
Balance carried forward	60,000	15,000	(10,000)	10,000

Activity

Activity 1: Calculation – Cash-flow forecast

1 Complete the chart below with the following information.

   a Under the heading 'Sources of income', list the different sources of income that you normally have, e.g. paper round; job; parents; birthday, etc. Use a separate line for each source of income.

   b Under the heading 'Expenditure', list the main expenditure types which you normally expect to have, e.g. entertainment; bus fares; make-up; music; mobile phone top-ups; DVDs; magazines, etc. Use a separate line for each main type of expenditure.

   c Use the chart to record the income and expenditure you:

   i *have had* over the *last* four weeks. Use the columns headed weeks 1 to 4.

   ii *expect to have* over the *next* four weeks. Use the columns headed weeks 5 to 8.

   d Calculate the amount of money you carry forward at the end of each week.

2 List the weeks where you have:

   a surplus of income and explain what you might do, or did, with the money.

   b deficit of income and explain how you overcame, or expect to overcome, the shortage of money.

3 Explain why it was harder to forecast the information for weeks 5 to 8 than it was to record the information for weeks 1 to 4.

	Week 1	Week 2	Week 3	Week 4	Week 5	Week 6	Week 7	Week 8
Balance brought forward	NIL							
SOURCES OF INCOME:								
TOTAL INCOME								
EXPENDITURE								
TOTAL EXPENDITURE								
Balance carried forward								

Is a negative cash-flow balance a problem?

A negative cash-flow balance may:

- only be temporary and may not necessarily cause a problem for the business
- require the business to obtain additional finance in the form of an overdraft to help it overcome a shortage of cash
- mean that the business has to delay payment of money owed until finance is available
- result in the business being unable to buy some equipment until its cash position improves.

In Figure 1 for the month of March, the balance carried forward was (£10,000). By the end of April, the balance carried forward had become positive because income during the month was greater than expenditure.

The business will be in serious financial trouble if it forecasts a negative balance or cash flow at the end of several consecutive months. Unless things start to improve, the possibility exists that the business may go out of business, not because it is unprofitable, *but because it has run out of money.* A business will always need money to pay for its day-to-day running costs.

For the month of March the balance carried forward was (£10,000)

Activity

Activity 2: Calculation – Cash-flow forecast

The cash-flow forecast below has been partly completed. Fill in the missing boxes by working out the cash-flow forecast.

	April £	May £	June £	July £
Balance brought forward	1,000		1,000	
INCOME:				
Income from sales	10,000		9,000	10,000
Rent	1,000	1,000		1,000
TOTAL INCOME	12,000	15,500	11,000	10,000
EXPENDITURE:				
Wages	3,000	5,500		4,500
Raw materials	5,000	4,000	3,000	2,500
Transport	1,000		3,000	2,000
Energy	500	2,000	1,000	500
TOTAL EXPENDITURE	9,500	14,500	12,000	9,500
Balance carried forward	2,500	1,000		500

Activity

Activity 3: Missing terms – Cash-flow forecast

Use the words below to help you fill in the gaps in the following paragraph.

- run out of money
- estimate
- increase
- accurate
- plans
- too much
- out of business
- profit
- expenditure

Cash-flow forecast is only an _____ of the amount of income and _____ which a business expects. The main purpose of the calculation is to estimate when the business may have _____ or too little cash. It does not calculate _____. When a shortage of cash, to pay bills, is expected, the business may need to change its _____ so that costs are reduced and attempts are made to _____ its income. Without sufficient cash, the business may go _____, not because it is unprofitable, but because it has _____. Short-term forecasts are likely to be more _____than long-term forecasts.

Evaluation points

1 How accurate are forecasts of income and expenditure likely to be? Recognising that they may not be 100 per cent accurate is important when assessing what the cash-flow forecast is telling you about the business.

2 You will need to consider, and be able to explain why most businesses, when forecasting, tend to *understate* expected income and *overstate* expected expenditure.

3 One of the most important points to completing a cash-flow forecast is for the business to consider how best it might respond to forecast surpluses of cash and, more importantly, shortages of cash. Being realistic is also important. There is no point in deciding that you will try to sell more products or services if the demand for them is likely to fall. Equally, cutting costs by sacking workers will not always work if those workers are needed to provide the goods or services which the business provides. Looking carefully at the situation in which the business finds itself and making realistic and achieveable changes to the forecast in order to improve the cash flow, will be necessary for the business to survive. Make sure you are able to explain this.

4 Not all businesses expect to have a cash flow surplus at the end of each month. It may be normal for the business to experience a shortage of funds for one or two months and then have a cash-flow surplus. Recognising the type of business, the likely level of demand month by month and the market in which it trades will be important factors in understanding what the cash-flow forecast is telling you about the business.

Cash flow and profit

Profit and a **cash-flow surplus** are *not* the same. Nor is a loss and a cash-flow deficit.

A business with a negative cash flow at the end of a month need not be making a loss. It might just happen that the flow of money out of the business for that month is greater than the flow of money into it. Equally, a business with a positive cash flow at the end of a month need not be profitable. The flow of money into the business for that month is greater than the flow of money out of the business in that month.

Unit 3.4.3 gave details on how different types profit are calculated.

Why forecast cash flow?

Most businesses will attempt to forecast the flow of cash into and out of the business for some or all of the following reasons:

● to identify when the business is likely to have a shortage or surplus of cash, and what it might do about the situation

Where will the money come from?

● to help the business plan for the future

● to provide targets to be achieved by employees of the business. The cash-flow forecast may have been devised on the assumption that the sales staff will achieve a given level of sales in one month. If this figure is not achieved, the business may run into cash-flow problems.

Sales staff have been doing their job

Problems and limitations of cash flow

● Cash-flow forecasts in the short term, covering the next few months, are likely to be more accurate than those for more than one year ahead for a variety of reasons. For example:

  ● the prices of goods sold and/or the cost of materials may be different to the forecast

  ● the possibility exists that a new competitor might enter the market and take sales away from the business

  ● the tastes of customers may change meaning that fewer goods are sold

  ● new technology may allow new and better products to be developed.

● The figures included in the cash flow forecast are only estimates.

● Estimates are likely to be more accurate when based on previous experience.

● The business may not have much control over some of the figures it has included in its forecast, e.g. prices of raw materials or energy.

● The forecast will need updating at regular intervals.

Activity

Activity 4: Calculation – Cash-flow forecast

1 Complete the cash-flow forecast by calculating the figures that are missing.

	March £	April £	May £	June £
Balance brought forward	20,000			
INCOME				
Sales revenue	100,000	125,000	130,000	80,000
Rental income	10,000	10,000	10,000	10,000
TOTAL INCOME				
EXPENDITURE				
Wages	20,000	25,000	20,000	30,000
Goods for resale	100,000	120,000	70,000	80,000
Electricity	0	10,000	0	0
Phone	5,000	0	0	5,000
TOTAL EXPENDITURE				
Balance carried forward				

Cash-flow forecast for Bowton Electrical Ltd

2 List *two* businesses that will probably have a fairly even flow of income from sales throughout the year and another *two* businesses which might only receive income from sales during two or three months of the year.

3 Using the cash-flow forecast you have completed for question 1, state the month in which the next phone and electricity bills are due. Give reasons for your answer.

4 Explain why Bowton Electrical Ltd might still be profitable, despite the fact that it has a negative cash flow during one month.

5 Explain the problems which there might be for this business when attempting to forecast income and expenditure after July.

Examination questions

Read the following information.

Tom and Sue own and run a farm. They have recently decided to set up a farm shop and have prepared a cash-flow forecast for June to September, predicting a cash surplus of £8,000 at the end of September.

They have now found that some of their figures are inaccurate and they need changing for the following reasons:

● Sales for June are likely to be disappointing – £400 because of bad weather

● Sales estimates for July to September are now:

   July £4,000   August £4,000   September £2,500

● The insurance premium due in June was £500.

● Workers wage costs are:

   July £700   August £700   September £500

a Using the information above and the cash-flow forecast below, rework and complete the cash-flow forecast for July to September to show how these changes will affect the business and what the cash surplus will now be at the end of September.   (8 marks)

Tom and Sue's cash-flow forecast June to September

	June £	July £	August £	September £
OPENING BALANCE brought forward	2,000	(200)		
Sales	500			
TOTAL INCOME	2,500			
EXPENSES				
Contribution to farm expenses	500	500	500	500
Wages	500			
Insurance	400	–	–	–
Advertising	100	200	100	–
Maintenance	200	200	200	500
Miscellaneous	300	100	200	100
Sue's wages	700	1,000	1,000	1,000
TOTAL EXPENSES	2,700			
CLOSING BALANCE Carried Forward	(200)			

b Identify three problems shown by the new cash-flow forecast and explain how Tom and Sue might solve them.   (6 marks)

Advice on how to answer the question

a You will need to read the information in the text and the cash-flow forecast very carefully. Working systematically through the information about the changes to the forecasts, write in the revised figures on the cash-flow forecast. When this has been done, you can start to work out the totals and the balance to carry forward at the end of each month to the start of the next month.

b Having worked out the new cash-flow forecast, you will need to look for three problems. These might be at times when the business is spending too much, or when its income is insufficient. An explanation of ways in which these problems may be solved will then need to be provided for each problem you have identified.

Key facts

- Businesses need to forecast the flow of cash to and from the business so that plans can be made for the future.
- Cash-flow forecasts are only estimates of expected income and expenditure.
- Cash left over at the end of one month is carried forward to the beginning of the next month.
- A negative cash flow does not mean that the business is unprofitable.
- A positive cash flow does not mean that the business is profitable.
- Cash flow needs to be managed so that the business does not run out of cash.
- Good cash-flow management is vital for the future success and survival of the business.

Key Terms

Make sure you can explain each of the following Key Terms

Income Money which the business receives.

Expenditure Money which the business pays out.

Cash-flow forecast A statement showing the expected flow of money into and out of a business over a period of time.

Balance carried forward The amount of cash left over at the end of the month. It is taken forward and used at the beginning of the next month and becomes the balance brought forward. It is sometimes called the **closing balance**.

Balance brought forward The amount of cash available at the beginning of the month which was left over at the end of the previous month. It is sometimes called the **opening balance**.

Positive cash flow During one month, more cash is flowing into the business than is flowing out of it. It is sometimes called a **cash-flow surplus**.

Negative cash flow During one month, more cash is flowing out of the business than is flowing into it. It is sometimes called a **cash-flow deficit**.

Unit 3.5.1

Competition

Introduction

Would you like to fly to the South of France for a weekend or a short break? A few years ago this was unthinkable for the vast majority of people. Nowadays a number of airlines offer cheap flights to destinations in Europe, making short trips abroad affordable for many more people. These airlines are usually called 'no-frills' airlines. What had happened was that a market where there had been little competition between businesses had become a competitive market. It was the traveller who was the biggest winner.

How the market for air travel changed

Before the 'no-frills' airlines came in to existence there was not a lot of competition in the market for air travel.

- There were a few large firms responsible for most of the sales.

- There was very little competition between airlines in terms of the price that they charged. If one airline did reduce its price, any competitors would do the same. The result would be that the airlines would keep the same level of sales but would reduce their profits.

- The airlines used non-price competition – competing on routes, quality of service, advertising and other forms of promotion.

After the 'no frills' airlines entered the market, it became more competitive.

- There were more firms in the market.

- The airlines began to compete with each other on price.

● There was still competition using advertising.

Examples of 'no-frills' airlines that helped to change the market are Ryanair, Jet2.com, bmibaby, Go, and EasyJet. EasyJet was founded by a man called Stelios. He believed that there would be a demand for cheaper flights. The secret was to make it profitable to provide these by reducing the costs as well as prices. This was achieved in several ways:

● People were encouraged to book directly, using the internet. This saved money because travel agents were not involved, nor did EasyJet have to employ large numbers of staff to handle bookings.

● A 'no frills' service was offered. Passengers were not provided with a free meal during flights. Instead, they could buy snacks on the plane if they wanted to.

● EasyJet flew from airports that were not very busy and where landing fees were cheaper.

● Planes stayed only for a minimum period of time at an airport, leading to further savings on airport fees.

The rest, as they say, is history. EasyJet has grown. Other cut-price airlines have also done well though some, like 'Go', no longer exist. Some of the major airlines have introduced their own cut-price subsidiaries. The market for air travel has been changed. It has become more competitive. There are now more firms than before and price competition is now more important.

Activity

Activity 1: Research activity – Types of markets

Using the internet, plan a flight to somewhere in Europe. Find out which airlines fly to the destination you want to go to. Try the 'no-frills' airline websites such as Ryanair, Jet2.com, bmibaby, and EasyJet and compare them with airlines such as BA, Air France, KLM and so on. Compare the cost of the flights. When you calculate the cost, make sure you compare like for like. For example, does the cost include travel insurance, carrying bags in the hold or hand-luggage only? Compare what you find out with those of other students. What conclusions can you draw from your research?

Stelios, the owner of EasyJet, helped to increase competition for air passengers.

Market types

There are two main types of markets – competition and monopoly. In practice these are two extremes. Some markets will have a lot of competition; this is called **perfect competition**. In others, there may be no competition at all; this is **monopoly**. In-between these two extremes, there will be a range of different markets with different degrees of competition. Figure 1 shows the idea of a range of market types – A, B, X and Y – between the two extremes of competition and monopoly. The words at the bottom describe the amount of competition.

Figure 2 summarises the main features of the two extremes, perfect competition and monopoly.

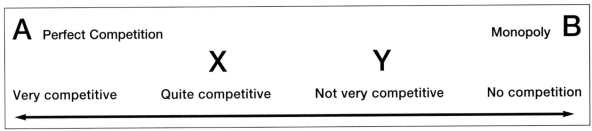

A Perfect Competition			Monopoly B
	X	Y	
Very competitive	Quite competitive	Not very competitive	No competition

Figure 1 The range of market types – competition to monopoly

Competition	Feature	Monopoly
● *Many* firms	*Number of firms*	● *One* firm
● *Many* products, all very different	*Products*	● *One* main product available
● *Low* prices (usually)	*Prices*	● Often *higher* prices than under competition – but not always
● *Advertising* is used to attract customers from other businesses ● *Branding* is used to build customer loyalty (usually to try to reduce competition) ● *Location*s are used that are convenient for customers	*Other ways of competing* *Barriers that prevent competition*	● *Advertising* may be used to stop competition and keep the monopoly ● *Patents* prevent other firms copying a product or production process ● Large monopolies can get *economies of scale*, leading to low costs and prices ● Firms may *collude* (work together to prevent competition) ● *Government rules* may create a monopoly ● High *start-up costs* stop new firms from entering a market

Figure 2 Features of competition and monopoly

Activity

Activity 2: Matching terms – Types of markets

Read the three case studies below. Match them to the type of market – is there perfect competition, competition (between competition and monopoly) or monopoly?

Case Study		Type of market
Case study one Southern Water supplies all the households with water and sewers in Kent, Sussex, Hampshire and the Isle of Wight. It owns all the water supply pipes and sewers and no other firms are allowed to use these to supplywater and sewage services to the households.	 Southern Water supplies counties in the south of England	Competition (but not perfect competition)
Case study two The Wholesale Fruit and Vegetable Market in Liverpool opens at around 4 a.m. The wholesalers bring their goods and set up stall. Grocers, mainly owners of small shops, come to the market to buy stock. The fruit and vegetables on offer vary little from stall to stall. Buyers go from stall to stall looking for the best prices.	 Fruit and vegetable wholesale market	Monopoly
Case study three The main petrol retailers in Britain are BP, Esso, Shell and Texaco. There are some independents, but none of them match these firms for sales. Many of the garages that sell petrol for the large retailers are franchises. They are strictly controlled in terms of the price that they can charge for petrol. In practice, the price charged by one petrol station will be the same as that charged by others owned or controlled by the big companies. One of the main ways in which they compete with each other is in terms of sites. The best sites for petrol stations are on the main trunk roads. The retailers also compete with each other by offering loyalty cards – points collected on these can lead to money off a future purchase or to free goods.	 Garage on a busy trunk road	Very, very competitive (perfect competition)

Activity

Activity 3: Zone activity – Advantages and disadvantages of different market types to consumers

Use the statements about market types to complete the table of advantages and disadvantages of the different types of markets. You may use some statements more than once.

Competition		Statements
Advantages	**Disadvantages**	a Consumers may benefit from lower prices because they can shop around to find the best deal.
Monopoly		b There is little or no choice of goods.
Advantages	**Disadvantages**	c Prices may be high – the seller knows that customers have no alternative.
		d A wide range of goods with different features may be available.
		e A firm may be able to get economies of scale and may be able to charge lower prices than if competition existed.
		f Firms must be efficient to survive, meaning costs and prices must be low.
		g A firm does not need to be efficient to survive – costs and prices may be high.
		h Producers may collude with each other to fix a high price.
		i Prices may be high to cover spending on advertising.

Market shares

Information is collected about the share of a market that businesses have. To calculate the share of a market that one business has, its sales are expressed as a percentage of the total market sales. Suppose that the total sales in the market for gloves are worth £50m per year. A producer of gloves, 'Handy Gloves', has total sales of £10m in that year. The calculation for its share of the market is:

$$\frac{\text{sales of the business}}{\text{total sales in the market}} \times \frac{100}{1} = \text{market share}$$

$$\frac{£10m}{£50m} \times \frac{100}{1} = 20\%$$

This kind of information is often presented using a pie chart. The pie chart on page 330 shows the **market share** that Handy Gloves has.

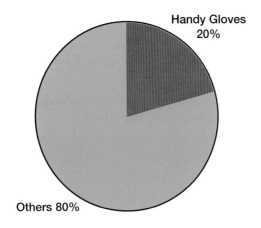

Activity 4: Calculation – Pie chart of market shares

Using the information provided, draw a pie chart to show the share of the market of each of the following firms. This can be done on a computer by entering the data into a spreadsheet and then creating a chart from it.

Total market sales = £100
Firm A: £25m
Firm B: £10m
Firm C: £40m
Firm D: £15m
Others: £10m

Market shares and market forms

Information about market shares can be used to decide what kind of market exists:

Monopoly. In law, a monopoly exists when a business has a market share of at least 25 per cent. Any firm having 25 per cent or more of the market is called a **monopolist**.

Perfect competition. Competition exists when there are many firms, all with a small share of the market.

Competition may exist among a number of firms who share out sales between them, but where there are not a lot of firms. The figures in Activity 4 show a market in which there are four large firms who sell most of the share of the market. There may be quite a lot of competition between them.

Changing the competitive environment

Businesses can change how competitive a market is by what they do.

1 *Increasing competition:* Competition can increase in a market by any of the factors shown in Figure 3:

Figure 3 How competition in a market can be increased

New firms entering a market	This is what the "no-frills" airlines did in the air travel market. The increased number of sellers increased the competition. Many markets in the UK have become more competitive because of foreign firms entering the market (see Unit 3.5.5 Globalisation).
Privatisation	Governments have encouraged more competition through privatisation; this is when government-owned businesses have been sold to private owners. They have allowed firms to enter some markets which used to be monopolies. For example, electricity and gas retailers can now compete with each other to supply power to households, which was not possible before the 1980s.
Selling new products	Existing businesses can increase competition by introducing new products and services. Competition by mobile-phone producers has increased as they have brought out more and more models.

Cutting prices	A business may try to get more sales by reducing its prices so that its goods are cheaper than those of its competitors. This may succeed if other firms do not also reduce their prices and there is no difference in quality.
Increasing advertising	A business may do this to persuade customers to buy from it, rather than its competitors.

2 *Reducing competition:* If competition is reduced a lot, a monopoly may be created. Firms can reduce or restrict competition through any of the means described in Figure 4:

Figure 4 How competition in a market can be decreased

Taking over competitors or merging with them	BA wanted to merge with American Airlines, partly to reduce competition on air routes to and from America. A merger would reduce competition
Using the marketing mix to increase their share of the market at the expense of other businesses	Businesses promote products to create 'brands', though it is not easy to do this. This can lead to **internal growth**.
Taking out a patent or copyright on what they produce	A patent means that no other firm can copy the product or process without the permission of the patent holder. For example, Pilkington Glass have the patent for the 'float-glass' method of producing glass. A copyright is a similar restriction but applies to artistic creations such as books, fims and music.
Collusion (working together)	Firms may agree to charge the same price for a product rather than compete and sell at lower prices. This is now illegal. When firms work together to fix the price of a product they are known as a **cartel**.
Internal growth	A firm can grow by increasing its sales. If this is at the expense of other businesses, competition falls and it is possible that it will become a monopoly.

Government and competition

In general, government in the UK has encouraged competition because of the advantages it can bring. However, monopolies can also have advantages and where they do they are allowed to remain in existence. The government is against 'restrictive practices' such as cartels. This is when businesses work together to prevent free competition between each other.

Evaluation

Competition between businesses is often a good thing, bringing many advantages such as lower prices, more choices for the consumer, better service and more efficient methods of production. Monopolies can abuse the fact that there is no competition by exploiting consumers through, for example, charging high prices. Why, then, are monopolies not illegal in the UK? The reason for this is that sometimes a monopoly can bring greater advantages than competition. A large business that is a monopoly may, because of economies of scale, be able to sell goods more cheaply than lots of smaller firms that compete with each other. Also, because a monopoly may make big profits, it can afford to do research and development to invent new and better products. So whether a monopoly is good or bad depends on what it does – the advantages and disadvantages of a monopoly need to 'weighed up' to see which is greater. Organisations like the Office of Fair Trading and the Competition Commission collect evidence on behalf of the government to decide whether monopoly businesses and the things that they do are actually good or bad.

Activity

Activity 5: Explanation – Increasing competition

Read the following passage about the Competition Commission and BAA.

> In 2008, BAA owned seven airports in the UK, including the three major airports in London – Heathrow, Standsted and Gatwick – meaning that BAA had a monopoly in London. Airlines that wanted to serve London had to fly to these airports; travellers had little choice. The Competition Commission wrote a report in which it criticised BAA. It said that because the airports did not have to compete with each other, they provided poor-quality services to the customers. It also said that the airports had failed to expand by building new runways so that it was not possible for them to meet the increased demand for air travel. The Competition Commission recommended that BAA should be forced to sell two of the airports to another company so that there would be more competition.

BAA has been told to sell off Gatwick Airport

Explain the benefits that would result from increased competition between airports in London owned by different companies.

Activity

Activity 6: Missing words – Office of Fair Trading and cartels

Read the passage below.

> #### Three imprisoned in first OFT criminal prosecution for bid rigging
>
> *Peter Whittle, David Brammar and Bryan Allison pleaded guilty at Southwark Crown Court to dishonestly participating in a cartel. Allison was the managing director of Dunlop Oil and Marine Limited whilst Brammer was its sales director. The company makes hoses to carry oil between tankers (large ships used for transporting oil) and storage facilities. Whittle traded as an independent consultant but in practice was employed full-time by Dunlop Oil and Marine Limited. He worked with other hose producers in different countries in the world. He arranged for the various companies that sold hoses, including Dunlop Oil and Marine Ltd, to take it in turns to get contracts to supply hoses. This meant that the different producers of hoses did not have to compete with each other to earn a sale – they would agree which firm should have the contract, then they would fix the prices which they tendered so that the firm got the contract. The court case followed an investigation carried out by the Office of Fair Trading (OFT).*
>
> *Source: Adapted from a Press Release by the Office of Fair Trading [OFT], 11 June 2008*

Complete the paragraph below about cartels using the words provided.

● higher   ● compete   ● profits   ● tender
● illegal   ● lowest   ● good   ● bad
● anti-competitive   ● fix   ● turn   ● cartel.

A cartel exists when a number of firms work together to _____ the price of a product and to share out work between them. Suppose there are four building firms, A, B, C and D, that _____ to build new housing estates in a region of the country. To get the work, they must _____ a price to the property developer. The developer will often give the work to the firm that quotes the _____ price. This is _____ for the developer who gets the work done at a low price but _____ for the building firms because the profit they may make may be low. If the building firms work together as a _____, they can increase their _____ by not competing on price. Between them they may be decide that firm A should get the first contract. It tells B, C and D what price it will tender and they tender a _____ price so the developer chooses firm A. Next it might be firm B's _____ and so on. A cartel is an example of an _____ practice. A cartel is _____.

Activity

Activity 7: Research – Anti-competitive practices

Use the internet to research examples of anti-competitive practices and the work of the organisations that are responsible for maintaining competition in the UK. Useful websites are those for newspapers like the *Guardian* and *The Daily Telegraph*, and organisations like the Department of Trade and Industry and the Office of Fair Trading and the Competition Commission.

Write a short report about the case that you have researched.

Examination questions

1 Ormskirk is a small town in Lancashire. There are four supermarkets and a number of grocery shops in the town. State and explain two advantages to the buyers of groceries that this competition will bring. (4 marks)

2 Steptoe Ltd has a monopoly in the specialist footwear market.

  a What is meant by a monopoly? (2 marks)

  b Why should the Government control monopolies? (6 marks)

Advice on how to answer the questions

1 The buyers will be able to choose which of the shops to buy from. Think about how the shops must compete to get their custom – these will be the advantages that the customers gain.

2 The first parts of both questions require clear definitions of terms. The answer to Part (b) of question 2 is that government should control monopolies to stop their disadvantages. You need to explain these possible disadvantages.

Key facts

- Businesses operate in markets.
- There are two main forms of markets – competition and monopoly.
- The form of market influences the way that firms in the market behave – the prices it can charge, how much it advertises and so on.
- Different forms of market have different advantages and disadvantages.
- Government controls markets so that they work in the interest of the public.
- Generally the government prefers competition.

Key Terms

Make sure you can explain each of the following Key Terms

Perfect competition A market in which there are a large number of sellers.

Monopoly A market dominated by one seller.

Patents The right to the use of an invention for a number of years.

Market share The percentage of the total sales in a market accounted for by a firm.

Monopolist A firm that accounts for at least 25 per cent of the sales in a market.

Privatisation When organisations owned by the state are sold off to private owners.

Cartel A group of firms that work together to fix prices.

Business ethics

By studying this unit you will be able to:

● **Explain what is meant by the term 'ethics'**
● **Discuss examples of ethical and unethical business practices**
● **Discuss ways in which businesses can behave ethically**
● **Evaluate the benefits and costs to businesses of behaving in an ethical manner.**

Introduction

Primark is one of the largest sellers of clothing in the UK today. Manthseeth was an 11-year-old girl born in Sri Lanka. Her parents were killed by terrorists' bombs. She moved to India, where she found work in a textile factory in a refugee camp. The people who ran the factory knew that refugees were desperate for work.

In India, Mantheesh worked in a house in a camp. She worked on clothes which had labels attached, from which it was possible to work out that they were for Primark. On a good day, she could earn 40 rupees (60p). She sewed beads on to the clothes. If it was night, they worked by candlelight because the electricity in the camp was not good enough. This practice was discovered during an investigation for the BBC Panorama programme and *The Observer* newspaper. The clothes were bought by a business, which then sold them to Primark

When Primark was told about this, it immediately stopped buying the clothes from the firm that supplied them. It also created the Primark Better Lives Foundation, which is designed to improve the living standards of people like Manthseeth by giving financial help. Primark said that it was an ethical producer, that it had not been aware that its supplier was using child labour. It also claims that its prices are low not because it uses child labour, but because they do not spend a lot on advertising, or have large mark-ups on their goods. However, critics have said that Primark only sacked the supplier because it wanted to avoid bad publicity. Other investigations have shown that some other clothing retailers have bought clothes made with child labour. Another famous example was Gap.   *Source: Adapted from* The Observer *newspaper, 22 June 2008*

Activity

Activity 1: Explanation – Ethical issues

a What are your opinions about the following?

- One in six children in the world today is involved in **child labour**, doing work that is damaging to his or her mental, physical and emotional development.
- Globally, between 210 and 240 million children are child labourers.
- 126 million of these children are engaged in dangerous work.
- Every year 22,000 children die in work-related accidents.
- 73 million working children are under 10.

b Primark was buying clothes from an area in India where a lot of child labour was being used. Do you think it should continue to buy clothes from this area in India?

c Would you stop buying goods from a shop that was found to be buying its supplies from a firm that used child labour?

The meaning of ethics

Ethics is about what it is morally right and wrong to do. It is not always easy to decide what is right and wrong in business and it can change over time. Two hundred years ago, many people thought it was right to trade in slaves, taking people from Africa and selling them in America. Nowadays, most people would think slavery is wrong.

Ethics is concerned with many areas of business activity today. Figure 1 gives some business activities and ethical issues connected to them. Some people may think it is morally acceptable to do these things, others will think it is wrong.

Figure 1 Examples of ethical issues for business

Area of business activity	Examples of ethical issues
Accountancy	<ul><li>Bribing others, perhaps to buy from you or sell to you</li><li>Business executives giving themselves large bonuses even if the business does not perform well</li></ul>
Human Resources	<ul><li>Discriminating against workers because of their age, gender or race</li><li>Spying on workers</li><li>Randomly testing workers to check whether they are taking illegal drugs or not</li><li>Preventing workers from being members of a trade union</li><li>Having poor health and safety at work practices</li></ul>
Marketing and sales	<ul><li>Fixing the price of a product by making an agreement with a competitor</li><li>Using sex in advertisements</li><li>Selling inhumane military equipment such as nuclear, chemical and biological weapons, or weapons such as landmines and cluster bombs</li><li>Selling to countries that violate **human rights** – some people think that Saudi Arabia violates rights by using capital punishment without</li></ul>

	proper legal procedures, carrying out corporal punishment (such as amputating the hands of thieves) and by oppressing women and homosexuals
Production	• Selling faulty or dangerous products • Causing pollution • Testing products on animals • Using child labour • Buying very cheaply from Third World producers • Having goods made in **sweat shops**: factories that may not have good health and safety practices and which pay very low wages
Intellectual property rights	• Photocopying a larger part of a book than copyright laws permit • **Pirating** films to sell on DVD

Unit 2.3.1 discussed the main types of stakeholders and how they were affected by business activity. Each type of stakeholder is affected by ethical decisions. Ethics places a right and a duty or responsibility on the stakeholders. The following are examples of these rights and duties:

• **Owners** take a risk and have a right to make a fair profit. They have a responsibility to look after their employees and to care for the environment.

I only do it for the fans

I have the right to make a fair profit!

• **Workers** have the right not to be exploited. Also, they have the responsibility to do a fair day's work for a fair day's pay.

• **Customers** have the right not to be exploited. They may have the duty not to buy goods and services from unethical producers.

• **Government** (local and national) has the responsibility to protect and provide for its citizens.

Activity

Activity 2: True or false – Ethical and unethical activities

Tick the true or false box next to each of the statements below to say whether or not they are generally thought to be ethical practices.

Statement	True ✔	False ✔
It is ethical for a football manager to take a bribe because other managers do the same.		
It is not ethical to sell arms to rulers who might use them to crush opposition in the country.		
It is ethical to employ very young children as long as they are paid a fair wage.		
It is ethical to copy films because the producers make a lot of money from them.		
It is ethical to buy goods from Third World countries, in order to help their businesses to develop.		
It is ethical to save money by reducing health and safety measures, as long as it helps the business to survive and so protect jobs.		

Activity

Activity 3: Zone activity – The ethics of spying on workers

Some employers spy on their workers. Spying may involve tracking records of how they use their computers – tracking emails they send and internet sites they visit while at work. It might also involve listening in to telephone calls, or using cameras to monitor what they are doing. The following are arguments for and against employers spying on their employees while they are at work to control what they do. Put the statements under the correct heading in the box below, 'for spying at work' or 'against spying at work'.

a Spying can help to stop people stealing at work.

b Workers should be allowed to carry out some private business at work, such as arranging a visit to a dentist or booking a holiday.

c The business pays for the equipment and for the time of the worker so it can make sure they are used for business purposes.

d The business can benefit from workers chatting with each other by phone, email or in person because it can lead to new ideas that help the business.

e The workers may not like being monitored so may not feel good about their employer and may not work as hard as they might otherwise do.

Arguments for spying at work	Arguments against spying at work

Activity

Activity 4: Research – Ethical issues

a Using the internet, find out about cases involving either (i) pirating copies of films or (ii) the use of animals in testing products. Describe what has happened. State the arguments for and against the practice. Use the Google search engine, the BBC website or a newspaper website such as www.guardian.co.uk or www.telegraph.co.uk.

b Choose one other ethical issue, either from Figure 1 or from your own knowledge. Write a newspaper article to explain the issue.

Ethical business practices – case studies

The Co-operative Bank

The Co-operative Bank adopted an ethical policy in 1992. In 2007, it estimated that it lost £14m worth of business because of its policy. The bank will not lend to firms that undertake animal testing, those that cause damage to the environment and those that deal with oppressive regimes and military hardware (guns, tanks, etc). Despite losing this business, the profits of the Co-operative Bank rose in 2007 by 11.7 per cent, from £49.3m to £55.1m.

Evaluation point

Sometimes doing the right thing may cost a business some profit. It may lose out on sales or may have to buy more expensive materials. This could be the cost of being ethical. However, being ethical could also lead to more profits. Many customers would not like to buy from unethical businesses and would be prepared to pay a little bit more if necessary to buy from **ethical businesses**. One of the reasons for the growth in the profits of the Co-operative Bank in 2007 may have been because customers want to deal with an ethical organisation. Primark was very quick to avoid the possibility of being labelled unethical when it was discovered that child labour was being used in the production of clothes that it sells. Being ethical may not always lead to lower profits.

Fairtrade

The Fairtrade Foundation exists to 'bring justice and sustainable development' to trade so that 'everyone, through their work, can maintain a decent and dignified livelihood and develop their full potential'. To achieve this it tries to help those who live and work in poor countries. It uses the Fairtrade Mark. This guarantees to the consumer that the retailer has paid a fair price to the farmers' groups, which produced the goods, so that they have extra money to pay for the education of their children and other social needs. Many retailers in the UK are increasingly selling Fairtrade products. Sainsbury's supermarket will only sell Fairtrade bananas, Marks and Spencers work with 600 Fairtrade cotton farmers and Top Shop sells Fairtrade tunics. Figure 2 below shows the growth in sales of Fairtrade produce between 1998 and 2007. It shows significant increases in the value of the sales of Fairtrade items.

However, some people criticise the Fairtrade idea. Producers in Third World countries may become dependent on their Fairtrade sales. In India and China, many people, who have not been protected by Fairtrade, have managed to increase their earnings by producing the right goods at the right prices. Other critics say that the prices the producers are paid are not a lot more than they would be and that the focus should be on developing and providing the farmers with new technology, which would increase the amount they could produce.

Product	2002 £m	2007 £m
Coffee	23.1	117.0
Tea	5.9	30.0
Chocolate/cocoa	7.0	34.0
Honey products	4.9	5.0
Bananas	17.3	150.0
Flowers	n/a	24.0
Wine	n/a	8.2
Cotton	n/a	34.8
Other	3.5	90.0
TOTAL	63.0	493.0

Figure 2 Estimated UK retail sales by value 2002 – 2007: Fairtrade goods

Evaluation

Consumers who want to buy eco-friendly goods will pay more than those who do not, according to research by Family Investments. If they wanted to buy eco-friendly or ethical goods for their babies, they were paying £700 more per year. (Source: Adapted from the BBC website). Ethical baby food, for example, was 79p a jar compared with 63p for a regular baby food. Not everyone can afford to buy the ethical products. Perhaps it is easier for rich people to be ethical than poor people! Or perhaps it is easier for us to be ethical when the economy is doing well and incomes are growing, rather than in a time of high unemployment and falling incomes.

Activity

Activity 5: Calculation – Sales of Fairtrade goods

Using the figures in Figure 2:

a   Construct a bar chart to show the value of sales of coffee, tea and chocolate/cocoa in 2002 and 2007.

b   Calculate the increase in the value of the sales of chocolate/cocoa between 2002 and 2007.

c   Calculate the percentage increase in the value of the sales of tea between 2002 and 2008 (you might like to round up the 2002 value to 6.0 to make the sum easier).

d   Which product had the largest increase in the value of sales between 2002 and 2007?

Activity

Activity 6: Missing words – Ethical business

Complete the paragraph using the words given below:

- child
- less
- human rights
- competitive
- more
- right
- survive
- safe
- money.

Ethics is about _____ and wrong. An example of an unethical business activity is when a firm buys products made using _____ labour. Another unethical practice would be a firm that does not provide its workers with a _____ working environment. A business that sells arms to the rulers of a country who do not give proper _____ _____ to their citizens may not be ethical. Sometimes it saves a business _____ by not being ethical. This may be important if the business is in a very _____ market. Some of the competitors may not be ethical and so they can charge _____ for their product. The result might be that the ethical business cannot _____. However, many customers are now prepared to pay _____ for products that are sold by ethical producers.

Examination questions

Nicole and Colin own a café business.

Question 1

a   Explain what is meant by ethical behaviour.   (2 marks)

b   Give two examples of ethical practices that Nicole and Colin could use in their business.

     (2 marks)

Question 2

Brooklyn Fashions sells mass-produced fashion clothing. It is in a very competitive market. The directors think that it should be operated as an ethical business. Discussing the advantages and disadvantages to Brooklyn Fashions, recommend whether or not it should operate as an ethical business.   (8 marks)

Advice on how to answer the questions

1 a This question needs a short definition.

   b Make sure that the examples that you use are relevant to a café.

2 Write about advantages and disadvantages of ethical businesses in the context – it is about making and selling mass-produced and, therefore, cheap clothes and it is a competitive market, so costs will be important. Being ethical may mean slightly higher costs and prices. Whether or not it will be successful may depend on how well it can sell the idea of ethical production to its customers, which may also depend on who they are, how well off they are and how well the economy is doing.

Key facts

- Ethical production is about doing what is morally right.
- There is now a much greater awareness of ethical issues in business.
- More and more consumers are concerned with ethical issues.
- Being an ethical business can bring advantages in terms of sales.
- Being an ethical business may bring costs in terms of lost sales opportunities, or higher costs and prices, or lower profits. It may even threaten the existence of the business.

Key Terms

Make sure you can explain each of the following Key Terms

Child labour This is the use of young children in order to achieve low-cost production.

Ethics This is about what is morally correct and what is morally wrong.

Human rights This is the idea that all people should have basic rights and freedoms such as liberty, freedom of speech, equality in law, the rights to food, education and to work.

Sweat shops These are factories where people are worked very hard, often in poor conditions, and paid a low wage.

Pirating Illegally copying films and music.

Ethical businesses Businesses that behave in a morally correct way.

Environmental influences on business

Learning Outcomes

By studying this unit you will be able to:

- **Explain the importance of the environment to consumers and to businesses**
- **Explain how consumers and businesses may cause harm to the environment – the social costs of production**
- **Discuss how businesses may become more environmentally friendly through 'sustainable production'**
- **Explain what actions governments can take to reduce the damage to the environment caused by consumers and businesses**
- **Evaluate the effects on businesses of actions by governments to limit damage to the environment.**

Introduction

The previous unit in this book looked at ethical production. How businesses use the environment is also a part of business ethics. Environmental issues are dealt with separately in this unit because there is a lot to cover. Read about The Shanks Group, then answer Activity 1.

The Shanks Group owns businesses in different parts of the UK and in mainland Europe. It disposes of rubbish. In the UK, it dumps nearly 75 per cent of the rubbish in landfill sites. Just over 25 per cent is recycled. Its businesses in Holland recycle 83 per cent of the rubbish they deal with, while those in Belgium recycle 51 per cent. The Shanks Group intends to build more recycling centres

Many EU countries use landfill less than the UK

in the UK. It intends in the future to process organic waste (rubbish that will rot) to produce methane gas, which can then be used to generate electricity.

Activity

Activity 1: Explanation – Recycling waste

a Explain what a landfill site is.

b Why is it necessary to reduce the use of landfill sites?

c Explain what is meant by 'recycling' rubbish.

d Are the plans of the Shanks Group to process organic waste good? Give reasons for your answer.

The importance of the environment

In this unit, the environment means our natural world. Households and businesses make use of the environment in three ways:

1 *It provides us with natural resources.* These include agricultural crops, fish, animals, wood, metal, oil, coal, gas and the land itself. Businesses provide goods and services using these, which results in profits and good standards of living.

2 *It is something from which we get pleasure.* We like fresh air and enjoy a walk in the park, fishing and swimming in rivers, lakes and the sea, looking at scenery, climbing in the mountains and so on. Again, businesses may make profits by, for example, providing leisure activities, such as coach tours or outdoor pursuits, for consumers.

3 *It is somewhere to dump waste* produced by households and businesses. Land may be filled in using rubbish; businesses may

dump waste in the sea, or in the rivers; and gases may be put into the atmosphere. Businesses like the Shanks Group earn money by dealing with waste. However, some businesses have lowered their costs and increased profits by dumping waste in a way that may harm the environment.

The social costs of production

When we make use of the environment, either as consumers or as producers, we can cause problems for society – these are called the 'social costs of production'. Some of the problems are as follows:

- *We are using up* **non-renewable resources**. Non-renewable resources are those that can be used only once and cannot be replaced. If we take oil from the ground, that oil is not replaced. Some scientists are saying that the world will run out of oil in the next 20 to 30 years.

- *We are spoiling the look of natural resources.* If we quarry stone from a mountainside, or build a motorway through countryside, or construct a housing estate in a rural area, it may reduce the pleasure that people get from enjoying the scenery or walking in the country.

- *We are causing congestion on the roads.* This has become a major problem in the UK. It costs time and money for businesses and people, as well as adding to the pollution of the atmosphere and increases our use of petrol and diesel, which are made from oil.

- *We are causing pollution and global warming.* The main kinds of pollution are:

- Air pollution. This is created when gases such as carbon dioxide are put into the atmosphere from cars, planes, factories and power stations. It is thought that 4.6 million people die each year from illnesses caused by air pollution, 310,000 of these are people who live in Europe. The types of illness that air pollution causes include asthma, bronchitis, emphysema, lung and heart diseases and respiratory allergies.

- Noise pollution. This occurs when people's peace is disturbed by noise from cars, factories and so on.

- Pollution of the sea and rivers. This occurs when, for example, businesses pump waste produce, such as chemicals, into the sea and rivers.

Global warming

When we burn fossil fuels such as coal and oil, **carbon emissions** result – carbon dioxide (CO_2) is put into the atmosphere. These emissions are causing **global warming**, which is a rise in average temperatures. This is causing the ice at the North and South poles to melt, raising the levels of the seas. Scientists think this will alter the weather and our ability to grow crops, and will threaten some species of animals.

Activity

Activity 2: Poster drawing – Using the environment

Think about the local area around your school. Individually or in groups, draw a poster that shows the costs to the environment in this area that result from consumers and producers using it. Also, show the benefits that consumers and producers gain from their local environment. The rules for drawing this poster are that you can use lots of pictures and symbols and numbers, but you cannot use more than ten words. Once you have drawn it, you need to explain it either to the whole class, or to some of the other students in your class.

Activity

Activity 3: Research activity – Environmental problems

Research a global, national or local environmental problem. A good place for information may be the local newspaper (you can read many of these on-line now). You could come across problems of litter, pollution of the atmosphere, the use of land such as greenbelt or threats to areas of scientific interest, problems with rivers, congestion on the roads and so on. Write a brief report about the problem.

'Green' business – sustainability

More and more people have become concerned about our use of the environment. Organisations like the pressure group, Greenpeace, have made people more aware of the problems. More consumers now want **'green'** products and businesses now offer lots of 'green'' products. One way of being 'green' is to use **renewable resources** rather than non-renewable ones. This means that production is **sustainable**, since the resources used are renewable or have been recycled. Here are some examples of businesses that are changing their products or services:

- Nokia's ReMade. This mobile phone is made from 100 per cent recycled materials. Additionally, this phone has energy-saving graphics and other eco-friendly features.

- Rosedale Funeral Home in Wymondham near Norwich uses coffins made from pineapple leaves, willow and bamboo.

- The Visit Scotland website advertises green tourism, giving a list of hotels and guest houses that are efficient users of energy. It also encourages cycling holidays.

- Bulldog makes men's toiletries such as moisturisers, shower gels and shaving gels using natural ingredients rather than chemicals.

- Tesco Supermarket transports some of the wine it sells by canal to reduce the carbon emissions which would come from using road transport.

- Supermarkets are trying to cut back on the use of plastic bags, plastic being made from oil.

- Marks and Spencers produces polyester clothing made from recycled plastic bottles rather than from oil.

- Electricity is being generated by wind power, wave and water power and solar panels to reduce the use of coal and oil.

- Bio-diesel is made from processed crops like rapeseed. Bioethanol, which is a substitute for petrol, is made from cereals and sugar beet. As well as being renewable resources, they are also carbon neutral – i.e. when these plants grow, they take out CO_2 from the atmosphere. Using the diesel or petrol puts about the same amount of CO_2 back.

- Some car manufacturers have already developed hydrogen-cell (battery) powered cars, e.g. Toyota have developed the Prius which runs on petrol and battery power.

- Some businesses are reducing the amount of packaging they use; others are using packaging made from recycled resources, while others are designing packaging to be recyclable.

Renewable energy – but do these spoil the environment?

Evaluation

It is true that people have become more aware of environmental products. However, they usually have to pay more for these. Sometimes this is because the producer has to pay more for natural materials but sometimes it is because the producer knows that many consumers are prepared to pay slightly more and so the firm can increase its profits. Also, if there is a recession and incomes are low, people may switch back to non-green products because they cannot afford to pay the extra for green products.

Activity

Activity 4: Research – green and not so green products

Imagine that you are buying Christmas presents for you friends and family – toys, toiletries, bags, clothes and so on. Research gift catalogues to find presents that are eco-friendly. You will be able to find these on the internet – use Google or a similar search engine. Write down your list of presents and explain how each one is environmentally friendly.

OR

Find out about environmentally friendly cars – use the internet. Fuel-efficiency (miles per gallon) is one measure that can be used; another is the CO^2 emissions of the car. Compare hybrid cars such as the Toyota Prius with petrol and diesel cars. Write down a list of about ten cars from the best to the worst, in terms of fuel efficiency. Explain why you have put the cars in the order that you have.

'Green' advice to business

Businesses can also reduce the damage they cause to the environment by encouraging good practices. The following list of advice is taken from several websites that advise firms how to make production more sustainable:

- Switch off lights when not used, or install sensors that switch lights off automatically when there is no one in the room. Do not leave computers on standby.

- Dispose of waste properly. Recycle things like paper and toner cartridges.

- Buy recyclable materials. Use fuel-efficient vehicles.

- Encourage staff to cycle, to use public transport or to car-share to get to work.

- Only print documents when necessary. When printing is necessary, print on both sides of the paper.

- Use water carefully. Check for leaks, install taps that switch off automatically.

- Insulate the building well to reduce heat loss. Close windows when it is cold outside.

- Use solar or wind power to generate electricity.

- Use video-conferencing for meetings to reduce travel.

- Use crockery, not polystyrene cups and dishes.

Renewable energy sources save money

Activity

Activity 5: Explanation – Making your school green

Individually, or in groups, think about your school. Discuss whether or not it is green – use the list of advice above to help you to make a start and add any other ideas that you have. Write down two lists. In the first, write all the things you can think of that happen in school that are green. In the second, write down all the ways in which your school could become greener. Briefly explain the things that you have listed.

Government and the environment

Governments can take action to deal with environmental problems. Some of the actions that are carried out are listed below.

Taxes

The government can tax products that cause damage to the environment. Car owners must pay Vehicle Excise Duties or 'road tax' each year. The amount of the tax to be paid depends on how much carbon the car emits. Large 4x4 cars often have high carbon emissions and are taxed very heavily. These taxes on petrol and cars can be justified by saying the money brought in can pay to deal with the pollution caused by the motor car.

Rules and regulations

These are designed to prevent or limit damage to the environment. For example, all cars over three years old must pass an MOT. Their carbon emissions are checked and any that are thought to produce too much fail the test. Another example of a rule is 'green belt', which is land that cannot be built on. It is usually found in or around towns. The idea is to stop the area becoming too built-up. The EU has introduced rules about how products like fridges and freezers can now be disposed of. This is because they contain CFCs (chloro fluoro carbons), i.e. gases that are damaging the ozone layer of the sky.

Advertising and labelling and education

Governments can encourage and control labelling that indicates how environmentally friendly a product is.

- The European energy label indicates the efficiency of electrical goods, such as washing machines and freezers.

- Farmers who use organic farming methods can label their products to show that they have been certified by Organic Farmers & Growers (OF&G), which is the certifying body.

- The government controls advertising and labelling so that businesses do not make false claims for their products.

The government promotes the idea of being environmentally friendly in many ways.

- It educates businesses by providing information on websites.

- It is educating pupils in schools to think about environmental issues. You may have done some work on green issues in citizenship or PSHE lessons, as well as in subjects like science, geography, design and technology, and you are doing it now in business studies.

Carbon permits

These are a method of making businesses and households pay for the pollution they cause. Under the European Union Emission Trading Scheme, businesses are given a permit or credits, which allow them to produce a specific amount of carbon. If a business wants, or needs, to produce more carbon emissions than its permit allows it must buy credits from another business that does not want to use all its allowance.

How carbon permits work

Suppose there are three factories – A, B and C, in an area. Each factory is given 100 credits, which allows them to create 100 tonnes of carbon dioxide emissions each.

- By restricting the total credits to 300, there is a limit on how much carbon dioxide the three businesses can put into the atmosphere – 300 tonnes worth.

- Factory A needs to produce more than its allowance. It will have to buy credits from Factory C, which does not need to use all its allowance. To reduce this cost, Factory A may try produce in a way that causes less carbon emissions in the future.

- Factory B may try to reduce its emissions so that it can make some money by selling unwanted credits.

Some MPs in the UK want to apply this kind of scheme to households so that it would limit the use of energy and fuel and make us pay for extra credits if we wanted to use more than our allowance.

Recycling

The government encourages **recycling**. Local councils are set targets for the amount of rubbish that they collect that should be recycled. While the recycling of household waste has increased in the UK, as was shown in the introduction to this unit, the country is still behind many other European Union countries in the percentage of the waste that we do recycle. Part of the problem is encouraging people to separate their waste for the different collections that local councils now make. Another problem is the cost of recycling. If businesses have to pay extra to recycle, it may make it difficult for them to compete with businesses in other countries that do not have to recycle.

Grants and tax relief

The government may give grants towards the cost of developing greener technologies. It did charge lower rates of tax on biofuels.

FACTORY A
Allowance
= 100 credits

Uses 200 credits

FACTORY B
Allowance
= 100 credits

Uses 100 credits

FACTORY C
Allowance
= 100 credits

Uses no credits

Evaluation point

Environmentalists want governments to take action to reduce pollution. However, there are problems.

1 If, for example, a tax is imposed in one country but not in another, the producer may switch production to the country that is not taxed. In 2008, firms in Germany were threatening to move to the Ukraine because the cost of carbon credits had been raised from €23 to €30 (£19.20 to £25) per tonne of carbon dioxide. They said this was raising their costs and making them unable to compete with firms in countries that did not have to buy carbon credits.

2 The countries in the world that produce the largest amount of atmospheric pollution are the USA and China. The US has not been willing to sign up to international agreements about limiting pollution and this gives their businesses an advantage. Another issue is whether or not it is fair to ask developing countries such as China to take costly measures to reduce pollution. When the UK started to develop, for example, there were little or no controls on pollution. Should Chinese businesses be allowed the chance to develop and then be asked to take measures to control pollution? The problem, though, is that if the newly developing countries do continue to cause pollution, they are adding to the problem of global warming.

3 Some environmentalists say that it is time to stop increasing production in order to raise living standards because it is not sustainable to do so. The problem is that many people in the world do not have very high living standards. In countries that are developing, such as China and India, people are enjoying rising living standards. Perhaps it would be fairer if we in the advanced countries agreed to reduce our living standards and share out resources more if we want to do something about environmental concerns?

Activity

Activity 6: True or false – Government and the environment

Place a tick next to each statement to say whether it is true or false.

Statement	True ✔	False ✔
By having a high road tax on large 4 x 4 cars the government hopes that car manufacturers will find ways to make them emit less carbon.		
Businesses must create carbon emissions that are equal in value to the carbon permit they are given.		
Taxes on petrol are low so that people in Britain can enjoy cheap transport.		

Labels on products can help consumers to know if the products are 'green' or not.		
The government hopes that by educating people about environmental problems they will choose to buy green products.		
Recycling our waste will help to reduce the problems of dumping waste.		

Examination questions

1 Acme Accident Management Services (AAMS) deals with insurance claims on behalf of clients. It wants to reduce the costs of running its offices by making them environmentally friendly. State and explain two ways in which it may achieve this. (4 marks)

2 Aston Plastics plc is based in the UK. It refines oil into plastic. It competes with other plastics producers in the European Union and some non-EU Eastern European countries and the Far East.

The EU has decided to increase the cost of the carbon credits that firms must buy if they wish to put carbon dioxide into the atmosphere. As a plastics producer, Aston Plastics plc produces a lot of carbon.

a Explain how the rise in the cost of the carbon credits will affect the competitiveness of Aston Plastics plc when competing against (i) the other European Union producers and (ii) the non-EU Eastern European producers. (4 marks)

b The Directors of Aston Plastics plc have considered moving production to Azerbaijan, which is not in the European Union. Discussing the advantages and disadvantages of moving to Azerbaijan, recommend whether or not Aston Plastics plc should move its production.
(8 marks)

Advice on how to answer the questions

1 The question is about an office. Think about the different ways in which businesses may be able to reduce costs using environmentally friendly practices and make sure that you apply them to the office situation.

2 a When comparing the effect of the rise in the price of the carbon credits on the competitiveness of Aston Plastics you must consider how the change will affect its competitors, if at all. Will other EU producers be affected in a similar way or not? Will the non-EU producers be affected in the same way?

b There is a lot that you can write about in answer to this question. Moving abroad may bring advantages. But there will be costs connected with moving the business – explain what these might be. Also, Aston Plastics plc may lose some benefits of producing in the UK (which is in the EU). Explain these – see Unit 3.5.7 on the European Union. Finally, this is an evaluation question. You may wish to make a decision and give reasons for it. Alternatively, as with many evaluation questions you may wish to answer that you need more information to make a decision and explain what this is and why it is relevant.

Key facts

- Some resources are renewable, others are non-renewable.
- As we produce and consume more and more, we are using up the earth's non-renewable resources.
- Consumers and businesses are becoming more and more aware of environmental problems.
- Sustainable production is increasing.
- As consumers demand more green products, businesses are designing new products and ways of producing goods and services to meet this demand.
- Many businesses have realised that they can cut their costs by acting in an environmentally friendly manner.
- The government can act to try to reduce damage to the environment caused by consumption and production.

Key Terms

Make sure you can explain each of the following Key Terms

Non-renewable resources Resources that can only be used once, such as oil.

Carbon emissions Carbon dioxide that is put into the atmosphere.

Global warming. The rise in average temperatures that scientists say is taking place.

Green An adjective that describes consumers and businesses that act to make production sustainable.

Renewable resources Resources that can be used more than once, such as the wind, or that can be recreated such as crops.

Sustainable production Production that involves the use of renewable resources and recycled resources. It also minimises waste and the use of energy.

Carbon permits Permits under the European Union Emission Trading Scheme which allow businesses to produce a certain amount of carbon.

Recycling When resources are re-used to produce something.

Government and business – demand

Learning Outcomes

By studying this unit you will be able to:

- **Discuss how businesses are affected by changes in consumer incomes and employment – economic growth and recession**
- **Calculate the interest to be paid on a loan, or to be earned from saving money**
- **Explain how the Bank of England can influence businesses through changes in interest rates**
- **Explain how changes in government spending and taxation can affect business**
- **Evaluate how much businesses will be affected by changes in interest rates, government spending and taxation.**

Introduction

This unit looks at how businesses are affected by demand. The case study below about Darlows Estate Agents sets the scene.

Estate agent offices to be closed

An estate agent in south west Wales is closing two branches and a third is being reduced in size because of the credit crunch.

Darlows' offices in Llanelli and Neath will be closed. Eight members of staff will lose their jobs or be asked to work in the Swansea offices.

In the late 2000s, the banks in the UK started to lend out less money and charge a higher rate of interest on the loans that they did give. People who want to buy houses usually take out a mortgage. These became more difficult to get and more expensive. There was a fall in the number of houses sold and estate agents like Darlows did not have enough money coming in to pay all its bills. Darlows was not the only business to suffer a fall in sales. Lots of businesses depend on the housing market – DIY stores, electronic goods and furniture businesses, as well as estate agents, solicitors and financial advisers are just some of the businesses that do well when house sales are high.

Source: Adapted from the BBC website

Economic conditions

Darlows Estate Agents had been affected by economic conditions.

Rising employment and rising consumer incomes – economic growth

When employment and consumer incomes in a country are rising it is called **economic growth**. There is a high **demand** for goods and services. As businesses produce and sell more, they employ more people, pay people more and make more profits for themselves. Consumers and businesses, because of their high earnings, are willing to borrow money and so spend even more. Businesses, workers and consumers are confident.

Falling employment and consumer incomes – recession

When employment and consumer incomes are falling in a country it is called a period

of **recession**. It is usually bad for businesses. The demand for goods and services falls in a recession. Many businesses will reduce the amount they produce and the number of people they employ and profits will fall. Some businesses will stop trading, as they cannot sell what they produce. Consumers reduce borrowing. Consumer spending falls. Businesses, workers and consumers are not confident about the future.

The trade cycle

It is common for economies to go through periods of economic growth and then of recession. This is known as the trade cycle. Between 1992 and 2008, the UK had an unusually long period of economic growth. Businesses and workers prospered during this period. House prices increased a lot, car sales boomed and many people were able to afford two or three holidays or short breaks each year. This period of economic growth

Evaluation point

Some businesses are affected more than others by economic growth and recession.
A firm that sells basic foods is less likely to be affected than one that sells luxury items. In a recession, people still need to buy basic food. However, they may cut back on luxuries. So, how much a business is affected depends on what it produces. Also, consumers will start to buy cheaper items. In the recession of 2009, the sales of more expensive products, such as organic food, fell but the sales of cheaper foods, such as Tesco's value range and baked beans, rose.

Activity

Activity 1: Zone activity – Economic conditions and business

Leisurestyle plc is considering expanding its chain of leisure centres. The statements below describe different economic conditions. Put the statements under the correct heading 'advantage' or 'disadvantage' in the box below to state whether or not they would help Leisurestyle plc to expand.

a Employment is rising.

b Consumers are not confident as they fear that a recession is coming.

c Spending in the economy is high.

d Many business are saying that their sales are falling.

e Earnings are rising steadily as businesses increase production.

Advantage – it will help Leisurestyle plc to expand	Disadvantage – it will not help Leisurestyle plc to expand

came to an end when the 'credit crunch' started. The banks in the UK, the USA and many other countries had made too many bad loans. They reduced their lending dramatically which led to falling demand for many products. The housing market, car manufacturing, building industry and sales of clothes were particularly affected. Many workers lost their jobs or were put on short-time working or had their pay cut. Many businesses closed including some famous businesses such as Woolworth's shops and JCB which made diggers.

Interest rates and businesses

The **interest rate** is a cost or a reward. It is a cost for borrowing, or a reward for lending or saving. It is usually written as a percentage of the amount borrowed or saved. The 'amount of interest' is a sum of money that must be paid on a loan. It depends on the *interest rate* and the *amount of money borrowed*. It may be calculated using the formula below:

$$\frac{\text{Amount borrowed} \times \text{Interest rate}}{100} = \text{Interest paid}$$

For example, suppose a business borrows £20,000 from the bank, which charges a rate of interest of 8 per cent. The interest that it would have to pay on this loan in a year would be:

$$\frac{£20,000 \times 8}{100} = £1,600$$

Activity 2 illustrates this formula for calculating interest when applied to someone's savings.

Activity

Activity 2: Calculation – Interest on savings

Elsie Logan has put £12,000 into an account at a building society. She will receive 5 per cent on her savings. Calculate how much she will receive in interest from the building society at the end of the year. *Tip:* You will need to replace the 'amount borrowed' in the formula for calculating interest paid with the 'amount saved' to calculate the interest received.

How the interest rate affects businesses

Interest rates affect businesses in three ways.

It is the cost to the business of borrowing money

Businesses borrow money to finance things – mortgages for a new factory, an overdraft for materials, etc. (For more information on sources of finance read Unit 3.4.2.) The amount of interest a business pays is a cost of production. Like any other cost, it affects the profits it makes. A rise in the interest rate will cause business costs to rise and profits to fall.

It is the cost to the consumer of borrowing money

Consumers borrow money to buy many things – a house with a mortgage, a car with a bank loan, holidays and furniture with a credit card. If the interest rate goes up, consumers may decide they cannot afford to borrow as much and so they reduce their spending.

Consumers who already have loans pay more in interest. This results in less demand for the goods and services that businesses produce that may require a loan, causing sales and profits to fall.

It is the reward for saving

When people receive money they either spend it or save it. If the interest rate is high,

The interest rate is the cost of a loan and the reward for saving

people may prefer to save some of their money rather than spend it. A rise in the interest rate may cause the sales and profits of businesses to fall.

The Bank of England, inflation and interest rates

Inflation is when prices of goods and services are generally rising. The government has made the **Bank of England** responsible for controlling inflation in the UK. It has been set a target rate of 2 per cent. The Bank of England sets the main interest rate, the base rate, to control the rate of inflation.

- If inflation is too high, the Bank of England will raise the interest rate. This should reduce demand for goods and services.

- If inflation is too low, the Bank will reduce the interest rate. This should lead to a rise in demand.

Activity

Activity 3: Explanations – The effects of a change in the interest rate

Explain how the following may be affected by a **fall** in the rate of interest:

a Sally Knox, who has savings of over £10,000. You need to discuss how this will affect the interest on her savings and her willingness to save and the effect this might have on her spending.

b Denby Builders Ltd, who borrowed a large amount of money to buy land to build houses on. You need to discuss the effects on (i) costs and (ii) sales.

Activity 4: Explanations – Changes in interest rates and how they may affect businesses.

a Suppose that the Bank of England predicts that a recession will affect the UK in the next six months. Recommend whether or not the Bank of England should raise or lower interest rates. Give reasons for your recommendation.

b Charman Electronics Ltd sells goods in the UK such as cameras, TVs, hi-fi systems and computers. Explain how Charman Electronics Ltd would be affected by the change in interest you recommend above.

Government spending and taxation

Government spending

The government spends money for several reasons:

To provide goods and services

Both the central government and local councils provide many goods and services to help people. Some examples are as follows:

1 Street lighting, the police and the armed forces help to keep people safe.

2 Education helps people to get jobs; it provides skilled workers that businesses need.

3 The health service helps to keep us healthy, and businesses need healthy workers.

4 Roads help people to travel, and businesses to transport goods.

Refuse collection is one of many services provided by the government

Activity 5: Explanations – how government spending affects businesses

a Read the following then answer the question.

Catherine Dams visited her doctor at the NHS health centre that had just been built. The doctor prescribed a course of drugs. She went to the pharmacist to buy the drugs. The doctor also gave Catherine a prescription, which entitled her to six months' membership of a local leisure centre at a reduced price.

Identify four businesses that have benefited because of the health service paid for by government funds.

b Aled Jenkins runs a business renting out houses that he has bought. Explain how social security spending may help to provide him with customers.

c Your school is building a new 'Performing Arts' block at a cost of £1.5 million. Explain how the following businesses may benefit from this spending:

i a firm supplying bricks

ii a sandwich bar near the school.

To help poorer or unfortunate people in the community

Social-security benefits include housing benefits, free school meals, disability benefit.

To help businesses

Grants may help to pay for a factory to be built or new machines to be bought. Building new schools and roads helps construction firms. This has a **multiplier effect**. The workers who build the schools and the roads have more money to spend, which increases the demand for other businesses.

Taxation

The government makes us pay taxes for several reasons:

- It uses the money raised from **taxation** to pay for the goods and services it provides, including social-security benefits.

- It uses taxes to raise the price of some goods that cause external costs so that people buy less of them. Examples of goods that have external costs are cigarettes, alcohol and petrol.

In the UK, we pay taxes on income and when we spend. The main taxes we pay on income are shown in Figure 1.

The money that we are left with after we have paid income tax and National Insurance is known as '**take-home pay**'.

The main taxes that we pay when we spend are shown in Figure 2.

Income tax	This is a tax on income. Some of the people who pay it are: i workers on their wages ii savers on the interest they earn iii shareholders on the profits they receive iv sole proprietors and partners on the income they take out of their businesses.
National Insurance Contributions	Workers pay this on their wages and salaries. It is used to provide health services, sick pay, state pensions and other social security benefits.
Corporation Tax	This is a tax that limited companies pay on their profits.

Figure 1 Taxes paid on income

VAT	This is a tax on spending, currently charged at 15 per cent on most of the goods and services that we buy. The normal VAT rate will go back to 17.5% at the end of 2009.
Excise duties	These are special rates of taxes on goods we buy, such as petrol, cigarettes and alcohol.
Business rates	This is a tax paid to the local council by businesses on the property that they use.

Figure 2 Taxes on spending

Activity

Activity 6: Matching activity – The effects of changes in taxation on a business

Adnan City Breaks specialises in weekend trips to cities throughout Europe. Draw a line from the statement about a change in taxation in column A to the statement in column B that describes the effect on Adnan City Breaks.

Column A – Change in tax	Column B – Effect on Adnan City Breaks
1 The government raises the income tax rate and this reduces disposable income.	a Sales of weekend breaks falls because the price that Adnan charges is increased to cover the extra costs.
2 The government raises corporation tax.	b The demand for weekend breaks falls as people have less money to spend.
3 The government raises the tax on air travel to reduce damage to the environment.	c Adnan City Breaks makes less profit after tax.

The importance of demand to business

Demand is really important in business – it influences how much businesses sell. The higher the total of the demand for goods and services in the UK the more that businesses generally will sell. However, not all businesses may have high sales at this time – if a business sells a product that has gone out of fashion or is sold more cheaply by foreign producers, its sales may fall.

The Bank of England and the government can influence the level of demand in the economy. The Bank of England can change interest rates. The government can increase or decrease government spending or taxes.

Evaluation point

How much changes in government spending, taxation and interest rates affect a business will depend on:

- the size of the change in the interest rate, or government spending, or taxation
- the amount that a business has borrowed – the greater the amount, the greater will be the interest it must pay, the greater the effect on costs and profits
- the type of product the business sells. If it sells expensive luxury products, demand may change a lot as government spending, taxation and interest rates change. For example, a change in the interest rate may have a big effect because people may need to borrow money to buy the expensive products. If it is a cheap product, or something that is a necessity, the change in the interest rate may have little effect on demand because people will buy it anyway.

Activity

Activity 7: True or false – Government and demand

Place a tick next to each statement to say whether it is true or false.

Statement	True ✔	False ✔
If the Bank of England raises interest rates, businesses may sell less because it is more expensive for customers to borrow money.		
If the government reduces income tax the demand for goods will fall because people have less disposable income.		
A rise in VAT will reduce the prices of goods in the shops and increase the demand for goods.		
A rise in the amount that government spends on building new schools and hospitals will be bad for construction firms.		
A fall in the interest rate will increase business costs, reducing the profit that they make.		
A reduction in government spending on the health service may reduce the sales of drug companies.		

Examination questions

George Weir runs 'Good Sport', a shop in Burton that sells sports goods.

a George has taken out a loan of £80,000 to build an expansion to his shop. The interest rate on the loan is 10 per cent. Calculate how much interest George will pay on the loan in the first year. Show your working. (2 marks)

b Explain how George's business is likely to be affected by a recession in which consumer incomes fall in the UK economy. (4 marks)

c The local council decides to build a leisure centre in Burton, costing £3 million. State and explain **two** reasons why the sales of Good Sport may increase as a result. (4 marks)

d The Bank of England decides to reduce the interest rate. Evaluate how much the profits of Good Sport may be affected by the fall in interest rates. (6 marks)

Advice on how to answer the question

a When you are asked to calculate something always show your working – the question usually includes a command to do this. This is because if you get the answer wrong you will still get a mark if your method is correct. In this question, you should use the formula for calculating interest paid.

b The command word is 'explain'. This means you need to state the effect that the recession will have on sales and then explain why it has this effect. To do this, you will need to state what a recession is and how and why it affects the spending of consumers.

c You need to think of two ways in which the demand for sports goods will be increased. More people may take part in sport. Also there may be a multiplier effect, resulting in people in the town earning and spending more money.

d The focus of the question is on the profits of Good Sport. First, analyse how a change in interest rates affects the *costs* of the business and *how much it will sell*. Then make judgements – will there be large changes in these and, therefore, large changes in profits? A useful evaluation technique is to say 'it depends'. For example, the amount that the costs of Good Sport change will depend on how much it owes in loans – large loans may mean a big effect on costs.

Key facts

- Whether or not businesses are successful is influenced by the economic conditions in the country.
- A time of falling unemployment and rising consumer incomes (economic growth) is usually good for businesses, as it means lots of demand.
- A time of rising unemployment and falling consumer incomes (a recession) is usually bad for businesses as demand falls, making it difficult to sell what they make.
- A rise in the rate of interest is bad for businesses because it raises their costs and can lead to a fall in demand.
- The Bank of England is responsible for setting the key rate of interest in the UK. This rate influences the rates that are charged by the banks.
- Government spending leads to the demand for goods and services from private-sector firms. Government spending may have a multiplier effect.
- Rises in taxes are bad for businesses because they may reduce demand for goods and services and because they may raise business costs.

Key Terms

Make sure you can explain each of the following Key Terms

Economic growth A period of rising consumer incomes, demand and output.

Demand The total amount of goods and services that all customers want to buy. It may refer to the amount that the customers of one business want to buy, or to the customers of all businesses in general.

Recession A period of falling consumer incomes, demand and output.

Unemployment The number of people who are out of work.

Interest rate The charge made to people and businesses for lending money. Alternatively, it is the reward to people and businesses for saving money.

Bank of England The organisation that sets the basic rate of interest, which influences the interest rates that the banks charge. It changes interest rates to control inflation.

Government spending Money spent by the central government or local council to provide goods and services, to help poorer people in the community and to help businesses.

Multiplier effect The amount by which an increase or decrease in spending on a specific item is multiplied in its effect on total spending in the economy.

Taxation Charges made by the government to people and businesses. Taxes may be on income or spending.

Take-home pay The amount of income a person receives after deductions from their pay for income tax and National Insurance Contributions.

Globalisation

Learning Outcomes

By studying this unit you will be able to:

- Explain what globalisation is and give some examples of global business activities
- Evaluate the advantages and disadvantages of globalisation to businesses and people in the developed and developing countries
- Calculate the costs of goods in different currencies depending on the exchange rate of those currencies
- Explain and evaluate the effects of changes in exchange rates on businesses
- Explain how businesses may respond to changes in exchange rates.

Introduction

Globalisation is how businesses in different countries have become increasingly dependent on each other. Case Studies 1–7 give examples of this interdependence.

Case Study 1: The shirt on your back – International trade

Visit a local clothes retailer and it will be like going to a bazaar of goods from all over the world. Looking through shirts on sale in Blacks (outdoor specialists), everything I saw had been imported. Table 1 gives the names of some of the main brands and the countries where some of their clothes are produced.

Table 1: Where shirts are imported from

Brand	Country	Brand	Country
Columbia	Cambodia	Polartec	China
Berghaus	Indonesia	Oakley	Turkey
Animal	Syria		

Case Study 2: Calling for help – Production abroad

If you have ever had to call a technical help centre to deal with a problem with your computer or broadband connection, the chances are that you will have spoken to someone in India. Banks, insurance companies and many other service providers have moved call-centre work abroad. Manufacturers have also moved production abroad. In 2002, Raleigh closed its factory in Nottingham with the loss of 280 jobs. It opened a factory in China, but kept design and marketing in the UK. Moving production of manufacturing and service work abroad can save money.

Case Study 3: Your iPod – Outsourcing

You would be wrong if you think your iPod is made by Apple. While it has been designed by Apple, the production of iPods is **outsourced** to Asustek, a company in Taiwan, and they are branded as Apple products.

Case Study 4: Your Mobile Phone – MNCs

The mobile phone that you have, whatever the make, was probably made by either Flextronics, a company in Hong Kong, or Selectron, an American-owned company. Selectron produces a wide range of electronic goods in 23 countries around the world, employing 70,000 people. It is a multinational company (MNC).

Study 5: A McDonald's world – Global branding

Some products have developed as global brands that are known and sold all over the world. McDonalds and Coca-Cola are two of the best-known examples. Coca-Cola claim that 98 per cent of the people on earth know what Coca-Cola is.

Case Study 6: Brammer plc – The movement of workers from country to country

Brammer plc sells ball bearings and other technical products. They have taken over other similar businesses in Europe, including Roulement Service in France. English workers have gone to work in the headquarters of Roulement Service in Strasbourg, France to run the business. A lot of people have moved to work and live in the UK in recent years, many from Eastern European countries such as Poland and Latvia.

Case Study 7: The UK Car Industry – Globalisation

Most of the mass-produced cars that are made in the UK are produced by foreign-owned multi-national companies. Toyotas are made in Derby, Nissans in Sunderland, Hondas in Swindon, and Jaguars in Speke. The cars are assembled from parts made in different countries around the world. For example, tyres from Italy, engines from Japan, body parts from Canada and electrical parts from Mexico. The production may be done in a factory that the car company owns, or it may have been outsourced to another business. Designers, perhaps from Italy, are employed in the UK. In this one industry all the aspects of globalisation occur. They have all become global brands. Jaguar cars sell on all five continents, while the Toyota Corolla is the world's best-selling car – ever.

Globalisation

Meaning

The examples in the case studies above all illustrate globalisation. Globalisation is when business activities in different countries become more and more connected to each other. It affects the production of primary goods, manufactures and services. Globalisation involves different forms of business activity – see Figure 1.

International trade	Companies in one country produce goods and services and sell them to companies in another country.
Production abroad	Firms may decide to set up *their own* factories and offices abroad.
Outsourcing abroad	A firm in one country may pay a *different business* in another country to produce goods or services for it. As well as manufacturing the goods, a business may **outsource** other functions such as accounting and marketing to businesses in other countries.
Multinational Corporations (MNCs)	These are companies that have plants in different countries of the world – like Selectron.
Global branding	The product becomes a brand name known and sold worldwide.
People movement	Workers move to work in different countries.

Figure 1 Forms of business activity involved in globalisation

The importance of globalisation has increased significantly in recent years. Better methods of transporting goods, such as the use of containers, have reduced costs. Improved ICT has made communications more effective and cheaper. Business in some countries has started to develop very quickly, particularly in India and China.

The use of containers has reduced the costs of transporting goods

Activity

Activity 1: Matching activity – Activities that are part of globalisation

Match one of the examples in the Introduction to this unit to each form of globalisation.

Form of globalisation	Example from the Introduction
a International trade	1 UK workers employed by Roulement Service in France
b Production abroad	2 Shirts sold in Blacks
c Outsourcing	3 Call centres in India
d Multinational corporations	4 The selling of McDonalds all over the world
e Global branding	5 Selectron
f People movement	6 iPod production by Asustek

The benefits of globalisation for the UK

For consumers and businesses in developed countries, like the UK, there are many benefits:

● **Consumer choice.** Consumers can enjoy goods that cannot be produced in the UK, such as bananas. Competition between businesses in different countries means that a greater variety is offered to customers. For example, wide choices of clothes and cars from all over the world are available in the UK.

● **Lower prices.** The prices of many goods such as clothes, electronic goods and many toys are lower now than they were ten or fifteen years ago because of lower production costs abroad. Competition between businesses in different countries also helps to keep prices low.

● **Cheaper labour.** It is often cheaper to produce abroad. The wages paid to workers in developing countries, like China and India, are much lower than those paid in developed countries like the UK. UK businesses that produce in, or outsource to, businesses in these countries will have lower costs and higher profits.

- **A larger market.** By trading with other countries, businesses have a much larger market for their goods and services, so they can sell more and make bigger profits.

- **Economies of scale.** If a firm is selling on a large scale to a worldwide market, production costs often fall because of economies of scale. (See Unit 3.4.3)

- **More jobs.** Successful companies have grown bigger because of globalisation and have often increased employment. **Inward investment** has also created jobs in developing countries – for example, the building of factories in Britain by Japanese car producers has created many jobs.

Activity

Activity 2: Matching activity – Advantages of globalisation

Match the example of globalisation with the main advantage that it has brought to UK consumers.

Example of globalisation
a   The assembly of cars, such as Toyota, in the UK
b   UK workers employed by Roulement Service in France
c   Shirts sold in Blacks
d   Call centres in India
e   The move of production to China by Raleigh
f   iPod production by Asustek

Main benefit to UK people
1   Services are provided more cheaply.
2   Jobs have been created for workers in the UK.
3   Consumers have a greater choice of makes and styles to choose from.
4   Consumers can buy goods at low prices because they are produced using cheap labour.
5   British workers have found jobs abroad.
6   UK businesses are still able to compete and so survive by moving production abroad.

The problems of globalisation for the UK

- **Lower profits** A firm in the UK may be forced to cut prices because of competition from abroad.

- **Lower sales** A British firm may find that sales fall because of competition from foreign firms.

- **Business closures and the loss of jobs** If goods and services are produced abroad, firms in the UK may not need to employ as many workers.

Globalisation and developing countries

There is a lot of debate about whether or not globalisation is good or bad for developing countries like China and India.

Xiamen Port

XIAMEN PORT As many as 35,000 police continued to raid illegal brickworks and mines across central China yesterday, as public anger intensified over the fate of kidnapped children being forced to work as slave labourers in appalling conditions.

So far, 548 people have been rescued in Henan and Shanxi provinces. At least 38 of those are children, with state media reporting the youngest to be eight years old.

Source: www.telegraph.co.uk (18 June 2007)

Culture. Local cultures are being affected as global branding, advertising and production methods influence the way of life in developing countries. This changes the way of life, making it different from what it may have been for thousands of years.

Pollution. The developing countries often suffer from bad pollution as businesses want to keep costs low and governments do little to control them.

The good

Jobs and living standards. Jobs are being created in these countries and wages are rising. Multi-national companies often pay wages that are twice as high as those paid by the country's own businesses. As a result, the living standards are getting better and people are living longer. Levi now makes jeans in countries in Africa and Asia. In 1991 it drew up a code of conduct that bans the use of child labour and imposes strict health and safety standards. It supports good causes

The bad

Exploitation. Workers in these countries may be exploited – paid very low wages and having to work long hours in dangerous conditions. The problems are often ethical problems (see Unit 3.5.2). The extract below illustrates some of the problems that can arise:

such as AIDS charities in South Africa, where it has opened a home to look after children who have suffered physical or sexual abuse.

Globalisation and the environment

Globalisation is causing many environmental problems. The controls on businesses causing pollution are often less strict in developing countries. Many parts of China, for example, suffer badly from smog. The greater amount of transport and travel that results from globalisation is increasing carbon emissions, particularly from aircraft, and this is adding to global warming.

Activity

Activity 3: Zone activity – advantages and disadvantages of globalisation for developing countries

Put the following statements under the correct heading, 'Possible Advantages' or 'Possible Disadvantages' of globalisation for developing countries.

a Children are used as workers.

b New jobs are created.

c There may be poor heath and safety conditions.

d People can earn higher wages.

e Living standards rise.

f Workers work long hours for low wages.

g People are living longer.

h Production may harm the environment.

The possible advantages and disadvantages of globalisation for developing countries

Possible advantages	Possible disadvantages

Evaluation point

It is difficult to say how an individual developing country will be affected by globalisation. Its own government may or may not take steps to prevent the exploitation of workers and children. The MNCs that locate in them may, like Levi Jeans, impose their own high standards to avoid exploitation or damage to the environment. However, If they are in very competitive markets, where prices and profits are already low, it may be that they cannot afford high standards.

Government and international trade

The government can help businesses in the UK to deal with international trade in two ways:

- The government can help UK businesses to compete better with businesses in other countries. This is discussed in more detail in the next Unit, 3.5.6.

- The government can protect UK businesses from foreign competition. This is called 'protectionism'.

Exchange rates

If you go abroad for your holidays, you will know that you have to buy foreign currency if you want to buy goods in that country. If you are lucky enough to holiday abroad on a regular basis, you might have noticed that the amount of foreign currency you can buy with one pound changes from year to year. The amount of a foreign currency that you get for £1 (pound sterling) is the **exchange rate** for the pound against that currency.

Businesses face similar problems if they deal in any way with goods and services from abroad. A UK business buying imports from an American business must change pounds sterling into dollars to pay the American seller. An American business buying from a UK seller must buy pounds sterling with its dollars, so it can pay the seller in pounds. The exchange rate fixes the price the buyer pays for imports and the amount sellers receive when they export goods. Businesses prefer a **stable exchange rate**, which means the exchange rate between different currencies stays much the same and a business can plan ahead, knowing what price it will pay or receive for goods from abroad. This is one of the aims of having a single European currency – the euro (see later in this unit).

A high exchange rate

High exchange rates are *a problem for exporters,* as they make the prices of the exports dearer for the buyer. The example in Figure 2 is based on a UK business wanting £100 for a piece of pottery that it produces. It shows how many dollars the US buyer must pay to get the £100 needed to pay the UK seller at two rates of exchange, £1 = $1.5 and £1 = $2 (the higher exchange rate).

A high exchange rate is *good for importers* because it makes imports cheaper. Suppose a UK buyer wants to buy clocks from an American firm which sells them at $200 each. The $ price now needs to be changed into £s – see Figure 3.

Exchange Rate	Price of the pottery in £s	Sum to change the £ price to $	Price in $s to the US buyer
£1 = $1.5	£100	Product price in £s × the dollars per £ = 100 × $1.5 =	$150
£1 = $2	£100	100 × $2 =	$200

Figure 2

Exchange Rate	Price of the pottery in $s	Sum to change the $ price to £s	Price in £s to the UK buyer
£1 = $1.5	$200	Product price in $ ÷ the dollars per £ = 200 ÷ $1.5 =	$133.3
£1 = $2	$200	200 ÷ $2 =	£100

Figure 3

Activity

Activity 4: Calculation and explanation – A fall in the exchange rate

Suppose the value of the £ has fallen against the euro, from £1 buys €1.5 to £1 = €1.2.

a i Complete the sums in the table below to show the effect of the fall in the value of the £ on the price of British exports to businesses in countries that use the €.

Exchange rate	Price of the export in £s	Sum to change the £ price to $s	Price in $ to the buyer
£1 = €1.5	£500	Product price in € × the euros per £ =	= €
£1 = €1.2	£500	=	= €

   ii Will the fall in the value of the £ against the € have helped British firms to export to countries that use the €? Explain your answer.

b i Complete the sums in the table below to show the effect on the price that British businesses must pay in £s for imports from countries that use the €.

Exchange Rate	Price of the import in €	Sum to change the € price to £s	Price in £s to the British buyer
£1 = €1.5	€50	Product price in € ÷ € per £ =	= €
£1 = €1.2	€50	=	= €

   ii Will the fall in the exchange of the £ against the € have helped British firms who import from countries that use the €? Explain your answer.

c Using your answers to the questions a) and b), explain whether a low value of the £ against another currency is good or bad for British businesses.

d i Explain what is meant by stable exchange rates.

   ii Explain why businesses that trade with other countries prefer stable exchange rates.

Changes in exchange rates summary

Exchange rate falls	Exchange rate rises
Exporters benefit. More goods are sold abroad; possibility of business expansion, increased sales, more employment and rising profits.	**Exporters have problems** with effect of price increase in other countries; possibility of sales falling, redundancies and business closure if problem persists. The exporter may need to reduce their prices, reducing the profit they make per item. Also they could try to export to countries whose currency has not risen instead
Importers have problems due to the increase in price of imported goods measured in pounds. As a result, sales could fall, workers may be made redundant and the business could close if the problem persists. The importer may need to raise its prices to cover the extra costs. Also it could try to buy the same goods from a different country which produces them more cheaply, or whose currency has not fallen against the £.	**Importers benefit**. The cost of imports will fall as fewer pounds are needed to pay for them. This will mean that sales and profits could rise, more jobs may be created as the business expands.

Evaluation point

The effect of a fall in the exchange rate on an importer depends on the following:

- If the fall in the exchange rate is large or small – a small change will not have a big effect.

- If the cost of the import is a large or small proportion of the total costs of the business – if the proportion of total costs is small, the change will not have a big effect.

- If the importer could buy the import from another country instead, which sold them more cheaply, or whose currency had not risen.

- If the cost can be passed on to the buyer in the form of higher prices and this will depend on how many competitors there are, and whether they, too, have to raise their prices to cover increases in costs.

- Can you work out what determines the effect that a rise in the exchange rate would have on a business that exports?

The Eurozone

The Eurozone is the name given to those countries in the European Union that use the euro (€) as their currency. It is intended that one day all EU countries will use the euro – there will be a single currency. Currently there are 15 countries using the euro. The UK is not a member as it still uses the pound sterling (£).

Advantages of using the euro

- **No exchange costs** Not having to buy a foreign currency will make trade cheaper. When a business buys a foreign currency to pay for imports, the banks usually make a charge – often as a commission or percentage of the amount of currency bought.

- **Reduced uncertainty** It will not be possible for the exchange rate to change after a deal has been arranged. A change in the exchange rate could make the deal less profitable, though it could make it more profitable.

- **Comparing prices** It is easier to compare the prices of goods if they are all in the same currency so the best deals are more obvious.

Disadvantages of using the euro

Interest rates will be set by the European Central Bank (ECB). In Unit 3.5.4, we saw that in the UK the Bank of England changes the interest rate to help businesses. It will increase the interest rate when demand is low and reduce it if the demand for goods is not high. If the UK starts to use the euro, the interest rate will be set by the ECB to help businesses in the Eurozone. If the main problem in the Eurozone countries other than the UK is that demand is too low, the ECB would reduce interest rates. This would raise demand in all Eurozone countries, including the UK. If demand in the UK was too high, the cut in interest rates would only make UK problems worse while reducing problems in the other Eurozone countries.

Examination questions

1 Carlton Press Ltd publishes educational textbooks. It imports coloured ink from America at $300 per drum.

   a Explain how a fall in the exchange rate from £1 = $1.5 to £1 = $1.2 could affect the price of the ink.   (2 marks)

   b Evaluate the effect that the fall in the exchange rate may have on the sales of educational textbooks by Carlton Press Ltd.   (4 marks)

2 a Good Sports plc manufactures and sells branded sports clothes. It currently sells clothes in two ways – through its own chain of shops in the UK and through other retailers. Explain two ways in which Good Sports plc may have benefited from globalisation.   (4 marks)

   b Vietnam is a country that is developing as a result of globalisation. Evaluate whether or not globalisation will be good or bad for Vietnam.   (8 marks)

Advice on how to answer the questions

1 a You should show how the fall in the exchange rate will affect the price of the ink. Using simple figures and calculations will make your answer clearer.

   b You are asked to evaluate in this question, so you must try to make some judgements. You cannot know for sure what the effect of the rise in the exchange rate will be so you must speculate with some 'it depends' statements. Two statements with each one explained will comfortably get you the four marks.

2 a You need to use the list of forms of globalisation and work out which of them Good Sports plc could benefit from. It may benefit in terms of the costs of manufacturing the clothes – explain how. There may be benefits on the selling side of the business as well. There are more than two possible answers to this question.

   b This is another typical evaluation question in which there is no single correct answer. There are 8 marks for the question, so write about three or four advantages and disadvantages (you must write about both) and then say what the overall effect will depend upon.

Key facts

- Globalisation is increasing.
- Globalisation has brought a lot benefits to both developed and developing countries.
- Globalisation has brought problems to both developed and developing countries.
- For businesses in developed countries like the UK, globalisation is a threat because it increases competition. It can also be an opportunity to reduce costs and increase sales.
- Globalisation is contributing to environmental problems.
- The exchange rate is an important influence on the prices that businesses must pay for imports and can charge for exports.
- Changes in exchange rates will cause the amount of imports and exports to rise or to fall.

Key Terms

Make sure you can explain each of the following Key Terms

Globalisation The process by which business activities in different countries are becoming more and more connected to each other.

Outsourcing When a business pays another business to do part of its work for it, such as producing goods, keeping accounts or marketing its produce.

Multi-national Corporations Companies that operate in different countries.

Global branding Where a product becomes a brand name and is sold worldwide.

Inward investment This is when foreign businesses set up factories and offices in the UK.

Protectionism The name given to methods used to protect business from the problems that international trade might cause.

Exchange rates The amount of one currency that another currency can buy.

Stable exchange rate An exchange rate that does not change greatly over a period of time.

Government and business – supply

Introduction

The following two articles were written within a month of each other. They introduce an important debate about the future for UK business.

James Caan: 'The UK can kiss manufacturing goodbye'

Dragons' Den investor James Caan stirred up angry debate among business owners at yesterday's Entrepreneurs' Summit by claiming that British manufacturing is dead.

'In our lifetime, I don't think we will compete with India and China', he told the audience of 250 entrepreneurs.

'We don't have manufacturing anymore. If somebody approached me tomorrow to invest in a business where they were going to manufacture something in the UK, I probably wouldn't invest. Within six months, that same product in India or China would be a third of the price.

In Britain, we are – and we will continue to be – a service country. I think that is where our income's going to come from."

Kate Pritchard – RealBusiness Website

Lord Bhattacharyya confident for future of UK manufacturing

'As a Professor of Manufacturing, I am more optimistic about the manufacturing sector today than I have been for years', said Professor Lord Bhattacharyya, head of the Warwick Manufacturing Group.

'Manufacturing output is 22 per cent higher than it was at the start of 1980 and manufacturing productivity has grown by 50 per cent since 1997. Many British manufacturing companies have become global success stories. For example, Rolls-Royce has a third of the global aerospace engine market.

'Some companies that were regarded as failures have come back to make successful products and big profits, Land Rover is a consistent profitable performer, and Jaguar is, on the back of innovation, growing once again. We've seen innovation and growth too. Renishaw, the precise measurement company, has developed new technologies in its sector that have opened up new markets

'These successes have been on the back of good management and product innovation. I wouldn't say that we have never had it so good. But we are having it OK.'

Birmingham Post, 23 May 2008

The problem of foreign competition

Will British manufacturing business survive?

There is a lot of competition:

- **Developing countries** such as China and India (See Unit 3.5.5 on Globalisation) have a lot of cheap labour. Now they make a lot of manufactured goods that used to be produced in developed countries, such as clothes, toys, furniture, electronic goods and so on. These countries are also improving their education systems, which will help them to grow even more.

- **Developed countries** from Europe, North America and Japan also have manufacturing businesses which compete with UK firms. They, too, are competing with the developing countries.

What about service businesses?

Many service businesses are not competing with firms from overseas – think of businesses like hairdressers, restaurants, the leisure centres, transport and the like.

However, other types of service business are facing competition from abroad.

- With the growth of internet shopping, retailers have to compete with overseas sellers.

- Competition in financial services such as banking, insurance, pensions and savings has always been tough.

- Now the newly developing countries are starting to compete by, for example, providing call centres for banks and insurance companies and services such as IT and accountancy.

This is all about supply – how well British businesses can produce and sell

This unit is about how UK businesses must compete to supply the goods and services that are being demanded.

Activity

Activity 1: True or false – The problem of foreign competition

Read the following statements and place a tick in the box to show if the statement is true or false.

Statement	True	False
Businesses in newly developing countries have the advantage of cheap labour over businesses in the UK.		
British firms only compete with businesses in developing countries like China and India.		
Britain no longer has manufacturing businesses, it only produces services.		
Service industries do not need to compete with firms from abroad.		
Newly developing countries produce both manufactured goods and services.		

How UK firms can succeed

To compete, UK firms need to sell in the UK and in exports markets across the world. The strategies that UK business must use to compete include those set out below.

Produce the right goods and services

UK businesses need to do market research (See Unit 1.2.1) and innovate to create new goods and services that meet the needs of customers better than existing products. **Innovation** comes from research and development.

Producing at the right price

UK businesses need keep costs low to keep prices low. Improved **productivity** – increasing the output of each worker – leads to lower costs. Productivity can be improved by investing in new technology (see Unit 3.3.1) and by improving the skills of workers (see Unit 2.4.3).

Good marketing

This is essential for any business. UK businesses have done well when they have created a strong brand image for their products (see Units 1.2.3 and 1.2.7).

Delivering the goods and services at the right time

This means that production must be carefully planned so that the goods and services are ready when they are needed. It requires efficient distribution so that the goods are delivered on time.

Outsourcing or moving production abroad when necessary

Not all the activities of a business need to be done in the UK. UK businesses may survive by having some parts of their work done abroad to reduce their costs.

High value-added

This describes production that takes materials or components and makes them worth much, much more. Many people believe that UK businesses will not be able to produce goods like plastic toys more cheaply than they are produced in China and other developing countries. These are "low value-added" goods. The examples of success that Lord Bhattacharyya talks about are all high value-added businesses which require a lot of technical expertise. He mentions engines for aeroplanes, motor cars and precision measurement instruments. He might also have mentioned pharmaceuticals (drugs), telecommunications and chemicals amongst others. All these products are high **value-added**.

Inward investment

This is when foreign firms decide to set up in Britain. Unit 3.5.5 on globalisation describes how car manufacturers from Japan have set up in the UK. Many other foreign businesses have also come to Britain. Google, Astrazenca, the HSBC Bank and General Electric are just some of them. These businesses may be competition for UK-owned businesses. However, when foreign firms set up in the UK they create jobs and they help other businesses. For example, British firms may supply the building materials and construct the factory, they may supply services like catering and cleaning and so on. There is a *multiplier effect* when **inward investment** takes place.

Activity

Activity 2: Matching pairs – Definitions of terms connected with competition strategies

Draw a line from the competition strategy in column A to the definition in column B.

Column A – Competition strategy	Column B – Definition
a Innovation	1 The amount produced per worker.
b Research and development	2 Investment by foreign firms in the UK.
c Productivity	3 Experimenting and testing to develop new products.
d Brand image	4 Developing new products, services and methods of producing.
e Value added	5 How well-known a product is.
f Inward investment	6 The increase in the value of the inputs used by a business and the value of what it produces.

Activity

Activity 3: Explanation – Competing in the global economy

a Explain what is meant by the term 'productivity'.

b Explain why improving productivity helps UK firms to compete with businesses from other countries.

c Explain two ways in which a business may improve its productivity.

d What is meant by the term 'high value added production'.

e Explain why good marketing is important if businesses are to succeed in the global economy.

Activity

Activity 4: Explanation – Inward investment

Suppose that a French company decides to build a large new factory in the town where you go to school. Explain how this may help:

a other businesses in the area

b the people who live in the town.

What the government can do to help business

Figure 1 shows some of the policies that governments can use to help UK business to compete better.

Policy	How it can help	Why
Cuts in taxes on business profits	This will help businesses to invest and innovate in new products and new technology.	Businesses will keep more of the profit they make so can reinvest it.
Grants to businesses	This will help business to invest and innovate.	The grant from the government reduces the cost to the business.
Cuts in income tax	This will encourage people to work harder and costs will fall.	• Workers will keep more of the money they earn. • Businesses may be able to pay lower wages if less tax is taken.
Education and training	This will help businesses to have better managers and more skilled workforces.	People will be better educated and trained in schools, colleges and universities.
Improving the infrastructure	This will help businesses to distribute goods more efficiently.	Roads, railways, ports and airports are being developed.
Information provided by government	It may help businesses when they want to export goods.	Businesses can find out about markets, laws and product standards in other countries.

Figure 1 Policies the government can use to help UK business to compete better

Activity

Activity 5: Star diagram – Government policies to help UK business compete

Create a star diagram to show the main policies the government uses to help UK businesses be competitive. Use key words to explain how and why each policy helps businesses.

Activity

Activity 6: Explanations – Government policies to help UK business compete

a Explain two ways in which the government can help businesses to invest.

b Explain how businesses may benefit from low rates of income tax.

c Explain how improving the **infrastructure** in the region in which you live may help businesses in that area.

Activity

Activity 7: Research and poster drawing – Encouraging inward investment

a Use the internet to research how inward investment is being encouraged. Try the website www.northengland.com or Google the term 'inward investment' and the name of the region you live in.

b Using the information you find, draw a poster advertising the region to foreign businesses.

How people can make business succeed

More on education and training

Have you been nagged by your teachers about working hard to gain good qualifications? Yes? Good! Although there will be low-paid jobs for people without skills and qualifications in the future, we have seen that UK businesses need *highly skilled people* if they are to compete in the global economy. So, if you want to help the country (and get a well-paid job while doing so), follow the advice of your teacher – education and training really are very important!

The government has made big changes to education. Schools and colleges now provide more vocational courses – Applied A levels and GCSEs, BTEC courses, diplomas, NVQs, functional skills and so on. The government is also encouraging more people to go to university to get a degree-level education. It set a target that 50 per cent of eighteen year olds should be going from school into university education.

Activity

Activity 8: Explanation – The importance of education

Explain why your education may be (i) good for you and (ii) good for businesses.

Immigration

Immigration has always affected the UK. People have come, and still come, to the UK from all over the world – from Europe, Australia, North and South America, Asia and Africa. In the 1950s and 1960s, encouraged by the UK government because of labour shortages, large numbers of people came to live and work in Britain from India, Pakistan and the Caribbean. In the mid and late 2000s, there has been another large wave of immigration, this time from Eastern European countries.

In 2004, several Eastern European countries became members of the European Union. This meant that people from these countries had the right to move to other EU countries, including the UK, if they wanted to. Around a million people have come to the UK from Eastern Europe. Polish builders, Slovakian nannies and Lithuanian fruit and vegetable pickers are just some of the people who have come to Britain. They help UK businesses in two ways:

- Eastern Europeans have a reputation for working very hard and not demanding high wages.

- The immigrants are creating extra demand. Go to a town like Peterborough where there are many Polish immigrants and you will find Polish shops and restaurants. Most supermarkets in most towns stock foods typically eaten by East Europeans. There is also an extra demand for housing as the immigrants need somewhere to live.

However, there are costs:

- Schools in areas of high immigration are crowded. One school in Peterborough has said that the teaching materials it uses need translating into 24 different languages. Doctor's surgeries are reporting thousands of extra patients who they are struggling to see. All this costs the tax payer money.

- Some British workers are complaining that because immigrants are willing to work for low wages, wages offered to them have fallen.

Evaluation point

Has immigration helped UK businesses? This is very difficult to weigh up. The people who came from Commonwealth countries in the 1950s and 1960s and from Eastern Europe in the 2000s came when businesses were short of labour. They helped UK businesses to grow. As well as helping businesses to produce, they also demand products from businesses, helping them to make profits. There have been costs – the pressure on public services in particular, although the immigrants have paid taxes like everyone else. The Migrants Impact Forum estimated in the late 2000s that immigrants from Eastern Europe were contributing about £6bn a year to the UK economy. In practice, it's very difficult to measure the benefits and costs accurately. The statistics in Figure 2 were provided by the Home Office in 2007. They show the kinds of work that Eastern Europeans do in the UK, as well as which countries they come from. Figure 3 shows the number of people from Eastern European countries who were given approval to come to the UK in the first three months of 2007.

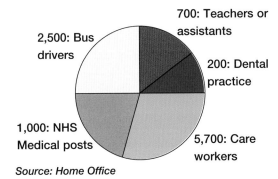

700: Teachers or assistants
2,500: Bus drivers
200: Dental practice
1,000: NHS Medical posts
5,700: Care workers

Source: Home Office

Figure 2 Eastern European nationals in public-sector style jobs

*Bulgaria
Czech Rep
Estonia
Hungary
Latvia
Lithuania
Poland
*Romania
Slovakia
Slovenia

Total approved workers = 613,305
Total applications = 640,670

0   50   100   150   200   250   300   350   400
*First approvals Jan–Mar 2007   (000's)   *Source: Home Office*

Figure 3 Number of approved workers by country

Activity

Activity 9: Zone activity – Advantages and disadvantages of immigration

Put the letters of the statements under the correct heading, 'Advantage' or 'Disadvantage' in the table below to state the effects of immigration.

a The increase in the number of immigrants has increased the number of workers in many areas.

b Local councils have to spend more on services such as schools.

c New businesses have opened to meet the needs of immigrants.

d Local workers are concerned that wages have fallen because some immigrants are willing to work for less money than they are.

e Businesses have been able to keep costs down by employing immigrants.

Advantage	Disadvantage

The ageing population and business

Another change affecting the population is the number of people who are living longer – our **ageing population**. Life expectancy in the UK is now over 78 years (76 for men and nearly 82 for women). This has caused an increase in demand for health services, nursing and sheltered homes, holidays for older people and many other goods and services that older people want. It has created many business opportunities. SAGA is a very successful business selling insurance, travel, health and money services to the over-50s. There is, however, also a cost. Government spending on the NHS and on pensions has increased. It is likely that people will be expected to work beyond the current state pension age of 65 in the future – you may not be able to retire until you are 67 or 68 years old. Many people do work beyond this age already. The oldest new employee to attend the B&Q University (training centre) for an induction course was 84 years old! Some employers like older workers, saying that they are more reliable than the young and better with customers.

Activity

Activity 10: Explanation – The effects of an ageing population

a Explain two ways that businesses may benefit from the increase in the number of old people in the UK.

d Explain the problems caused by the increase in the number of old people.

Examination questions

1 Jenkins Pharmaceuticals Ltd (JP) is a UK business that produces medicines. It competes with similar businesses in other developed countries. Its products are sold in developed and developing countries around the world.

   a Medicines are a high value-added product. Explain what this means. (2 marks)

   b JP spends a lot of money on research and development each year. Explain why this is important for a business like JP. (2 marks)

   c Assess the importance of good marketing to JP. (4 marks)

   d Explain why businesses such as JP need skilled workforces to compete. (4 marks)

2 A large number of people from Eastern Europe have come to live and work in the town of Peterborough. Discuss the factors that need to be considered to decide whether or not this immigration has been good for the town. (8 marks)

Advice on how to answer the questions

1 For part a) give a clear definition of the term. In part b) state what research and development is and then explain why this is important for a business in a competitive market for highly technical products. For part c) discuss the importance of developing a strong brand image and explain how this will help sales in different countries in a very competitive market. For part d) link the nature of the business to the need for a skilled workforce – what kind of workers are needed to do research and development, to produce and to sell medicines.

2 This is an evaluation question. Identify the benefits that immigration can bring and the costs. Write a conclusion. You could quote some research which has looked into the benefits and costs of immigration (use the internet to research this), or say it depends on the amount of the benefits and the costs and how these could be measured.

Key facts

- The development of the global economy has increased competition for UK businesses.
- UK businesses need to produce the right goods at the right prices and at the right time to be competitive.
- Governments can help businesses in the UK to be competitive.
- Changes in the population have helped businesses in the UK.
- Changes in the population have increased the demands on public services.

Key Terms

Make sure you can explain each of the following Key Terms

Developed countries Countries that have strong economies, where most workers earn high wages and living standards are high. They usually have very large service sectors.

Developing economies Poorer countries that are starting to grow, usually expanding production of primary and manufactured goods but also possibly services.

Exports The goods and services a country sells to other countries.

Imports The goods and services a country buys from other countries.

Innovation Developing new products and new ways of making products.

Productivity The amount that each person produces. Increasing productivity reduces business costs.

Value added The difference between the cost of the raw materials and the value of the product when it has been produced.

Inward investment Investment in the UK by foreign firms.

Infrastructure The provision of roads, railways, ports and airports in an area or country.

Immigration The movement of people from abroad to live in the UK.

Ageing population The increase in the proportion of the population over the age of 65.

The European Union

Learning Outcomes

By studying this unit you will be able to:

- **Explain why the European Union exists and be able to name some of the member countries**
- **Discuss how the UK membership of the European Union may help UK businesses but may also lead to increased competition for them**
- **Explain what the Eurozone is**
- **Discuss the possible benefits and problems for UK businesses if the UK starts to use the euro instead of the pound sterling.**

Introduction

The **European Union** has been good for many UK businesses. It may not be good for all of them though. UK membership of the European Union leads to both opportunities and threats for UK businesses.

Sales of Jaguar XF surging in Europe

Jaguar has been increasing the sales of cars in Western Europe. In 2008 it sold 70.3 per cent more than in 2007. In April of 2008, Jaguar sold 3,949 vehicles compared with 2,319 in April 2007. The most popular model was the XF. Jaguar's main rivals did not do so well, with Audi up 9.5 per cent, BMW 26.7 per cent and Mercedes 14.7 per cent.

A UK success in Europe

European Union expansion threatens UK manufacturing

Over two-thirds of the UK's manufacturing engineers are worried that they will be unable to compete against lower-cost East European countries. This was the finding of a survey about the effects that increasing the number of countries in the European Union would have.

What is the European Union?

The European Union (EU) is a collection of 27 countries in Europe, which aim to co-operate on trade, social affairs and certain laws.

Growth of the EU

The EU has grown since it was started in 1957 – see Figure 1.

Year	Countries joining the European Union
1957	Belgium, France, Italy, Luxembourg, Netherlands, West Germany
1972	United Kingdom, Denmark, Eire
1980	Greece
1986	Portugal, Spain

Year	Countries joining the European Union
1995	Austria, Finland, Sweden
2004	Czech Republic, Estonia, Latvia, Lithuania, Hungary, Poland, Slovenia, Slovakia, Cyprus and Malta.
2007	Bulgaria and Romania

Figure 1 The growth of the European Union

Three more countries are hoping to become members of the European Union in the near future – Macedonia, Croatia and Turkey.

The EU – benefits to business

- **A bigger market.** The population of countries in the European Union is nearly 500 million people. This makes it possible for a business in Britain to sell goods and services to a larger market than just the UK, with its population of 60 million. This means that businesses can take advantage of economies of scale. Also, the enlarged market may give businesses an opportunity to extend the life-cycle of a product by exporting to new markets. UK businesses do more trade with other European Union businesses than with businesses from the rest of the world.

- **Common standards.** Throughout the European Union there are common standards on safety, quality and labelling of products. This means that a business no longer has to make different products for the different countries it trades with in Europe. This can save costs.

- **Free trade.** There are no **tariffs** (taxes) or **quotas** (limits to the amounts that can be traded) on trade between member countries.

- **Free movement of goods.** There are no customs barriers to delay the movement of products.

- **Freedom of workers.** Workers from an EU country are free to work in other EU countries. This is one of the reasons for the number of Eastern Europeans working in the UK (see Unit 3.5.6).

- **Freedom of movement of services.** This has really affected the banks and other financial services in Britain, who can now sell their services throughout the member countries.

- **Grants and subsidies.** The European Union pays grants and subsidies to businesses in the poorer areas of Europe. This has greatly helped the coalfield and steel communities in Britain, which have seen great job losses and need help to rebuild businesses. Money has been spent on building new factories, improving transport systems and training workers in new skills. Farming areas have been given grants and subsidies to guarantee the price for certain crops, and to help create jobs not in their traditional farming roles but in industries such as tourism.

A bigger market is an opportunity for more customers

The EU – problems for business

- **A bigger market.** Although a bigger market can bring benefits to business, it can also cause problems. Just as a business in Britain can export more easily to other member countries in Europe, all those other member countries can also export more easily to Britain because Britain cannot impose tariffs and quotas. This means that if a business in Britain is not as efficient as competitors in Europe, it may well see sales and profits fall as consumers switch to imported goods from Europe. In total, the UK does import more from other EU countries than it sells to them.

- **The Social Charter.** This Charter was introduced by the European Union to help protect workers against bad employers. Although it should not cause problems for businesses that treat their workers well, it has had an effect on a number of different businesses. The main items within the **Social Charter** are:

  - full-time and part-time workers should have the same rights

  - a limit of 48 hours per week for workers. At present the UK has 'opted out' of this – workers here can work more than 48 hours if they wish to do so. There is pressure from Euro MPs to end this opt out.

  - the **minimum wage**. This has meant that some businesses have had to increase the amount they pay their workers, which in turn adds to costs; this may then mean that sales and profits fall. Some businesses have claimed that this may even force them out of business, causing a rise in unemployment. However, many British businesses were already paying *more* than the minimum wage before the law was introduced.

- **Environmental standards.** The European Union has introduced new standards on water quality, waste recycling and pollution. While these measures should improve the environment by providing cleaner beaches, less need for waste disposal and less pollution in the atmosphere, they do add costs to the businesses that are involved, and may cause some redundancies as firms try to reduce costs to pay for the improvements. One of the environmental measures that the European Union has introduced is the use of 'carbon credits'. (See Unit 3.5.3.)

Free trade with the EU has increased competition for UK firms

Activity

Activity 1: Zone activity – Advantages and disadvantages of the EU to UK businesses

The following statements describe either advantages or disadvantages to UK businesses caused by the UK membership of the European Union. Put them under the correct heading in the table below.

a The large population of the EU means that UK businesses have more customers to sell to.

b Tariffs and quotas cannot be used to restrict the sale of UK goods in other EU countries.

c UK firms face more competition from EU firms because they are free to sell their goods in the UK.

d UK firms have found it easier to employ labour because people from other EU countries have been free to come to work in the UK.

e The EU has created common standards so UK firms do not need to change the goods they produce to sell in another EU country.

f The EU has increased stricter environmental controls, which have increased costs for UK businesses, making it more difficult to compete with non-EU countries.

g The EU has given grants to help businesses develop in some parts of the UK.

h The government in the UK introduced a national minimum wage partly because of the EU Social Charter.

Advantages for UK businesses

Disadvantages for UK businesses

Activity

Activity 2: Leaflet – Advantages and disadvantages of the EU

Design a leaflet explaining the business advantages of an enlarged market in Europe. Use IT for the design if you have it available.

Activity

Activity 3: Explanation – Advantages and disadvantages of the EU

How could UK membership of the EU affect the following UK businesses? Give details of any laws and regulations that apply to the situation.

a A water-treatment company that discharges water into the sea.

b A farm that has been short of workers.

c A business that exports a range of electrical goods to Europe.

d A cleaning business that pays all its workers £2.50 an hour.

e A computer business that is very busy and expects all its workers to work 55 hours per week.

f A business that wants to expand in a former coalfield area.

g A security business that said its part-time workers should have fewer rights at work because they worked less than full-time workers.

The Eurozone

This is the name given to the 15 countries that use the European currency, the **euro** (€). It was first used in 1999 by the following countries:

Austria, Belgium, Finland, France, Germany, Ireland, Italy, Luxembourg, Netherlands, Portugal and Spain.

Greece started to use the euro in 2001, Slovenia in 2007 and Malta and Cyprus in 2008. Over 320 million people live in the eurozone.

There has been a great deal of discussion about whether joining the Euro will benefit British business or not – see Figure 2.

Advantages	Disadvantages
Cost savings. When a business trades with another country, there has to be an exchange of currencies. This is costly, and can only put up the costs of goods and services. Having the same currency will help lower prices.	**Adds to costs.** All the business in Britain is in pounds, so all the machinery, computers, tills, etc. will have to be changed to euros. This will cost businesses a lot of money to do. The change-over costs should only be seen as short-term.
Most trade is with Europe. As most of Britain's trade is with Europe, it makes sense to have the same currency.	**Loss of the pound.** A number of people will need to be educated on the use of the euro. Any change-over might cause some confusion, especially amongst shoppers.
Stable exchange rate. As Britain's main trading countries will have the same currency, there will not be the changes in exchange rates that cause businesses so much concern. It is therefore better to join.	**A final decision.** Once any change has taken place, it will be difficult to change back. Any decisions to do with the Euro in the future may not please some of the member countries, but they have to accept them.

Figure 2 Advantages and disadvantages for British business in joining the euro

Activity

Activity 4: True or false – The euro

Tick next to each of the following statement to say whether they are true or false.

Statement	True ✔	False ✔
Vending machines in the UK can already take euros so they will not need to be changed if the UK starts to use the euro.		
Businesses and consumers will not need to exchange currencies to buy from other Eurozone countries, so this will save them money.		
If the UK starts to use the euro it will not have very much effect because businesses do very little trade with other European Union countries.		
There will be no fluctuations in the exchange rate of the £ against the €, so this will remove one of the risks in international trade with other Eurozone countries.		
Some people think the UK should keep using the £ because it is a part of our history.		
Once the UK starts to use the euro it would be almost impossible to go back to using the pound because it would cost so much.		

Examination questions

1 Germany and the UK are both members of the EU.

   a What do the letters 'EU' stand for?   (1 mark)

   b State **one** other country that is a member of the EU.   (1 mark)

2 Explain how membership of the EU helps businesses in the UK to trade with businesses in other member countries.   (6 marks)

3 Explain how the UK's membership of the EU might bring disadvantages to British firms.
                                                                                           (4 marks)

Advice on how to answer the questions

1 a In this question simply write the two words which the two letters stand for. No further writing is needed.

   b Only one country is required. Writing any more will not add to your marks!

2 This is a longer, 6-mark question in which you are instructed to 'explain'. You should try to think of at least three separate features of membership of the EU that help businesses in the UK. Make sure you explain how the features you use will help business. Remember that the question is about trade with other member states, not with any other part of the world.

3 In this question you need to think of the disadvantages of EU membership to British firms (not British people in general). The question is for 4 marks, which would indicate that two features, well explained, will enable you to achieve full marks. Once again, you must show how the features you use will cause problems for British firms.

Key facts

- The European Union is made up of 27 countries.
- It exists to increase trade and co-operation between these countries.
- It provides an opportunity for UK businesses to sell more because it is a bigger market than just the UK and there is nothing to stop them selling their goods and services in the other member countries.
- The European Union has increased competition for many UK businesses because firms from mainland EU countries can now export freely to the UK.
- The euro is the currency that is now used in 15 of the European Union countries. The countries that use the euro are known as the Eurozone.
- In many ways the euro helps businesses that are involved in trade in the Eurozone countries.
- There may be some problems for UK businesses if the UK starts to use the euro.
- Whether or not the UK should start to use the euro is a matter of debate.

Key Terms

Make sure you can explain each of the following Key Terms

European Union (EU) The collection of 27 countries in Europe which trade together and aim for closer co-operation.

Tariffs Taxes on imports that raise the price of imports so that it will be harder for foreign firms to sell their goods.

Quotas Limits on the amounts of a good or service that can be imported. This restricts competition from foreign firms.

Social Charter Measures to protect workers in the European Union from unfair working practices.

Minimum wage Part of the Social Charter, which guarantees certain wage levels for workers.

Eurozone A name given to the countries in the EU which use the euro.

The euro The currency used by 15 of the EU countries.

Index

Note: page numbers in **bold** refer to key word definitions.